Who's *Really* Running Your Life?

Who's *Really* Running Your Life?

Free Your True *Self* from Custody,

and Guard Your Kids

Fourth Edition

Peter K. Gerlach, MSW

This book was printed in the United States of America.

To order additional copies of this book, contact:
Xlibris Corporation
1-888-795-4274
www.Xlibris.com
Orders@Xlibris.com
95176

Contents

PART 1

PART 2

PART 3

PART 4

To my parents and grandparents, with respect, compassion, and sadness. You gave us your wounded best, and died unaware—long before I met my true Self and yours.

PREFACE

This book has been gestating since 1938. As a young Stanford engineering graduate in 1959, I had no clue that my life path would lead to writing these words. I also had no clue that my younger sister and I had been raised in a terribly troubled family—that our lively, social, "normal" parents were functional alcoholics.

The society in which Mom and Dad raised us hadn't discovered what caused substance addictions, or the other kinds of addiction (relationships, activities, and mood states). Most people didn't know what addiction *meant* to addicts, their families and descendents, and our culture. Because addiction was deemed shameful, the pioneers who founded the 12-step alcoholism recovery movement in 1935 used the (shaming) adjective "Alcoholics *Anonymous*," which endures and proliferates today.

My sister and I grew up in a middle-class family that ignored God, spirituality, or family worship. We kids were bundled off to church for social convention, while Dad and Mom stayed home. This was one of many, many double messages we unconsciously adapted to.

One day in 1985, a divorced friend who's Mom was alcoholic mentioned therapist Claudia Black's book "It Will Never Happen to Me." My friend said she saw herself and her sibs in the book as being normal "Adult Children of an Alcoholic (family)," or "ACoAs." She said she'd found validation, insight, and hope in the pages for herself and her two young daughters. I'd never heard of Black or her book.

Four years earlier, I'd begun a new midlife career as a therapist, as my remarriage and stepfamily were dying. I thought "I ought to read this 'ACoA' book. Some of my clients are from alcoholic families, and my clinical master's-degree training didn't focus much on that."

A few days later, my mail included a flyer for an upcoming seminar by Claudia Black. Noting the "coincidence," I registered and went. Two hours into the conference, my life changed completely. The dynamic, eloquent speaker kept describing *my* life. In a 5-minute epiphany, my lifelong denial shattered, and I saw the beginnings of the awful, freeing truth. Our extended family had been massively "dysfunctional"—i.e. very low in emotional and spiritual nurturance. We kids and relatives all accepted this as *normal*. Of my generation's seven first cousins, two died before their 40th birthdays, and the rest of us accumulated seven divorces.

Since that pivotal conference, I have been in personal recovery from the inner wounds that low childhood nurturance promotes. Like many early recoverers, I felt compelled to "learn everything" about alcoholism, then "addiction," then "recovery." I read dozens of books, attended seminars and early ACoA conferences, and (I suspect) wore my friends out with my obsession.

Three years later, I "chanced" on a seminar on "Inner Family Systems Therapy" by local psychologist Dr. Richard Schwartz. I'd never heard of him or that topic. It appealed to me as an ex engineer and as a student of clinical hypnosis. I dimly perceived that the God I was beginning to acknowledge via Unity Church in Chicago had put that flyer before me.

That seminar led to two long externships, and more intense study and practice of this newly emerging form of "talk therapy." During that time, I met my own *inner* family of over 20 "subselves"—and *more* lights went on. I worked on my own recovery with several different therapists, while working with hundreds of unhappy clients in troubled and divorced families and stepfamilies. As my life became clearer and more centered, purposeful, and peaceful, I saw "inner-family work" helping many clients regain some measure of control of their lives. My spirituality and "attitude of gratitude" steadily increased, amazing my unreligious friends and me. Before 1985, I had somewhat belligerently identified as an atheist.

Motivated by my fine/awful experiences as a stepson, stepgrandson, stepbrother, and divorced stepfather, my therapeutic specialties became teaching communication skills, and helping divorced families and stepfamilies. I learned how awesomely complex these families are, and speculated why so many are significantly troubled. Trying to understand and help my clients (and myself) led to hundreds of hours of post-graduate study of child and human development; attachment, loss, and grief; relationships; outer and *inner*-family "functioning;" and the nature of human change.

In the last 25 years, these learnings have gradually illuminated a predictable hidden pattern among my divorced and/or remarried clients. The various problems they sought to resolve were real—and were *always* symptoms of three underlying problems these adults weren't aware of:

- Their lives were largely controlled by a misguided, chaotic psychological "false self;" and . . .
- They were ignorant of healthy marital, parenting, and grieving realities and principles, and effective communication skills; and . . .
- They weren't aware of their unawarenesses and ignorances, and our society promoted that.

Since 1985, I have witnessed scores of courageous, wounded people free themselves, with temporary help, from life-long protective false-self captivity. Those who are ready to work toward true recovery always report and manifest growing inner and relationship harmony, peace, and productivity—"happiness." I have heard similar stories from many clinical colleagues.

At this time, there are few books or programs that help to heal the widespread false-self wounding that I believe burdens most American adults and their kids. I believe spaceship Earth is spiraling into an accelerating era of new human *awareness* as profound and impactful as the discovery of fire, the wheel, and the atom. The acceleration is due to the interactive advances in computer systems and information sharing, medical science, and psychiatry. The increasing pace of awareness is steadily fueled by the primal human yearnings for comfort and joy, and for raising healthy, contented kids.

Our descendents will probably be as amused at the old illusion that we each are "one person" as we now smile at our ancestors' *certainty* that the Earth was flat, and the hub of the cosmos. I vision enlightened future generations working together to help their kids grow up in higher-nurturance homes and communities, and empowering their own and their kids' true *inner* harmony and well being.

I hope you find the ideas between these covers intriguing, validating, freeing, and empowering. If you're being held in "protective custody" by a misinformed, well meaning "false self," I encourage you to experiment with the ideas here. *Bon Voyage*!

The third edition corrects some terminology and Web-page addresses. The content remains the same.

The fourth edition corrects all cross-reference page numbers.

PKG
Portland, OR—February, 2011

ACKNOWLEDGEMENTS

I'm grateful to *many* people for what you'll read here . . .

- Frank McNair, who made it all possible;
- Devera Denker and Claudia Black, who turned the lights on for me.
- Psychologist-authors Hal and Sidra Stone; and Richard Schwartz, Ph.D. and a group of clinical colleagues and clients with whom I studied the "Internal Family Systems Model."
- Annette Hulefeld, LCSW; who skillfully and compassionately led our inner-family recovery group for eight years. Equal loving thanks to Jane, Jeff, Ronnee, Danna and her infant son Sam, and the others.
- Dozens of my clients, and their subselves and spirits. Special thanks to mentor Elizabeth Bormann, A.C.S.W., and to Jayne G. and her inner family for inspiring us (my inner crew) to finally sit down and write this.
- Each of the dozens of lay and clinical authors and speakers whose collective wisdom and insights have shown me the way since 1985.
- Profound thanks to psychiatric pioneer Dr. Milton Erickson, and the colleagues and students who explored and applied his work. They taught the rest of us about the amazing potentials and dynamics of our several minds.
- Warm appreciation to my unexpected virtual colleague Gloria Lintermans, for her verve, spirit, wisdom, and encouragement; and . . .
- Over all, I wordlessly acknowledge the patient, loving presence of the One who provided the darkness, the light, the path, the teachers, the mission—and in recent years, the peace beyond all understanding.

INTRODUCTION

We want the facts to fit the preconceptions. When they don't,
it is easier to ignore the facts than to change the preconceptions.
—Jessamyn West

Before you continue, spend a quiet moment with yourself. Reflect: "Why am I reading this book? What am I interested in, or looking for? What do I *need*?" Notice your thoughts, and take a moment to note inside the front cover the key reason/s you picked up this book. "I'm not sure" is a valid reason. I'll invite you to refer to your reason/s, as you finish the book. You may find that your unconscious mind had it's own motives for urging you to read, which become clearer as you do.

Have you ever . . .

- Said or thought "Something just came over me"?
- Acted "impulsively"—and later delighted in, or regretted that?
- Felt *torn*, *confused*, and unable to make an important decision?
- Felt love and "hate" for someone at the same time?
- Found yourself doing things you knew you shouldn't do "anyway"?
- Experienced frustrating arguments among different inner "voices" (thought streams)?
- Been unable to sleep because your mind "wouldn't let you"?
- Had an obsession, compulsion, or addiction?

Most kids and grownups experience these occasionally or often. What causes them? What if "someone else" was secretly running your waking and sleeping life every day—controlling your perceptions, thoughts, emotions, goals, plans, actions, and the quality of your life? What if this was true of many of the key adults and kids in your life?

Recent advances in medical radiology and psychiatry suggest this *is true* for most of us, to some extent. We seem to be a bustling, noisy, troubled nation of sleepwalkers and hostages in individual protective custody—and most don't know it yet. Are you one of them? Based on 18 years study and clinical experience, this book offers a way to find out.

The fundamental premise of this book is this: though we have one brain and one body, our personalities are routinely composed of a dynamic group of "parts", or "subselves." This is based on the recently demonstrated "multiplicity" trait of our brain—it's inherent ability to have a group of separate neuronal regions operating simultaneously, to produce "one experience" like "I see my hand." Each subself has its own values, perception, goals, and role—which often conflict with other subselves and other people. Only a small fraction of the population has this fragmenting to extreme. Most of the rest of us have it "a little" or "significantly."

Adults and kids who have significantly troubled lives seem to be under the short-sighted, well-meant, impulsive control of a group of personality parts called (here) your **"false self."** The alternative is inner leadership by an innately skilled, wise personality part—your true Self. Basic questions this concept poses each of us are: "Who is controlling my personality—my true Self, or some other subselves?"—and "How do I like what they're doing, so far?"

Another basic premise here is: if your false self is running your life too often, you can shift that, over time, to the expert leadership of your true Self and any Higher Power that's meaningful to you. Notice your thoughts and reactions to these ideas, so far . . .

Is This Book For You?

I write this to lay and professional men and women who are enduring recurring periods of significant emotional pain, numbness, or apathy: people who . . .

- had a difficult, painful (low nurturance) childhood—i.e. who were significantly neglected emotionally, spiritually, physically, and/or mentally. Many people who think they had a "normal, happy childhood" didn't.

- feel socially isolated and unhappy, and/or have had a series of unhappy relationships.

- are divorced single parents of minor or grown children, custodial or not, conflicted or not.

- are considering forming a stepfamily together, or have already committed to forming one. A "stepfamily" is one where one or both partners have children with prior mates.

- have chronic "money problems," including bankruptcy and compulsive spending or gambling habits.

- have chronic "mental" and/or physical health problems.

- have no clear life purpose, and feel they are "drifting."

- And I write to you, if you . . .

- are in a troubled primary relationship, and truly want to improve it and your life.

- are the anxious co-parent of a child who is "in big trouble" socially, scholastically, or personally.

- are struggling to free yourself from one or more addictions to substances, relationships, emotional states (like *excitement*), or activities—like compulsive work, gambling, sex, Web surfing, working out, eating, fantasizing, etc . . . .)

- are clinically diagnosed as having a "character disorder," a "mood disorder," or "personality disorder." These can include diagnoses of being "chronically depressed," "manic depressive," "bipolar," "borderline," "dissociated," "hyperactive," "Adult Attention Deficit Disorder," "Narcissism," and many others. I believe every one of these is a symptom of significant, undiagnosed false-self wounding (dissociation).

- are the parent of a divorced or maritally-troubled child, and/or care about troubled grandchildren.

- are working with a therapist, psychiatrist, counselor, or personal coach—and feel "I'm not getting anywhere."

- And I write this to student and veteran clinicians and other human-service professionals of all disciplines and levels of experience—and to the people who supervise, employ, evaluate, and teach them. This includes clergy; family-law professionals, including enforcers; educators; welfare workers; and divorce mediators. Many of your present and future clients, students, and patients are burdened with underlying false-self dominance—but will rarely present that as their problem.

Will This Book Help You?

If your well-meaning false self is controlling you now, the subselves that comprise it may be alarmed by and/or skeptical about what you (they) just read. I want to reassure those parts of you about several things:

You (subselves) will find that this book genuinely respects each of you as helpful, valuable parts of your host person. This is not a trick, a con, or a soft sell. I'd bet that you have done spectacularly well at keeping your person and other subselves safe and well enough, through some *very* difficult times. I'll also bet no one has ever acknowledged or thanked you.

This book is not about "killing" you, "throwing you out," "banishing," "forcing," or harming you in any way. You are cellular-chemical-spiritual part of your host person, and can't ever be "fired" or disregarded. This book *is* about . . .

- Recognizing and affirming your energy, devotion, resilience, anxieties, and positive intentions.

- Helping you meet and grow trust in some inner and outer helpers, so you can relax a little—*safely*—and share your inner-family responsibilities with competent others.

- Growing teamwork and cooperation among you and other subselves, so you can all get more done, enjoy it together, and rest when you need to; and . . .

- Eventually finding it safe enough to shift to some interesting, safe, satisfying new work—if you wish to.

You don't know me or my motives, so you may not trust these words. I invite you to keep an open mind. Please try to reserve final judgment about these ideas until you all have had a chance to read this whole book, try the exercises, and glimpse "the big picture" of what's possible for you and your host person.

I can't emphasize enough: this book is not about *blaming* any of your subselves, or your person's parents or other people, for being "wrong," "evil," or "bad." It may take more reading and some related new experiences for you to start believing this. If one or more of you (e.g. *Inner Critic*) are used to judging and criticizing your person, and/or other subselves, people, events, "fate," or God—you're apt to eventually find that there are more satisfying ways to get what you want.

If there are minor or grown kids in your life now, the ideas in this book can help your person help them have a happier, safer, more peaceful life. The ideas here are not magic answers. They point toward a healthier, safer, more satisfying way of purposeful living.

Pause, breathe well, and notice with interest what your inner voices and body are saying right now . . . What was it like to have me write to your personality parts as a group, separate from "you"—your Self? Common subselves would have reactions like these *all at once*:

Inner Cynic—*"Live a better life, huh? Yeah, sure—yet another hokey way of saving the world. Stupid."*
Catastrophizer*: "Oh, my God—multiple personality! I knew I was crazy and messed up. Oh, NO! Padded cell ahead!"*
Inner Saboteur—*"Huh? What did I just read? This psychobabble is too heady and complicated. Forget this."*
Deflector—*"Better put the book down. What are you gonna do about the funny noise that the car just developed?"*
Anxious Child—*"Does this mean something bad will happen if we keep reading—or if we don't?"*
Blamer/Judge—*"Low childhood nurturance, eh? So Mom and Dad really messed us up? Great, just great. Why were we born to that pair of losers?"*
Righteous One—*"What a horrible thing to say! You know the Bible says 'Honor thy Father and they Mother. You know what will happen if we . . . "*
Health Director—*"Wait a minute. This sounds promising and important. Keep reading."*
Nurturer—*"Forget the car noise, and keep reading. It's more important to find out if the kids have this 'false self' thing, and how to help them if they do."*
Shamed Child—*"See? I knew it! I'm 'wounded' and ruined. No way anyone is ever going to love me—I'll be alone forever."*

(Food) Addict—*"Hey, hey there! Picture this delicious chocolate sundae. Imagine the taste and feel of it. Ahhh! Why not get one right now?"*

Health Director—*"No, not a good idea—we don't need the sugar and calories!"*

Analyzer—*"You know, these 'subself' ideas are intriguing. Might explain why Charlie can't 'get it together.' I wonder if this 'false-self' thing affects physical health. Can it cause warts? Tooth cavities? Hiccoughs? How do 'subselves' relate to schizophrenia and manic depression? How could dreams fit in? Are Alaskans more wounded than Norwegians? Do dogs have false selves? Let's learn more!"*

Fixer—*"We ought to give a copy of this to Marsha. I'll bet it would help her and her therapist to make progress. You know, Jeremy too, and Alex, and . . ."*

Observer—*"These ideas have really stirred everybody up."*

Spiritual One—*"Listen . . . "*

Self—"H-E-Y! If you all would just calm down and talk one at a time, we could discuss what we ought to do next, here . . . Please—chill out, OK?"

Note that the false self in this example has almost a dozen discrete subselves. Who among them will prevail to determine whether "you" continue reading or not? Have you ever been in a group of people who were all talking and interrupting like this, and no one was focusing, *listening*, or leading? This is what "mind racing" or "mind chatter" is like for a person ruled by a false self. It's a sure sign that their true Self (capital "S") is being ignored, paralyzed, or held in protective captivity.

Pause now, close your eyes, if that helps you concentrate, and "listen in" on what your subselves are "saying." Breathe comfortably, and just . . . *notice*, without judgment. Anything like the example you just read? As the "listener," you (your Self) just did a little "parts work."

Book Overview

This four-part book is modular. There are several ways to use it, depending on your needs, knowledge, and inner compass. Here's an overview:

Part 1 outlines a set of ideas about your personality: who comprises your *inner* family, where they came from, how they behave, and *who's in charge of them, most of the time.* You'll meet your natural decision-maker and leader here—your true Self. You'll also meet your "false self"—a normal group of personality parts who may have taken you into protective custody some or much of your life, to date. Part 1 closes with a summary of major implications of false-self wounding for you, your relationships and kids, for human-service professionals, and our society and global ecology.

Part 2 overviews recovery from inner wounds, and "parts work"—a safe, effective way of harmonizing your *inner* family, over time, under the wise leadership of your Self and Higher Power. Doing Self-motivated parts work (or "inner-family work") can improve the quality of your life, and protect any dependent kids from the hidden risk of developing their own false self. Part 2 includes a glossary of inner-family and recovery terms.

Part 3 offers 11 self-assessment checklists. These will help you reach an initial conclusion on (1) whether you're significantly dominated by a false self or not, and if so, (2) which of five related psychological wounds that may stress you. The array of checklists lowers the chance that your well-intentioned false-self committee will prevent you from learning the truth.

Part 4 offers a group of recovery resources, including selected readings and inspirations. The book ends with an index.

If your inner family permits you, read Part 1 of this book for meaning. Then decide if it feels safe and useful enough to use the wound-assessment worksheets in Part 3 *honestly*. Doing that will help you (all) grow a clear sense of (1) who has been running your life, and (2) what that *means* to you, and key adults and kids around you. If your true Self has usually led your inner crew, you can expect to enjoy and savor the outcome.

An option is to read about recovery from false-self dominance (Part 2) before you assess yourself. That may help your subselves understand your options, and feel safer and more grounded before assessing.

If your false self supervises your reading this book and using the checklists, those distrustful subselves may urge your Self "This was a waste of time." They may distract you, make you procrastinate, scare you, or distort your perception in small or large ways. If so, appreciate that they're diligently trying to protect you. Typically, false-self personality parts focus only on the short-term, and instant gratification. They lack your Self's wide-angle, long-range vision, and often have little patience for it. Their tolerance for making short-term sacrifices to earn long-term rewards grows, as they trust your Self more and see what s/he can do.

Are you curious to know if your false self is controlling you right now? Bookmark this page, scan checklists B and E in Part 3, and return here. If you identified with "a lot" of these traits, and/or felt uneasy, numb, upset, distracted, irritated, or blank reading them, your watchful false self is probably in charge. If your Self is leading, you'll feel some combination of *light, focused, clear, calm, grounded, purposeful, energized, patient, interested,* and *realistically optimistic.* Do you know how often you feel mixes of those? Do you trust your judgment of that?

If your distrustful false self discourages you from using this book now, that's OK. Each new day is another chance to use it and others like it, and/or to explore some recovery options. These include trying some form of parts work, (Part 2), and learning more about your subselves and your options. Scan the selected readings in Part 4 now, to get a sense of what's "out there." There's a lot, though very few authors try to paint the whole picture, so far!

Benefits of Recovery

If your Self decides that you may benefit personally from some kind of recovery program, you (all) can expect other payoffs. Over many months, recovery (inner-family harmonizing) will foster your . . .

- Evolving a rich, meaningful, spiritual awareness and communion.

- Exchanging currently stressful relationships and settings for high-nurturance, wholistically healthy relationships and surroundings.

- Protecting any dependent kids from a low-nurturance environment, and lower the odds of their developing an impulsive, short-sighted false self.

- Finding work content and environments that empower your recovery, wholistic health, and life-purpose, and foster your . . .

- Living your old age well satisfied with the life you've chosen, and the unique contributions you've made to the world.

Notice how your inner crew reacts to that vision . . .

Get the Most From Reading

If your false self crew agrees, "OK, read more," consider these ways of harvesting the most from this book:

Now and at random times, reflect: **"Why did I pick up this book?"** What caught your eye and curiosity? What do you need? Pause, and notice how this sentence completes itself:

"I'm reading this book because . . . "

Your unconscious mind may identify your need before you "realize it." If you need to change something fundamental about how you're living your life—do you know what it is, yet?

Can you recall a time in your life when *learning* something genuinely excited you? How does that compare with how you feel right now? If your Self is in charge, you'll probably **have the open "mind of a student,"** as Zen teachers request. Notice everything, and question everything, including your questioning. You'll probably find many ideas here that feel alien, and challenge you to change some core beliefs about yourself that you've held for years. Do you equate *change* with *growth*?

As you read, coach yourself (or selves) to **become routinely aware** of your body, breathing, thoughts, feelings, and of your *awareness*. Build the habit of noticing *without judgment* the rich "conversations" that happen in your minds and your body all the time. If you're not in some form of personal-growth or recovery work, you probably don't know what you don't know about the amazing world going on inside you.

Consider journaling, as you read and react. If you do, affectionately ask your inner *Editor* and *Perfectionist* to relax! There is no right or wrong here—just *awareness* and *meaning*. You may discover one or more protective subselves who fear those, and will try to block, numb, paralyze, or blank you, when you "look inside." All your subselves will gradually learn to trust that inner awareness is safe and *useful*. You've already got all the abilities and faculties you need to learn do this—no Ph.D. required.

Take all the time you (all) want in reading and absorbing these ideas. Meeting and harmonizing your inner family under your Self's expert leadership—with loving spiritual guidance and encouragement along the way—is a lifelong process. If there are specific ways you'd like to improve your life, over time, keep them clearly in your mind's eye as you go. With focus, patience, and awareness, you can probably attain them, through some version of recovery and inner-family work. The exception is if your vision is coming from your inner *Magician*, who's talented at creating entertaining fantasies and protective illusions.

Note the difference between skimming and reading for meaning, and notice which you're doing, along the way. There is a place for each of these. Your Self knows when to do which, so . . . *listen*, and *trust*!

If you encounter times of unusual times of confusion, anxiety, boredom, or elation as you read, try this and see what you learn: Pause. Focus on sorting out and naming each of your feelings, and sense which of your subselves is bringing that feeling to you—and why. Trust the first thing that occurs to you, and try not to "logic" everything. Be lovingly alert for attempts to derail you (your Self) by your narrow-focused *Skeptic*, *Catastrophizer*, *Critic*, and/or restless inner *Teen(s)*.

The most meaningful thing you can do while reading this book and afterward is to develop a real interest in learning "**Who is running my life at this moment**—my Self, or some other subselves?" With practice, this self-awareness becomes a reflex, and you don't have to "do it" consciously. Who's in charge of you right *now*? A normal reaction is "*I* am." Which of your subselves is that?

Ready? Here we go . . .

PART 1

Discover who is really running your life

"The ego states of 'normal' people in our culture are not truly integrated into a cohesive, yet fluid self. Everyone in our culture could benefit from . . . therapeutic . . . subpersonality work . . . "
Colin A. Ross—Past president, International Society for the Study of Dissociation; in "*The Plural Self—Multiplicity in Everyday Life*," edited by John Rowan and Mick Cooper; Sage Publications, 1999; p. 193

1) Our false-self legacy

2) Your many-sided *personality*

3) Meet your *inner* family and its leaders

4) The effects of false-self dominance

1) OUR FALSE-SELF LEGACY

ARE YOU WOUNDING
YOUR CHILDREN?

This chapter presents 13 related premises that form the foundation of this book. Choose the open, curious "mind of a student," and see how these ideas compare to what you now believe. Note with interest what your "inner voices" (thoughts) have to say, as you read, encounter, and ponder. I encourage you to highlight, scribble margin notes or symbols, underline, and express yourself as you go. Use paperclips to mark parts of the book you want ready access to as you read and learn.

Are You In Protective Custody?

If you're ready for it, this book can help you uncover whether you've been unaware of being held in "protective custody" for years, why, and by whom. If you find that a distrustful, protective false self has dominated you, Part 2 will show you options toward *recovery*—taking control of your life back safely. Notice without judgment your mental and physical reaction to what you just read. "No reaction" *is* a reaction.

You're in the first generation of people in Earth's history who can see video-screen scans of live human brains in action. In the last quarter century, CT (Computed Tomography) and PET (Positron Emission Tomography) body-tissue scans have disclosed a startling fact: up to a dozen or more interconnected brain areas "activate" simultaneously to produce single ho-hum experiences like "I smell-taste-chew-hold-feel the candy bar."

We're the first generation to visually confirm that we have many specialized centers in each of our *three* multi-part brains (stem, cerebrum, and cerebellum) that automatically work together to create "meaning" from our sight, taste, hearing, and touch sensations; our emotions, and our several levels of memory. *Thinking* happens in several parts of your brain, and memory and emotional and physical *feelings* happen in other regions. Combined, these unconscious processes routinely seem to be "one experience." Since early childhood, when you have thought and spoken the word "I," you've assumed there was a single "you"—yes? Ponder why we English-speakers don't ask, "How *is* you?"

Lacking credible evidence to the contrary, generations of parents—probably including yours—have taught their kids the ancient "logical" belief that because we obviously have one body and one physical brain, we must be "one person." Physiologically true. Psychologically *wrong*. Accelerating advances in medical radiology, computers, and psychiatry since ~1975 now show this to be an illusion, just like the old popular and religious *certainties* that "gods," or "devils" caused illness, plagues, and insanity. You're in the vanguard of a profound new global awareness about who we humans really are—and aren't. The evidence is everywhere, if you're aware of what to look for.

Most adults resist accepting an emerging new reality because it's alien and *scary*. The reality is that our *personality*, or *psyche*, *character*, or *identity*, is not one entity, but a shadowy group of "parts," "subselves," or "subpersonalities." These subselves interact in combinations below our conscious awareness to shape our waking and sleeping perceptions, goals, desires, moods, and behaviors. This *multiplicity* of personality parts is a natural, normal human feature, *not* weird or "crazy." Multiplicity seems to be the way we humans have been designed to survive and adapt to our early-childhood environment. Developing an inner crew of subselves is as automatic and unconscious as our breathing, digesting, and heartbeat.

If this is true, which subselves are normally in charge of your personality group, or *inner* family? How effective is their leadership, measured by the quality, health, productivity, and satisfaction of your life to date? Who is *really* running your life? Would you like to change that if you could, and improve your life? You can, if you wish to discover and free the *real* "you."

I suspect you already know what that "you" feels like. Reflect for a moment on whether there been periods of minutes, hours, or days in your life when you have notably felt some blend of these:

- *Centered, grounded,* and *focused*, vs. distracted, unsure, and confused,

- *Clear* on who you are, what you're doing, and why

- Calm or *serene*, vs. worried, stressed, or "upset"

- Upbeat and *light*, vs. gloomy, heavy, and "down"

- Purposeful, sure, strong, and firm

- Rested, healthy, energized, and *alert*; vs. apathetic, tired, or "out of sorts"

- Resourceful, resilient, patient, and good humored

- Empathic, compassionate, and appreciative of yourself and others around you

- Delighted to be alive, and proud to be *you*.

These contribute to feeling *good*, or *happy*. The degree that you experience a blend of these traits at the moment and over time measures your wholistic "well-being." Some people experience these even if they're in the midst of crises, conflicts, losses, or emergencies—they somehow stay "cool and *collected* under fire."

Do you?

If you don't usually feel many of these, what *do* you feel? Have you ever wondered why sometimes you feel *great*, and other times you don't? What your life would feel like if you could feel the traits above more often? Would you like to help your kids feel these traits more often?

Do you often hear "inner voices" (have "thoughts")? Observe with interest what your inner voices are saying now. How many voices do you have? Who are your inner "speakers," anyway? If there's a committee governing you, who are they—and who usually leads them? To begin forming answers, see how your inner committee reacts to each of these . . .

Premises

After 72 inquisitive years on Earth, I propose some bad news and some really good news about your life. These proposals are based on these decades of life experience, earning engineering and social work degrees, and 29 years' postgraduate study and clinical and classroom experience with over 1,000 single, married, divorced, and stepfamily co-parents and their kids.

Here's the bad news:

1) Families exist across centuries and cultures because they're uniquely able to fill core human needs for nurturance, belonging, support, and protection. Evidence suggests that caregivers in most past and modern American families *unintentionally* have provided too little *emotional* and *spiritual* nurturance (Part 3, worksheet A) for their kids and each other—and haven't known that, or what to do about it. Judged by their behavior rather than their words, most co-parents haven't *wanted* to know.

2) Because low family nurturance is so widespread and impactful, it is personally, socially, and politically accepted and denied, so far. When extreme or obvious, our society calls low nurturance "parental *neglect*," and judges it a criminal offense. *Self* neglect is rampant in our society. It is condoned and largely ignored, because we adults hold each other responsible for our own lives—and our false selves want to deny it. Megabillion dollar examples are our fast food and advertising industries, which relentlessly promote unhealthy eating habits and diets, while justifying or denying that. These industries flourish because we (our ruling subself committees) *want* them to. Unhealthy obesity in American kids and adults has steadily risen in recent years, causing major personal and social problems.

3) Very young personalities automatically adapt to too little emotional and spiritual nurturance by forming personality "parts" or "subselves"—neuro-chemical brain regions. Each subself (region) develops a specialized protective function, *and its own goals, perceptions, priorities, strategies, and limits.* Our subselves naturally learn, interact with each other, and change over time, just like our bodies.

Adaptive personality fragmenting seems to range from mild to extreme in adults and kids, in a normal bell-curve social distribution. The "extreme" sufferers, about 5% of Americans, make lurid media headlines. They have been dubbed "Multiple Personalities," and sensationalized in books and films like *"Sybil"* and the *"Three Faces of Eve."*

I propose that the gloomy American statistics about mental health, crime, divorce, abortion, addictions, homelessness, chronic illness, and premature death are symptoms of the great majority of us who *aren't* extremely wounded. The symptoms of significant false-self wounds are everywhere—and are largely unrecognized, so far. I suspect they have impacted your life in many painful ways without your knowing the real causes. More bad-news premises . . .

4) Your group of personality subselves forms an *inner* family, committee, squad, troupe, cast, or team. You call them "my personality" and "me," just as students and their instructor call themselves "my class." Like classes, sports teams, committees, and musical groups, some personalities are more productive and harmonious than others. With leadership and resources, any inner or outer group—like yours—can soar!

5) A key personality part that every adult and child seems to have can be called our ***true Self***—capital "S." When other subselves permit it, your Self consistently produces wholistically healthy short and long-term decisions to routine and emergency situations. These decisions promote *inner* family security, harmony, and pride ("self esteem")—which foster the traits of "happiness" above. Your Self is a naturally talented leader, like a gifted athletic coach, orchestra conductor, board chairperson, or passenger-jet captain.

6) If other dominant inner-family members (your **"false self"**) don't know or trust your Self, they automatically and impulsively "take over" to guard and protect each other ("you"). If chronic, these takeovers usually produce a mix of up to six characteristic inner wounds:

   • Dominance of a reactive, short-sighted false-self, which promotes . . .
   • Excessive shame and guilts;
   • Excessive primal fears—e.g. of abandonment (aloneness); and . . .
   • Trusting too easily, or too little. These four cause . . .
   • Reality distortions, like denials, psychoses, and illusions, and . . .
   • Trouble genuinely bonding, committing, and loving—which
   • amplifies the other traits.

7) Most adults and kids, and many human-service professionals and their trainers and evaluators, don't know much about inner families of subselves—in general, or inside their skins. Probably like *you*, most people aren't conscious of who is usually running their daily lives:

a wise, reliable, stable *Self*, or a highly camouflaged, well-meaning, limited, impulsive, misinformed false *self*. For a net comparison of true Self and false self behaviors, see the Web page at **http://sfhelp.org/ gwc/compare.htm**.

8) Unaware of their false self's dominance and misjudgments, **adults and teens *unconsciously* pick equally-wounded partners over and over again.** Perhaps this is because toxic shame, or "low self esteem," covertly seeks its own level. Typical false selves will vehemently deny or justify these toxic relationship choices—*even if they're harmful* to themselves and others, including kids. This appears to be an unremarked core cause of our unfathomably costly U.S. divorce epidemic. Divorce is a years-long process, vs. a courtroom event. It's a *symptom* of deeper personal, marital, and social problems—usually based on unseen wounds, denials, unawareness, and couples' lack of key knowledge.

9) Two mates who each (a) aren't aware of being controlled by a false self, and (b) haven't developed a set of relationship, parenting, and communication skills, will *predictably* co-create low-nurturance family environments, *against their conscious wills*. **This unintentionally promotes false-self formation in their kids**, who grow up and—without awareness and personal recovery—spread the low-nurturance wounding cycle down the generations. For credible recent research that validates this, see the Internet page at **http://sfhelp.org/site/research.htm** (Lesson 1).

10) If a false self often controls one or both adults or kids in a relationship, they will have difficulty communicating effectively. Conversely, two people with their Selves solidly in charge of their inner families will often communicate effectively. That is, they'll each consistently get (a) their current needs met well enough, (b) in a way that feels mutually satisfying. False selves fight, argue, manipulate, blame, submit, abuse, and avoid. True Selves respectfully assert, negotiate, brainstorm, and compromise with mutual respect.

11) The inner-family chaos or harmony of any human group's leaders will manifest in similar chaos or harmony among the group's members, over time. People dominated by false selves produce, and even covertly seek, conflictual, stressful environments—against all "reason." They truly don't know why, and will deny or defend it, if confronted.

12) Social research on these 11 premises is spotty, uncoordinated, and hampered by (a) universal social denials and superstitions, and (b) the lack of common concepts, language, interpretations, and protocols, so far. The scope of all these premises together appears too broad to test in one classic research study. Nonetheless, credible evidence of widespread multi-part personalities is accumulating. For example, see John Rowan's recent books (Part 4, Selected Readings.)

The Good News

Together, these dozen propositions are pretty gloomy, aren't they? There is a clear, demonstrable reason for hope and cautious optimism, based on our quenchless human drive for health, security, and self-actualization. My personal and clinical experience, affirmed by a swelling group of other mental-health professionals, suggests a final premise . . .

13) Any adult or child can grow more of the true-Self traits above via a safe, learnable process called "*inner* family therapy," or "parts work." The process is no different than taking an unruly orchestra, sports team, or mob of bus passengers, and working respectfully and patiently to build trust in, and loyalty to, the skilled conductor, coach, or bus driver. In your case, the resident leader of your *inner* family is your Self.

Inner family therapy usually benefits from using temporary human consultants, empathic supporters, and openness to spiritual help, along the way. This transformative process is basically about _ greater self-awareness and _ spiritual growth. Its success depends on your learning what's possible, "putting away the things (attitudes) of a child," and taking full responsibility for raising the quality of your own life. Typical false selves are too busy squabbling, infighting, and putting out today's brush fires to commit to working toward a long-range vision of wholistic health and happiness.

2)   YOUR MANY-SIDED PERSONALITY

WHO *ARE* YOU (ALL), ANYWAY?

Have you ever tried to define "personality" to a child? It's not easy, is it? Here, *personality* means "The whole ever-changing mosaic of an infant's, child's, or adult's non-physical traits that make her or him unique from other persons." These traits include the rich mix of core values, priorities, preferences, reflexes, motives, beliefs, attitudes, needs, mental associations, memories, "instincts," and self-perceptions, which all shape how a person (like *you*) characteristically reacts to perceived changes in their inner and outer environments.

For perspective, let's take a brief tour of the human concept of "personality."

Personality "Parts" Aren't New

About 2,400 years ago, Greek philosopher Socrates wrote that his inner life was controlled by "daimons" (demons). Just as he did, people have tried for millennia to explain their thoughts, dreams, actions, and "natures." All cultures have evolved beliefs that spirits, gods, imps, leprechauns, fairies, goblins, cosmic and planetary rays, witches, angels, "ethers," ghosts, and space aliens cause humans to feel, experience, think, and do weird and wonderful things.

Freud's Three Parts and Three Minds

Early last century, Austrian psychiatrist Sigmund Freud proposed a startling new idea that changed beliefs worldwide. He proposed that we each have three personality parts that determine who we "are": our Id, Ego, and

Superego. These, he felt, drove us to act from "instincts" and "drives"—with pleasure-seeking and pain-avoiding as their primal motivations.

He also taught that we all have three *minds*: the *unconscious* (never "knowable"), the *preconscious* (eventually knowable), and the (fully) *conscious*. He felt that these three interact in ways we can't comprehend, causing inevitable mystery in what we think and do—or don't. Freud's ideas revolutionized at least the Western world's views on how to understand and heal "madness," depression, and many human "mental" problems.

Around 1950, some psycho-medical researchers focused on the ancient realm of "psychotropic" or "psychoactive" (mood-altering) drugs. Ethyl alcohol compounds, which now fuel our vehicle engines, are among the oldest. That produced a new class of mass-produced prescription drugs like Valium and Xanex, which reliably relieved (some) depression, controlled violent mood swings, and improved other troublesome human emotional behaviors, like mania, anxiety, and Attention Deficit Disorder (A.D.D.). The combination of Freud's ideas and the new chemicals turned (many) exorcists and shamans with rattles into psychiatrists with couches, in just three generations—an evolutionary fingersnap.

(Outer) Families Become "The Patient"

Also in the mid 1950's, a few pioneering mental health clinicians began exploring the novel idea that putting the client's whole family on the couch at once, so to speak, could ease the sufferer's mental/emotional problems. "*Family* therapy" flowered, bringing impressive results for many, specially when combined with emerging *communications* and *systems* theories. Clinicians increasingly began to work on outer families—while a dedicated core kept focused on taming and balancing Ids, Egos, and Superegos.

Because Freud's ideas were obscure to many, they were recast in the 1960's by professionals who used "Transactional Analysis" (TA). In 1967, working with the ideas of psychiatrist Eric Berne, Dr. Thomas Harris published "*I'm OK—You're OK.*" His book popularized the idea that we each had several versions of inner *Parent*, *Child*, and *Adult* parts that determined our feelings, beliefs, and behavior. A therapeutic goal became helping people understand and balance these three inner entities, and keeping their *Adult* in charge. Family therapy was too new for any reputable mental-health leader to propose using its principles *internally*.

While the TA idea was spreading through our (Western) culture, more psycho-biological facts were unearthed. These included growing evidence that alcoholism—long thought to come from a "weak will," a "defective character," or a "demon" (e.g. rum)—really came from a combination of the addicts' genes, and childhood (family) trauma. It's now clear that true addicts metabolize ethyl alcohol differently than non-addicts because of a genetic inheritance. Social factors seem to mediate if and when such people become addicts or not.

Our Inner Child Becomes Famous

In the late 1970's, a new set of mindscape pioneers suggested that the grown children of alcoholic families—addicted themselves or not—had common emotional traits and troubles. For instance: depression, low self-esteem, and chronic relationship conflicts. It gradually became clear that kids in "alcoholic" families were usually deprived of key emotional, spiritual, and sometimes physical nurturing—just as one or more of their caregivers had been. In the next decade, a flood of books, conferences, support groups, magazines, and two national advocacy groups erupted across the country for millions of troubled Adult Children of Alcoholics (ACoAs) to help them toward emotional and spiritual *recovery*.

The principles underlying this movement were strongly shaped by the 12-step recovery philosophy of Alcoholics Anonymous —"AA"—born in Akron Ohio, in 1935. The unprecedented global spread of that philosophy attests to the universal need to manage "addictive (i.e. false-self dominated) personalities." This new "Higher Power"-based philosophy seemed to be far more helpful in combating lethal addiction to ethyl alcohol than any other medical or psychiatric "cures" of the day. Still, many who tried AA *relapse* permanently or cyclically into lethal addiction behaviors. Others quit drinking, but keep their "stinkin' (addictive) thinkin'" and attitudes. Some AA chapters have added special meetings for recovering "Adult Children" (ACoAs).

From this fledgling "Adult Child" movement came an explosion of national interest in nurturing and healing our "Inner Child," who retained the fear, sadness, and shame of real birthfamily neglect and abuse. Two kinds of people excited by this idea were women and men coming from any kind of painful early years ("Adult Children"), and healers and entrepreneurs who wanted to help them. Because of unintended childhood neglect and abuse, our (single) "Inner Child of the Past" was clearly "wounded," "orphaned," or "lost." Unrecognized, s/he seemed to cause many of us serious personal problems.

One such problem was eventually dubbed *co-dependence* It began as *co-alcoholism*: being toxically obsessed with the welfare of an alcoholic.

As recognition of this affliction spread, it came to be seen by many as a relationship compulsion as harmful as any chemical addiction. Since the mid-80's, hundreds of Codependents Anonymous (CoDA) 12-step support groups have bloomed in every state. They serve a rainbow of people who admit and struggle to break free from powerful *relationship* addictions to a lover, parent, child, media star, or some other person. Related groups help people to control *love* addiction, and *sexual* addiction—e.g. "Sex and Love Addicts Anonymous" (SLAA). The *Anonymous* still promotes the undeserved attitude that addiction is *shameful*—despite the growing awareness that addictions of any sort are unconscious attempts to self-medicate against the relentless pain of toxic shame inherited in childhood. The "cure" promotes the "disease," so far. False selves at work.

Theorists proposed that co-dependents' inner children were terrified of abandonment, because as very young real kids, they had felt searingly neglected and rejected by caregivers. Where true, it often turned out that the *caregiver's* parent/s had been similarly abused and/or emotionally abandoned. "Toxic parenting" and the crippling shame that it causes were wryly labeled "The gift that goes on giving."

From the surge of public interest in (and identification with) these ideas, programs and books now abound on healing from dysfunctional families, abusive parents, and "emotionally absent" fathers and mothers. An awful and hopeful current offshoot is the mushrooming U.S. awareness of how common childhood *sexual* abuse has been, and is.

Sociologists have recently estimated that one of four American females, and one of seven males, are sexually molested by their 18th birthday. The emotional and spiritual trauma from this is usually devastating. To survive it, people normally appear to "go to (inner) pieces." Like many people experiencing war, torture, and natural disasters, sexual abuse survivors are often diagnosed as having "Post Traumatic Stress Disorder" (PTSD). I believe this is a mis-diagnosis of severe, protective false-self wounding.

Multiple Personalities

From studies across the world, mental health researchers now agree that adults and children surviving cataclysmic natural and man-made disasters "dissociate," or "split." One form of dissociation is that survivors numb themselves, and (temporarily) feel no pain from a terrible physical or emotional injury. Other forms are escaping from agony by believing that the current horror is happening to "someone else" ("projection"), or isn't happening at all ("denial"). Many (most?) delusions, hallucinations, neuroses, paranoias, and psychosomatic illnesses stem from this automatic reflex to protect us from perceived outer and inner horrors.

False-self reality distortion allows a helpless child or adult being abused to "float up to the ceiling," "become an eagle soaring free," "visit the beach," or "become an observer." They detach from the overwhelm of their physical and emotional agony. Children enduring intolerable sexual, emotional, physical, or spiritual abuse or neglect appear to do the same thing. To escape unbearable terror, shame, hopelessness, and loneliness, such kids' false selves invent invisible companions or retreat into dream worlds which are absolutely real to them. See informed descriptions of this in Dr. James Masterson's "*Search for the Real Self*," and Brenda Schaeffer's "*Is It Love, or Addiction?*"

Since ~1980, it's become well documented that up to ~5% of our population has *extremely* fragmented ("multiple") personalities. These people repeatedly show patterns of hidden or obvious changes in thinking, abilities, and behavior—as though they literally become "another" person at times. Videotaped studies have documented that each *subpersonality*, or *alter*, in the host person can have it's own IQ, memories, skills, voice, likes, and even unique allergies and eyeglass prescriptions! This is unarguable evidence of our brain's ability to "fragment" (rewire itself) to promote survival.

Frequently, some alters don't know about each other. If they do, they can be deeply loyal, indifferent, or suspicious and fiercely competitive for control of the host person. Almost always, these extremely wounded people have experienced agonizing traumas in their early life. The public hears of only the most sensational of such cases, like "*Sibyl*," "the *Three Faces of Eve*," and "*When Rabbit Howls*."

People who suffer from "multiple personality disorder" (MPD) are understandably terrified and embarrassed by it's inexplicable symptoms. They live with what feels like an uncontrollable inner—and hence outer—life. Most try hard to deny or mask the evidence of their alters. Someone in your life now may have MPD without you suspecting it. Professionals working with these trauma-survivors patiently assist them towards awareness, acceptance, and eventual "fusion" and permanent integration of some alters.

Many subjective reports of this happening are now documented. The prestigious American Psychiatric Association (APA) first formally acknowledged this dissociative condition in 1980. They included it in the third edition of it's clinical standard "Diagnostic and Statistical Manual of Mental Disorders (DSM)." In the 1994 edition of the DSM, the APA revised the MPD term to "Dissociative Identity Disorder," or D.I.D. "Dissociation" means "personality splitting." Public recognition and understanding of this extreme form of false-self formation is limited—and growing. D.I.D. and the childhood trauma that seems to promote it may be more common in our population than previously thought. The ignorant ancestral stigma and fear of being "crazy" promotes shame-based people to camouflage and deny their symptoms of inner-family chaos and its effects—just as alcoholism, abortion, and sexually transmitted diseases have.

The Millennium of the Inner Family?

In the last four generations, then, at least (part of) our Western society has gone from believing in moon rays (making "lunatics") and devils to Freudian id-ego-superego "analysis," to (outer) family therapy, to *inner* children, adults and parents; to psychological woundedting and multiple personalities.

The concept of ordinary persons *normally* having a whole inner family or team simply extends these ideas. Evidence is growing that the high majority of us are not full multiples—and do have *some* personality fragmenting. Some people have more than others, depending on their genes, brains, and mix of pain, fear, confusion, and nurturance experienced as a child. Since I began studying *inner* families in 1988, I've met many average people who have 15 or more subselves *without being "crazy" in the least*. At times we certainly can feel "nuts"!

These personality parts seem to be like a group of related people living in the same dwelling. They each have different skills, jobs, ages, values, and needs, and may or may not know about, understand, and accept each other. They can ally, fight bitterly, or ignore or hide from some others, just as members of any group do. And like any crowd working together, if the individual members are acknowledged, respected, and effectively led, stress drops, and serenity and achievements soar!

Child development researchers propose that while our personality or *character* changes across our life, its basic structure (our core beliefs, values, perceptions, and priorities) is largely set by the time we're about five or six years old. Thus how *nurturing* we experience our earliest years to be has a profound effect on how our neuro-hormonal system develops—and on the rest of our life. *Nurturance* is the empathic, informed process of filling basic developmental needs.

You and your children may be among the first wave of people to start recognizing and accepting that normal people are really dynamic, talented, conflictual groups of subselves. One implication is that any two-person "conflict" is really three conflicts at once; one inside you, another inside your partner, and a third between both of your inner squads! Notice how your inner crew reacts to that idea . . . Small wonder many of us have trouble negotiating and compromising, including parents and kids!

So—Who Are You?

Your human *personality*, or *psyche*, or *self*, (small "s") . . .

- Is *not* a single monolithic aspect of your Being, but a rowdy, talented crowd of "subselves;" which . . .

- Changes in significant ways over time—within limits. Your many "sides" . . .

- Evolve from your unique organic mix of (neurological + hormonal + cellular + spiritual) components. Some of these are predetermined by inherited DNA, and others from your life experience and nutrition between conception (vs. birth), and your first three to six years of life; and . . .

- Your personality is dynamically guided or controlled by one or more *semi-independent* brain regions (modules) at any moment, and across time. These systems have no widely accepted name yet. Historically, they've been called many things . . .

• Selves	• Imagos
• Streaks—e.g. "yellow	• Sub-identities
• Alter egos	• Subselves
• Energies	• Daimons (demons)
• Sides—e.g. "musical	• Modes of being
• Higher selves	• Domains
• False selves	• Identity states
• Aspects	• Potentials
• Elements	• Self schemas
• Multiminds	• Subpersonalities
• Character flaws	• Internal objects
• Sub-regions	• Small minds
• Inner voices	• Possible selves

- Complexes
- Alters
- Moods
- (Mind) states

- Parts
- Agents
- Traits

See researcher/clinician John Rowan's interesting book "*Subpersonalities—the People Inside Us*" (Routledge, 1989) for a mind-stretching, well-researched historic and clinical perspective on this. The 1999 (Sage) book "*The Plural Self—Multiplicity in Everyday Life*," edited by Rowan and Mick Cooper, is even more compelling and convincing.

Based on a decade of parts-work study and experience, I believe that each of your personality parts has it's own unique perceptions, goals, motives, modes and styles of communication, priorities, capabilities, limits, tolerances, rhythms, developmental cycles, "moods" and ranges of emotional sensitivity and expression. "You" are a group of inner "people"—like a boarding house full of various relatives who may or may not know of, like, or "love" each other. Following the work of Dr. Richard Schwartz, (*Internal Family Systems Therapy*, Guilford Press, 1995) your whole group of active and inactive personality parts is called your "*inner family*" in this book.

Meet Your Inner Leader—Your Self

One of your personality subselves is naturally skilled at harmonizing and leading all other parts, and making optimal decisions *if allowed to do so by your other parts*. When their Self (capital "S") is trusted by, and leading their other subselves, people universally report feeling mixes of *grounded, clear, light, centered, purposeful, energized, aware, alive, confident, "up," resilient, focused,* and *serene.*

Your Self develops wisdom and ability from life experience. As an infant, your Self was undeveloped, so you (your inner family) had to depend on the inner families of your caregivers to fill your needs. Your other young personality parts got used to depending on these "big people" to satisfy your needs, and you became unconsciously skilled at trying to please and manipulate your caregivers to comfort and protect you.

If your caregivers' Selves were usually in charge, they gradually encouraged you to like, trust, and depend on your emerging Self, rather than theirs. Unfortunately, most of us didn't get that loving, sensitive encouragement consistently, or at all. Where true, that's more from caregivers' wounds, unawareness, and ignorance rather than "bad parenting." If that was your situation, then your "growing up" really meant finding a way to shift from *unconsciously* depending on others' inner families to fill your needs, to learning of and trusting your resident Self. Most of us faced with that implicit life challenge had little informed help with it, or even knew that's what we needed to do.

Reflect for a moment. How does your inner crew react to this question: *"Who do you usually depend on and expect to fill your daily needs and wants?"* Note that "me" now means a group of psychological subselves—so which subselves are "you" depending on in yourself or others around you?

Typical *emotional* needs for kids and adults alike are . . .

- Appreciation
- Companionship
- Patience
- Respect
- Potency (power)
- Validation
- Pride
- Affirmation
- Purpose
- Clarity

- Encouragement
- Humor
- Stimulation
- Play
- Hope
- Touching
- Tolerance
- Acceptance
- Usefulness
- Trust (security)

Put these primal needs together and they become a need for "love." Recently, have you looked to other people (lover, boss, friends, parents, child, guru . . .) to fill your mix of these needs, or looked inside and to your Higher Power, if any?

We've covered a lot, so let's recap: your *personality* . . .

- **Operates like a dynamic group of people.** Each of your personality parts can be aware of the other subselves or not; communicate with, ally, fight, or ignore each other; be active or passive; and react unconsciously and consciously to other parts'—and other people's—opinions of them. Your inner crew . . .

- **Interacts with your body** in ways we don't really understand yet. Some subselves seem to communicate via headaches, insomnia, nausea, chest pain, numbness, dizziness, hot flashes, dreams, and many others.

These *psychosomatic* signals can cause other parts to react—and cause other bodily symptoms (signals). And moment to moment . . .

- Your "inner family" **can experience itself** in a range from . . .
    (*chaotic / out of control / disorganized / frantic / panicked /*
    hysterical . . .)
    to . . .
    (*numb / blah / empty*),
    to . . .
    (*centered / harmonious / grounded / serene / calm / clear / sure / . . .*)
    to . . .
    (*enraptured / transcendent / enlightened / at One*).
    And your one-of-a-kind inner family . . .

- **Is neither *good* nor *bad*, by itself.** The *effects* of your personality's behavior on your wholistic health and on living things around you can be judged as being between *nurturing* (promoting wholistic health, growth, and full potential) and *toxic* (inhibiting these things).

From this, *personality* now becomes a word like *team, troupe, corps, gang, community, congregation, and family.* It follows that the words "I" and "you" have different situational meanings. They can refer to the whole (mind + body + spirit) entity, or the whole multi-sided personality, or the current false self (a group of subselves), or the true Self. Clarity on word meanings is key in recovering from false-self wounds.

You'll learn much more about the traits and characteristics of your inner team and your Self in Part 2.

Why Isn't Inner Wounding Widely Known?

Since I learned this *inner*-family concept over a decade ago, my experience is that most people are (1) unclear on what "personality" is, and (2) have never encountered the concepts you just read, in one place. When they do, they either say something like "Yeah, that makes *sense*," or "So you're saying we're all *crazy*?" Their automatic (fearful) association is "having personality subselves means 'a multiple-personality psycho.'"

If false-self wounding is so commonplace, why isn't it making top headlines in the media and personal growth bookshelves? Why aren't

clinical schools teaching about assessing and "curing" (vs. preventing) it?
I suspect a combination of interactive reasons:

- All our formal and informal training says, "Each human is one person, with one brain, and one mind"—and we're not encouraged or motivated to question that old assumption; plus . . .

- Widespread ignorance of brain architecture and functioning, and therefore of the modular-personality concept. This ignorance is slowly shrinking, as teachers learn what to teach with new multi-media help; and . . .

- Our media sensationalizes *excessively* wounded people, rather than empathically explaining their origins and behavior.

- Perhaps the most powerful reason that the inner-family concept is not yet widely understood and accepted is that we have a natural (false-self) *terror* and horror of feeling that . . .

     "I'm controlled by a shadowy, inept group of weird personality parts, and maybe I'm really crazy;" and . . .

     "My parents were probably wounded, and didn't nurture me well enough," vs. the Christian God's stern commandment "(Burn eternally, if you don't) honor thy Father and thy Mother"; and the horror of feeling . . .

     "My God, I've unintentionally passed on false-self dominance to my kids!" And . . .

- If most people are ruled by false selves, then our (unaware, wounded) policy makers are denying that **low-nurturance families are our societal norm**. Ignoring this amounts to implicitly sanctioning child neglect on an incomprehensible scale. To correct this, legal regulations about "family nurturance," and maybe "child-conception fitness" would have to be set and enforced. The barest public suggestion of this would probably cause riots. Notice your own reaction.

Together, these premises suggest why *normal* (vs. extreme) false-self wounding remains our cultural secret—our "elephant in the living room." If we are a nation of wounded people, our distrustful false selves have a common interest in helping each other deny our denials. What do you think? The false selves I've met often reactively equate conscious awareness of them ("exposure") with certain *death*. The more forceful subselves also enjoy the power and control they have, and resist "giving it up" to a Self they distrust, scorn, or don't know. Such parts also can reject relying on a Higher Power, because they'll lose inner-family status or control if they do.

Recall that widespread acceptance of the new idea that our *families* greatly shape our "mental health" is less than 50 years old. Also recall that the prestigious American Psychiatric Association only formally acknowledged "Multiple Personality Disorder" (MPD) in 1980—one short generation ago. The rules about our *personalities* are changing dramatically. Any core conceptual change like these evokes caution, doubt, confusion, disbelief, and "resistance."

So it takes great courage to acknowledge that a misinformed, biased, myopic, reactive false self may unconsciously dominate many of us—including "disturbed" kids, warlords, politicians, and eccentric geniuses. It takes even more courage (or pain) to square off and say—"I'm going to honestly assess myself and my partner for significant psychological wounds."

The long-term personal price for *not* assessing honestly for false-self dominance is even higher. It involves risking the lifelong wholistic health and happiness of your minor kids and grandkids, which is a form of unintentional neglect.

To help make this assessment project more credible and interesting, relax. Choose the "mind of a student" (curiosity and openness), and . . .

3)   MEET YOUR *INNER* FAMILY

WHO'S *REALLY* RUNNING
YOUR LIFE?"

Your personal group of subselves is as unique as your fingerprints. Yet most of us have some personality parts that perform common functions. They can be called by a wide range of names, but their inner-family *"jobs"* seem to be the same.

Three Groups

Just as Freud, Eric Berne, and Thomas Harris proposed, our inner team members seem to fall into three or four groups. From their key traits, our subselves can be grouped into Managers, Inner Kids, and Guardians, or Protectors. While each inner-family member (subself) brings us unique and special talents and abilities, those in each group have common traits.

All Manager and Guardian subselves have one goal: to *protect* us from extreme discomforts and dangers, and to s*urvive* in the world, moment to moment. However, subselves often have conflicting ways of trying to do this. Therefore, they need co-ordination and effective leadership.

Your **Managers** are the "general staff" of personality parts that (ideally) guide you through daily life situations when things are not threatening. Your Self is one of your Managers. This subself's natural talent is *excellent* inner leadership. This inner-family member can either help us be marvelously effective and serene, or may be blocked from doing so by other agitated, reactive parts. The word "self" (small "s") means all our parts together as a group. We'll see other common Managers in a moment.

Developmentally, **your Inner Kids** range from pre-verbal infants to teens. All your "inner children" fit here—you probably have *several*.

Because they're inexperienced, naive, and dependent, they're easily excited, and can be very reactive and impulsive. Just like physical children, that excitement can cause "us" (our mind-body) surges of sudden fear, confusion, rage, guilt, shame, sadness, joy, excitement, and elation. They're vulnerable to misinformation, misdirection, mistreatment, and unintended neglect.

Your young subselves can be intensely needy. When they are, or when they're joyous, amazed, or thrilled, they seem to infuse or "take over" your Self. Inner-family pioneer Dr. Richard Schwartz calls this **blending**. As this happens, our conscious and physical awarenesses are flooded with this young part's perceptions, thoughts, intense emotions, and motives, and we react impulsively ("Jack can be so childish.") Typical Inner Kids carry burdens of learned shame, fear, guilt, and distorted beliefs from your childhood. Fairly often, one or more of them lives every day in your long-ago past. They need to be identified and gently "rescued" from life conditions that have long since disappeared in the outer world—like an "uncaring" or abusive parent, sibling, or relative.

To protect your needy, reactive inner kids, your **Guardian personality parts** stay constantly alert to imagined or actual inner and outer danger. They seem to watch even while you sleep. They're like a Green Beret or SWAT team of dedicated specialists. Normally inactive, one or several Guardians spring into action whenever they believe that one of your Inner Kids is upset or in danger. They too can blend with, paralyze, or override your Self then—causing extreme or "irrational" reactions and behaviors that are hurtful to you and/or others. Some Guardians watch all your Inner Kids, and others devotedly protect individuals.

Typical signs of your alarmed Guardians taking over your Self are "failing," forgetting, spacing or numbing out, procrastinating, apathy, screaming, seduction, stealing, abuse to self or others, lying, sickness, depression, insomnia, physical pain (like migraines) or illness, delusions, phobias, suicidal or murderous thoughts, addictions, "spells," rages, and *many* more . . .

Such harmful protective actions may seem crazy or paradoxic. Our subselves seem to have their own kind of logic. With narrow views, short-term focus, and often badly distorted information, they're fiercely dedicated to protecting your defenseless inner kids and themselves.

Your Guardians stand down only when they trust that your Self and other Managers can reliably keep your young subselves safe—as *they* define "safe." You *blend* whenever one or more Inner Child and/or Guardian subselves take over your Self. Some people have *never* had their Self in charge—and don't know it. Could you be one?

Building inner-family trust over time, and freeing your Self from blending to competently harmonize and lead your three groups, is the goal of *inner* family therapy. Part 2 outlines this concept. Patient work at reorganizing your inner team or family yields the priceless goal of personal and family peace and self-actualization.

Now let's expand this abstract idea of three functional groups of personality parts, and make them more real. See who you recognize among your inner kinfolk . . .

Typical Subselves

Who comprises your three inner-family groups? Though we each have a unique roster, some parts seem to be very common in *function* among us all. Some personality functions (roles) are performed by one subself, and some by several parts together. You probably have most of these . . .

Typical Manager Subselves (Parts)

- Self / Leader / Coach /
- CEO / Chief / Director
- Spiritual One
- Organizer / Planner
- Health Director
- Analyzer / Thinker
- Striver / Do-er / Driver
- "Pusher" / Achiever

- Wise One / Sage /Old One / Crone
- Observer / Reporter
- Adult / "Common Sense"
- Judge
- Survivor
- Historian
- Nurturer / Good Mom / Good Dad
- Creative One

Typical Inner Children (Parts)

- Innocent / Naïve Child
- Playful Child
- Shamed / Guilty Child
- Hurt / Wounded Child
- Artistic Child
- Awed / Delighted Child
- Abandoned Child
- Lonely / Lost Child

- Terrified Child
- Curious Child
- Selfish Child
- Joker / Clown / Trickster
- Fetus or Infant (pre-verbal)
- Sexy / Lusty One (often a teen)
- Dreamer / Fantasizer
- Defiant / Rebellious Child

Typical Guardian or Protector Subselves

- Warrior / Amazon
- Indulger / *Addict*
- Controller / Manipulator
- Hermit / Loner
- Catastrophizer / Pessimist
- Abuser / Rager / Sadist
- Saboteur / Spy
- Entertainer / Clown / Joker
- Black Sheep / Scapegoat
- Rationalizer / Explainer
- Hypochondriac / Sick One

- Anesthetist / Numb-er
- Assassin / Suicider
- Evader / Avoider
- Perfectionist
- Witch / Bitch / Harpy
- Rebel / Activist
- Liar / Con artist
- Procrastinator
- Psycho / Weirdo
- Saint / Martyr
- Pleaser / *Nice* One

(more) *Typical Guardian / Protector Subselves*

- Idealist / Fanatic / Zealot
- Hoarder / Miser
- Distracter / Confuser
- Illusionist / Magician
- Vagabond / Drifter / Bum
- Daredevil
- Worrier / Panicker

- Idiot / Crazy One / Dunce
- Victim / Helpless One
- Thief / Crook
- Hero(ine) / Star
- Critic / Shamer / Blamer
- Impatient One
- Seducer / Tramp / Tease

The function of each personality part is more important than its name here. With some editing, do you see the whole "You" represented here among the three groups? Who *are* "y'all" anyway? Does it make more sense now to use the words *personality* or *character* as denoting an inner group or community of semi-independent specialists? *Now* who do you feel is really running your life?

Higher Parts: A Fourth Group?

Many believe we each have one or more *spiritual* parts. They reside inside us, "somewhere else," or both. People speak of special experiences with their *Higher Self*, a *Collective Unconscious*, *Mastermind*, *Soul*, *Higher Power*, *the One* or *Old Ones*, and/or *Guardian Angels*. Many followers of Jesus experience the *indwelling Christ*, or *Spirit within*, guiding us by a "still, small voice." Millions of oriental and other peoples venerate and obey wise ancestral *spirits*.

Other millions seek their "Buddha Nature." Many Native Americans and others *know* they have a Totem, Manitou, or Spirit Guide—a special visionary Being who watches over, guides, and protects them. In her interesting 1990 book "Recreating Your Self," therapist Nancy Napier proposes that we can meet and be advised by our wise and caring *Future* Self. I have witnessed many normal clients in my office conversing with this aspect of themselves.

Some people regard such spiritual energies as ridiculous, fanciful, or absurd. Others are certain of them from personal experience. Do you, or *could you*, have spiritual inner-family members who nurture, guide, and protect you? How might they communicate with "you" (your inner family), and vice versa? Do you have a "still, small voice?"

After a decade of inner-family work with hundreds of clients, Dick Schwartz reported experiences of some (not all) of them becoming aware of an external spiritual "councils" or "watchers" that sent caring guidance at crucial times. Could this be the source of "hunches" and "intuition"? Recently, his belief is that our Self is akin to our *soul*. Since "the truth" here can only be known intuitively and subjectively, there are many points of view.

Before answering some common inner-family questions, let's see . . .

A False self and True Self in Action

Let's compare how a typical divorced parent's false self and a true Self might handle unacceptable behavior from their ex mate. If you're divorced, imagine this example to be about you and your ex. If you're non-custodial, try to "be" your ex mate. If you're not a divorced parent, think of a divorced family you care about, and imagine being the custodial partner as you read this.

During your relationship years with your ex mate, you've each built unconscious patterns of thoughts, feelings, and behaviors with the other. You've formed assumptions and expectations about how the other will think and react to you, in certain situations. *You*, here, means the members of your inner family or team. Thus subselves will probably have "standard" (semi-conscious) reactions to your ex mate's violating your boundaries in ways like these . . .

- Walking into your dwelling without calling or knocking, saying righteously *"Hey—my child lives here, so I have a right to come in!"*

- Repeatedly asking your child for personal information about you, despite their discomfort.

- Showing your pre-teen child x-rated videos, despite your strong objection.

- Sarcastically criticizing you as a parent or a person to your child.

- Frequently sending the child support check late, and ignoring your protests.

- Insisting on telling you personal information about themselves that you don't want to hear.

- Calling your over-talkative parent or sibling for personal information about you.

- Repeatedly changing child-visitation arrangements at the last minute. And . . .

- Frequently ignoring the terms of the legal parenting agreement, and refusing to discuss that.

The way you react to behaviors like these depends on your history, your perceptions, and how your inner family is composed and led.

Common *false-self* (young and Guardian subselves') reactions to behaviors like these include automatic responses like . . .

- "Blowing up" at your ex-yelling, name-calling, threatening, disparaging.

- Sulking, obsessing, and badmouthing (blaming/attacking) your ex behind their back.

- Numbing out, ignoring your feelings, and passively enduring and "making the best of it."

- Muffling or manifesting your hurt, resentment, and anger by overeating, overworking, working out, or "getting depressed."

- Asking a child or someone else to tell your ex to stop violating your boundaries.

- Punishing (hurting) your ex mate in some way, and denying, justifying, or flaunting that.

- Praying humbly for patience and tolerance, and piously or righteously "turning the other cheek."

- Whining and complaining to others, and avoiding confrontations with your ex.

- Sending your ex spouse mixed messages like "I want you to stop that (but I won't do anything if you don't)."

- Guiltily relishing wonderful fantasies about awful things happening to your ex "some day." And . . .

- Generalizing critically—reminding your ex angrily of all the rotten things s/he's done over the years.

- When your true Self is leading your inner family, s/he typically would . . .

- Carefully weigh the overall situation against your current and long-term needs and goals,

- Collect opinions from other subselves and trusted people,

- Review your Bill of Personal Rights (p. 350), and then . . .

- Calmly decide:

    1) *Specifically* what you need from your ex, right now;
    2) How to *assert* that firmly and respectfully, and *handle probable reactions without giving in, defocusing, or "losing it"*; and . . .
    3) What *specific* action you'll take if your ex chooses to continue violating your or your child's boundaries.

- Then follow through, by . . . Asking your other personality parts to not interfere; confronting your ex, when neither of you is distracted; and firmly asserting your boundary, and your consequence for violating it. S/He means this respectfully as clear, factual information, not a threat or manipulation.

If your ex is wounded, her or his false self may need to interpret your assertion as "controlling," "manipulating," or "threatening." Your Self knows s/he can't control that, feels compassion, rather than blame, and guides other inner-family members to not over-react to it.

Which of these reaction-types is more familiar to you—false self, or true Self?

Here's how typical *inner* and outer dialogs would go for each type, if, say, your ex spouse insists on changing visitation arrangements at the last minute, despite your repeated requests not to.

The scene opens with your ex (Pat) calling 10" before he's due to pick up your kids to say he can't come because "something's come up." Expecting your daughter Anne to be with her Dad, you're dressed and ready to go to dinner with a special friend. This has happened several times in the past months, with your ex offering insincere apologies, and/or giving no explanation at all. You're on the phone now, Annie's within earshot, and you're unconsciously controlled by your . . .

False-self Personality Parts

They all "speak" (think and react) at once. *Italicized* words are your *thoughts* . . .

Inner Critic—*"Pat is such an insensitive, selfish JERK!"*
Catastrophizer—*"We'll have to put up with this for the rest of our life. We'll never be able to have friends or good social times again!"*
Peace Maker—*"Now c'mon, everyone, calm down. Let's not get into a . . . "*
Rager/Warrior—*"Oh shut up, for God's sake. You are such a pitiful doormat!"*
Righteous One—*"Remember, 'act not in anger . . . "';*
Perfectionist—*"People have to do what they commit to! Pat has to . . . "*
People Pleaser—*"Agh! Sal (friend) will be so disappointed and inconvenienced! We'll send a card, after calling now and explaining that . . . "*

Scared Child—*"Please—is something really bad going to happen? Did I do something wrong?"*

True Self—*"WAIT a minute! What we need to do now is . . . "*

Critic and Rager together (distrustful)—*"Ah, be quiet! We'll handle this."* They blend, and use your lungs and larynx to say "I am so *sick* of you being so unorganized and irresponsible, Pat. You *always* disappoint the kids, and you make it impossible for me to have a social life (reality distortions). I can't believe how *selfish* you are! (name-calling, blaming) I've already made plans to . . . " (Implied disrespectful message: "I'm 1-up.")

Pat's false self (sarcastically)—"Well, here we go again—demanding your way without ever considering what *I* need. You didn't even bother to ask why I can't pick the kids up, did you? How do you know my leg isn't broken? You really don't give a damn about me, you're just focused on your wonderful social life." (Implied message: "No, *I'M* 1-up!") A well-practiced power struggle is starting to evolve, based on *unawareness* and mutual false-self dominances.

Your daughter Anne (nearby) looks at you, her subselves alert and anxious . . .

Inner Good Parent—*"I have to tell poor Annie what's going on, without bad-mouthing Pat . . . "*

Critic *(sarcastically)*—*"Hey, way to go! How come you let Annie get whipsawed by this stupid jerk? She keeps getting hurt, and you never stand up to Pat. Some 'parent.' You're* pathetic.*"*

Shamed Child—*"I don't know how to parent! I'm no good at anything. I'm so stupid and worthless . . . "*

Addict (Comforter)—generates a vivid multi-sensory image of a delicious martini, butterscotch topping, or slices of high-fat pizza) *"Hey, wouldn't this taste really good right now? C'mon, let's . . . "*

Judge speaks—"So what's your stupid excuse this time, Pat?" (Condescending voice tone implies "I'm 1-up") . . .

All this took under 10 seconds to happen. Neither true Self is in charge, and neither "you" nor Pat is listening to the other, objectively aware of your inner and interpersonal processes, or intentionally problem solving. This example omits Pat's inner chaos, which is just as confused and raucous as "yours." There are probably well over 20 combined subselves activated here, including Annie's inner Worried Girl, Critic, Hurt Girl, Angry Girl, Numb-er, and Good Girl (Pleaser)!

What might this inner and interpersonal exchange have sounded like if your Self was solidly in charge of your inner family?

Your True Self Leads

You're on the phone, and Pat's just said "Something's come up." Again, *italics* are thoughts.

Your Self—"So you're not coming? Pat, this is really short notice!"

Pat's false self—"Yeah, I know. I'm sorry, but a key client called just as work was ending, and my boss wants a report on her desk at 9 AM tomorrow. She's a real hardnose, and I have to get on this tonight . . . "

Critic—*"What a jerk! Pat probably wants to drink beer, and rent a sleazy video."*

Historian—*"This is the fourth time in five months that Pat's cancelled at the last minute."*

Practical Adult—*"We better call Sal right away, and let Annie know what's happening . . . "*

Perfectionist and Idealist—*"This is wrong! People have to honor their commitments!*

Your Self—*"Hang on; hang on, all of you."* (Forcefully) "Pat, when you tell me of changes at the last minute like this, I feel disrespected, hurt, frustrated, and *really* irritated!" I need you to give me more warning. I also need you to get more assertive with your boss. I feel like she's running my and Annie's life, because you choose not to draw the line with her." (a clear, respectful "I-message" assertion.)

Pat's false self (defensively, voice rising)—"Oh, I suppose *you* never had things change suddenly without being able to control anything, eh? Remember all the times you . . . ?"

Guilty Child—*"He's right! Remember when we messed up by . . . "*

Critic/Blamer—*"What a sorry excuse for a man. As usual, if we try one more time to act civilly to him, he whines and tries to squirm out of facing the truth and being responsible. Isn't that just like him—avoiding and pointing fingers like a guilty kid. We should . . . "*

Cynic and **Amazon**—*"Look, talking has never worked. Let's cut this short, and call the lawyer."* (They stop short of blending with Self.)

Self—*"Let me handle this."* (Calmly, to Pat) "You need me to acknowledge that you couldn't forecast this client's call and the demand from your boss." (Empathic listening, not *agreeing*.)

Pat's false self (feeling *heard* and affirmed)—"Uh, yeah! (pause) I don't like last minute changes either, but I really don't have a choice here."

Your Self—"Well, I see it differently. At the least, you could confront your boss factually with your having an important commitment with your daughter, and then brainstorm a compromise. You also could have called me right away, and given me more warning of your choice to change our plans, so I could change mine."

Critic—"Way to *go!*" (Your other subselves agree)

Doubter—*"Easy does it! You know how unreasonable Pat can get if he feels guilty . . . Are you overdoing the confrontation thing here?"*

Self (firmly)—*"No. This has to stop."*

Pat's false self—"Well, I'll try. Look, I really have to start on this report, so would you tell Annie that I'm really sorry that . . . "

Critic (sarcastically)—*"'Well, I'll try.' What an indecisive weasel!"*

Spiritual One—*"You misunderstand. Pat is wounded, not bad."*

Practical Adult—*"This is a real opportunity to not only adapt to this change, but start doing what we can to avoid this happening again. We should (1) have Pat explain this to Annie, (2) call Sal, and (3) assert with Pat to try renegotiating with him respectfully and patiently."*

Nurturer—*"Right, Annie needs . . . "*

Self—*"Thanks."* Calmly: "Two things before you go, Pat. I need to sit down with you and work toward changing visitations. I'm not sure you're aware how often you abort, and how that affects Annie and me. I know you don't have time to talk right now. Please check your schedule and call me about whether you can work on this with me next Tuesday or Thursday night, all right?"

Pat's false self—"You want to change visitation *again*? You know we've been over and over this. I don't think we need to change anything."

Self—"I know we've struggled. This is *my* need, Pat . . . "

Critic (not blending)—*"Tell Pat how unreliable and irresponsible he's been!"*

Self—*"Not right now. That'll only cause defensiveness, and get in the way."*

Self reasserts—"So will you let me know if you can talk next Tuesday or Thursday—say 8:00 or so?"

Pat's *true* **Self**—"Yeah, OK. You said there were two things?"

Self—"Yeah. I'd like you to explain to Annie what's happened here. While you do that, I have to call Sal on the other line and say that our dinner's off."

Pat's false self—(feeling guilty and defensive) "OK, put her on . . . "

Self and Nurturer, holding out the phone—"Annie, Hon, our plans have to change. Come and talk to your Dad, OK?"

Pause and notice with interest what your inner crew is saying, right now. Who's "speaking"? When you've listened (your Self), note the themes of this two-minute vignette:

- Your inner family members trusted your Self to handle this unexpected situation. They were relatively quiet, and (mostly) didn't interrupt, babble all at once ("mind churning"), or take control (blend), as they needed to in the prior example.

- Your true Self was aware, direct, and *respectfully* assertive, vs. aggressive ("I'm 1-up") or submissive ("I'm 1-down").

- Your Self stayed aware of the concurrent inner and interpersonal processes, and intentionally stayed focused on problem solving in the present and near future. She didn't allowing other inner-family members to blame, complain, name-call, or rehash the past. Your Self was assertive with Pat *and* your protective (narrow-viewed) Inner Critic, which avoided defocusing and escalating into an argument or a power struggle.

- With the counsel of your Practical Adult subself, your Self stayed balanced, and attended the immediate needs of you, Pat, Annie, and Sal; and . . .

- By calmly proposing several specific meeting times, your true Self laid the groundwork for you to declare your boundary with Pat about aborted visitations with your daughter. Between now and the meeting, your inner family will need to debate what options you and Pat have, what you need, and any consequences you'll need to assert if Pat chooses not to change.

Can you imagine having this kind of Self-managed inner and vocal conversation with your ex or other conflictual people? Notice with interest what your inner voices are saying right now. Which of your subselves are "speaking"? Imagine a similar exchange between you and an upset "Annie," or manipulative parent or sibling. The themes are just the same.

Unless a Guardian part needs you to defocus or blank out what you've just read, I suspect you have some . . .

Typical Inner-family Questions

After first digesting the inner-family and false-self concepts, people often wonder . . .

- What are my subselves like?
- Where did they come from?
- What do my parts *want*?
- Who am "I"—who's "*Me*"?
- What is my Self like?
- How do I know when my Self is leading?
- How do subselves behave?
- Is there any danger in "meeting" my personality parts?

Let's look at each of these.

What Are My Subselves Like?

While unique within each of us, our subselves seem to have common traits. Part 2 explores how to use them, in some detail. From the reports of hundreds of people who have done parts work, our inner-family members . . .

- Seem to be semi-independent regions of our brain. As such, subselves can't be killed, fired, ejected, or gotten rid of. They can each be refocused and retrained. Parts are often eager to change their burdensome or harmful protective roles, when they see value to that and feel it's safe. This enables us to reorganize our inner team. And your parts . . .

- Are benign. *From its own viewpoint*, every subself means us well.

- Can be developed or not, depending on inner and outer events and environments. That means that some parts can have latent abilities that you haven't experienced yet.

- Activate or rest, depending on perceived current inner and outer life conditions;

- Have unique individual talents and abilities, and a primary job or mission that uses these.

- And your inner-family members . . .

- Each have their own thoughts, ideas, feelings, and perceptions of the inner and outer world—which are sometimes very distorted and outdated;

- Can quickly and permanently *change* values, roles, and goals, *when that seems useful, safe, and viable.* This gives you the ability to make second-order (core attitude) changes, which underlie major behavioral changes. Reality check: recall some major habits that you've intentionally changed, over time.

- Want inner and outer respect, recognition, and appreciation for their efforts, and respond to these "just like people do;"

Further, your inner-family members . . .

- Are *extremely* self-protective of themselves and of you—though paradoxically, their ideas of "protection" may cause you or others great pain and harm. This is largely because typical parts have very narrow vision;

- Are of equal value to you. As in any true team, there is no one "best" part, overall. Each part excels in certain situations;

- Live in the present *or the past.* When feeling safe enough, subselves trapped in the (usually traumatic) past can come to live in the present. Until they do, they habitually react just as they did many years ago. "Reasoning" or trying to persuade them of this seldom works, until you find a safe way to have them tour your present environment (rescuing)."

- Communicate with each other, and with you (your Self/conscious mind) via thoughts, "voices," hunches, feelings, images, visions, memories, "senses," day and night dreams, and physical sensations. The latter can include "tight" stomachs and throats, neck and back pains, cramps, headaches, tinglings or numbnesses, "floating anxiety," "panic attacks," warm or cool skins, thumping hearts, "crawling" feelings, and many others;

- Are male, female, or neither, *regardless* of your physical gender.

- And your three or four groups of subselves . . .

- Often don't know each other, or misunderstand, fear, distrust, scorn, and compete with, each other, alone or as allies. Self-motivated (true) recovery can greatly improve this, over time;

- Can disguise themselves and/or hide from you (your conscious awareness) and each other, if feeling confused or unsafe.

- Have chronological (developmental) ages, preferred names and titles, and sometimes favorite locations in your body—which can change.

- May perceive that they have their own "body," which may be "lost" via real-life trauma, and regained via "parts work" (Part 2).

  And your subselves can . . .

- Return to remembered real-life traumas, and—with planning and new inner-family awareness, leadership, and alliances—"re-do" these events to greatly reduce old fears, guilts, and compulsions.

- Cause and relieve many physical and emotional symptoms; and . . .

- (Eventually) function as a true co-operative team, led by your unblended Self or its delegates, in any situation.

Notice what your mind and body are doing now, including your breathing and posture. Do you need a break? Now that you have part of the big picture, let's look a little closer. What you're learning here is the basis for your subselves meeting each other, and your Self respectfully reorganizing them, over time.

More Detail on Your Subselves' Key Traits

Your parts can give you "voices" and/or (often) images of themselves on request. The images are either clear and accurate, or symbolic or disguised. Many of your parts (usually) want to be noticed and heard! Often very distrustful at first, they may hide silently until they feel it's safe to be known by other parts or people. One scared part may block another from identifying itself. Some people only have different inner "voices," while others have voices, images, feelings, or a combination.

Your parts may use images of real or imaginary children or adults; cartoon or fiction characters; males, females, or neither; plants, animals, or objects in Nature; geometric or abstract symbols—just about anything. One client's part chose the image of "a pile of black dirt." Another portrayed itself as "a pack of ferrets."

Your subselves can change their images as they feel more trusting, or use alternating images, depending on how they feel. *Your subselves are brain regions, not their images*—so if a part looks or sounds like your Father—it's not *him*!

Some of your inner members live in the present, and *others are trapped in your past*. The latter are usually young Inner Kids or Guardians who literally don't know or believe that the world is different than when they started developing. That may have in your mother's womb, or when you were four days, or three, seven, or 13 years, old. *They react and pursue their goals based on conditions that are no longer true*—but they minimize, deny, or don't know that.

Personality parts may know they're in the past, but can be afraid to shift to the present—or they may want to, but not know how. Your Self can invite them to tour your present life, and to ultimately come *here* to live, when that feels safe to everyone. When they do such "time travel," people usually report feeling noticeably more "together" and "better." Does "Get it (your 'act') together" take on a new meaning here?

Each subself brings you one or several special abilities, like compassion, wisdom, joy, humor, concentration, playfulness, curiosity, creativity, patience, bravery, and so on. Building inner-family awareness and cooperation lets these talents be used in combinations that best fit any moment. Once trusted by your crew, your Self can delegate, coordinate, and direct your parts to fit their talents to any given situation—just like a coach skillfully adjusting her team to play against a new group of challengers.

Your subselves can learn, and change their minds about themselves, each other, and the real world. They can switch goals and strategies within you *quickly*, and work cooperatively and peacefully with each other. Like most team members who feel useful and appreciated, they really prefer this, once they believe it's really possible. This cooperation can build over time, with loving patience and intentional inner-family education, negotiation, and problem solving.

What inner voices are you experiencing now? Who's "speaking," and who's silent?

Though some parts may seem "bad" or "evil" at first, they all *truly* mean to help. They intensely fear that some catastrophe will happen to a Young subself or the physical you, if they stop what they're doing—even if their actions cause pain or harm. You and others have *no* inherently "bad" parts. There *are* misguided, misinformed, terrified, distrustful, myopic subselves, who can change over time.

Such parts see no viable alternatives to their way of keeping you *safe*. They also may greatly fear losing their "job." When they learn of trustworthy alternatives, there's often another inner job that they'd much rather do.

For example, a woman plagued by repeated "uncontrollable" failures at work eventually found a *Saboteur* part that was responsible. It feared that if the woman was as successful as she was capable of being, she would "get a swelled head," reap scorn and ridicule—and *be rejected again*, as in her childhood. The *Saboteur* used the inner image of a curly-haired five-year-old girl. She acknowledged that by making the woman "forget" things, procrastinate, and not propose innovative ideas, she was hurting the woman—but this Guardian subself saw no options to protecting her from *certain* rejection and greater agony.

After meeting the woman's Self, and some negotiation and retraining, the *Saboteur* said she would rather become a spiritual director for all the other parts. With their collective agreement, she tried that out. The woman reported feeling "different" about herself, and that her life changed "for the better . . . "

A controversial implication of this idea is that *there are no intrinsically "evil" or "bad" people*. Notice your *Inner Critic*'s reaction to that idea. There *are* enormously *wounded* people; whose chaotic inner families live in a distorted, terrifying, shameful inner past. They *do* cause real pain and suffering to themselves and others—and have the potential to stop, with informed help, via Self-directed inner-family work. People controlled by false-selves who believe in Hell and Satan or the Devil *must* reject this idea, or confront the horror that they and key people around them (like their family and church denomination) have lived their lives from a false belief.

Other people have real physical and neural disabilities, and imbalances of hormones and other key body chemicals and processes. They too can do "bad" things—but (I believe) are not *immoral* or "*evil*" by nature. Working with subselves offers genuine hope of positive change to the former people, while new drugs and medical procedures can relieve some of the latter.

When enraged, terrified, or deeply hurt, guilty, or ashamed, your subselves can try to "take you (your Self) over." Like "outer" people, your inner parts fight with each other regularly, each believing it's right, and wanting it's way with and for you. Without internal trust and leadership, these battles often hurt others and you. When this happens, you feel *torn*, *confused, uneasy*, and perhaps awash in conflicting feelings about a person, idea, or event.

These times are just like a group wrestling over control of a moving vehicle: one part wants to go faster, another to hit the brakes, a third holds their head and screams, while a fourth pulls on the wheel and yells "we've got to *turn*, right *now!*" The skilled onboard professional driver (Self) is quickly overwhelmed. Do you ever feel anything like this? Who usually "wins" and "drives your bus"?

At such times, you and others lose the ability to react calmly to situations, make balanced decisions, and coordinate and use your subselves' talents wisely. A common reaction at such times is "I don't know *what* got into me (or *you*)!" That is literally true, until you become aware of your inner crew. Note with affection that typical kids' Selves don't yet know how to "drive their bus," and frequently stall, run out of gas, or run into or over things . . .

Parts who take "emergency" control may only appear (blend) at times of great stress or felt threat. In reality, it's not really "us" (our Self) reacting, but an overexcited, reactive subself. If asked, "Who's scared in you?" we reflexively answer "*I* am!"—rather than "Jinx, my abandoned four-year-old inner child."

Someone living in fear all the time (i.e. constant blending with a terrified Young subself) may never realize this is happening. They may have never experienced the serenity and power of having their real Self trusted and in charge! Without Self and inner-family awareness, such kids and adults live as terrified and deeply unhappy children, guiltily masquerading as adults their entire lives. Do you know anyone like that?

Doing "parts work" or inner-family therapy (Part 2) helps people see their daily *inner* conflicts in a new way. It helps their Self or a competent, trusted delegate to lead. This skilled leader part takes in the advice of other inner team members involved, adds its own wisdom, and calmly makes decisions that best fit both short and long-term situations with available information. The more this happens, the greater the trust your other parts feel in your Self's ability to value and listen to them, and keep everyone safe and productive.

Before meaningful parts work, the average peace or chaos in your inner family usually (1) mimics the emotional environment in your childhood years, and (2) creates and seeks similar conditions in your present outer family and work lives. Until in true recovery, we (our false self) often unconsciously reproduce our early-family low-nurturance over and over, because that's our dominating subselves' definition of *normal* . . . Even if uncomfortable, blah, or painful, it's safer than the fearsome unknown. Once freed to lead, your Self probably has other ideas.

Where Did My Subselves Come From?

We'll cover this in some detail in Part 2. Here's a preview: as mentioned before, we're all born with the normal capacity to develop subselves—semi-independent brain regions—like seeds, specially the Managers and Inner Kids. Based on the observed human ability to grow new neural pathways and "rewire" old ones, this natural ability to evolve semi-independent subselves is called "multiplicity" by some inner-family and personality students. Guardian parts seem to "start" (develop) after some major traumatic incidents or periods of too little emotional/spiritual nurturance that we experience as infants and pre-teens. New subselves may appear in later life, but that seems unusual. New *functions* (inner-family *roles*) can and do appear as recovery unfolds or people age. Veteran subselves' deciding to change their old inner-family role is like reprogramming a computer, vs. creating a new computer—a new subself.

"Trigger times" that breed Guardians are those when we young kids felt agonizingly hurt, shamed, confused, stressed, or terrified by caregivers, teachers, strangers, animals, or nature (e.g. a tornado). Often these traumas are so shocking and painful (e.g. abandonments and sexual abuse) that a Guardian protectively helps us "forget" they happened. The personality fragments (parts) that appear after these events seem to *never* forget, tirelessly guarding us against similar wounding and harm—*long after any real threat is gone.*

What Do My Parts Want?

Every subself seems devoted to keeping their host person and themselves safe from pain and harm—as *they* define "safe." Like people, subselves strive fiercely to keep their roles or "jobs" intact, and to be free to use their gifts productively. Each inner-family member also appears to long to be recognized, trusted, respected, and appreciated for what they're trying to do for us.

In early parts work, some subselves typically fear that other parts, or an external person, will misunderstand and dislike them—and want to reject, demote, kill, or banish them. Such insecure parts can resist your meeting or disclosing your inner teams (inner voice/s: "What *stupidity*! A *real* waste of time! Don't be a jerk! You're weird! This'll *never* work! *Stop*! You'll uncover a *horror* you can't handle! You'll flip *out*!")

Or they can try to hide themselves by blocking any thoughts, sensations, and images; or inwardly saying "I *won't* talk to you or let you "see" me! These are *normal* defenses, which subside as parts come to trust that they and you are safe enough.

Protective subselves can also be terrified that if you explore your *inner* territory, you'll find and "free" a paralyzed part they see or sense as very dangerous to you or them. Patience, empathy, and small, safe risk-takings change this. Other subselves—specially young ones—will welcome you ("I've waited SO long to be noticed and cared for! *Please* don't leave me!")

Who Am "I, Myself"—Who Is "Me"?

Terms can be confusing here! "Me," "myself," and "I" each usually mean *all* your physical, emotional, and spiritual parts together—the whole person called by your name. Your *Self* (capital "S") denotes your inner leader/coordinator part. When agitated parts take over or blend with your Self, you may experience their feelings, thoughts, and goals as "me." They are *not* you *as a whole*.

If one or several subselves are controlling your Self, the words "I" and "Me" refer to them—*not* you as a whole person. Can you think of someone constantly obsessed with others' opinions and being "right"? An alliance of their hyperanxious *Critic*, *Perfectionist*, and *Shamed One* may "always" control their Self. So "I" refers to several or all of them, when they're in charge. Pronoun and name confusions subside when your Self is free, trusted, and solidly in charge.

Incidentally, Managers can take over your Self just like Inner Kids and Guardians. Know anyone who's "always in their head"? Their Self is probably controlled by their distrustful *Analyzer* part, which may fear that allowing emotions would be disastrous to the person. For most wounded people, distrustful Inner Kids and Guardians are usually holding their Self hostage, and "driving the bus."

What's My Self Like?

Reflect—are you aware of a real or fictional man or woman whom you feel was an effective, gifted *leader*? Have you ever been in a group that was competently guided and directed through various situations by a respected, reliable chief, chairperson, teacher, scoutmaster, director, minister, president, or coach? Your Self is an innately skilled leader.

Like all personality parts, your Self has special abilities. It is *not* more "powerful" or "better" than any other inner-team member. Its main talent and aim is to be an excellent leader. As such, your Self's talents are to (1) realistically perceive situations in light of your major abilities and life goals, (2) invite and evaluate the counsel of inner and outer advisors, and then (3) calmly and firmly coordinate other parts in making effective decisions and acting on them.

Your Self is like a naturally talented musical conductor, drama or dance troupe director, congregational minister, or an athletic team's coach. S/He skillfully clarifies and communicates goals, resolves impasses; delegates responsibilities; and builds group morale, loyalty, identity, and teamwork. Your Self can give recognition and praise; coach; and make artistic, complex, and "tough" judgments *well—most times*. When trusted by all other parts and free to lead, s/he can reliably counsel, encourage, and empower other confused or overexcited parts in all kinds of life situations. Your Self also has misconceptions and limitations, makes mistakes, and can feel stumped, at times. Can you imagine having such a part in charge of your life?

When you were a child, your Self was unwise and inexperienced. S/He *couldn't* make healthy decisions for you. Ideally, your caregivers' wise Selves and empathic advisors did that for you. As your new protective Guardian subselves evolved, they had little reason to trust your own inept Self. They adapted by chronically depending on "outsiders," or themselves, as the safest leaders. No one knew this was happening. The most effective parents are those who lovingly encourage kids to begin to trust their own judgments, including "I don't know enough in this situation—I need help."

"Growing up" can be seen as the process over time of (1) your Self growing into it's full potential as an instinctive, knowledgeable leader; and your other parts (2) gradually learning to appreciate and trust that leadership and related spiritual guidance, rather than anxiously depending on inner Guardians and outer hero/ines or caregivers. This outer-to-inner *trust* shift is much more likely if the person is *aware* of their subselves and this process. Do you know anyone who is aware of this—and is teaching it to the kids in their lives?

At any moment, your Self may be (1) free to lead and coordinate, (2) strongly influenced or controlled by, or (3) blended or paralyzed by, other subselves. Your Self is unlike a coach or musical conductor in that s/he can't *fire* or *sanction* distrustful or rebellious team members. S/he can't stop other parts from interfering or taking control. There is no "board of directors" or "police" s/he can appeal to. S/He needs trust and willing co-operation from your other parts to be *really* effective for them and you. Other subselves can come to believe in the judgment and leadership of your Self only from experience. They then want to follow that gifted subself from *respect* and trust, rather than fear, resignation, or duty.

As your eye can't behold itself without a mirror, your Self can't "see" itself in an inner image. Your Self is the one *doing* the seeing. So if you "go inside" and image "your Self," know that it's *another* part. The "you" who's focusing *is* your Self. If your (unblended) Self says "I," it may mean either your whole person, or your Self alone. This gets clearer as you do more parts work (Part 2).

Some researchers believe that our inner family, or "cast of characters," has *no* Self. They feel our momentary thoughts, feelings, and actions are a blend of all our parts, which get along by group consensus, as some human communes do. Leader Self or inner-family consensus—which concept fits better for you? Based on a decade of research and experience, this book follows the idea that we each have a skillful, dedicated true Self inner-family member.

How Do I Know If My Self is In Charge?

Have you ever belonged to a harmonious team of people with a common purpose and a leader you all liked, respected, and really trusted? Recall how you *felt* in that group. When this happens in their *inner* family, people say they feel *calm* or *serene, centered, light, clear, firm, focused, sure, confident, patient, energized, compassionate, aware*, and *grounded*—even in a crisis. These feelings are sure signs your Self is unblended, undistracted, and free to lead. Do you "know" such feelings? How often do you get them? Would you like to have them more often? Any sarcastic inner laughter at that dumb question?

Some people have rarely or never felt those for long—or ever. They may understandably not relate to, and scoff at, the idea that such inner harmony is an actual option for them or anyone. Does this describe *you*? Your Mother? Your Father? Your mate?

How Do Parts Behave?

A true story: A single mother holding a very stressful and responsible managerial job began to develop severe back pains that woke her up in the middle of most nights. As she tried to fall asleep again, she usually experienced "mind racing," obsessing on the chaos at work, and the difficult situations she faced both there and personally. Her doctor and a chiropractor could find nothing physically wrong. Meditation, aspirin, and prayer didn't help. She was becoming more and more exhausted, irritable, and distracted both at work and with her early-teen daughter and friends.

Respectful inner-family inquiries revealed a Guardian part that said clearly it was responsible for the back pain and mind racing. It chose the inner image of a "hulking" teenage boy. He said he knew he was causing the woman distress and pain, but saw no other way to ensure that she had enough time to carefully think through the next day's activities. He only vaguely knew of her Self, and had no trust that it or any other part could reliably protect her against "failing" and being humiliated and shamed at work. It developed that the woman had a very young part that believed she was "no good," and the "Hulk" was single-mindedly devoted to protecting that Shamed (inner) Child.

When respectfully and sincerely acknowledged and *listened to*, "The Hulk" was willing to meet with the woman's Self, and other competent Managers. Over time, Hulk said he was willing to try to let them prepare adequately for the day's work. Her back pains stopped immediately, and stayed gone.

I recall describing this real event to a group, after an introduction much like what you've read. One woman raised her hand, and said, "Up until now, I was staring to believe this (inner family) stuff. Now I don't, because of what you just said (about the vanishing back pain.)" My best guess is that the concept plus illustration had hit too close to home for (became too frightening to) one or more of her Guardian parts. The woman's *Cynic* took over (blended), and used her lungs and vocal chords to recreate safety by debunking the implications of the story, and by implication disqualifying me as trustworthy or credible. Her Self, I imagine, would have said something like "Isn't that interesting," while perhaps wanting more information before judging the credibility of the story and me.

This vignette illustrates common parts' behaviors: once focused on and *listened to respectfully*, your subselves will usually disclose their purposes and strategies, which other parts they know, and their key beliefs and values. They'll listen to other inner and outer viewpoints, and will negotiate for safe change. When conditions are "right" (safe), they'll meet with other parts, and start to harmonize and co-operate with them. I have witnessed these dynamics in scores of people who had the courage to explore their inner families—and felt it in my own.

Is There Any Danger In Meeting My Parts?

No! At first, your Guardians or Inner Kids may normally feel alarmed, and strongly resist. As they gradually come to trust that your Self's intents are to (1) learn about, *appreciate*, and help each member use it's gifts fully and effectively; and (2) to reduce inner and outer conflict and stress; their resistances shift to enthusiastic co-operation, over time.

From inherited ancestral ignorance and superstition, our culture links independent subselves and "multiple personalities" with mental illness, and *craziness*. In a decade of experience and research, and listening to other inner-family therapists, I have not encountered a single instance of anyone being harmed by meeting and harmonizing their subselves.

When first hearing about their *inner* family, many people are naturally skeptical, scornful, or amused by the idea (how about *you?*). This may be one or more of their Guardian parts (e.g. *Skeptic*, *Doubter*, or *Pessimist*) doing their defensive job well. *It also may be that such people truly have no inner team, and really do "have it together."*

Some Guardian and/or young subselves fear that doing parts work will unleash some awful "force;" "demons;" indefinable, destructive "things;" or overwhelming feelings. I've seen and heard *nothing* to support this. What can happen—*when your Self and Guardians clearly believe you're strong enough*—is that some repressed experiences, and the memories and feelings attached to them, can be *safely* accessed, experienced, and released. Such recall usually signals breaking old, protective emotional repressions, and the release of frozen grief. These are tolerably uncomfortable, growing and healing times.

From experience, I believe that over time, such cathartic releases can free many people from unconscious bondage to some (not *all*) . . .

- Physical conditions like chronic pain, asthma, headaches, and insomnia;

- Emotional states like panic or rage attacks, depressions, "hyperactivity," "Seasonal Affective Disorder," or "numbness;" or . . .

- Self-harmful habits like obsessions, reflexive pessimism, addictions, over-isolation, and self-sabotage.

Doing inner-family work is fail-safe: you (all) control it. You do only what you wish, when you wish, and how you want to. This work is not magic, and it's not a cure-all. It *is* often an effective way for many people to feel calmer and more confidence and enjoyment in their life, over time. Parts work can frequently help resolve some vexing relationship problems like codependence, marriage, and parent-child struggles, *when both partners' Selves use it cooperatively.*

Pause, and poll your inner crew. How are they feeling about this attempt to generalize about who they are, as individual subselves and a whole personality? Did the inner-family questions you just read answer most of their questions, or do they have new ones? How are *you* (your Self) feeling about your marvelous collection of Managers, Inner Kids, Guardians, and "Others"?

Reflect for a moment. Recall picking up this book and deciding to read it. Can you recapture your motives, thoughts, and feelings? What have you learned, so far? Are you different in any way than when you began reading? How do (each of you) feel about all these pesky questions? (*My Guilty Kid* and *Pleaser* parts are feeling anxious.) My queries invite you to use *awareness* to appreciate some aspects of your marvelous inner crew. Breathe well, stretch, and take a break, if any of the passengers on your "bus" need to. Who's driving, right now? When you return, poll your inner committee to see what you (all) want to do:

- Put this investigation down now, and resume "some (other) time."

- Get undistracted, and journal about your awarenesses and reactions so far, including trying out transcribing or tape-recording a discussion among those of your parts who have some "public opinions" about the 13 premises or any spinoffs. Or . . .

• Use your new *personality* knowledge and the 11 checklists in Part 3 to begin to assess "Who Is *Really* Running My Life?" You now know enough to decide if such assessment has any merit for you—i.e. researching whether a faithful, distrustful false self has been holding you in protective custody without your conscious awareness. Or you can . . .

• Defer that, and read the next chapter on some vital implications of false-self wounds—to yourself, to committed mates and co-parents, to mental-health clinicians, and to our society and it's policy makers (below); or you may choose to . . .

• Learn more. Scan the selected readings list in Part 4, get some, and sample other authors' opinions and experiences on multi-part personalities, and true and false selves to give you more perspective; or your inner leader/s may feel it best to . . .

• Begin learning how to use some version of parts work to empower your Self to reorganize your inner family. See Part 2. Or . . .

• Get very still, comfortable, and relaxed. Respectfully and firmly quiet the chatter in your mind, breathe well, and ask your still, small voice, "What should I do now?" Then trust whatever answer you receive. Or . . .

• Do something else. Whatever you decide, try to *sense* who's making your decision, and why. Your inner voices and your body will give you clues.

4) THE EFFECTS OF
FALSE-SELF DOMINANCE

SIX WIDESPREAD INNER WOUNDS

Fualse-self wounds in yourself and/or others probably stress your daily life in many direct and indirect ways. This chapter explores the key ways. Seen together, the impacts of psychological wounds are challenging, to say the least. My purpose here is to widen your view, and encourage you to assess yourself for false-self control and guard your dependents against it. I hope it spurs a few special readers to act on a community or societal level.

Recently, almost half of American first marriages, and probably a *higher* fraction of stepfamily marriages, have broken up. Millions of other (re)married co-parents elect to live in the daily misery of psychological divorce. It seems probable that the majority of us Americans live in a significant degree of personal, marital, and familial unhappiness and stress. This is happening amidst a dynamic culture with unprecedented freedoms, opportunities, resources, and services. We live in the best of times and the worst of times—as our ancestors did.

In my work as a family-life researcher, educator, and counselor since 1979, I've met or talked with over 1,000 average Midwestern divorced co-parents and re/married couples. Most of the re/marriers had previously divorced, and a few were widowed. Almost all were veteran bioparents. Others had never married, or were newly wedded to a bioparent. Most were in their late 30's to mid 40's. Does this describe you or someone you care for?

They came to tell me their stories about unexpectedly confusing relationship struggles with ex-mates, troubled kids, and each other. They spoke in pain, bewilderment, blame, and anger. Sometimes they laughed, but seldom from the belly. A common theme: "I never knew it'd be like this . . ."

Perhaps like you, these women and men all deeply wanted a happy re/marriage and a loving, normal family—and were finding these elusive. Many re/married co-parents were reluctant to say, "We're a stepfamily," or "I'm a stepparent." Those who were seasoned spouses and caregivers often seemed uncomfortable describing their family conflicts and frustrations, or vehemently blamed "the ex."

Men in particular found it hard to look in their partner's eyes, or mine. Having a second marriage start to wobble *forces* (some) self-reliant people to seek help—specially if they live with one or more beloved kids in obvious pain.

Nina and Tom were one such couple. A vivacious 40-something, redheaded mother of teenagers Bill and Anita, Nina had recently quit work because of severe depression. Several years before, she had divorced her first husband. She had endured nine years of his drinking-and-remorse cycles, punctuated by many episodes of physical and verbal abuse. "I kept hoping he'd change, and we'd be all right," Nina said. "Finally, I had to accept—he wouldn't."

Tom sat close to his new wife on the couch. They held hands and leaned into each other as they talked. They had remarried eight months before, sure that their shared love would iron out the modest complexities of their three-home stepfamily. Tom had not seen much of his two pre-teen kids recently, who lived with their mother. "She and I don't talk much," he said. "She won't listen to me. She's pretty bitter about our divorce—though she asked for it. Never have figured that out."

Nina had called for the appointment. "It's about Tom's rages," she said intensely. "They really *scare* me and the kids. He gets totally out of control. We have to do something, but I don't know what . . ." Their story was unique in detail, old in theme: Tom was hurt and frustrated by his teen stepdaughter's "ignoring" him, though he was now the sole breadwinner for her, her brother, mom, and grandmother. When he blew up at her daughter Anita, Nina felt caught in the middle: the standard stepfamily *loyalty conflict*. Her husband became enraged when she seemed to side with Anita. "We just don't know how to talk together about this," the redhead said. "I feel so *torn*." Tom smiled, in his pain. "Yeah, my anger scares me too. We . . . I . . . have to knock it off. It's *hard*."

From long experience, I began to ask about their childhoods. Almost offhandedly, Nina said, "My mom was tough, at times." I asked how. "Oh, she broke a lot of plates over my brother's head. He was pretty wild. She used to hit us with a 2-by-4 until I hid it. She was alcoholic back then, but she's 84 and mellowed, now." Tom grinned. "Yeah, that's another thing we have in common: my Dad was a heavy drinker too." I tried to catch his eye. "Do you think he was addicted?" Tom looked at the ceiling. "Hard to say. I suppose so—never really thought much about it." Familiar ground.

I asked quietly "Do either of you know what 'ACoA' stands for?" Tom nodded, and his wife looked blank. "It stands for 'Adult Child of an Alcoholic (family).' Each of you may be an ACoA. You both probably come from pretty low-nurturance childhoods, through no fault of your parents. If so, that's *normal*—and it's related to both your divorces, Nina's depression, and Tom's rages." They looked sober, and said nothing. Further questions disclosed that Tom and Nina's first mates *also* grew up with little consistent emotional and spiritual nurturance.

Since I began studying family "dysfunction" in 1985, I've made it a point to ask troubled co-parents (divorced bioparents, and stepparent-bioparent mates) about their childhood years. I've found that most, like Tom and Nina, were *unintentionally* neglected emotionally and spiritually, and that many were abused spiritually, emotionally, physically, and/or sexually. Their young years were spent in environments lacking too many of the traits on p. 257.

Few are aware of this, or what it means to them and their kids. Fewer *want* to be aware, because of awful implications. Their parents weren't monsters. Almost always, they *too* were accidentally deprived of adequate emotional and spiritual nurturance, and were significantly wounded as children—and didn't know it. They loved and parented as best they could.

Are you "Nina" or "Tom"? If so, what does that mean to you and your kids?

Common Inner Wounds

The six psychological wounds from low childhood nurturance in adults and kids seem to be:

- Living in chronic denial of false-self dominance, these other traits, and this denial.

- Excessive shame ("I am a flawed, bad, worthless, unlovable person") and guilts ("I've done terrible, *bad* things").

- Excessive primal fears of abandonment, emotional overwhelm, risk and change ("the unknown,"), "failure," and "success."

- Trusting too easily, and being repeatedly betrayed and hurt; or trusting too little, and living in anxiety, suspicion, and social isolation. Together, these four traits promote two more . . .

- Reality distortions, like denials, repressions, fantasies, exaggerations, paranoias, and illusions, and . . .

- Trouble *feeling* and genuinely bonding, committing, and loving, while longing for these.

If you're being held in protective custody by a well-meaning, short-sighted false self, your mix of these traits has major implications for your personal wholistic health and longevity, your primary relationships, and your child conception and/or co-parenting decisions and outcomes. The traits also have profound implications for any clinical practitioners and other human-service professionals you seek help from (or don't), and the society in which we all live.

This chapter highlights key implications of psychological wounding in each of these domains. We'll outline an effective way to recover from it in Part 2.

Wounds and Your Wholistic Health

Your wholistic (usually spelled "holistic") health is the combination of your emotional, physical, spiritual, and mental well being. Significant false-self wounds degrade each one of these areas, directly and indirectly. That diminishes the quality, productivity, and length of your life. One of the insidious things about false-self dominance is it inherently makes living a degraded life appear "normal" to us—reality distortion at work.

My Mother died "of lymphomatic cancer" at age 50. My Father died "of lung cancer" at 63. The average life span of Americans then was about 74 years for men, and 78 for women. Both these good people were clearly addicted to ethyl alcohol, nicotine, and high-fat "comfort foods." I now believe they both were burdened with codependence—relationship addiction (p. 316). Like many Depression-era men, Dad was also a workaholic, like his stern German-born father.

These are symptoms of *major* psychological wounding. Unseen and untreated, it cost Dad 10 or more years of life, and Mom ~25 years of hers. For the last decade or more of their lives, they were very unhappy, and privately discussed divorce at times. Because their peers and our (very judgmental, nonspiritual) relatives decreed addiction and divorce were *shameful*, they settled for depleting psychological divorce. I believe both my parents were majorly wounded people. They, our relatives, and their society had no inkling that these good people were each captive of a protective false self. Both were college graduates—and woefully ignorant of the world *within* them.

Since I began to study and do recovery in 1985, my observation of hundreds of significantly wounded adults and kids leads me to conclude that my parents are typical of significantly wounded people. Ceaseless inner conflict among chaotic subselves, plus toxic outer environments promote (1) unhealthy eating, work/play/rest, and exercise habits; (2) self neglect—avoidance of preventive and curative medical care; and (3) spiritual poverty or anxiety (vs. fulfillment and serenity). The false-self reality-distortion strategies like denials, repressions, minimizations, and rationalizations make these toxic factors seem acceptable and "normal." It's possible that significantly-wounded ancestors bequeath "genetic predisposition" to certain diseases like diabetes and cancer. I am not medically trained, so this is intuitive speculation.

Bottom line: if you are significantly controlled by a false self, I fear that puts you at greater risk of chronic or serious physical illness and premature death. Recent research seems to support this (**http://sfhelp.org/parent/news/ucla.htm**). Without real recovery and retraining, significant false-self dominance also puts your descendents at higher risk of these than if their true Selves ran their inner families.

False selves and Primary Relationships

People seek relationships to fill a set of deep emotional, spiritual and physical needs. Like most people, you're probably motivated to choose and live with one special adult. That universal urge is powered by a mix of primal needs for companionship, affirmation, stimulation, and intimacy. You may have other semi-conscious needs to feel needed, useful, impactful, "known," *special*, and "secure." Still other behavioral wellsprings may be longing to send your genes and beliefs into the future by co-creating and raising one or more kids, and to feel that you're personally and socially and "normal."

Unseen inner-family chaos will relentlessly limit your satisfying your needs in two ways: if, who, and how you choose a partner; and how you relate to her or him before and after your commitment rite. How well you satisfy these ceaseless needs over time will have a major affect on your and your partner's wholistic health. That in turn will affect the wholistic health of any dependent kids you two care for—and whether they develop major false-self wounds.

Inner Wounds and Courtship

If a false self dominates your life, you risk avoiding a primary relationship commitment and living a solitary, impoverished life, or picking "the wrong" partner—a wonderful, exciting, alluring, *significantly wounded* person. Two wounded mates rarely seem to have a long-term, mutually fulfilling relationship. My clinical experience since 1981 with hundreds of couples, and my own redivorce, suggests that many people ruled by false selves pick (1) the wrong person/s to commit to, (2) for the wrong reasons, at (3) the wrong time. In America 2000, over half ultimately divorce, legally and/or emotionally.

Clinical veterans Harville Hendrix, and Hal and Sidra Stone propose that we all have "disowned" personality parts. We (our false self committee) fear and are ashamed of them, so they unconsciously "hide," "exile," or "repress" these "awful" subselves. (Got any of those?) Hendrix, the Stones, and others believe we react strongly to people who display repressed parts of ourselves—both desirable and despicable. For instance, if you are "shy and introverted by nature," you might find a gay, extroverted "social" partner intensely alluring. Have "opposites attracted," in your life?

Conversely, if you're unaware of repressing a shameful Voyeur part, and you meet someone who's Voyeur subself is flamboyantly out for all to see, you (your *Inner Critic*) proclaims righteously "What a disgusting *creep.*" Your *Inner Magician* causes you to distort reality and be oblivious of *your* "disgusting" *Inner Voyeur.* I accept the idea that the persons we're most strongly attracted to and repelled by are often displaying personality parts that our Guardian subselves have repressed without our awareness.

After decades of clinical experience, Dr. Hendrix proposes another way parts affect our courtship choices. He and his many followers believe that most of us *unconsciously* marry "Imagos"—delusional images of the best and worst *parts* of our main childhood caregivers. Imago therapists propose that we do this for two unconscious reasons: to . . .

- Regain the best-remembered traits of our caregivers via our delightful new partner—like patience, tenderness, strength, playfulness, and humor (and unconditional love, if we were so blessed); and to . . .

- "Finish" major unresolved emotional/spiritual conflicts with our original caregivers.

One type of such conflicts is ridding ourselves of undesirable traits we "somehow picked up" from our caregivers—e.g. a need to shade the truth and manipulate, to control, be "cold," or to interrupt others. The other kind of conflict ("old baggage") is gaining the courage to do as adults what we were unable to do as dependent kids—e.g. confront a controlling, demeaning (wounded) parent (in the guise of a similar new mate), and successfully assert our needs, feelings, and opinions, despite ridicule, shame, and disinterest. A major aspect of typical recoveries is leaning the art and skill of effective assertion, based on evolving a Bill of Personal Rights. See the sample in p. 350.

If true, these two ideas combine to suggest that if typical "love-struck" (needy) co-parents aren't aware of being controlled by their narrow-visioned false selves, they're at high risk of choosing an alluring *illusion* as a (new) partner. Hendrix proposes that *if you don't heal your personality wounds, you'll keep remarrying the same partner (parts of one or both caregivers) until you do.* Notice your thoughts and feelings now . . .

Many theorists preach, "Heal your wounds, guilt, shame, and anger with Mom and Dad *before* saying 'I do.'" Others say, "No, you have to commit to a primary relationship to heal your childhood wounds—you can't do it alone." Either way, your opinionated *inner*-family members conduct your courtship dramas. I believe significant inner wounding and romantic-love hallucinations are two of the five main causes of our largely ignored U.S. divorce epidemic.

Once you exchange rings and vacuum up the rice, how can camouflaged inner wounds affect your wedded bliss?

False selves and (Re)Married Life

Your and your mate's subselves interact all the time, like two debating or sports teams. Your Inner Kids and Guardians are regularly activated by perceived threats of attack or rejection by "your mate" (i.e. her or his inner family), and vice versa. People with a history of relationship struggles may have seldom or never experienced a steady pairing of (my Self's in charge) and (your Self's in charge) with a friend or lover. Have you?

Many of the frustrating "automatic" cycles we have with special people become clear—and can *change*—via working with inner subselves. For instance: Jack is attracted to Anita, both emotionally (*Adult Man, Needy Boy*, and *Good Father* subselves) and sexually (*Lusting Teen* part).

Anita responds unconsciously to each of these with four complementary parts: her *Adult Woman, Good Mom, Lonely Child*, and *Sensual Female* subselves. If Jack seems to pull away, her *Lonely Child* gets scared and sad, based on early real emotional abandonment by her father. One or several distrustful Guardians quickly blend with her Self and "make" her be shaming, seductive, rejecting, abusive, controlling, and/or pitiable.

Jack can respond to these in many ways. If Anita's dominant Guardian is a *Guilt Tripper*, Jack's sensitive *Shamed Child* will feel awful. His *People-Pleaser* Guardian will spring to life, so Jack apologizes to Anita and becomes attentive again. Her *Scared Child* is reassured, so the *Guilt Tripper* stands down, freeing her Self. His *Shamed Child* gradually feels better, and his *Pleaser* gives way to his *Adult* and Self.

This whole sequence might take two weeks, or five minutes. Without awareness of their parts' interactions, and their Selves being disabled (blended), Jack and Anita's relationship goes on until the next version of this (or another) avoid-approach cycle repeats. Seen this way, there is no "Jack and Anita"—there are eight or more subselves interacting to create a complex and dynamic relationship between two (physical) "individuals." Notice your reactions to this idea . . .

Similar cycles occur in all relationships: friend-friend, clerk-customer, parent-child, boss-employee, student-teacher, and so on. Large groups like real families become stunningly complex, if member's Selves aren't regularly in charge. Few of us are aware of the *amazing* interactions that happen at lightning speed within and between us. Does this make sense to you?

A remarriage implication is that if false selves often control stepkids' other bioparents (and their new mates), the new couple is highly likely to face *years* of strife with one or more "hostile, crazy" exes over child-related conflicts. Because there are so many stepfamilies—and wounded, bitter ex mates—a new post-divorce problem is emerging. It is unofficially labeled "Parent Alienation Syndrome" (PAS), and centers on one parent appearing to maliciously discredit the other bioparent in their kids' eyes, and/or prevent contact. I have worked with scores of such families, and find that the warring co-parents are *always* highly wounded (as are most of their new partners), and their shame-based false selves fiercely deny that.

People ruled by false selves are not famous for effective communication skills, empathy, or respectful assertion. Their minor kids get caught in the middle, in a low-nurturance environment maintained by (shame-based) blameful pointing fingers.

I believe false-self wounds cause or combines with three other factors to cause most psychological and legal (re)divorces:

- Ignorance of family-nurturance factors (p. 257), the seven effective-communication skills, healthy relationship principles, and healthy three-level grieving,

- Blocked grief from prior agonizing personal and family losses (broken bonds), and . . .

- Inevitable romantic-love (courtship) distortions and illusions.

For information on these, see the companion volumes. *Satisfactions* and *Stepfamily Courtship* (Xlibris.com) or **http://sfhelp.org/hazards.htm** on the Web.

Two majorly-wounded partners who each are in meaningful real (vs. pseudo) recovery can have an exceptionally strong, rich relationship. They're uniquely able to help each other break the chain of unconscious bequests of low nurturance and false-self wounds down the generations.

Do you have—or want to have—one or more children? If so, I assume you long for (usually) enjoying them, as you guide them towards adult independence. I suspect you look forward to the shared satisfaction of their happiness, health, and success. If you are significantly ruled by a false self, how may that affect you and your mate realizing your co-parental dreams? How may it affect your kids?

Inner Wounds and Parenting

Here *parents* includes biological parents, stepparents, and any other adult providing primary care for minor children. The implications of false-self wounds and co-parenting effectiveness easily justify a whole book (See *Build a Co-parenting Team*, Xlibris.com). Understanding the implications starts with defining "What is an *effective* parent?" A superficial answer sounds like "Someone who raises a happy, healthy child." A more thoughtful answer might be something like . . .

"An *effective* (vs. 'good') parent . . .

- Can accurately name most of the traits of a high-nurturance family (p. 257), and most of the behavioral symptoms that suggest these traits exist (p. 281);

- Is clearly aware of __ who comprises their *inner* family, __ who usually leads it, and __ the *inner* nurturance level that results from that;

- Can accurately name what normal kids need spiritually, physically, emotionally, and cognitively, as they develop from fetuses through young adulthood;

- Deliberately __ chooses a wholistically-healthy (true-Self led) partner, and then __ makes timely, consensual child conception or adoption decisions with their partner; and then . . .

- *Wants* to dedicate major high-priority effort to consistently filling their dependent kids' normal and special needs from *love*, vs. duty or anxiety. And an effective co-parent (mostly) enjoys steadily . . .

- Protecting, encouraging, teaching, and guiding (loving) each dependent child toward wholistic health and adult independence, and competence at their own child-conception and nurturing; while . . .

- The co-parent nurtures and heals themselves of significant psychological wounds, and . . .

- Stays intentionally aware, balanced, and wholistically healthy while they do all this, one day at a time, for several decades or more."

More concisely, "An *effective* parent is someone who—as judged decades after child co-conception or adoption—successfully co-provided a high-nurturance environment for the kids *and adults* who comprised their immediate family."

How do these three definitions of an "effective co-parent" compare to yours? Do they describe each of your parents? Your grandparents? If you have kids, do these definitions describe *you* and your mate/s? Pause, breathe well, and notice what's happening among your inner committee.

Denied false-self dominance usually hinders biological, foster, adoptive, single, and step moms and dads from doing each of the high-nurturance things above. Also, parents controlled by false selves are likely to be part of a low-nurturance extended family, which lowers the odds the parents are getting the wholistic nutrients they need from key relatives, over time. The lower the family nurturance level that caregivers provide for themselves and their minor kids, the more likely it is the kids will develop protective false selves.

False-self wounds manifests in many ways between parent and child. One of them is chronic double messages, which no one notices, questions, or confronts. They can sound like . . .

- "I really love you . . . (one subself speaking) " . . . now leave me *alone!*" (another subself);"

- "I'm so proud of you . . . (*Nurturer subself*), " . . . even though you're a stupid klutz;" (*Inner Shamer*);

- "I am *not* angry at you!" (clenched jaw, red face, sarcastic tone)

- "Of course I want to know what you feel . . . " (no eye contact, busy doing something else)

- "Kids go to dentists and doctors. Adults don't have to."

Variations are boundless. They all produce confusion, mistrust and doubt, and for young kids, guilt, frustration, and shame. Double messages *produce the same effects among inner-family members*, and with primary adult partners. Some inner-family therapists believe that subselves can have their own inner families, but that's another book!

Other classic ways parents' wounds affect minor kids are either expecting them to be over-responsible "little adults," or smothering ("over-controlling") them and blocking them from learning self-competence. Typical shame-based or fear-based (wounded) caregivers, including teachers and baby sitters, will vehemently deny doing these, or endlessly justify them. *"You don't understand. I have to do it for Joanna because she always . . . "*

Another way is non-verbal: some parents ruled by false selves avoid hugging or kissing their children, or are overly physical—including unconscious sensual or sexual touching, caressing, and kissing.

A fourth way parental wounds affect children is modeling self-neglect to them—poor hygiene, grooming, medical care, diet, and exercise habits, while possibly preaching otherwise (another double message.)

A hero of mine, psychiatrist Milton Erickson, wrote of work with a patient which adds perspective to our topic. His patient was a young man who had been burdened by major stuttering since early childhood. Conventional speech therapy hadn't helped. With permission, Dr. Erickson hypnotized the man, and skillfully got him to regress to a time he was about four years old. The little boy haltingly described his huge, gruff father scolding him fiercely for spilling soup from his spoon. He tearfully recounted his father saying angrily *"Always* be careful what goes in *and out* of your mouth!" His father, a military pilot, crashed and died the next day, and the boy had stuttered terribly, ever since. Erickson worked with that repressed awareness, and had the man's *Adult* subself gently explain to his inner four-year-old what his father had meant, and that the soup spilling had *not* caused his father to die. After coming out of trance, the young man's stutter immediately dropped "by about 80%"—and stayed there. Many similar stories of working with the unconscious mind sway me to believe that parents' false-self wounds unintentionally promote wounds in their dependent kids.

I contend that emotional and legal divorce is major sign of false-self dominance, ignorance, and denials. Other probable signs: adult and child addictions; chronic illnesses; "major school problems," (some) Attention Deficit Disorder (A.D.D)," teen runaways, pregnancies, and abortions; child suicide gestures or fantasies; all forms of abuse and parental neglect; and "over-serious, over responsible" kids.

After 29 years' clinical study and experience, my guess is that most (all?) "parenting" and "family" problems involve significant psychological wounding plus lack of knowledge, in one or more co-parents and relatives, and any kids involved. As suggested in Chapter 1, only professionals and researchers specializing in dissociation and inner-family therapy hold this view, so far.

If these premises are true, the personal, family, and societal implications of adaptive childhood false-self formation (wounding) are profound. They probably have affected your life in direct and indirect ways you're unaware of—so far. You may well be aware of the *symptoms* of the six inner wounds . . .

False selves and Human-service Professionals

Your life will be significantly affected if (1) you hire wounded human-service professionals to help you and/or your family, and (2) if you've chosen a human-service career—specially in some branch of "mental health."

Since learning of multi-part personalities in 1988, I've noticed in many clients and colleagues that significantly-wounded men and women often spontaneously express interest in some aspect of "psychology" and "human behavior." Many of my clients have chosen in a human-service profession, like beautician, day-care supervisor, nurse, lawyer, customer service rep, mediator, coach, salesperson, teacher, waitress, and—counselor. Several have been highly interested in nurturing and healing animals.

Many of the clinical texts I've read since 1979 humorously or dryly surmise that we in the medical, pastoral, and "mental-health" fields are really seeking to heal our own wounds by helping others to heal and prosper. I've seen no research that bears this out, but the persistence and prevalence of the idea implies some truth to it. If so, there are several major implications worth pondering.

It's probable that any human-service professional you hire (clinician, lawyer, mediator, doctor) to help with your life is (or was) significantly wounded themselves. Professionals who deny a dominant false self risk providing you with well-intentioned, skewed service. That can manifest anywhere between ineffective, unethical service to compulsively over-responsible, *enabling* assistance. Like "overprotective" (enmeshed) parenting, the latter blocks you from evolving your own self-sufficiency and self-confidence by assuming the responsibility for fixing your problem. Either of these types of "help" is likely to provide temporary solutions, and to hinder empowering your Self. You'll find suggestions for shopping for an effective recovery counselor in chapter 6.

If a childish false self is influencing your life, s/he will probably urge you to seek professional helpers who will act like a parent—i.e. helpers who will take responsibility for filling your *surface* need, or symptom. For example, filling your cavities or surgically bypassing your blocked artery doesn't touch your underlying self-neglectful attitudes: eating poorly, ignoring dental hygiene, rarely exercising—and denying, minimizing, or rationalizing these. Self-neglectful or self-abusive attitudes are typically fostered by (1) a Shamed Child ("I'm bad—I don't deserve health or happiness"), and (2) ever-alert Guardian parts who focus on providing *temporary* comfort to that child ("Sure you can have that bag of yummy chocolate morsels, Honey—don't let that scary adult talk about cavities and cholesterol worry you.")

Doctors, dentists, oculists, pastors, and therapists who are guided by their true Selves can only show you or confront you about the *real* cause of your symptoms—they can't direct your daily life as your protective, short-sighted false self does.

If you're in a human-service profession yourself, or wish to be—I suspect that the odds are better than even that you're often unwittingly held captive by a protective false self. If so, that shapes your choosing this work, limits the effectiveness of your service, and perhaps stunts or exaggerates your satisfaction from providing it. Note your immediate reaction to this premise. (Who is that?)

Another implication: if the 13 premises about multi-part personalities in Chapter 1 are largely true, most of your clients or patients offer you presenting problems which mask their deepest need: to discover and empower their Self to release them from false-self domination. Working on resolving presenting problems nets out to symptom-relief, so the core false-self wounds will resurface again in other guises. As long as this happens, your clients' minor kids are at significant risk of inheriting false-self wounding themselves. Are you professionally responsible for them if their caregivers are unaware? If not you—who?

Do you believe in "psychosomatic" illnesses—bodily maladies caused or promoted by emotional "disturbances"? (What is an "emotional *disturbance*," anyway?) Our emotional/spiritual stability undeniably affects our bodily functions and organs, and vice versa. Could common troubles like allergies, migraines, insomnia, and "indigestion" be mute subselves trying to express something important? Could hidden false-self dominance weaken our immune systems and raise susceptibility to viruses and bacteria—e.g.

to flu, asthma and pneumonia? Could severe or significant psychological wounding promote some forms of cancer and "hormone imbalances"? In the last decade, credible studies imply that faith-based group prayer promotes certain medical healings. Could that be because sincere prayer is a way of calming inner families so they can receive spiritual "nutrition"?

This raises practical and ethical dilemmas in prescribing or relying on mood-altering drugs to stabilize or reduce "emotional problems." Using prescription drugs to reduce emotional discomforts is a socially sanctioned version of using alcohol, cocaine, or sugar to ease current misery. While genuinely relieving current discomfort, it avoids confronting the (scary) root cause, and *spreads* the problem, long-term. This is because dependent kids inherit their drug-taking caregiver's false-self dominance and pass it on.

Those who argue "psychological cures don't work as well as drugs, or at all" are often right—so far. I suspect that's because patients, practitioners, and society don't understand or accept the concept of multi-part personalities, and their false selves unite in fiercely guarding the secret. As a medical layman, my current perception is that science still can't say *why* people have "hormone imbalances." Medical researchers can't accurately predict why some people with proven "genetic predispositions" for alcoholism become addicted, and others don't. I believe a major determinant is the nurturance level of the gene-carrier's childhood family—which is shaped by the inner-family harmony or chaos of their caregivers. The Nature-nurture debate rages on—probably between passionate armies of false selves.

In my generation of mental-health training (1980-90), the schism between "(substance) addiction counseling" and "psychotherapy" was clear and unremarked. We were taught by implication that these were two similar, separate fields. My clinical study and recovery experience since 1985 strongly suggest that "addiction" is just another manifestation of low inner and outer family nurturance. I now believe that effective recovery from a true addiction *does* require specialized clinical skill and resources—*and* strategic use of some form of inner-family work as outlined in Part 2.

Note that we're all pioneers here: "addiction recovery" theory and programs just emerged in the last several generations. Validating "multiple personalities" and acknowledging widespread childhood abuse and neglect have barely had one generation to seep into public consciousness. Inner-family therapy is even newer.

If you're a mental-health professional, I respectfully that suggest you refocus from reading this book "to help other people," to helping yourself first. Use the 11 worksheets in Part 3 honestly, and see where that leads you.

I also recommend you rethink your paradigm about individual vs. couple, vs. family therapy. Teaching adult partners and whole families about their inner families can open major new options for desired therapeutic change. For a clinical overview, I highly recommend *"Inner Family Systems Therapy,"* By Dr. Richard Schwartz.

Wounding, Society, and Ecology

A core proposal here is that children unintentionally deprived of enough emotional and spiritual nurturances automatically develop a protective, dominant false self. The resulting inner wounds seem to promote or cause chronic illness and unhappiness, stunted or toxic relationships, unrealized human potentials, and premature death. Typical false-self personality parts work hard to remain hidden from the host person's conscious awareness.

As Colin Ross has observed, we appear to be an entire culture of significantly-wounded people in a mass delusion. Our inherited individual denials have blended to produce an unnoticed "elephant in the living room" that spans most (all?) nations and cultures. The social and ecological implications of this are almost incomprehensible. See how you (your inner crew) feel about a few of them . . .

Dominant false selves are typically concerned with short-term individual comfort and security. Other than *Idealist* and *Zealot* Guardian subselves, parts have little or no real interest in local, national, or global needs, because personal needs and conflicts are far more vital. Usually they don't care about other person's individual needs—unless keeping another person healthy and happy fills the false self's need. Altruistic people do genuine social good, and often don't really understand their core motives for doing so—e.g. to offset gnawing toxic shame and guilt, and avoid their inner pain and lack of true life purpose. Yes, of *course* there are exceptions to this.

Before meaningful recovery, false-self personality parts operate largely below conscious awareness. Their thoughts, feelings, and perceptions are the only "normal" the adult or child has known. This promotes confusing inner-family and social double messages. For example, "I love my child, *and* (I'll pretend) I'm not toxically addicted (i.e. wounded), and that my addiction isn't harming my child. If anyone points out this contradiction, I'll justify, argue, deny, attack, or ignore them."

I believe most of our major social problems are (1) symptoms of epidemic false-self wounding and ignorance, and (2) our lack of effective *preventive* policies and programs. Our national, state, and local attempts to "fix" teen suicide, school dropouts and murders, abortions and pregnancies, drug dependence, and obesity are well-meant attempts to cure the symptoms, while tacitly agreeing to ignore the root social problem: inherited, socially-condoned irresponsible child conception, and low-nurturance, ignorant parenting.

This is just as true for our national adult mood-control (e.g. anti-depressant) drug industries; and the criminal justice, welfare, and mental health systems. Most of the billions of tax dollars poured into these programs aim to treat the symptoms, not *prevent* the root cause.

To protect our citizens, most states require applicants to qualify for a license in order to legally become a barber, beautician, food purveyor, accountant, plumber, lawyer, vehicle operator, or even an angler. We sternly require aspirants to pass rigorous examinations to earn college diplomas, and professional licenses and certifications to sell real estate, lead a church congregation, or wear a law-enforcement badge and gun.

The tragic paradox (societal double-message) is—to my knowledge, no U.S. state yet requires two adults to *demonstrate* their competence and readiness to (1) co-create and maintain a lasting, high-nurturance committed relationship, and to (2) conceive and nurture a wholistically-healthy new citizen, over two decades of committed sacrifice and joy. This is crudely like societal officials covertly agreeing to hand out handguns or infected needles to every preschool child in the land, urging parents to ignore that, and then focusing all policies and programs on making beautiful, cost-effective cemeteries. Note your reaction to this metaphor. To protective false selves who avoid pain by distorting reality, the absurd and tragic becomes perfectly acceptable.

One recent result: almost half of U.S. first-marriages fail. Most of them involve minor kids. A higher percentage of remarriages breaks up—most of them affecting young or adolescent kids. Unmeasured millions of other adults and kids live in solitude or unhappy marriages, households, or homeless enclaves, lacking viable alternatives. The implacable, awful truth seems to be: we inherited, live in, and condone a low-nurturance society. We piously wring our hands at the ills and struggles of our "poor children," and revile evil drug growers and importers, and the human rights atrocities of other countries' politicians.

We are the first generation of global citizens to be able put all the puzzle pieces together and have clear, verifiable knowledge of what's *really* happening inside our skins and homes across the land. So far, we don't like the picture that's emerging, for it implacably shows we are avoiding ourselves—and most of our kids and grandkids are our unintended victims.

Until we evolve national and local policies of mandatory parental screening and education, and meaningful, humane, and dignified legal sanctions against low childhood nurturance, we will continue to pass on the silent epidemic of psychological wounding to our descendants—and reap the consequences.

The very real human stakes are increasing exponentially. We face at least three concurrent global challenges unlike any other human era: global warming, depleting potable drinking water, and unbalancing the delicate global biosphere that sustains all life. The latter includes loss of rainforests and wetlands, over-fishing and polluting our freshwater and saltwater habitats, depleting our fossil-fuel reserves, and steady loss of arable croplands. Many speculate that this overall process is accidentally freeing new viral scourges like HIV and Ebola, which humans are vulnerable to. Every one of these is due in one way or another to our exploding human population, and our increasing ability to affect the biosphere in complex ways we don't yet understand.

In his sobering 1971 book *"The Closing Circle,"* ecologist Dr. Barry Commoner vividly illustrated the point. He wrote that the common flashlight battery you throw in the trash gets incinerated. The resulting toxic, insoluble mercuric compounds rise into the atmosphere, and then fall to the ground and lake-bottoms via rain. The mercury compounds are ingested by microorganisms, and move up the food chain into the tissues of fish or livestock. These are sold in supermarkets and wind up on your dinner plate. The mercury from your discarded battery takes up toxic permanent residence in your and your kids' livers.

Most false selves have "more important things to think about." How about yours?

Most individuals—specially those in developing nations—are preoccupied with immediate personal and family problems. Their covert false selves cause many of these concerns, and loudly blame other factors for them. As long as this is so, average elected politicians will have little demand to frame policies to *really* combat these combined global eco-challenges. Fortunately, there is a dedicated group of people around the world who are trying to understand the eco-changes we're causing and their impacts, and lobbying for effective policies to balance our incessant population growth and resource depletion. The average person on the street may intellectually acknowledge that these eco-events may affect his or her descendents, but most of us (our false selves) aren't concerned enough to work for social change. We're too busy fending off imaginary and real *pain*—fear, shame, emptiness, and guilt.

I feel that adults whose inner families are solidly guided by their true Selves are more apt to take a balanced interest in their personal welfare, their grandkids' well being, and the welfare of future life on Earth. By honestly evaluating whether you are significantly wounded, and then evolving a meaningful personal recovery program, if needed, you act in a small way to save life on Earth. If you have an *Idealist* on your inner team, s/he should get excited about that possibility!

False-self dominance seems to be the unseen norm in our culture. If denied or ignored, their key long-term implications are profound.

If your true Self is paralyzed, you'll probably experience increasing personal emotional, physical, and relationship "problems," as you age. These cause chronic inner conflicts and anxiety—"stress." These diminish your daily satisfaction, and can impair your organs and immune system—which promotes your dying before living up to your full potential. You also risk unconsciously picking significantly-wounded partners over and over again, and reproducing your and their low birthfamily nurturance. That unintentionally passes on false-self dominance to your kids, just as your ancestors did.

High-nurturance childhood families promote harmonious, Self-led personalities in their children. This happens partly because the adult caregivers have harmonious, Self-directed inner families. They consistently shield their kids against excessive shame, guilt, and fear, rather than cause or allow them.

Through no fault of our caregivers, we *all* were shamed, hurt, and frightened as children. When these were severe and prolonged, Guardian subselves allow us to minimize, "forget," or deny our emotional and spiritual deprivations. "Finding your Self" is the essential task of gradually learning which subselves have protectively led you all your life, and helping them trust your *true* Self to guide you safely and serenely through each day toward discovering and fulfilling your unique life purpose.

To evaluate yourself or another for false-self traits now, go to Part 3. If your inner troop would rather get an overview of personal recovery first, continue with Part 2. Another option is to scan the selected readings in Part 4 to learn other authors' viewpoints on the ideas you've read so far. If you've done all of these, (re)read "Summing Up" on p. 336. Yet another choice is to find reasons to postpone any of these, and "never finish" the book.

Before you do any of these—get quiet, breathe well, and notice what your inner-family members are saying and feeling. Take stock:

Do you (they) feel it's possible, probable, or certain that a hidden committee is running your life? If so, what does that *mean*? Who has been running your life—a well-meaning false self, or your wholistically-healthy true Self? If a false self rules you now, those well-meaning subselves will convincing distort your answer.

Focus inside. Ask all your inner voices (thought streams) to quiet down for now. Then ask "What should I do now?"—and trust the quiet answer . . .

PART 2

Wound Recovery: harmonize your inner family

> "The truth will set you free—but first it will
> make you miserable."
> —Celestial Arts poster

Note: these *Recovery* chapters and the related wound-assessment checklists in Part 3 are on the Internet at **http://sfhelp.org/gwc/links1.htm**

5) OVERVIEW: RECOVERY FROM FALSE-SELF WOUNDS

HARMONIZE YOUR *INNER* FAMILY

This section outlines an experience-based framework for readers who want to recover from . . .

- Living unhappily under the domination of a well-meaning false self, and not knowing that there is a far better way to live.

- Excessive shame ("I'm unlovable, worthless, and disgusting"), and guilt ("I've done really bad things to myself and others").

- One or more excessive fears, including fear of fear.

- Major reality distortions—like denial, repression, projection, minimizing, intellectualizing, emotional numbing, "neuroses and paranoias," and exaggerating (catastrophizing).

- These four combine to promote . . .

- Chronically overtrusting or undertrusting—including distrust of Self, and of a benign Higher Power, and . . .

- Stunted or blocked abilities to feel, to bond (emotionally attach), and to exchange healthy love with other people.

This recovery framework centers on a demonstrable reality: people like you can intentionally "meet" and reorganize the different parts of your inner family (personality). That can lead to misinformed, anxious subselves relaxing their old distrusts and fears, and empowering your Self to resolve inner conflicts and make healthy life decisions. This inner-family reorganizing gradually replaces the six wounds above with their polar opposite traits, over time.

Part 2 will probably make more sense if you've done the 11 assessment worksheets in Part 3 *honestly*. Alternatively, reading this overview may help grow your motivation to use the worksheets. Get quiet, and listen to your inner voice!

This book can be a starting point for your personal recovery. There are many ways to free your wise, far-seeing true Self to lead your team of talented subselves. "Inner-family work" seems an unusually effective way, for a wide range of people. The next two chapters will outline it for you in some detail. This chapter is an introduction to recovery from the six false-self wounds.

True (vs. pseudo) recovery is about you taking full responsibility for the quality of your own life, and accepting *on faith* that you can raise your enjoyment of it. Recovery is about committing to making safe changes in your key attitudes, priorities, and surroundings, and noticing what happens when you do.

Because of knowledge and communication (media) breakthroughs in the last 20 years, swelling millions of people are now in various stages of recovery. You have *a lot* of company! I've been recovering since 1985 from growing up in a low-nurturance (double alcoholic) home. I was in total denial of our family's terrible wounds and unawareness until I was 47. Recovery has made a *major* positive difference in my life, as I've seen it do for many, many others.

I've been privileged to work clinically with, and learn from, scores of courageous women and men in various phases of their own recoveries. My teachers include well over 30 lay and clinical authors. Overall, their general observations and experiences are very similar to mine, and shape what follows. I conclude there are some general guidelines that will fit most significantly-wounded people—perhaps including *you*.

Before exploring inner-family work, let's tour an . . .

Overview of the Healing Process

Remember what it was like to wake up in the morning as a teenager? You thought you knew how to live, if only your caregivers would let you do so.

You felt you understood many things about people and the world, and many adults seemed stupid, boring, and unfair. Or possibly you were confused and anxious, and the world *didn't* make much sense to you. How would you summarize the main shifts in your attitudes and priorities since you were a fledgling adolescent? If you could talk and listen to your younger self about life on Earth and *your* life, what things would you say s/he "doesn't understand yet"? How accurate were your young forecasts about how your adult life would be?

True recovery from false-self control will bring you as many new awarenesses and attitudes as changing from adolescence to middle aged adulthood has (or will). You can't forecast them. At each point along the way, you think you've found "the truth," only to discover a new truth emerging gradually or suddenly. There are no shortcuts, because the healing changes can only accrue from experimenting with new beliefs and behaviors a day at a time.

Recovery is like a wise, patient consultant reorganizing an undisciplined sports team, or an uncoordinated orchestra, to learn to follow the leadership of a highly qualified coach or conductor. Your recovery process is also like the professional driver of a moving bus patiently and respectfully convincing the chaotic, anxious passengers to relax, and trust her or him to get them all safely through hazardous conditions to their destination. The "conductor," "coach," or "bus driver," is your true Self. The "players" or "passengers" are the semi-independent subselves, or personality "parts," that make up your *inner* family, community, or team.

The healing process is complex and multi-faceted. This section provides a general framework, from which you can tailor your own unique process. If you haven't yet, scan the selected book list in on p. 369 for some of the many titles available now on "Adult Child" recovery. None focus on freeing your true Self, so far—and the list is growing . . .

Recovery has three parts:

- Protective development of a false self beginning in early childhood;

- Some form of "hitting bottom," usually in midlife, and then . . .

- Dissolving old protective denials and beliefs, and breaking free of false-self dominance.

The first phase is living in increasing pain for many years, under the well-meant control of a protective, myopic, impulsive, misguided false self.

This gang of determined young and Guardian subselves tries a series of things like drugs, sex, overwork, isolation, religion, "depression," marriage, adventure, repressions, addictions, geographic moves, denials, and illness. These *always* fail to permanently reduce the inner pain—which inexorably increases, over the years. The learnings that accrue as the pain increases are rich resources for later recovery.

This first phase ends with some moment of "hitting true bottom." Finally, something internal or external happens ("the last straw"). Like a dam giving way, your inner family exceeds an ultimate tolerance limit for accumulated pain, weariness, and hopelessness. This can follow hitting "trial bottoms," and relapsing—i.e. falling back under the dogged control of your false-self personality parts. It can also follow a period of **pseudo recovery**, in which your subselves acknowledge the inner pain and cleverly make surface changes, but don't really shift their underlying toxic attitudes and distrust of Self and spiritual realities.

"Reaching your limit" has an infinite number of forms: a heart attack, a drunken-driving arrest, bankruptcy, divorce, a loved-one's death, or injury, a spiritual event, or just "one time too many." Something triggers the healing years of recovery. This phase begins with breaking lifelong denials in stages—"peeling the onion." This results in growing clear, painful awarenesses of your living as a prisoner to excessive shame, guilt, fear, and distrusts . . .

"I am addicted to my anti-depression medication."
"I am not living my truth—I'm living a lie."
"I am *tired* of living in fear!"
"I am harming my child(ren)."
"I am living my life to please (or defy) my parent/s"

The ultimate recovery trigger is . . .

"If I continue to live the way I have—I will die early, and/or filled with agonizing regret."

Full awareness dawns that you are ultimately responsible for the quality and achievements of your own life. This *feels* far different than understanding it intellectually.

The early healing phase of recovery is marked by a series of small and large attitude, behavioral, social, and environmental changes. You will probably end long-standing toxic relationships, work and habits like overeating, and compulsively putting others' needs before your own. You may move to a wholistically-healthier locale. These life changes each cause waves of inner and social reactions, causing a cascading series of new awarenesses, which promote more inner and outer changes . . . Gradually, personal recovery evolves into an authentic life philosophy that's serenely different than the core beliefs and values of your early caregivers.

Later in the healing phase, many veteran recoverers find spontaneous satisfaction in helping others prepare to hit bottom, or to evolve their own recoveries. People in true recovery tend to choose each other because they "talk the same language." They manifest genuine empathy and compassion for those in earlier stages, not superiority, pity, disdain, or smugness—though some subselves in transition may still need to hold on to those old comforting attitudes!

The three phases of recovery are complex, dynamic, organic, agonizing, and confusing. Each process takes decades to evolve. The healing phase is also freeing, scary, exhilarating, joyous, peaceful, and awesome. It is literally life transforming. It's fair to say that this phase is what "growing up" *really* means! At the core of this whole transformation process is a spiritual awakening. It nurtures a marvelous sense of clarity, acceptance, gratitude, compassion, serenity, creativity, and frequent gusts of awe, wonder, and delight. These often blend into real *love* of yourself and all other beings.

My many recovery students and teachers have demonstrated that we each craft our own unique healing program. There is no cookbook "right way." There *are* some elements of real (vs. pseudo) recovery that appear to be true for everyone, but the details vary richly.

Pause for a moment and reflect: where would you place yourself on the timeline that spans both these recovery phases? Have you hit your true bottom yet? How do you know? Do all your inner-family members agree? If you haven't hit your bottom, the following will help some of your subselves understand what you all may choose to do "up ahead."

This book is about one of two possible ways to recover—inner-family work. Many have healed without working with their subselves. Both ways can work, over time, to raise the satisfaction and productivity of your life. The two ways are determined by a single core belief you hold—either "I am one person, with one personality," or "I am one person under the control of many subselves. I need to identify, appreciate, and educate each of them, and harmonize this group that has been making my life decisions and controlling my body."

Despite advanced educational degrees and broad life experience, few people are aware of our brain's normal capacity to form a network of interactive subselves (regions). Therefore, few are able to take advantage of the second way to recover—and break the ancestral bequest of low childhood nurturance. This book outlines this second way of healing, to widen your choices.

In this inner-family type of recovery, your healing process begins with . . .

- Your understanding the concept of personality fragmenting (false-self formation) in low-nurturance environments, and then . . .

- Accepting that protective development of a false self is *certain* in very young children, including *you*. The next step is to . . .

- Understand how your caregivers' *reactions* to (1) your needs for emotional and spiritual nurturance (p. 257) and (2) your adaptive behavior over your first three to six years, affected you. Their own woundedness (low to high) and their reactions to your emerging false self largely determined to what extent false-self dominance became "a problem" for you and them.

Genes, ignorance, and unawareness pass false-self wounds on to minor kids, unless parents intentionally heal themselves, and nurture their kids to avoid doing so. If your parents were in denial and trying to cope with their versions of the six inner wounds without knowing it, it's very unlikely that they could prevent your false self from expanding to control you. Does this make sense?

Because false-self formation passes down the generations, trying to define "where does it start?" is like picking a beginning point on an infinite spiral. Let's start here: *significantly wounded people seem to choose each other*. Choice of mate is clearly a largely unconscious process, engineered by each partner's team of subselves. Our tragic (re)divorce rates since ~1950 imply that roughly half of American false selves pick . . .

1) The wrong people to wed (an alluring, well-camouflaged false-self dominated person), for . . .
2) The wrong reasons—like . . .

- legitimizing an accidental pregnancy,

- rescuing a needy person (co-dependence),

- gaining social approval and/or financial security,

- power,

- avoiding abandonment and loneliness (i.e. avoiding facing

- yourself),

- legitimizing sex,

- independence from parental control or abuse,

- revenge,

- excitement and adventure, or

- "the right thing to do;" . . .

3) At the wrong time—i.e. before developing Self awareness; self love; *inner-family* harmony; a clear life purpose and direction; clear, firm personal boundaries; clear understanding of how to communicate and problem-solve effectively; and healthy emotional and financial independence.

Unaware of their controlling false selves and the related five wounds, most couples intentionally or accidentally conceive one or more kids. I'd guess that as they do, under 5% of American mates can name over half of the ~30 high-nurturance family traits (p. 257) that their newborn will need consistently to develop without a harmonious Self-led personality. Our unaware, wounded society and the parents' relatives encourage this ignorance without knowing it.

Multi-part Personalities Are Normal

Two factors guarantee some inner wounding in young children—like *you*: First, infants and toddlers obviously can't care for themselves. If their caregivers aren't there often enough physically and emotionally, infants *automatically* develop subselves (new brain paths) and false-self strategies to please or alarm their caregivers, so they'll keep coming back. See Dr. James Masterson's *"Search For the True Self"* for a clear, credible description of this inevitable birth of a false self. Masterson stops short of describing the dynamic group of Manager, young, and Guardian subselves that comprise your "false self."

A young child's true Self is inexperienced and undeveloped. It can't provide effective decisions yet, so the newly minted *inner*-family members of young kids get used to depending on other people to fill their needs. That inherently breeds self-doubt, anxiety, and self-scorn—"I can't fill my needs by myself." Aware, sensitive parents gently and patiently offset this dependence with encouragements and safe challenges, to help their child develop staged self-sufficiency and self-reliance over their pre-adult years.

Significantly-wounded caregivers can't do this, because they're unaware, uninformed, and distracted by inner and/or outer conflicts and crises. A parent's chaotic inner family repeatedly gives naive youngsters double messages, like "I love you, you're so stupid." The well-intentioned caregivers are also apt to criticize, ridicule, or impatiently squelch their child's inept attempts to get their needs met ("Stop that. I'll do it.")

Over time, these parental responses inevitably promote self-doubt, confusion, self-blame, guilt, hurt, anger, repression, withdrawal, numbing, and shame in young kids—i.e. they *unconsciously* amplify the child's false self, and hinder their true Self's development and leadership. No one is aware this is happening, including early teachers, doctors, and grandparents.

Did you get confusing mixed messages or shaming criticisms too often from the adults who raised you? Do you give such messages to your kids? How do you know?

Despite conscious vows not to, couples' hidden false selves often recreate a home environment lacking too many of the ~30 traits of a high-nurturance family. If that's what they were raised in, it feels *normal*. Low or inconsistent emotional nurturance deprives average young kids of enough focused encouragement, attention, touching, play, affirmation, validation, autonomy, guidance, comfort, and praise—i.e. *love*. Most caregivers who thoughtfully chose child conception genuinely love their kids. However, American statistics suggest that too often, they don't understand their own and their kids' deep emotional and spiritual needs, and/or know how to fill them well. Most parents don't know how to *nurture* emotionally and spiritually well enough. Others know how, but their anxious, impulsive false-self parts won't *let* them nurture consistently and effectively.

So false-self formation happens naturally in infancy. If the caregivers are significantly wounded, their child's false self gets stronger over time. This group of semi-independent Inner Kids and Guardian subselves learns to rely on themselves or other people, vs. their emerging true Self, to help the young child cope and survive. If unchecked, a mix of the six false-self wounds is firmly rooted well before adolescence.

Close your eyes, and breathe comfortably. Relax. Let your awareness focus on the thoughts and feelings that are happening right now. How would you label your emotions at this time? How does that feel? When you're ready, let's continue exploring early inner-family recovery.

The "One Brain—One Person" Myth

Besides infants' primal brain response to a low-nurturance environment, an ancient misconception contributes to hidden false-self dominance in parents and kids—i.e. to *you*. Your caregivers, relatives, and others around you were probably taught to believe that each of you is "one person," or an "individual." The ancient Latin root of that word is "in-" (not) "dividuus" (divisible). We persons teach each other to see ourselves as not-divisible. Though the signs of multi-part personalities are literally *everywhere,* people are rarely aware of it and its effects, until the first phase of true inner-family recovery.

Note the difference here between *understanding* the concept of your false and true Selves, and *experiencing* them . . .

Unaware of being held in protective custody by their false self, significantly wounded men and women (like you and your ancestors?) experience an inexorable growth of inner discomfort, emptiness, and emotional pain over their first 30 or 40 years. The false-self traits (toxic shame, fears, distrusts, reality distortion, and bonding blocks) amplify each other, over time. So do the inevitably unsuccessful attempts to ignore them, analyze them intellectually, or heal them with chemicals, distractions, or ineffective therapies. Many wounded, unaware people develop chronic physical illnesses and/or emotional conditions like mania, obsessions, delusions, "A.D.D.," obsessions, and/or "clinical depression." These may be mute subselves desperately trying to gain conscious attention.

The decades-long pre-recovery process may either be disguised by moderate or great social and professional successes, or clearly studded by obvious addictions, social or health problems, and/or a series of painful, embarrassing "failures." Tragically, many false selves shame themselves and others by judging divorce a "failure," vs. a clear sign of major childhood wounding and unawareness.

During these pre-recovery decades, fragmented people unconsciously evolve a set of personally-unique attitudes and behaviors to cope with the effects of their wounds. To a trained eye, ear, and heart, these characteristic symptoms stand out like a skyscraper in the desert. So do key traits of the person's family tree. You'll review them when you use the symptom-assessment worksheets in Part 3.

As inner pain and emptiness grow, and sustained "happiness" remains elusive, typical people formed attempts to minimize, rationalize, repress, numb, and/or deny their woundedting traits and their relentless painful effects on daily life. Many in denial try to medicate their pain, anxiety, and emptiness via addictions to chemicals (including sugar and fat), sex, activity, relationships, emotional states, power, "causes," and material things.

They may also try to blame their pain on others, fate, God, or Satan, rather than accept responsibility for facing and healing it. Others seek to heal their growing discomfort (e.g. "depressions" and "failures") through external "first-order" (pseudo) changes like shifting jobs, dwellings, locations, relationships, friends, hobbies, and churches. Their false selves generate persuasive illusions that such superficial changes will surely bring "a better life."

Though providing temporary distractions, none of these "solutions" work. The pain, anxiety, shame, hopelessness, and emptiness always return, amplified by new shame, guilt, self-doubt, confusion, frustration, and unease from the failed "cures." Accepting that these trial "cures" don't work can take decades. They are important learning experiences that contribute to eventually "hitting the wall," surrendering to what *is*, and starting true recovery.

A stark example of this is our billion-dollar American industry that endlessly sells miracle diets, and related products, tapes, books, and programs. These rarely keep unwanted pounds, flab, and bulges off for good. That's because most of them don't promote or successfully achieve *second-order changes* in the core attitudes that underlie the flab—the comforting rituals of buying, preparing, and "snacking" on wholistically unhealthy foods high in sugars, simple carbohydrates, and fats. U.S. obesity is a silent monument to the pain that millions of kids and adults carry. It's been said that "every fat cell is an unshed tear."

Relationships

Before the healing phase of recovery, typical people ruled by false selves have one or more "toxic" primary relationships. These are characterized by mixes of excess shame, guilt, frustration, rage, fear, excitement, anxiety, hope, loss of boundaries and identity, numbness, confusion, betrayal, disappointment and/or emptiness.

Such relationships are almost always with other significantly wounded people—perhaps because core shame seeks it's own level. The relationships are often complex approach-avoid or power-struggle "dances." Some lead to marriage and/or child conception, and others don't.

Literate societies have been absorbing the new concept of "co-dependence" (relationship addiction) since ~1980. The explosion of related support programs, materials, and groups (e.g. Codependents Anonymous, or CoDA) since then signals how widespread this symptom of false-self control is in our culture, and the yearning to break free of it.

Experience since 1985 leads me to suspect that we co-dependents are usually controlled by subselves that are (1) deeply ashamed, and (2) terrified of (re)abandonment—and *expect* it. Woman or man; white, black, red, or ivory; white collar or blue; we co-dependents are all dominated by *shame*-based and *fear*-based Inner Kids and their Guardians, until true recovery is well underway.

Typical couples that don't know that false selves are controlling them usually divorce psychologically or legally within seven to ten years of cohabiting or (re)marrying. Most of them have kids who are silently developing their own controlling false selves. Divorced or not, many American families outwardly appear "fine" and "happy," thanks to everyone's false selves' ability to avoid shame by generate convincing, charming social masks.

Other significantly-wounded people avoid any committed, intimate primary relationships. They approach middle or old age childless and alone, or a lonely (but *safe*) single parent who may depend emotionally on a child as a surrogate partner. Such troubled singles are often dominated by hidden toxic shame, guilt, fears, and an inability to truly trust and bond with other people—and work unconsciously every day to minimize, avoid, and numb the emptiness of that.

So—after hitting true personal bottom, your first early-recovery step is to understand and accept that this ancestral spiral has significantly affected your life to date:

- Your grandparents' and social ignorance, plus your ancestors' unseen psychological wounds, led your young parents to . . .

- Grow up wounded and protectively unaware; and to pick the wrong partner/s, too soon, for the wrong reasons. The latter choices led to . . .

- Uninformed and/or accidental child-conceptions (you), which led to . . .

- Your natural early development of a false self and dependence on outsiders, which is . . .

- Amplified over time by your caregivers' uninformed, unintentionally inadequate nurturing, which . . .

- Combines with your caregivers' false-self dominance to cause personal, "school and social," marital, and family "problems," causing . . .

- Your repeatedly unsuccessful attempts to solve them or blame others, to avoid confronting false-self dominance in your parents, yourself, and any children. This promotes . . .

- Shame and fear-based (false-self) denials of inner wounds and their effects—by you, your parents, human-service professionals, and our policy makers and media. These all manifested in your life so . . .

- You're reading this book—without previously knowing some or all of this cycle.

Pause for a while, and let the meanings of this begin to emerge . . .

During our pre-recovery decades, we can either develop exquisitely convincing false masks of happiness and material and social "success," or we display our mix of the six false-self wounds for all to see. President Clinton and Donald Trump are two of *many* prominent American examples. Many of us populate the legions that Henry David Thoreau described as "living in quiet desperation." Others of us are very noisy!

Pause and take stock now. You have a recovery decision to make. Does the ancestral cycle you just read make sense to you? If not—why? If it does make sense, could it be describing your parents, you, and your child(ren)? Your present and/or ex mates' ancestries and lives? Your in-laws? Your siblings?

If you answer "Probably," or "Yes," then read on. If your inner voices say "I don't know," or "No way"—then I suggest you shift gears and experience Part 3 now. Bookmark this chapter, and assess yourself honestly for symptoms of false-self dominance. Then return here and reread this chapter. See if the cycle summarized above is any more credible. Your false self may not feel secure enough to risk this.

For perspective, reflect: have you ever seen the ideas you've read here before? In six decades of exploring our world as a curious student and tourist, I have only seen a handful of people (authors) propose anything like them. A perpetual student, I never saw these ideas *anywhere*, before 1988. I again acknowledge that the 13 premises in Chapter 1 are not yet validated as a group by any formal research that I know of, and they should be. Nonetheless—while we're both waiting for that to happen, you may ponder if you should evolve some kind of recovery program.

What does the process of Self-directed recovery from false-self custody look like, over time?

Your recovery can proceed, when . . .

- You've hit your *real* bottom or wall, ("I will not live one more day with . . . "); and . . .

- You understand and accept *what* you're recovering from (toxic false-self dominance), and you . . .

- See *why* (to avoid living unhappily from the six wounds, passing them on to your kids, and dying too soon, well short of your potential); and then you have . . .

- Accepted full responsibility for empowering your Self, harmonizing your inner family, and improving the quality of life for you and any dependent kids.

Note that you may understand and accept the *what* and the *why*, and still take months or years before you feel really ready to start evolving and acting on a personal recovery plan. Unless you face a clear personal crisis every day, the motivation to make core second-order (core attitude) changes is erratic. Busy daily life and myriad responsibilities tend to distract us from our vital *inner* work. Is that true for you? If you rank your current priorities by where you generally allocate your waking hours—how high does "personal healing and growth" rate?

The elements of true (vs. pseudo) recovery are wonderfully varied. They usually include combinations of . . .

- A compulsive thirst for education: reading self-help books voraciously, listening to or watching recovery tapes, going to recovery lectures, talking with others in recovery, asking family-history questions of relatives, journaling, . . . The thirst is powered by consciously recognizing "I'm injured, and have been living life as a prisoner;" and "I see the real possibility of a far better life for me and my child(ren)!"

- A growing feeling of "AHA!," "rightness," or "centeredness" about your inner shifts—without being able to identify why; or . . .

- Starting to see (understand and accept) your childhood nurturance deficits; and the resulting toxic personality traits, attitudes, and behavior patterns, with laser clarity for the first time ("breaking denials.") Vague or laser-clear hopes for a "better life" increase;

Other symptoms of typical early recovery are . . .

- A gradual thawing of emotional and physical *feelings* frozen for decades, and/or a validation and *understanding* of lifelong "unexplainable" feelings. These are usually surges of rage, deep sadness ("depression"), guilts, and profound shame. This thawing may come in gusts and explosions, or gradual releases and unpredictable swells and spurts, over years.

- Growing awareness of these long repressed, legitimate feelings can evoke intense feelings of *anger* at parents, themselves, others, and/or at God. Long-repressed grieving of lost childhoods, relationships, and life opportunities begins or resumes;

As these emotions and awarenesses cascade, amplify, and billow, typical new recoverers may start . . .

- Seeking various kinds of recovery help. These can include combinations of individual and/or group therapy; self-help (e.g. 12-step) groups; inpatient addiction-treatment and aftercare programs; spiritual communion and guidance; Tai Chi or meditation classes; dance, massage, or art therapy; retreats and wilderness sojourns; . . .

All these experiences add to a growing wholistic (cognitive + emotional + spiritual) *awareness* of the original nurturance deprivations, the old coping behaviors, and a humbling, exciting vision of your true Self and a possible new lifestyle. Understanding leads to new understanding— "peeling the onion." Veteran recoverers smile, remembering successive phases of "seeing the whole thing," and discovering later "Oh—there's *more!*" Nature (mind-body-soul design + Self + Higher Power?) seems to pace us, so we don't hit overload, and have time to integrate and rebalance before the next leg of the pilgrimage.

As old denials and repressions continue to dissolve, recovering people confront a series of difficult inner and social conflicts. Continued healing *inevitably* requires intentionally changing or giving up and replacing key things including . . .

- *Toxic attitudes and beliefs* (e.g. "it's OK for me to work 65 hours a week" or "there is no real God");

- *Toxic relationships* with other people—e.g. significantly-wounded mates, friends, employers, siblings, and parents; and . . .

- *Toxic environments*—e.g. working in a shaming, guilt-promoting "dysfunctional" (low nurturance) organization, or attending an unfulfilling or low-nurturance church.

Toxic means any relationship, activity, or setting that consistently promotes major (1) mixes of personal shame, guilt, distrust (of self and others), anxiety, confusion, frustration, pessimism, anger, hopelessness, and "failure;" and/or (2) unawareness of, distrust in, and disability of one's true Self. In the context of personal recovery, *toxic* means anything wholistically self-harmful and self-neglectful.

As uncertain early recoverers try out these scary changes, other unaware people either withdraw in alarm, or may try subtly or harshly to block the changes. Alarmed, relatives' and friends' false selves try to pull the recoverer back into their predictable old ways of believing, thinking, feeling, and re/acting. Double messages may bloom—"I admire that you're going to counseling, but it seems like your main achievement is to be more uncooperative, selfish, and cranky." Real—vs. pseudo—recovery threatens everyone's securities, until things restabilize!

Pseudo Recovery

These combined inner and outer conflicts are scary, confusing, and painful. So some wounded people stop or pause initial healing, and (unconsciously) adopt a *pseudo* (false) recovery. They may *understand* their childhood nurturance-deficits, wounding, and recovery, but they (their anxious false selves) stop short of making true second-order (core attitude) changes. Their true Self remains a disabled hostage of distrustful, disorganized young and Guardian subselves (Chapter 3). These subselves will concoct ingenious and persuasive rationales and explanations, and/ or or blame or discount others people ("You obviously don't understand.") who confront them on their pseudo healing.

As I write this, a vivid image appears: a lively, articulate, bright, sincere 30-something single (divorced) Mom, who had read every self-help recovery book ever published. She could describe every term and concept, describe 12-step recovery groups and addictions, and clearly identify her own co-dependent "traits." She absolutely believed she was well along in personal recovery. Yet she had no stable job or home, was on the edge of needing welfare support, and weighed almost 300 pounds. She was sincere—even righteous—about describing others' needs for recovery, yet her false self had skillfully blocked her from seeing that she herself had deep personal wounds that she wasn't yet ready to admit. Her Inner Kids and Guardians were protectively denying her (their) denials. She left therapy when I tried gently to suggest that. I had become "unsafe." Toxic *shame, fear, and reality distortion* at work!

The Guardian *Magician* subself of a pseudo-recoverer will protectively distort reality, and deny their distortion and their denial. It will cause their host person to *believe* they're recovering—but they really aren't, yet. The person makes first-order (cosmetic) changes, rather than core attitude and priority changes. Their ranks include millions of people in 12-step meetings who control an addictive urge to use alcohol or hard drugs, and rigidly ignore, minimize, or deny their addictive use of nicotine, caffeine, sugar, or fat.

In AA, they're called "dry drunks," who have stopped using alcohol but have not changed their "stinking thinking" and related toxic behaviors. They're still controlled by a false self, and don't know it yet. Quitting alcohol dependency is a convenient way to "prove" "I'm OK, now."

Depending on many inner and outer factors, people living in pseudo recovery may hit the *real* wall one day, and start true recovery—or they may stay stuck and unaware of what living from their true Self would feel like and bless others with. Genuine recovery (second-order change) can't be forced or rushed. By definition, the motivation to heal must come from within.

Typical recovery from false-self wounds is not a smooth process. Between times of elation, freedom, resolve, risk, and reward, there are interspersed . . .

- Periods of "no progress," which are usually healthy periods of rest and integration;

- Episodic regressions to "the old ways"—which can be seen as reminders and course-correctors;

- Times of confusion and doubts, which are often symptoms of true transformation in progress; and some . . .

- Aimlessness—feeling lost, directionless, and temporarily overwhelmed.

As these accumulate, there is a growing calm acceptance that true recovery from childhood nurturance deficits is a ceaseless *becoming*, not an event. New frontiers and vistas keep opening up unexpectedly . . .

At this point, some of your inner crew may want to know "What's the point of this 'recovery' thing? What would we be trying to achieve?" Excellent question!

Recovery Goals

In this conceptual framework, recovery from false-self wounds can be described as a process of (1) becoming first aware of the six inner wounds and their effects, and then (2) using Self-motivated inner-family work (Chapter 6) to reduce them. Here's a summary of what these healings generally aim at, over time. Each recoverer has a unique set of these goals. Note in the following that "someone" is implied as directing your time and creative energy toward these targets and subgoals. That someone is your natural coach, conductor, or bus driver—your innately skilled true Self, aided by your other personality parts, your Higher Power, and selected other people.

Recovery Goal 1) Empower Your Self to Lead Your Inner family

The overall goal is to replace periodic or chronic false-self dominance with all your subselves relying on and following your true Self and Higher Power. Your false self is a group of shortsighted, impulsive, well-meaning personality parts that don't know or trust your true Self. When they perceive danger, one or more of these Inner Kids or Guardian subselves blends with, or paralyzes, your Self. This is like a group of anxious, emotional, zealous musicians each trying to lead an orchestra by paralyzing or ignoring the expert conductor. Healing the other five wounds below gradually converts this dominance to allowing the Self to lead, more and more often. This condition can exist occasionally, often, or all the time.

Typical **subgoals**:

• Identify all your active and disowned personality parts;

• Learn which of them regularly blend with, or take over, your Self. Then . . .

• One at a time, help these subselves to trust and follow your Self, other subselves, and your Higher Power, and each other. By doing this, gradually . . .

• Harmonize all your subselves into a secure, confidant, goal-oriented team, over time. The end goal of recovery is to live authentically and automatically from your true Self and Higher Power, in normal and emergency situations—i.e. to live with Self-confidence and serenity.

The next target has two interrelated halves—healing excessive shame and guilt. Because these are mutually reinforcing, they're treated here as one goal.

Recovery Goal 2a) <u>Convert **Excessive Shame** to Healthy Self Love</u>

This overall inner-family recovery goal is to convert semi-conscious toxic shame into genuine self-respect, self-appreciation, and self-trust—i.e. to self-love, while nurturing equal respect and love for other people and life forms.

Toxic shame and guilt ("I break important rules—and am *bad*.") block self-love and self-respect. That promotes self-neglect, which causes health problems and often premature death. From childhood training, one or several very young subselves believe "I am worthlessness, bad, incompetent, damaged, and unlovable." They often live trapped in the past, endlessly reliving old shaming incidents. Because they feel they are disgusting, inept, and worthless ("self hatred"), their frantic instinct is to hide from conscious or public awareness.

When activated, these young subselves blend with your Self to flood you with their feelings of *shame*. If other people see the external reason for this ("At the party last night, I forgot my best friend's name!"), some subselves feel *embarrassed*. Usually, a well-intentioned *Inner Critic* or *Judge* constantly reinforces these feelings of *badness*. A *Catastrophizer* can amplify them ("No one could possibly love me. I'll die alone, unloved, and maybe homeless.") Other Guardian parts work ceaselessly to calm, distract, numb, and comfort your shamed part/s. Shamed and shaming subselves are often the hardest to access and heal—and bring the greatest relief.

Typical shame-conversion recovery **subgoals**:

- _ Identify your shamed subselves and their Guardians, and __ confirm the presence of an *Inner Critic* or *Judge* (and maybe a *Perfectionist*) who constantly proclaim stern beliefs of worthlessness.

- _ Explore whether any shamed part is trapped in the toxic past—an "Exile." If so, _ build that subself's trust in your Self, your Higher Power, and other key parts (e.g. your *Nurturer*), and _ work to bring the Exile safely into the present. See "Rescuing" in the next chapter.

- Retrain your *Inner Critic* to _ trust the judgment of your Higher Power and your Self (recovery goal 4), and to _ switch their sarcastic criticism and self-blame to constructive feedback. Option: _ evolve a Bill of Personal Rights (p. 350), and _ teach it to all subselves. Then _ learn the communication skills of respectful assertion and empathic listening, and _ experiment *acting* assertively from your Rights. _ Expect and _ confront inner and outer resistance to these new values—they'll disturb insecure (wounded) people!

- Identify subselves who promote a core attitude of self-neglect ("I don't deserve to be healthy, happy, and fulfilled.") A common Guardian is a *Saboteur,* ("Oh, come on—another slice of cake won't hurt!") Another is an *Addict*, who pairs up with your reality-distorting *Magician* ("You are *not* addicted—you can quit any time. Don't sweat it.") Work with them to grow a new attitude of high-priority self-care, while caring selectively for key other people. Widen the inner-family influence of your *Nurturer* subself. As recovery progresses and inner team harmony grows, this pro-health attitude builds among all subselves. Option: use your subselves' ability to change their roles to retrain a subself to become or assist your *Health Director*, or equivalent.

- Patiently help your shamed subselves to change their toxic beliefs to genuine self-acceptance, respect, appreciation, and compassion—i.e. non-egotistical self-love. I have witnessed this life-changing transformation, over time, in many Self-directed clients in true recovery.

- Develop an effective *inner*-family strategy to _ avoid, or _ identify and _ assert limits with, shaming people. This step often results in reducing or ending some key toxic relationships with significantly-wounded mates, relatives, and/or employers. It can also cause major shifts away from shaming religious beliefs, practices, and environments ("You are an evil, unclean sinner by nature. Only a gracious God can save your soul from damnation.") Excessive shame seems to be one of the two taproots of co-dependence (p. 316).

Recovery Goal 2b) Identify, Reduce, and Avoid Toxic **Guilts**

Guilt is a normal emotion kids and adults feel when we (or someone) believes we've broken an important rule. False selves feel and promote unwarranted, exaggerated (toxic) guilts. That's partly because those misinformed subselves are still using their early caregiver's rules vs. their own.

The overall recovery goals here are to _ grow self-awareness of healthy and toxic guilt, and an effective way of releasing guilts. Then _ review your inventory of childhood *shoulds, ought-to's,* and *musts* ("rules"), and _ upgrade them to fit your current adult self and values. Then _ reduce old misplaced, unwarranted, or exaggerated guilts to normal healthy levels, and work toward selective, genuine (vs. pseudo) inner and social forgivenesses. Finally, _ learn to protect your inner family reliably against other people who try to manipulate you via guilt. ("If you *really* loved me, you'd know what I needed. I shouldn't have to ask you!")

Many of us have an overactive *Guilty Child* in our inner family. Do you? S/He reacts to outer criticisms and the *Inner Critic's* ceaseless (distorted) judgments ("You shouldn't have . . . ") by blending with your Self. That infuses you with her/his *guilt* feelings and related thoughts—e.g. "I (broke a rule)—I did something really bad, or wrong." Such thoughts and feelings feed your *Shamed Child's* blind certainty that "I'm a bad, stupid, worthless, flawed, unlovable person."

Your *Shamed Child* and *Guilty Child* may be the same subself, or two or more different ones. I have never met a significantly wounded person without these influential parts. They cause several Guardian parts (p. 49) to be ceaselessly vigilant and active, like your *Perfectionist, Catastrophizer, Critic,* and *Magician* (reality distorter.) Other common devoted Guardians are the *Addict, Rationalizer* ("You drink because of that shrew you married"), and the *Numb-er (Anesthetist).*

Typical guilt-conversion recovery **subgoals**:

* Learn _ what healthy guilt is, and why it's useful; _ how toxic guilt differs from shame, _ how guilt is created and maintained, _ what real (vs. pseudo) forgiveness is, and _ which subselves infuse your Self with toxic guilt feelings and thoughts.

* Methodically re-examine the old (childhood) rules that cause your *Inner Critic* to inflict guilt on your *Guilty Child* and other subselves ("*Never get angry with Dad!*"), and . . .

* Assess whether your *Guilty Child* is an Exile trapped in the toxic past. If so, evolve a plan to bring her or him to live in the present with your other subselves. See "Rescuing" in the next chapter for more on this.

* Gradually replace subselves' outdated "shoulds" and "oughts" with current ones that fit you, your environment, your new (harmonious) personality and priorities, and your unique life purpose. Then . . .

* Work patiently to _ accept full responsibility for your life, and forgive _ your self and _ other persons who have been significantly hurt by your (false self's) past choices and actions. _ Learn from these incidents and this process, over time.

* Evolve an effective way to identify and confront people in your life who choose to inflict guilt one you. Anyone come to mind? Learn effective _ assertion and _ listening skills, and use them to declare and enforce your evolving Bill of Personal Rights (p. 350). If necessary, end relationships with people who chronically "guilt-trip" you, with compassion, vs. blame. Such whiney, controlling, and/or critical people are usually very wounded, and don't know it.

Reflect for a moment—how is your inner crew reacting to these ideas (thoughts and feelings)? Is your Self in charge right now, or are some other subselves? See p. 67.

While building Self trust, converting shame, and reducing toxic guilts, another recovery target is . . .

Recovery Goal 3) Identify and Reduce **Excessive Anxieties and Fears**

Reflect for a moment on your favorite semi-conscious fears. How have they been shaping your relationships, finances, dwelling, and health? Complete and repeat this sentence until you run out of inner responses:

"*I'm often afraid (or 'worry') that* _____*; and* . . . "

The overall recovery goal here is to _ develop clear awareness of your current anxieties and fears, and _ learn to *use* them to guide current life decisions. Evolve an effective way of reducing exaggerated or groundless old fears to healthy levels, and/or safely letting them go for good. ("I used to fear traveling in strange places. Now I enjoy doing so, selectively, because I'm learning to trust myself (my Self) in unexpected situations.")

Fear is a natural survival reflex that helps you avoid injury, pain, and death. Individual members of typical inner families like yours vary widely in what they fear, why, and how intensely. Your Self and Manager parts can have healthy protective fears and anxieties. Typical false selves include young and Guardian subselves who are *excessively* scared of mixes of these:

- Social criticism, rejection, and abandonment. The usual underlying (infantile) core *terrors* are aloneness, hysteria, powerlessness, and *death*;

- Loss of internal and external control—i.e. fear of the unknown, and of lethal overwhelm (loss of personal "boundaries" and self due to emotional *flooding*—inner-family chaos);

- Intense emotions (loss of control)—and thus excessive fear of bonding, loving, intimacy, and conflict (p. 312);

- Success and/or "failure" (in someone's opinion); and subselves fear of . . .

- Excessive fear.

Often, well-meaning *Catastrophizer* and *Worrier/Doubter* subselves keep your insecure (untrusting) subselves anxious. They may be aided by a *Magician* part, who protectively distorts reality, and a *Numb-er*, who mutes or anesthetizes "unsafe" emotions. Often the *Critic* heaps scorn on other subselves for "being a wimp / scaredy cat / doormat / coward / lily-livered, / "weak" / yellow / timid / . . . ", which inexorably nourishes Inner Kids' toxic guilt and shame.

Typical toxic-fear recovery **subgoals**, using inner-family work from chapter 6:

- Learn _ the surface symptoms that mask repressed fear, and _ the difference between healthy and toxic anxiety and fear.

- Identify which subselves feel each of your major fears (above). If any are living in the past, _ evolve an effective rescue effort, and _ bring them into the (safer) present time.

- Validate and affirm each scared subself's feelings and beliefs, and _ promote honest dialog with them, your Self, and other parts like your *Nurturer* and *Spiritual One*.

- Work patiently to have your scared subselves _ begin to trust your Self's (and related subselves') ability to (a) avoid most real danger, and (b) manage unsafe situations effectively.

- Respectfully retrain your *Catastrophizer*, *Worrier*, and *Magician* subselves to _ trust your Self and a benign Higher Power, and _ stop scaring other subselves to the extreme.

- Retrain your *Critic* and *Perfectionist* to stop _ shaming other subselves for being afraid, and _ seeing normal emotions like anger or sadness as "negative" or "bad."

- Retrain your *Numb-er* subself to _ trust all subselves' ability to safely tolerate feeling, and then _ to permit feeling all emotions fully, and as they happen.

- Work to _ identify if certain subselves fear other subselves ("Keep that Nut locked up. She's going to kill us!"), and _ convert that to cautious trust. As inner-family understanding, respect, and trust in your Self's leadership grow, such fears will shift to tolerance and trust, and later to affection and appreciation.

- Investigate possible connections between terrified young subselves and their Guardians, and any chronic physical symptoms you experience—e.g. cramps, muscular tics or spasms, migraines, asthma, insomnia, "digestive problems," ulcers, . . . Isolated or mute subselves can promote such symptoms in a desperate attempt to be noticed and comforted. Work with medical professionals to reduce these, as your inner harmony grows—including letting go of depending on prescription or other chemicals. A growing number of recent books testify to the very real power of your mind to cause—and heal—physiological ailments. See, for example, titles by Larry Dossey and Dr. Bernie Siegel.

Recovery Goal 4) <u>Rebalance Chronic **Overtrusting and/or Undertrusting**</u>

Trust is a primal reflex of judging what and who is *safe*—i.e. who will bring us comfort and pleasure, and who will bring pain. Trust grows from direct and indirect life experience, starting in our first moments after birth. Our dis/trust reflexes begin to form well before we can talk or think "thoughts." Often they're unconscious for kids and adults alike, until recovery brings clear awareness.

This false-self wound manifests as blindly trusting abusive, selfish, dishonest, or indifferent (i.e. wounded) others; or often "irrationally" distrusting reliable others, and/or your own judgment or ability. Symptoms of *Self*-distrust are chronic ambivalence, indecisiveness, and "second guessing" key decisions. "Popular" Guardian subselves that provide this protection are the *Doubter/Worrier*, *Catastrophizer*, and *Skeptic*. Another symptom of toxic distrust is ignoring or rejecting the nourishment, guidance, and inspiration of a benign and loving Higher Power. Spiritual distrust can be promoted by insecure subselves who are terrified at the prospect of surrendering their illusion of control.

Undertrusting can imply the dominance of a *Cynic* and/or *Pessimist* subself who guards you by forecasting certain disappointments and betrayals. Your Guardian *Magician* may also try to help by distorting reality—e.g. "All / lawyers / politicians / cops / authorities / teens / Jews / foreigners / salespeople are out to get you."

A *Nice Gal/Guy* Guardian subself can rigidly urge overtrusting. S/He probably does so to protect your shamed, guilty, and lonely young subselves who fear repeating early-childhood abandonment agony. Extreme overtrusting results in being repeatedly victimized, exploited, abused, and betrayed, despite painful results. The *Critic* then may harp "It was *your own* fault. You should have . . . ", raising young Inner Kids' guilt, shame, and self-distrust.

On a scale of -10 to +10, how would you rate yourself as being a "trusting" person? Typical wounded people are at either end of that spectrum, vs. in the middle ("I'm calm and selective about whom I trust. I trust my own judgment in deciding.") Picture some people now that you "don't trust," and do. How aware are you, generally, about trusting your self, others, and your Higher Power? Distrust feeds toxic fear (and vice versa), and may feed toxic guilt and shame ("I *should* trust my spouse / boss / minister / child / mother—but I don't. I'm a bad person.")

The overall recovery goals here are to _ evolve a clear awareness of current trusts and distrusts, and _ rebalance the ability to trust your Self, _ your subselves (within limits), _ selective other people, and _ a credible Higher Power wisely and serenely. Then _ learn how to communicate and problem-solve effectively with *distrusted* subselves and people. _ Evolve an effective way of rebuilding lost trust among subselves and trust-worthy people.

Typical recovery trust-rebalancing **subgoals**:

- Evolve _ a definition of "healthy distrust"; and _ a clear explanation of how trust is created or regained. Grow a clear understanding of _ the behavioral symptoms of overtrusting and undertrusting; (p. 304); _ how each of those may be affecting your life quality, including nourishing other toxic traits; and _ which Inner Child and Guardian subselves usually blend with your Self to bring you _ overtrusting and _ undertrusting. Then . . .

- Inventory your known subselves, to learn which of them . . .

_   trust your Self and Higher Power, and which don't;

_   trust all your other subselves enough, and which don't; and learn which . . .

_   personality parts most influence your inner family in deciding which people you trust, when, and why. Then . . .

• Work with your inner-family's findings to increase all your subselves' trust in your _ Self and your _ Higher Power. Work also at _ raising the trusts among your various subselves, over time. Such trust gradually accumulates as you shift your attitudes and behaviors—and get different responses back from the environment. Part of this subgoal involves your _ exploring for distrustful parts being stuck in the (unsafe) past, and _ rescuing any you find.

• Consider the parts-work technique of internally re-doing old traumatic real-life events that generated major distrust in one or more subselves (p. 204). A series of such re-doings can raise the mutual awareness and trust level among all your inner-family members. You'll learn about re-doings and other inner-family techniques in the next chapter.

• As your Young subselves gain in trusting your Self and selected Guardian and Manager subselves, _ invite their Guardians (e.g. your *Cynic*, *Catastrophizer*, *Procrastinator*, *Perfectionist*, and *Magician*) to gradually relax their old vigilance, and try out new productive inner-family roles. Recall—personality parts can't be "fired," "killed," or ignored, because they're neuro-chemical areas of your mind/body. They can learn, and focus their valuable talents and energy in new directions—often very quickly, when they believe it's safe to do so.

Recovery Goal 5) Replace Protective **Reality Distortions** With Clear Awareness

Subselves learn in early childhood that distorting reality brings temporary comfort and relief. For example, believing in an invisible companion can banish unbearable loneliness and anxiety caused by unavailable caregivers. Blaming others for your own mistakes, lying, denying, repressing, projecting, minimizing, black/white thinking, and exaggerating are effective ways of avoiding unbearable fears, guilts, and shame. Enduring others' criticism of those behaviors is less painful.

Significantly wounded people (i.e. their false selves) automatically see things that aren't there (i.e. illusions, delusions, projections), and/ or don't see or experience things that *are* there (via denials, repressions, and minimizations). This hinders your making healthy life decisions, like balancing your and others' needs; doing real recovery; choosing key relationships, appropriate jobs and surroundings; and doing effective parenting. Reality distortions *always* degrade effective internal and interpersonal communication and problem solving—which raises frustration, self-doubt, guilt, and shame, over time.

The most pervasive reality distortion is denial of these distortions ("I do *not* shade the truth!"). The master distortion is "I am *not* 'controlled by a false self', and I do *not* have these inner wounds!" Recovery starts with dissolving this illusion. Protective reality distortions are often provided by a combination of tireless Guardians like your *Magician, Blocker, Distracter, Doubter, and Forgetter* subselves who are eternally devoted to keeping your Inner Children safe.

The overall fifth recovery goal is to raise your Guardian and young subselves' trust, over time, that honestly accepting reality is *safe enough*, so distortions aren't needed. Such safety grows from increasing inner-family trust in the wisdom and will of Self, your Higher Power, and selected other subselves and people. It also comes from learning a core set of relationship concepts and skills, like present-moment awareness, and effective thinking, communicating, and problem solving.

Typical recovery reality-clarification **subgoals**:

- Become aware of the _ concept of, and _ symptoms of, typical reality distortions (p. 308); and _ their typical impacts on your life quality.

- Respectfully identify _ the Guardian subselves who promote each distortion, and _ why they do—i.e. who they're protecting. By definition, Guardian subselves exist to protect and comfort one or more Inner Kids. So reducing reality distortions is really about finding a new way of protecting the inner kids (plural)—e.g. building their trusting in the vision, sensitivity, strength, and reliability of your Self and other Manager subselves. Until this safety is credible, typical Guardians see no options to distorting reality. They often fear being "killed" or rejected and spurned as useless, if they quit.

- As you recognize habitual reality distortions, _ work respectfully with your *Inner Critic* to reduce that part's inner shaming and blaming—"What a pathetic weakling you are to have to lie to people who care about you!"

- Over time, _ identify other people in your life who scare your inner-family members so they feel the need to distort reality. Then _ work toward the subgoals for reducing toxic fears (above). _ Intentionally choose people to be around you who are genuinely respectful, accepting, and empathic—including other recoverers working on these same goals.

- Retrain your *Magician* and other Guardian parts to experiment with allowing clearer and clearer views of the past and present ("Pat really is an addict.") to be "safe enough."

Healing reality distortions tends to happen "by itself," as you work on the other recovery goals. This comes from the inner security that increases as your subselves get to know and trust your Self, your Higher Power, each other, and trustworthy (non-wounded) other people.

Recovery Goal 6) Risk Feeling, **Bonding**, Intimacy, and Love

Toxic shame, guilt, fear, and reality distortions can combine to block your Young subselves from attaching to (caring about) other people and themselves, and from accepting others' real love as merited, genuine, and safe. The overall recovery goals here are to _ patiently heal the five prior wounding traits above, over time, and intentionally risk _ feeling self-love, and _ exchanging genuine love with others.

Bonding and Love barriers usually stem from all the other toxic traits. This sixth false-self wound centers on . . .

- An inability to genuinely love your self (your mind-body-spirit), from a mix of excessive old childhood shame, guilts, and distortions;

- Never having experienced or *trusted* genuine love from another person or Being;

- Unconsciously associating love with pain, duty, sex, power, "things," entrapment, loss, and/or fear; and . . .

- Spiritual unawareness, distortion, or distrust.

Excessive fear and distrust, plus reality distortion and toxic shame, can block true emotional/spiritual attachments. One symptom is difficulty committing to a long-term relationship. Bonding-blocks hinder exchanging real love *internally*, and with other people and living things. Your protective *Numb-er* or *Blocker* Guardian subselves can mute or block feeling love and other emotions. This can include numbing instinctual parental love—which promotes dependent kids adapting to feeling unlovable by growing their own protective shame-based false self.

Many significant-wounded caregivers can't really provide the full range of critical nurturances for dependent kids without meaningful personal recovery. Some are better than others at *pretending* to love (a reality distortion), when they really feel inept and disinterested. This usually sends a confusing double message: their *words* say "I really care about you," and their actions imply "I don't."

Since the various forms of *love* are spontaneous attitudes, feelings, and an ability, I see no realistic way of using "logic" and "a plan" to acquire these. I also know no way to heal this false-self wound without being in meaningful intimate (honest) relationships with other living things and an accessible, responsive Higher Power.

My experience is that the ability to bond and exchange love may grow spontaneously, as other recovery steps and experiences accumulate. In stark, tragic reality, some people seem to be too badly injured and unaware to regain the full human ability to bond, and feel, give, and receive love that they were born with. They can still live meaningful lives.

Four Recovery Themes

Notice four things from this summary of typical recovery goals. First, note that the six false-self wounds promote each other. For example, shame, distrust, fear, and reality distortion combine to promote difficulty bonding and loving—which promotes shame and fear. The silver lining is—healing each of the wounds makes healing the others easier, over time.

Second, note that each trait is the result of a group of inner-family members acting together: typically Guardian parts (p. 49) who distrust your Self or other subselves (like the *Nurturer*) acting devotedly to calm, comfort, or protect one or more shamed, guilty, scared, or lonely young subselves.

Third, notice that each of the main recovery goals is made up of many smaller steps. This makes setting current recovery targets and the overall process far less intimidating and overwhelming. What's your instinct about how long it might take an average person to make significant progress on all six of these goals (vs. "achieve them")? Do you see why true recovery from false-self dominance is not a short-term project?

Finally, note that the overall theme is helping the several personality parts who "cause" each of these traits to meet each other and your true Self, relax old perceptions and reflexes, and risk letting your Self and other Manager subselves take the lead. That leads to freeing up Guardians to learn new roles. See "Reassigning" (retraining) in the next chapter.

Typically, these six multi-part recovery goals aren't worked on one at a time, or in order. The recovery process is organic, like growing a garden. It yields progress and rewards irregularly, in fits and starts.

Some people have a structured recovery plan ("I'm working on healing my shame and increasing Self-love, this month.") Others evolve an unstructured healing experience without clear, explicit goals. Though the latter may take longer, the end results are the same: (1) a calmer, clearer, more focused, spiritual, enjoyable and productive daily life based on living from your true Self, and (2) increasing clarity on, and acceptance of, your strengths, limits, and real Life purpose/s. Where is your (your subselves') comfort zone between structured to unstructured recovery?

Types of Recovery Help

Though rarely devoted to "healing false-self wounds," personal recovery programs and resources have exploded since the 1980's. Options include . . .

- S elf-help books and workbooks;

- Audio and video tapes and CDs;

- Internet Web sites, message-boards, and chatrooms;

- Therapists and agencies specializing in aspects of "Adult Child" recovery—including inner-family therapy;

- Clinical outpatient recovery groups;

- Various public and private agency or hospital inpatient programs—typically two to four weeks, usually with an aftercare-program option.

- Local and national recovery conferences and workshops;

- Lay-led mutual-help groups, many of which are modeled after the successful 12-step Alcoholics Anonymous groups. These can include Al-Anon for ACoAs (Adult Children of Alcoholics); Co-dependents Anonymous (CoDA), Adult Children Anonymous, Adult Children of Toxic Parents (or Dysfunctional Families), Women Who Love Too Much, Incest Survivors Anonymous (ISA), Sex and Love Addicts Anonymous (SLAA), Gamblers Anonymous (GA), Overeaters Anonymous (OA); and many more. An increasing number of these have national headquarters.

- See p. 356 for a proposed revision of the traditional 12 steps to fit recovery from false-self wounds.

- Art, dance, music, and massage therapies and workshops;

- Personal journaling, retreats, and focused meditating;

- Spiritual/pastoral, exercise, and nutritional counseling.

The most successful recoverers I've seen have used several of these healing options over time, not just one or two . . .

Recovery Guidelines

Is there a "best way" to achieve these recovery goals? While each person heals in their own way, I feel your recovery will yield more, faster, if you evolve a set of ground rules. These are like precautions you'd heed in order to enjoy traveling safely in a strange new country. These are suggestions to your Self and your *Health Director*, who will co-manage your recovery . . .

- Coach your inner-family members to keep a patient, long-range outlook: "fireproof the forest," vs. constantly putting out local brushfires.

- Pace yourself: work, rest, and play. A key recovery goal is to stay balanced as you transform. Take your time!

- Work to accept full responsibility for the quality of your own life, and respectfully grant others responsibility for theirs—without guilt, shame, or anxiety!

- Accept that true recovery will require you to risk making core attitude, priority, and behavioral changes, over time. That implies "mistakes," and experiencing tolerable losses.

- Choose to avoid black/white thinking. On thoughtful examination, the high majority of "problems" have multiple options. Also, work toward a glass-half-full attitude, without becoming a blind optimist or rigid idealist.

- Adopt "the (open, curious, patient) mind of a student." Question everything—including these guidelines. Your Self and Higher Power ultimately know what's best for you, short and long term.

- Expect to need and accept help, along the way. Find recovery hero/ines and mentors, and risk using them. Accepting genuine help is a mutual gift, not a burden!

- Accept that at times, the best help is "no help." Avoid depending on (wounded) rescuers—they'll unintentionally hinder your recovery by blocking you growing your self-competence and self-confidence.

- Enjoy laughing (compassionately) with (vs. at) yourself, others, and at the recovery process, at times. We're funny!

- Let go of any need to blame others or yourself for "having to recover." It's a gift.

- Expect to find that recovery is, essentially, a spiritual-growth process; and . . .

- Know that true recovery usually includes re/learning how to grieve your many profound losses, old and new. That enables you to form healthy new bonds.

Pause. Notice your thoughts and feelings. How does your inner family react to these suggestions? Recall that "no reaction" *is* a reaction. If you have a notable response to one or more of these ("Spiritual growth? I don't need that junk!"), use that as a helpful clue to subselves that feel threatened in some way by these ideas. Option: copy the list above, and post it where you can see it every day, until it merges into your core daily values. Edit the list to suit your values, needs, and experience.

Here's brief perspective on these guidelines.

Keep a Long-range Outlook

The healing phase of true recovery takes *years*. It's studded with tiny and major breakthroughs, and subtle to obvious life changes along the way. Coach your subselves to be patient, take small steps, rest when you need to, and have faith that your steps will add up to a far better life. Some benefits come very quickly, once you start! Consider working from this book for many months. You'll probably have to affectionately frustrate a young *Impatient* part, who demands instant results and gratification. Sorry.

Pace Yourself

Because you have a kaleidoscope of needs each day, give yourself permission to rest, pause, and focus as your mind, body, self, and spirit request. Like all organic processes, recovery has spurts and lulls. Stay aware: *"doing nothing" (resting) is doing something valuable!* (Possible T-shirt logo?) If you need to put this book or other materials down for a week or several, then do so—without anxiety or guilt! Trust your Self to know when to pick up active recovery again.

Accept Full Responsibility for Your Life

Do this and respectfully give other adults responsibility for theirs. Carrying (enabling) or blaming others, and/or expecting others to fill your primary needs, are standard false-self ploys to protect you from facing what you need to face for wholistic health and fulfillment. Your true Self already knows how to handle this responsibility safely—and your false self probably doesn't trust this yet. This self-responsibility goes hand in hand with your forging and using your own Bill of Personal Rights (p. 350), as a dignified, unique individual with valuable talents and gifts to bring to the world.

Accept that Recovery Will Require You to Change

You'll find that you'll discard some key things that you've believed, thought, felt, and done since you were a child or young adult. Over and over again, your Self will ask your inner family to give up relationships, habits, and values that promote the six psychological wounds. *You* control when, what, and how to change, and how to decide which risks during change are "safe enough."

You'll learn along the way to be alert for "changeless changes"—an elegant strategy that distrustful false selves often use to make it seem like you're changing, when you're really not. Diets that don't work, and substituting one addiction (e.g. nicotine) for another (alcohol), are widespread examples. Part of our mega-billion dollar advertising industry caters to and promotes these illusions ("Improve your sex life—get a glorious tan in our studio for only $30!")

Here, such pseudo changes are called first-order (surface level) changes. "Pseudo recovery" happens when your distrustful, clever false-self crew persuasively promotes these changeless ("first order") changes. The alternative is *second-order* changes, which shift core attitudes and beliefs. True recovery evolves from—and promotes—a series of *safe* second-order changes. These produce permanent healthy shifts in your life.

A powerful second-order change in most recoveries is calmly giving up the old (false-self) need to *control* people, relationships, and situations. Veteran recoverers all acknowledge that paradoxically, things got better as they stopped their life-long attempts to control ("manipulate.") We learned (painfully) to *surrender* to the reality that many important things are beyond our ability to control or affect. Spiritual faith helps most of us to accept this scary truth calmly.

"The overall key to mental health: Settle for disorder in lesser things for the sake of order in greater things. Therefore, be content to be discontent in many things."

Here, "letting go" (of control) means to work patiently with your subselves to build *trust* that your Self, your Higher Power, and your "human nature" (instincts and DNA programming) will guide you reliably, step by step, toward what you want. Often, you won't see this at work, and will need to rely on faith that you'll see it "later." Shifting to a long-range outlook helps trust that short-term difficulties and "setbacks" have unseen future benefits.

More recovery guidelines . . .

Reduce Black/white Thinking

Many of us survivors of low-nurturance childhoods learned very early to adapt to overwhelming situations by reducing them to only two options: right or wrong, good or bad, safe or lethal, stay or flee, etc. This is a way of achieving the comforting illusion of *control* over overwhelming situations, and avoiding feeling inept and possibly failing at choosing among a range of options.

I learned this from recovery pioneer Rokelle Lerner. At an ACoA (Adult Children of Alcoholics) conference, she related an experience while driving home one day. She suddenly *saw* her lifelong tendency to do black/white thinking, and got an image of a piano keyboard. She thought, "A piano has 88 keys, not just two," and started to cry at the implications of this for herself and her clinical clients. Her story and analogy guides my recovery today, fifteen years later.

Recovery teaches that all internal and social situations have many, *many* options. Like Rokelle, you'll learn to see this as your subselves grow in patience, and in trusting your Self to identify, evaluate, and choose among them. This awareness and attitude is essential for choosing the "next best steps" in the strange new world of harmonizing your inner family. Incidentally, note the option of inviting a Guardian subself (e.g. the *Liar* or *Addict*) to shift to a helpful new inner-family role: being in charge of spotting "new options" in any confusing situation. Note your inner gang's reaction to that idea . . .

Adopt "the Mind of a Student"

Your recovery process is largely about learning new information and concepts, and unlearning others—i.e. changing toxic old perceptions, beliefs, "shoulds," and understandings, that unintentionally promote your inner wounds. Your learnings will come from many sources—media, people, meditation and journaling, and new social experiences. Enjoy becoming aware of *how* you learn—seeing, touching, moving, hearing, tasting . . . There's no best way but *your* way!

Risk Seeking and Accepting Help

Most recovery veterans say you can't really recover alone. We need others to encourage, confront, mirror, hold, appreciate, and inspire (i.e. to "love") us when the going gets tough, discouraging, or confusing. I'm confident that there are persons and groups devoted to true recovery in your community. They may not know about false-self dominance (yet), but they will know about versions of the six wounds. Experiment with using terms like "wholistic healing" and "personal recovery" in social situations, and notice how others react. There are *millions* of us Americans in various states of shedding our false-self camouflages! I trust that's true in other literate countries, but don't know, factually.

Part of building a recovery support network is identifying recovery hero/ines—people who are further along their version of your path. Be comfortably alert for such lay and professional people, and reality-check the premises you'll read here and elsewhere with them. Their terminology may differ from yours or mine, but they'll clearly *know* what you're trying to do.

Ask spokespersons for churches, mental-health clinics, and hospital outpatient programs if they know of any local lay or professionally led groups on recovery from childhood abuse or neglect. If you can't find any, and aren't motivated to start such a group, use the Internet to find fellow recoverers. See Part 4 for more on this.

Enjoy Laughing With Yourself and the Rest of Us

Do this compassionately and affectionately, not critically. Once you see your (and other's) subselves in action, they're often silly and absurd—even hilarious. The sage who said, "He who laughs at himself will be entertained his whole life long" offers us a fine recovery T-shirt slogan to keep us light and relaxed, as we change and claim what we're *really* capable of, over time. Recovery doesn't have to be a grim, white-knuckle experience! It also needs to be taken seriously at times.

Expect true recovery to cause unexpected gusts of resentment, anger, anguish, regret, sorrow, and guilt—even disgust and horror. These all can bring out old (shame-based) reflexes to identify "who caused this—who's at fault here?"

This healing process is *not* about blaming your caregivers, your ancestors, or yourself. It *is* about growing compassion, forgiveness, and acceptance of what *was* and *is*, along the way, and what's possible now.

Your caregivers were probably ruled by false selves, and living in normal denial of it. They gave you their best, even if it wasn't always enough. This doesn't mean you can't authentically feel *angry* with them—and with your unaware ancestors and our wounded, ignorant society.

Recovery is Basically a Spiritual-growth Process

"Spirituality" means believing that there is some force or power in you and the universe that is greater than all of us. A related faith is that this power can promote your healing *if invited and accepted.* You may call the power "God," or "Great Spirit," or "Atman," or "The One," or "The Force" or "my Higher Power," or something else. In 15 years, I have never met anyone in true recovery that didn't acknowledge the growth of a core spiritual faith that transcended "reason" and "logic."

It helps here to stay clear on the difference between *spirituality* and *religion.* "Religion" is a man-made system of spiritual beliefs and worship rituals, usually based on interpretation of a sacred text, like the Bible, Torah, or Koran. Some religions promote psychological shame, guilt, fear, and conflict, while piously focusing on "love" and "doing God's will." By doing so, they unintentionally promote false-self dominance, vs. true self-awareness and healing. Some (threatened) people will righteously disagree.

Recovery Involves Grieving Prior Losses

A "loss" is a broken emotional/spiritual bond, or attachment. The nature of life on Earth is that over time, many things we're significantly attached to are taken from us, or we choose to end the bond. The innate mental-emotional-spiritual process of mourning is nature's way of helping us to accept our losses—which frees us to form selective new bonds.

In a low-nurturance childhood, we're often discouraged from healthy grieving, and/or we block ourselves from feeling grief emotions (confusion, rage, and deep sadness). As effective recovery progresses, awareness of major old losses and these repressed feelings usually start to resurface, as your inner-family members start to unify and feel more secure. If you (all) expect this to happen, it isn't as likely to discourage or frighten your subselves.

A related part of the recovery process is to become non-judgmentally aware of people around you whose false selves inhibit you from healthy grieving. Once aware, your Self will decide whether you should change or end your relationship with them, in favor of others who support your grieving.

In true (vs. pseudo) recovery, you'll naturally become more aware of your thoughts, feelings, needs, bodily signals, and responses. Use your growing awareness to act on these guidelines (and your own) as you go. That will help keep you on track, avoid dead ends, and get the most from your risks and new learnings.

Recap

This chapter overviews recovery from false-self dominance: the general three-phase process, six key goals, types of help available, and a set of guidelines. The theme of all of these is intentionally freeing your Self from life-long "protective custody" of a distrustful group of personality parts called your "false self."

The next chapter outlines an effective way to free your Self, and help your subselves learn to trust him or her and team up together, over time. Here, this way is called "parts work," or "*inner* family therapy." As a therapist, I have studied and used this set of ideas and techniques for a decade, with scores of clients and my own inner crew. There is nothing in this set of ideas you can't master and benefit from by yourself—though having a skilled parts-work coach for a while usually helps, until you get the hang of it.

6) RECOVERY: *INNER*-FAMILY (PARTS) WORK

"Go within—or go without."

—*Neal Walsch*

This chapter aims to inspire and guide you toward harmonizing your *inner* family of subselves (personality "parts"). It provides outline concepts, terms, examples, techniques, suggestions, and exercises. The last part of the chapter offers options for applying these inner-family ideas to each of the six main recovery goals you just studied. There are a number of related readings in Part 4.

Because many of the ideas in this book may be new to you, I suggest you scan or re-read Chapter 3 to refresh yourself on the key traits of your inner family. Pause and reflect: do the ideas in that chapter seem generally credible? Does it seem reasonable that "you" are really made up of a group of wonderfully varied subselves? Does it seem possible that you (your Self) can *meet* and team-build your inner crew? Listen to your inner voices now (plural), and notice what your body is saying . . .

A fundamental element in successful recovery is to get clear on concepts and terminology. This is true to sharpen your own thinking and reasoning, and in your working with selected helpers. Because the concept of personality subselves is probably new to you, let's clarify some key words we'll be using together.

Parts-work Terms (Alphabetically)

Addiction—is a behavioral sign that a pair of Guardian Subselves have teamed up to comfort, soothe, and shield one or more Young subselves from unbearable pain. They will do so with one strategy or another (addictions to chemicals, activities, relationships, or mood-states) until trusting that the

Self, Higher Power, and safe others will take over this protection, and true recovery has well begun. Ending the *Inner Magician's* protective denials of addiction, and then having the *Addict* subself cautiously relax (stabilize), is necessary before *full* recovery can proceed. Thus 12-step "recovery" is often the first part of true recovery.

Awareness—is the changeable human trait that regulates recovery from false-self wounds. Here, *self awareness* means "consciously knowing," and "sensing," your bodily and inner-family dynamics moment to moment, and over time. "Dynamics" spans your current and chronic thoughts, feelings, emotions, fantasies, needs, priorities, values, habits, associations, fears, goals, joys, hopes, "hunches," intuitions, "urges,"—and paradoxically, becoming aware of what you've been unaware of. A core goal in inner-family harmonizing is to become instinctively aware of who's in charge of your life, moment to moment—your Self, or other subselves.

As true recovery progresses, your awarenesses—and awareness of them—grow naturally. This happens as your Guardians feel progressively more trust in your Self, Higher Power, other subselves, and selected persons. As your Inner Kids and Guardians relax, aspects of your inner and outer life that were distorted, repressed, or numbed-out become clear. Five key aspects of increasing awareness are . . .

• Noticing the still, small voice of your spiritual Guide/s;

• Becoming increasingly aware of your awareness—which often promotes consciously noticing your breathing, heartbeat, and muscular tensions—and what they *mean*;

• Learning to automatically see more than two options in complex, conflictual situations (reduce black-white thinking);

• *Empathy*—becoming more aware of what other people need, think, and feel *now*; and . . .

• Communication sequences and patterns: what's happening in you, in your partner/s, and between you and them, now and over time.

Forms of meditation like journaling, Active Imagination, breath work, dream work, Tai Chi, and Gestalt and movement therapies are some effective ways to increase your personal awareness, over time. Ongoing parts work (inner-family therapy) focuses specifically on raising your self-awareness. Many people value learning how to access the wisdom of their *unconscious* mind, as part of maturing and healing. See "Going inside."

Blending—This term was coined by inner-family pioneer Dr. Richard Schwartz. It describes one or more excited subselves infusing your Self with its feelings, views, perceptions, and needs. When this happens, you consciously experience what the blending subselves feel, think, want, and believe. Your Self's calm, balanced leadership is usually lost, until the excited part or parts calm down and/or "unblend." Blending is universal, and is implied by terms like these:

going to pieces	going nuts
spacing out	losing it
lost my mind	going crazy
flipping out	looney tunes
off the wall	obsessive
paranoid	beside herself
depressed	loose cannon
addicted	bonkers
Borderline	mentally ill
hysterical	paralyzed
meantal case	psycho(tic)

split (multiple) personality
a side of you I've never seen
s/he turned into someone else
s/he's from another planet
couldn't get it together / get a grip
lights on, but nobody home

Unblending is separating an excited part from your Self so s/he can manage the current situation.

Parts work can teach you how to unblend, fill the excited parts' needs, and build their trust and cooperation over time.

Blending can occur when you first focus on a subself that has been causing harm to someone. Your *Inner Critic* infuses your Self with his/her critical opinions (or fear) of that part ("I *hate* this part that makes me overeat!") Your *unblended* Self will typically regard such a part with interest and compassion. "Disliking" and "distrusting" another part usually signals blending in action.

Blending also happens automatically when your Guardian parts believe inner or outer situations are significantly threatening. Any part can blend with your Self, but your Inner Kids and Guardians are specially adept at it. People who seem "childish" at times probably have a young subself that's taken over their Self much of the time. Other people dominated by false selves can be seen as "cold," "critical," "controlling," "spacey," "sexy," "intellectual," and so on.

"Direct access" happens when an outside person (e.g. a therapist or inner-family supporter) speaks directly with one of your parts without your Self acting as a go-between. The alternative is "indirect access," which may seem safer during early parts work. This happens when the outsider asks your Self to query or inform the part in question—so "You" (your Self) act as an intermediary. As your parts learn to trust the inner-family process, they'll usually communicate directly with trusted outsiders, unless other anxious parts object and interfere. I've experienced scores of clients react with amazement the first time one of their subselves was willing to talk with me directly through their vocal chords, muscles, and bodily senses.

Disowned parts are those subselves you've been trained to dislike, reject, repress, and deny. For example, if you have a (young) part that really wants you to focus only on its needs, or to act violently, your inner *Judge* will probably have been trained to see that "selfish" part as "bad." Once so labeled, other parts will work fiercely to block, paralyze, shun, and ignore such "awful" parts, causing ongoing inner strife. Often we've lived with this strife for so long we're unaware of it. This is specially true of our *Shamed One* —usually a young subself.

In their intriguing, useful book *"Embracing Our Selves,"* psychologists Sidra and Hal Stone propose that we feel most intensely attracted to or repelled by people who act out their version of our disowned parts. Have you ever met someone you "couldn't stand"? The reason you dislike them intensely is probably an instinctive recognition of a part of yourself that you (some judgmental parts) "can't stand," displayed by the other person. Later in parts work, we come to calmly accept and embrace ("own") *all* our varied parts, and the array of talents and limitations they bring us.

Dissociation is the protective ability of our "minds" (subselves) to automatically separate one level of mind-body experience from another. Thus victims of abuse or other trauma can "go somewhere else" to endure it. Broadly, I believe too little early-childhood nurturance causes daily adult dissociation: false-self dominance. Psychiatrists have designated a family of related mental problems as "dissociative disorders."

Exile is Dr. Richard Schwartz's term for a part that is trapped living in a past (usually traumatic) time of your life. Such parts can be freed and brought safely into the present via the parts-work techniques of re-doing and rescuing (see below). Doing this can often release life-long anxieties, repressed feelings, and misperceptions and enhance inner-family harmony.

False self describes one or more Guardian and/or young subselves that protectively blend with your Self to take momentary or chronic control of your personality (inner family) and your body. Many adults from low-nurturance childhoods may have never experienced their *true* Self in consistent control. Their controlling subselves are understandably skeptical (distrustful) that the person has a reliable, gifted inner leader who can foster a new safe, serene, and productive lifestyle for them all. "Persona" means "false self." See "Self" (capital "S.")

Fear-based (personality)—having a dominating false self which is strongly influenced by (1) one or more frightened Inner Children, and (2) one or more Guardian subselves devoted to soothing, distracting, and comforting them. The young subselves may be Exiles stuck in the past—i.e. living a daily life where there are no reliable people to keep them safe. Recovery identifies these subselves, brings them to live into the present, if needed, and helps the Inner Kids trust Self, *Nurturer*, adult, and spiritual parts—and selected other people—to keep them safe. That eventually frees their Guardian parts to take up more productive inner-family roles. See Shame-based.

First-order change, or "changeless changing" is making a superficial mental or behavioral change (swearing off chocolate doughnuts) without changing the underlying core attitudes and priorities ("I now choose to eat much less sugar, fat, and carbohydrates, and to exercise four times a week, because I truly value my wholistic health and my life.") First-order changes are a favorite strategy of false selves to give the illusion of change without losing their control over your inner family. People in pseudo recovery are making first-order changes, which are rarely effective, over time (e.g. addiction "relapses," and "marrying another control freak.") True recovery requires second-order (core attitude and priority) changes—which signal a shift in inner-family leadership. These usually follow "hitting the wall"—i.e. exceeding a primal tolerance limit for pain, fear, emptiness, or despair.

"Go inside" means to get quiet and undistracted, and focus on your current thoughts, emotional and physical feelings, any inner images, and your inner thinking-feeling-sensing process. You experience "inner awareness" when you go inside. Alternatives are focusing only on your thoughts, or your feelings, or your body, or things outside your body. Most Americans are used to being automatically focused outside ourselves.

"Going inside" is a learnable skill and ability. Meditation, journaling, breath work, massage, Tai Chi, and being in Nature are some ways to cultivate inner awareness. Recovery is directly proportional to your ability to "go inside" comfortably, and become *aware* of what's happening in your inner family and body. Being "in a trance" happens when you focus on the happenings inside you. You do that daily, preparing to sleep, waking up, and at other times. See "Awareness."

Guardian—any one of the group of subselves whose primary mission (inner-family role) is to comfort, soothe, and protect upset young subselves. Guardians, "Protectors," or "Firefighters," seem to be eternally watchful. They activate whenever they perceive significant danger to one or more Inner Kids, themselves, and/or you as a whole person.

Activated Guardians typically blend with your Self, so you feel, think, and perceive as the Guardian part does. Blending happens below conscious awareness, like lightning. It's based on the Guardian's historic unawareness or distrust of your Self. Once convinced that it's safe to do so, Guardians readily change their "jobs" and redirect their talents and energy—permanently. This is one reason that recovery based on inner-family work succeeds, over time.

Harmonizing your inner family—Converting your disorganized subselves into a well-led, effective team. Recovery is necessary because many of us have lived with our personality (inner family) in moderate to severe chaos most of our lives. The chaos comes from your subselves not knowing and trusting each other, and fighting or hiding in certain situations.

Harmonizing is the process of building awareness and cooperation among your subselves, under the trusted leadership of your Self, Higher Power, and delegates. This healing process is an alternative to the traditional concept of psychological *integration* (see below).

Healing means (here) the process of transforming inner-family chaos to serene harmony, pride, and effective teamwork. This evolves from inner-family work like that described below, and other health-promoting choices, attitudes, and activities. Another definition of healing is "reducing the six false-self wounds, over time." See *Recovery*.

"Hit bottom" or "Hit the wall"—means "to experience something that triggers a lasting, second-order decision to start and maintain true recovery from false-self dominance." Common "walls" are drunk-driving arrests, legal suits, divorce threats, job firings, and major health problems. The "walls" and "bottoms" are as varied as snowflakes and fingerprints. Hitting bottom separates the "wounding" phase of recovery from the "healing" phase. A **"false bottom"** is an episode or temporary decision that results in a first-order (superficial, temporary) change.

"I," "Me," and "Myself" (or "my Self") can refer either to . . .

* Your true Self, or . . .

* The other part/s blended with your Self at the moment, or . . .

* Your whole mind-body self (small "s.")

Because of these multiple meanings, initial parts-work language and conversations can often be confusing. See "You" and "Yourself."

Indirect access—A safe way an outside person can communicate with your distrustful, anxious subselves using your Self as an intermediary. See Direct access.

Inner Child—one of a group of inner-family members who are impulsive, reactive (very emotional), naïve, narrow-visioned, focused on the present, and have little knowledge of the real world. They are usually young, developmentally. Some of your Inner Kids may be unaware of your Self, your *Nurturer*, and/or your Higher (spiritual) parts. You can help them meet and trust these subselves via effective parts work (Part 2).

Inner conflict —happens when two or more of your subselves disagree on perceptions, meanings, values (including priorities), and/or goals. These disagreements first increase in frequency and intensity and then fade, as true recovery progresses. Your Self is naturally skilled at resolving inner conflicts safely and effectively, if trusted, unblended, and free to negotiate, mediate, delegate, and lead.

Inner conflicts are characterized by *self doubt, anxiety, worry, confusion, mind racing, obsessive thinking, insomnia, indecision, procrastination, irritability, being spacey, avoiding,* and other traits—recognize any? Core reasons for inner conflicts are (1) lack of effective inner-family leadership; (2) mutual distrust among subselves, including spiritual; (3) unawareness of the seven communication skills (*Satisfactions*, xlibris.com); (4) excessive fears, shame, and guilts, (5) misinformation and misperceptions; and (6) lack of self and outer awarenesses. *All* of these can be improved, in true Self-directed recovery!

Most conflicts between two or more people are really at least three concurrent conflicts below the participants' awareness—*inside* each of them, and between their respective chaotic inner families. Small wonder that intentionally growing self and interpersonal awarenesses are needed for effective conflict resolution!

Inner family—denotes all your personality parts together as a group. You may prefer another term, like my inner *team, troop, troupe, squad, community, tribe, cast, clan,* or whatever. Experiment, and use the term that emerges as most comfortable to your inner *crew.* Depending on their members' dynamics and leadership, inner families (personalities) range from "numb" and paralyzed, to chaotic and "crazy" to "high spirited" to "controlled and rigid" to "harmonious and serene." How would you describe yours, so far?

Inner-family council—A parts-work technique in which your Self calls selected or all members of your inner family together, and has a moderated discussion of some important issue. A common example would be to collect feedback about having a veteran Guardian subself (e.g. *Pretender*) let go of their old protective role, and accept a new inner-family role (e.g. *Focuser*)

Inner-family system—encompasses your inner family plus the rules, values, and drives that govern how all your subselves behave, react, and interact. Similarly, your *outer* family system refers to all the people you designate as "family," the boundary that separates them from other people-groups (systems), and the rules and dynamics that connect and govern them.

Inner-family work—see Parts work

"Inner voice"—refers most often to current conscious thought streams. It may also denote hunches, intuitions, premonitions, "senses" (as in "I sense that you're distracted"), and expectations. Inner voices and physical and emotional *feelings* are major ways your parts express themselves. It's normal and common for us to have several inner voices going at once—some louder than others. Many believe the "still small voice within" is the voice of our Higher Power, or soul. Are you aware of this voice? Do you (your subselves) *trust* the One who "speaks" with it? True recovery will raise your awareness of who's "speaking" inside you, and what they're saying (or whispering).

Inner Wound—see wound

Integration—can refer to (1) re-including your disowned personality parts into your inner family; (2) fusing two or more subselves into one, during recovery; or (3) growing a common purpose and mutual respect, tolerance, loyalty, affection, and appreciation, among all parts that comprise your personality (inner team). The latter process can also be called "harmonizing" (see above).

Job retraining—happens when your Self negotiates with another personality part to shift its energies and aims to a new role in your inner family. This happens only after the subself comes to trust that your Self, and perhaps other parts and safe people, can reliably provide the protection for you that it has worked at all its life. Job shifts can happen very quickly, or gradually. See "Reassigning" in the next chapter.

Manager part—any of the group of "every day" personality parts that respond to the environment when no threat is apparent to an Inner Child or related Guardian. See p. 48 for typical Manager subselves. Your true Self is one of several.

Me—see "I"

Mental "illness"—seems to be caused by having a chronically chaotic inner family controlled by a false self. This produces observable mixes of the six inner wounds, whose combinations have been given a wide range of psychiatric labels. From this viewpoint, while "mood-controlling" medications like antidepressants, tranquilizers, and "sleep medications" may reduce uncomfortable *symptoms*; they also reduce the motivation to confront and heal the unseen *real* problem—denied or minimized false-self dominance.

Our generation may be the first to learn some science-based answers to the endless debate about which causes which: biochemical "imbalances," or "emotional disturbances" (inner-family chaos).

Mind—this noun and verb has many meanings. Here *mind* usually means the total set of brain-body aspects that determine your behavior and moment-to-moment perceptions and experiences. There's no question that we humans naturally have *conscious* minds and *unconscious* minds. Many believe we also have a *semi*-conscious mind. Each of these "processes" (i.e. sorts out and makes meaning of) inner and outer events, and helps shape our re/actions as life unfolds. "Awareness" happens in our conscious mind, as other levels of perception happen "below" conscious awareness.

Many researchers agree that each of our minds uses different rules to process life events. One school of thought says that your *unconscious* mind is more primitive, concrete, and black/white. If your *Inner Critic* says, "You are really stupid," the other subselves comprising your unconscious mind accept that without question—"Oh, OK, we're really stupid." In that sense, permitting self-critical thoughts is a form of self abuse. The current *meaning* that each of your minds perceives may be opposed—which causes "you" to experience *confusion*, *doubt*, *unease*, and *distrust*—i.e. to "get *upset.*"

Different groups of personality parts govern what happens in each of these regions of experience. Inner-family harmonizing is a way of reconciling both groups to understand, tolerate, and accept these differences, and work to compromise them respectfully under the leadership of your Self and Higher Power. *Multiplicity* and *inner-family* concepts give "Make up your mind," "What's on your mind," "playing mind games," and "I changed my mind" new meanings, don't they? A new question is "Who's running your (or other peoples') minds?"

Multiplicity—refers here to the natural ability of the human mind-body system to fragment or split (as in "split personality"), and develop many semi-autonomous *parts* or subselves, in response to threatening or traumatic childhood and other life conditions.

Myself—see "I"

(Personality) "part"—is a discrete (mental + emotional + spiritual + physical) "energy" in a normal infant, child, or adult, probably corresponding to a discrete area of the brain. Most adults and kids seem to have well over a dozen inner parts, without being "crazy" in the least. Like members of a committee or entertainment troupe, each part brings you one or more unique abilities and limitations. They can communicate with your Self and each other in various ways. All parts mean well, though they can be badly misinformed, biased, short sighted, and hysterical. They can hurt us, each other, and other people.

Writers across the centuries have described our personality parts as *sides* ("Jamie has a witty side"), *aspects, alter egos, subselves, inner voices, subpersonalities, demons, streaks,* "something in me," *character defects, talents, gifts* ("Mildred has a gift with teens"), *traits, weaknesses, strengths, tendencies* ("Max tends to be extreme"), *paranoias, complexes, spells, moods, mind (or mental) states,* and *personas.* What's your favorite? See p. 40 for even more descriptors.

See False self, Inner family, Personality, Self, and Subself.

Parts work—is the intentional process of meeting, assessing, owning, rescuing, re/training, and (eventually) harmonizing all your inner parts under the consistent leadership of your unblended true Self. Parts work is also called "inner-family work" here. An outline of parts work starts on p. 133, and Chapters 7-9 provide much detail.

Personality—traditionally, this word means all the traits, opinions, reflexes, values, memories, "quirks," associations, needs, and habits that distinguish you from another person. In one sense, all these factors do form a single "entity," like a "team" is a single group of individual players. In inner-family and recovery work, your "personality" refers to the whole inter-related set of subselves or "parts" whose collective traits and motivations make "you" up. Other words for *personality* are *psyche, character, identity, and "psychological makeup."*

"Multiple Personality Disorder," now called "Dissociative Identity Disorder (D.I.D.)" by the American Psychiatric Association, is an unusual condition where groups of parts comprising the personality are unaware of each other, and operate independently. It has been recently estimated that about 5% of the American population has this condition, though data is questionable. True D.I.D. can be hard to diagnose because of expert false-self camouflage. See Inner family, "I," Multiplicity, and Wounding.

Pseudo recovery—Some psychologically-wounded (blended) people can think and act as though they're in "real" (true) recovery, unaware that they have one or more terrified or uninformed parts that block it. Until such Guardian and young subselves feel safe enough, they will cause intense denial (reality distortion) of this protective inner deception. Effective parts work can calm and reassure these subselves over time, and resume wholistic inner healing—*true* recovery.

Managing an addiction without empowering the Self is a kind of pseudo recovery, specially if the person denies substituting a new addiction (like sugar, fat, nicotine, or gambling) for the old one (like alcohol or another drug). Our false selves are devoted, persistent, and extraordinarily clever at trying to gain us *short-term* comfort and safety, despite long-term harm. They'll do that until they're helped to accept (trust) the true Self's short and long-term judgments, and to have serene faith in the guidance and protection of a nurturing Higher Power.

False-self based pseudo recovery is similar to the widespread relationship phenomena of pseudo intimacy, pseudo-commitment, and pseudo-mutuality. I believe all are clear symptoms of significant denied false-self dominance.

Reassigning (Guardian subselves' to new inner-family roles)—see "Job retraining."

Recovery—refers to the ongoing intentional process of reducing the impacts of the six false-self wounds, and harmonizing an inner family under its resident true Self. *True* recovery causes noticeable emotional, mental, spiritual, behavioral, and sometimes physiological changes in the recoverer, over time. These are permanent second-order (core attitude) shifts. See Harmonizing, Healing, and Pseudo-recovery.

Re-doing—is a powerful parts-work technique. It involves planning and rehearsing, then vividly recalling a past inner and/or outer trauma, and revisiting it with your present Self and any other desired healthy parts or people. The goal is to intervene safely in the remembered traumatic experience, and help involved subselves experience a safer outcome. See p. 204.

Rescuing—involves identifying *Exile* parts stuck in the past (see below), patiently gaining their trust, preparing a safe, nurturing (inner) place for them in the present, and helping them transfer safely out of their traumatic environment to join their inner-family teammates in the *now*. Rescuing paralyzed (often young) parts can help thaw frozen grief, heal old shame, and seeing the world as it *really* is. A symptom of a successful rescue is having life-long fears, anxieties, and frustrations greatly recede.

This technique is based on subselves' unquestionable abilities to _ change, and to _ distort reality to absolutely believe they are living in a time that has long since vanished, despite daily evidence to the contrary. I have witnessed this phenomenon in dozens of typical recovering clients, and have heard clinical colleagues describe the same. Some inner-family therapists call rescuing "time travel." See p. 208.

self (small s)—denotes your physical body, spirit, and all your inner parts, together. S/He is the whole person who is called by your name, including all parts' dreams, genes, hopes, fears, skills, limitations, and history. Thus your *Self* is one aspect, or part, of your *self*. "My self" ("myself") may describe _ this or _ the part who is currently running your inner family. See "I."

Self (capital S)—refers here to the natural emotional-spiritual energy or brain center that every human has. Its innate, inborn talent is consistent, effective leadership of all other subselves. If trusted enough by your other personality parts and allowed to fulfill its goal of promoting your health, growth, and success, your Self is a naturally gifted coach and director. S/He calmly assesses, prioritizes, problem-solves, delegates, motivates, co-ordinates, facilitates, negotiates, and makes wise, wholistically healthy wide-angle, short and long-term decisions, based on current information and trusted counsel.

Your Self matures and develops skill, wisdom, and good judgment over time, just like all other parts. One implication is that kids' true Selves aren't usually wise enough to be trusted by other parts. Without consistently high caregiver nurturances (p. 257) that promotes false-self dominance. Do you believe you have such a true Self? Is it in charge of your life? How do you know?

Given the chance, your Self will help all your other parts to develop and use their individual skills and gifts. S/He will work to develop deep senses of inner-family safety, and subself and inner-family purpose and pride. Your Self is not more "powerful" or important than any other part. It can't protect itself from *blending* and being overwhelmed or paralyzed by other mistrusting, agitated personality parts.

When their unblended Self is clearly leading their inner crew, people universally report feeling *confident, serene, calm, clear, grounded, centered, focused, purposeful, energized, up, light, patient, empathic, alive, alert, aware, strong, firm, and "in the flow."* When is the last time you experienced that state? Can you imagine feeling that way most of the time?

"Self-talk"—is the ceaseless inner chatter of your personality parts. It ranges between a single clear momentary "knowing" to a rich, dynamic broth of thought fragments, memories, emotions, bodily reactions, intuitions, images, hunches, and "senses." The "noisier" your self talk, the more "confused," "unfocused," and "unsure" you feel. The noise goes down, over time, as chaotic subselves learn to see their collective identity as a team, and learn to trust that their Self will respectfully *listen* and respond to them, one at a time.

Mind racing and ***obsessing*** are forms of self-talk. Going "inside," and (your Self) calming tumultuous self-talk, is needed to hear the ***still small voice*** of your spiritual or Higher self. Adults or kids who "can't concentrate" are probably experiencing chaotic self-talk, and anxious subselves that don't feel *noticed, heard,* and *respected.* Whether situational or chronic, mind-racing and defocusing are sure signs of inner disharmony and false-self dominance.

Serenity is one outcome of effective true recovery from false-self control. It may be described as a temporary mind-body-spirit state of anxiety-free peace, clarity, awareness, acceptance, love, and inner and outer balance. It usually results if your inner family of subselves truly trusts your Self and Higher Power to move safely through current life situations. Many feel that true serenity is a state of spiritual grace. Serenity differs from *numbness* in that in it, you're fully alive, and aware of your thoughts and major current feelings.

Shame-based (personality)—A *shame-based* person is someone often or always controlled by a false self largely run by Guardians protecting an agonized *Shamed Child*. Shame-based people exhibit predictable behaviors like those on p. 293.

Shame-based behaviors imply the presence of (1) one or several Inner Kids who feel intensely worthless, disgusting, and unlovable; and (2) one or more protective Guardian subselves devoted to soothing, comforting, and protecting the anguished young subselves. Developmentally, typical Shamed Child subselves are often under six years old. They're usually stuck in an endlessly traumatizing past time.

Their Guardian subselves can produce a range of attitudes, perceptions, and behaviors that expertly camouflage the existence of these intensely ashamed young subselves. Recovery aims to gently identify these despairing subselves, and find ways to convert the Inner Child's core belief of unlovability to attitudes of self-worth, self-respect, and self-care—"self love." As this happens, the Guardian parts can gradually relax, and eventually shift to new inner-family roles. In my personal and clinical experience, significantly troubled adults and kids are *always* shame-and/ or fear-based (q.v.) personalities—i.e. majorly wounded.

"Stress"—is felt in direct proportion to the intensity and duration of inner-family disharmony. The polar opposite is *serenity*, which grows from effective (true) recovery and related spiritual growth, over time. Some Child and Guardian subselves *promote* stress, because they experience it as pleasurable excitement and/or an effective distraction from pain and emptiness. Some wounded people are addicted to excitement—i.e. they have a ruling *Addict* Guardian part, until in true recovery. Sexual addiction is one form of this.

Such excitement-seeking parts may chronically control some wounded people. They're labeled as "Daredevils," "Rebels," "Rash," "Troublemakers," "Adventurers," and "Risk takers." Our society dubs them "type A." They're among the people who like to compete obsessively and "pick fights." Their ruling personality parts seek the thrill of combat and *victory*, rather than effective conflict resolutions. The legal, military, political, and law-enforcement professions value and attract many such people. Many shame-based excitement seekers are obsessed with "winning" and "being number one." Others controlled by shamed and fearful subselves are subservient, and avoid conflict and competing to the extreme.

"Stuck in the past"—describes a personality part that fiercely believes it still lives in the calendar time and situation where its person was originally traumatized. Such parts are usually Inner Kids or Guardians. Thus a grown woman may have a young part who *knows* (believes) that any night, her (remembered) drunken father (or any man) may barge in and molest her—and that there's no one around who will believe or protect her. *Reassuring* and *reasoning* with such traumatized parts does not help them change, any more than someone trying to convince you that the sun rises in the North. Attempts at logical persuasion often make them feel self-doubtful, crazy, bad, frustrated, and even more anxious. *Experiencing*—like well-planned, safe "re-doing" and "rescuing" (Chapter 8) *does* help them change safely, when they and other subselves are ready.

If such Exile subselves feel secure, and are respectfully asked "What year is it?" they will often quickly respond (in your thoughts) "1971," or some date many years ago. After building trust and security, such terrified, misguided parts can eventually visit the present, and—when feeling safe enough—come to stay.

Subself—is one of well over a dozen terms that people have used to describe the different semi-independent parts of our multifaceted human personality. Individual subselves are probably discrete regions of our brain-mind-body system. Some equivalent terms are *subpersonality*, *alter (ego)*, *aspect*, *mini-mind*, *mind state*, *mood*, *trait*, *character defect*, *talent*, *inner child(ren)*, *ability*, *"flair"* (e.g. for politics), *potentials*, *(inner) voices*, *streak (e.g. yellow, and mean)*, *sides (e.g. musical, seductive, or analytic)*, *"bent"* (Wanda had a bent for fixing motors); etc. Subself is used interchangeably here with (personality) *part*. Subselves seem to fall into at least three functional groups: see Guardian, Manager, and Inner Child. A controversial fourth group is *Higher*, or *spiritual* subselves.

True recovery—see *Harmonizing Healing, Integration, Recovery, and Pseudo recovery*.

Wound, Wounding—*wound* refers (here) to any of six toxic psycho-spiritual traits that are caused by early-childhood trauma. "Wounding" means "causing a protective false self to develop, to survive a low-nurturance environment." See *Recovery*.

"You" and "Yourself" (Your Self) take on a whole new meaning in this inner-family context. When referring to another physical person, "you" can mean . . .

- Their whole mind-body-spirit entity, or . . .

- Their true *Self* (inner-family leader), or . . .

- Their *self* (all parts together—their "personality"), or . . .

- Their false self—one or several parts that have blended with their Self now and/or historically.

"You" can also be your Self referring to one or more of your other subselves in an inner dialog, as in "Seems like you don't trust me yet." See *"I."*

These inner-family and parts-work concepts, terms, and phrases are tools that can promote effective recovery. Many of them differ from traditional meanings, which were based on the old idea that people have a single-sided personality. Helping your inner family and your supporters agree on meaningful definitions of terms like these is an important part of early recovery. Use these definitions if they suit you, or evolve your own glossary and meanings. You'll develop your own inner and spoken language, over time, to fit who you are and the healing transformations you seek.

The Goal of Parts Work (vs. Recovery)

Working with the parts of your personality is a technique that promotes true recovery from false-self dominance, over time. It is one of many ways you can heal the six inner wounds from inadequate childhood nurturance. In this context, parts work aims to do some or all of these things . . .

- Coach all the subselves in your inner clan to eventually know, trust, and respect each other and your Self; in order to . . .

- Free your Self to lead (make healthy decisions), with other parts' help, through any life situation; and thus to . . .

- Fully empower your unique personal talents and potential through growing steady inner-family harmony and co-operation—i.e. to "Self actualize."

As this happens, people like you report increasing periods of feeling *light, centered, grounded, clear, serene, energized, resilient, patient, purposeful, peaceful, compassionate, firm, strong, aware,* and *focused.* If you live this way now, bravo! There's no need for you to read further. If your Self doesn't often lead your inner family (which seems to be our cultural norm), here's . . .

An Overview of Parts Work

Here are key steps toward harmonizing your inner family. Each person develops their own unique path in using them, so there is no "right" way. You measure parts-work success by the results you experience. You can do parts work by yourself, and/or with a trained helper or a supportive, informed partner. To make recovery more manageable, the steps are grouped into four phases: evaluate, gather resources, meet and harmonize your inner family members (parts), and extend parts work to others. Though you can skip around, I suggest that following the order of these phases and steps as shown will conserve your energy and time, in the long run. The sections after this summary describe key parts-work steps in more detail.

Phase 1: Evaluate

_ 1)   Study the basic inner-family concepts above and in Part 1, and clarify any questions or confusions about them. If you can describe the concepts lucidly to another person and answer most of their questions, you've "learned" the concepts well enough to start. This doesn't mean you accept or believe them yet. Expect to edit and adjust the concepts to fit you, as your experience unfolds.

_ 2)   Compare these inner family concepts to your life experiences, and see if they ring true "enough" to explore further. For example—have you recently experienced several inner voices arguing, or had major "mood swings"?

_ 3)   Try some initial contacts with one or several of your subselves to see what that feels like. Decide if you (all) want to go further. If not—pause and reflect: which part of you is making that decision? Is it your Self, or one or more protective, distrustful parts who are scared of risking losing their control of you? It may be hard for you to tell, at first.

Phase 2: Gather Resources

_ 4) Decide if you'll use a parts-work journal as a place where some of your parts can communicate, and where you record your experiences and discoveries. I recommend it, even if a (protective) part says, "Oh, I can't write!" Inner-family work is about trying new things safely, and learning . . .

_ 5) Rough-draft an initial list or roster of your parts. _ Group them tentatively into "Managers" (everyday parts), and "Others," who activate in "irregular" (conflictual) situations. _ Pick a label to describe all your parts together that feels right: imagine them as a *team*, a *family*, a *troupe*, an *orchestra* or *choir*, a *gang, squad*, an *expeditionary force*, a *community, committee, clan, tribe,* . . . Have some fun with this!

_ 6) Choose inspiring recovery targets: From all the people you know about, envision as clearly as you can . . .

- _ A recovery model, or hero/ine: i.e. a well-balanced, wholistically healthy, productive person whose life philosophy and actions you specially admire;
- _ What it feels like to belong to a truly effective, well-led family or team;
- _ A gifted and dedicated nurturer and mentor, and . . .
- _ Your life in daily detail, after you meet and harmonize your inner team.

_ 7) Review and edit your initial beliefs about what personal changes might really be possible with effective parts work. _ Adopt an initial tentative positive attitude about this work, _ your ability to do it, and _ each of your known and unknown parts.

_ 8) Rank how important parts work is to you now: decide what other life activities and responsibilities are more important (at this stage), and whether you want to allocate Manager time to reorganize and harmonize your subselves.

_ **9)**   Pick initial supporters. Decide who's "safe" to share your early inner family work with, and what kinds of things you're willing to tell. Decide if you want a professional guide. If so, select one. See p. 174.

Phase 3: Meet and Harmonize Your Parts

_ **10)**   Over weeks or months, use a series of stressful or pleasant current-life situations to _ discover which of your parts are involved, how, and why; and to _ develop the specific parts-work skills described below. Your main goals in this team-building phase are to:

* Evolve a complete "roster" of all your parts, and a clear profile of each one. You'll probably meet your "noisiest" Guardians and Inner Kids first, then your Managers. As inner awareness and safety build, different parts will reveal themselves to each other and your Self at different points along the way. Be open to sensing or affirming your spiritual part/s, as you do this.

* _ Identify any Inner Kids who carry an old terror of abandonment. Then _ identify the Guardians that ceaselessly attend them. _ Work to earn their trust in your Self, Higher Power, and any outside helpers. When all involved Guardians pronounce it *safe*, _ rescue the young parts safely from the past (p. 208). Then _ gently put them in the loving care of your Self, inner Nurturer/s, "Big Brothers or Sisters," and spiritual One/s.

* Identify any Kids that carry excess guilt and shame and the Guardians that protect them. Work patiently with them all to _ trust your Self, *Nurturer* (s), and Higher Power, and then to _ shift toxic shame and _ guilt to self-respect, self-trust, self-appreciation, self-nurturance, and self love (vs. egotism). Parts who have inherited early caregivers' excess shame are usually the best guarded, most hidden, and take the longest to meet, rescue, and heal.

* Identify any disowned parts, and respectfully include them as legitimate members of your inner family, over time. Patiently resolve inner conflicts that erupt as you do this. Your Self is good at that, if free to lead!

- Teambuild. Introduce all parts to each other and your Self, over time. Build mutual trust, group awareness, purpose, teamwork, and pride among all your parts. Try out Inner-family council meetings, with your Self presiding.

- Retrain (some) Guardian subselves. As your Inner Kids and their protective Guardians gain trust in your Self, your Nurturer/s, your Wise (spiritual) One/s, and key people around you, some Guardians will agree to "change jobs." Work with them to redirect their energies and abilities to goals better suited to your inner-family's wholistic welfare in the present. Occasionally, Guardians will "disappear," or merge together, when everyone agrees they've served well, and can "retire" with honor.

- Across all these steps invite your Self and all subselves to seek, experience, and increasingly trust the guidance and support from your Higher Power and/or indwelling spiritual subself. Experiment with identifying and replacing toxic old religious and spiritual beliefs and practices to new ones that feel more wholistically healthy—regardless of other people's reactions.

- _ 11) Continue to do steady or situational parts work as long as it feels useful and productive. Some people use it only for resolving one problem, like managing an addiction or stressful relationship. Others spend some years freeing and developing their true Self, and related spirituality, inner harmony, and daily productivity. Your Self will know what you need.

- As a set of evolving beliefs, discoveries, and realities, parts work may become a personal philosophy and a way of life for you. It may also remain just a concept, or something in between.

Phase 4: Extend Parts Work to Others

_ 12) Grow your abilities to _ compassionately recognize other people's parts in action, and to _ use your inner-family awareness to improve your relationships with them.

The most satisfying personal relationships are those between unblended, empowered Selves and their well-functioning inner families.

Do you know what that feels like? True recovery will gradually move you away from toxic relationships, toward people who's Self is in charge—or is learning to be.

These 12 inner-family steps and the various techniques described below may look like stand-alone projects. In real life, many of them overlap. Inner-family work is organic—it flows, grows, and evolves. Still, there can be an overall plan, meaningful structure and guidelines, specific tools, skills, and achievements, and eventually a "sensed" end to the process.

Pause and experience your thoughts and feelings. Some mix of simultaneous skepticism or disbelief, interest, anxiety, and excitement—is normal. This is a collage of several of your parts' reactions to this inner-family overview and what it means initially to them.

Does this parts-work overview seem daunting? Seen all at once, four years of high school or college work can seem like an overwhelming project. Looking at classes one at a time feels much more doable. Parts work is just the same. Take one step at a time, with time-outs for rest, integration, stabilizing, and relaxing. *You* set and adjust the schedule and the targets!

For now, these phases and steps are just words. They'll come to life when you actually start meeting your inner crew, and *experience* their reality. This work is basically about maximizing the quality and long-term productivity and satisfaction of your life. Can you name a more worthy project?

If you're controlled by a shame-based or fear-based false self now, those subselves will numb or blank you out, cynically trivialize or reject what you just read, or deflect your thoughts. Such personality parts can't imagine that you're capable of—and merit—a high-quality life. Reality distortion at work!

Prepare

Some preliminary learnings and decisions will boost the long-range effectiveness and value of your inner-family work. Investing energy in these initial steps before meeting and working with your parts is like planning for a long important trip: it can save you time, discouragement, frustration, trauma, and perhaps money in the long run. False selves aren't famous for patience, or tolerating delayed gratification!

As a first step, try an initial meeting with one or more of your subselves now. Here's how:

A First Hello

Read "Getting Ready," "Communicating with parts," and "First Meetings" starting on p. 158. Follow the guidelines in the first of those, as you wish. Have paper and pen/cil nearby, notice the clock time, for reference, and relax.

This exercise will probably take about five or 10 minutes. There is no "right" way to do it. To help all your parts hear what you're about to do, try reading these steps out loud before the experience. Some subselves learn better through your ears.

Close your eyes, if that feels OK. Breathe well for some moments. Remember vividly the last time you intentionally met a new person. Recall what you thought, felt, and did—and how they reacted.

Now imagine what you would think and feel if you learned you had a cousin or half-sibling that you'd never known of, who was about to join you. What would you want to know about them? Allow several questions to form clearly. Trust that other questions may evolve, in both you and your relative.

If you notice any thoughts ("inner voices") trying to distract you, or to discount or inhibit this exercise, think or say out loud something simple and clear like, "This will be a safe experience." Respectfully and firmly (your Self) ask the voice/s to hold their thoughts and feelings, and let you (all) have this learning experience. If the inner distractions or resistances continue, consider meeting that (anxious) part of your crew now.

If you experience several voices, assure them you're interested in meeting them all, in good time. Once some (lonely) parts realize someone is really interested in noticing and hearing them, they can get pretty excited and impatient! (Notice your reaction now) . . .

Breathe comfortably. Muse on all the qualities that make you up as a person. Pick one that stands out for you now, and start to wonder about the part in you who "carries" or brings you that trait. Get clear on what part you'd like to meet now (my *Babbler, Explainer, Critic, Organizer, Happy Kid, Lover,* . . .).

Clear your mental movie screen, and invite (vs. demand) an image of this part to form. (Option: think, "Please give me an image that represents you.") *Trust the first thing that comes up*—there is no right or wrong. If your *Inner Critic* proclaims something like "That's a stupid, weird image," acknowledge that protective opinion—and keep going. *You (your Self) do not have to please your Inner Critic!* If no image forms, that's OK. If an inner image does appear, know that it's your Self who's doing the "seeing." Like your eye without a mirror, your Self can't see itself . . .

Recall: your Self is reading this, as are some other subselves, and is taking these steps to meet another of your inner-family members. Focus on the part you want to meet, breathe well, and ask your first question silently or out loud. Be open to any reaction: thoughts, memories, emotions, or bodily sensations (warmth, coolness, tingling, tightness). *Numbness*, "*nothing*," and *silence* (no thoughts) *are* reactions. If you get any of those, consider that they're ways that distrustful, anxious, rigid Guardian parts may be protecting someone from this alien experience. (Who?)

Whether a clear inner image forms, an inner voice responds, or "nothing happens" (which *is* something)—note with interest what you feel and think. If you sense that another part is present now, including an alert *Blanker* or *Blocker*, ask yourself "How do I feel about this part now?" If you notice any critical, anxious, or indifferent feelings, respectfully ask the part who carries those feelings to step aside from your Self now—i.e. to unblend.

Now image and/or speak to the first part again. Notice how you feel about it now. Did your feelings shift? "No" and "I don't know" are OK. If you feel some degree of interest, curiosity, and/or compassion for this first part, your unblended Self is probably in charge now.

As you would if meeting a new relative, identify yourself (your Self), and describe what you're doing—e.g. "We're related, and I'm really interested in getting to know something about you.") Ask any questions of the subself that occur to you, one at a time. Be open to any responses you experience, without judgment. If they've given you an image, see how it acts.

If needed, ask your *Critic* to "talk to me later." If a dialog "wants to happen," let it unfold. Ask your subself if they have anything they want to know, or to tell you. If other "voices," feelings, or sensations intrude significantly at any time, ask their owners (other parts) to let you finish this meeting without distraction. If they insist—explain to the first part you need to attend the distracters, and that you'll return shortly. Refocus on the distracter/s, confirm that they know who "you" are, and ask what they need. Allow anything to develop, checking for your *Critic*, *Perfectionist*, and *Catastrophizer* making intrusive judgments or comments. Notice who's in charge of this process . . .

Trust your Self (vs. "yourself") to make any appropriate decisions on how to conduct and conclude this experience. If it feels OK, thank all parts involved—including those who didn't interfere. Notice your breathing, body, and feelings now with appreciative interest. If you want to follow up on something from this experience, mentally note what it is.

Finally, journal about this experience soon afterwards—even if some protective Guardian part wants you to believe the illusion "I don't write very well." No one else will read this, unless you wish them to. Like a tourist would, describe any parts involved (including your Self), and any awarenesses, insights, anxieties, questions, and "aha's" that you had during this inner adventure.

Feeling weird, strange, or a little anxious about this first exercise is normal! The more inner-family sessions you have, the more comfortable and familiar these meetings become.

Let some time pass. If you wish, try this initial experience again several times—perhaps with different parts. Among our Manager subselves, most of us have a neutral *Observer* part who simply views things calmly and objectively, like a scientist. Ask that part for feedback on what s/he noticed—and then *listen*!

An optional way to first meet several of your parts is to get quiet and undistracted, and reflect on a recent or current "dilemma" you face. Imagine your Self as a reporter who wants to understand all sides of the conflict, and then "interview" each of the inner voices that bring you opposing thoughts and feelings. You might have a dilemma (conflict) about this exercise: One or more "voices" (parts) say "Yes, let's do it!", and others may be arguing "Don't!" As you conduct the interview, notice whether other "voices" (parts) pipe up—specially your *Inner Critic*. Notice the different thought streams, images, and feelings you have, and try out the idea that each one is a *different part* of your personality communicating it's thoughts, perceptions, and needs.

After this exercise, reflect: does the overall inner-family concept seem any more real, credible, and personally meaningful now? Does your Self feel that doing further parts exploration seems "right" now? Review the changes you'd like to make in your life, and wonder what you might accomplish by meeting your whole inner family, and harmonizing them. If gaining further inner family experience doesn't seem "right," or "comfortable enough" now, know that you can do parts work any time.

If you feel ambivalent (wounded), confused, cautious, curious, or skeptical, try reading any of the inner-family books in Part 4 by Rowan, Satir, Carson, Nelson, Stone (specially recommended), Chase, or Schwartz. They use different terms and concepts, but the themes are the same as these.

When you (all) *do* want to experience and get to know your subselves, here are some options . . .

Getting Ready

Doing parts work can yield richer results over time if you take preliminary steps like these:

• Decide whether to use an inner-family journal.

• Draft an initial list of the parts you feel you have, and pick a comfortable way to think of them all as a group;

• Clearly envision inspiring models of a Self-led "hero/ine," a truly effective team or family, and a naturally loving Nurturer;

• Clarify your initial inner-family goals;

• Learn and fine-tune your initial parts-work beliefs and expectations;

• Decide how important inner family work is to be in your life, among your other current goals and responsibilities; and . . .

• Choose who to tell about your parts work, at first, what to tell, and if and whom to ask for help along the way.

Notice a theme here: if you truly value the quality of your own life, you'll feel genuine interest in exploring and trying these options. If you're controlled by a shame-based false self, you'll have thoughts that will distract or discourage you from reading and doing these preparation-phase steps. Let's look at each of them now. How do your parts seem to feel now about you (your Self) getting ready to meet, harmonize, build trust, and lead them? "Skeptical" and "anxious" (worried, or uneasy) are normal.

To Journal or Not?

One of my many instructors along the path said "A personal journal can be one of your best friends: you can tell it anything, and it will never talk back, criticize, discount, monolog, defocus, jeer, or ignore you." Do you have anyone in your life now that does that for you? How does it feel?

Serious (vs. superficial) parts work is like journeying into a rich, unknown land. If your style as an outer-world tourist is to take pictures and buy postcards and mementos, then consider keeping a notebook or journal for this inner adventure. This can be specially helpful if your parts tend to be disorganized and scattered. Your inner family productivity will rise if you stay clear and focused along the way on what you're doing, how, and why.

A major reason to create an inner-family journal is to give some subselves a place to communicate safely. Clients have taught me that some parts only "talk" by writing prose or poetry, or drawing pictures. Journaling opens up this channel—perhaps giving one or more of your parts a "voice" for the first time in their existence. How does that idea feel?

A part simply being able to express it's feelings, views, and hopes—and being *heard* and acknowledged by your Self and other parts—can release chronic emotional tension you may not have been aware of. Recording dialogs or group talks between several of your parts can be a powerful help in (your Self) understanding and resolving their (your) inner conflicts.

Also, inner-family journaling over time lets you compare how you feel now vs. earlier in your recovery. Doing this gives a concrete way of recognizing and affirming changes in your beliefs, priorities, feelings, and behaviors that evolve. That validates your inner-family process, your parts, and the effectiveness of your own efforts.

As you (all) make your initial decision about journaling, note with interest any "resistant" thoughts and related feelings. These can sound like "Journaling is dumb"; "I'm a lousy speller;"; "What if someone reads my journal?"; "Too much work!"; "I might uncover something (bad)"; and "I'll never reread it, so why bother?"

If you have any voices (thought streams) like these, know that they probably belong to some distrustful inner Guardian/s. Such thoughts probably don't represent your Self's belief or feelings. S/He might say something like "Mmm, this idea seems to scare some of you. We've never tried journaling before. Maybe it could help. Can't hurt to try it, and then decide."

Finally, note the power of words. Does "make a *workbook* or a *log*" feel different than "keep a *journal*"? How about "keep a *record*," "a *diary*," or "a lab(oratory) *notebook*"? If you have some uneasy part/s, sometimes the label you use to describe your inner-family writings can make a difference to them.

As with all parts-work decisions, if keeping a journal doesn't feel right at first, don't force it. You can start one at any time along the way.

Inventory Your Known Parts

Who are you? If your personality wasn't a dynamic group of subselves, the question would be "Who *is* you?"

Recall: each of your inner-family parts is probably a discrete brain region that affects your emotional, physical, and spiritual experiences. Each of your personality parts has it's own thoughts, feelings, goals, plans, role, time frame, and worldview. Usually they each have a developmental age, a gender, a preferred name or job title, a unique "voice," and may use one or more inner images to represent themselves to you (your Self). Keep reminding your anxious parts that subselves are a *normal* part of our being human, not some shameful pathological condition! Yes, many people don't yet accept that, so far. False selves at work!

The first step in making an initial personnel roster is to check a key attitude (belief): are you now open-minded about the possibility that you really *do* have such parts, including a true Self? Some people instinctively know they do. Others are understandably skeptical, or even scared of the idea. If a part of you has some doubts, acknowledge them respectfully, and ask your *Doubter/s* to be open to experimenting with parts work. Their (protective) attitudes will either be validated, or they won't.

What you're about to do is like a reporter walking into an interesting small business or organization, and identifying the staff on hand. There are probably other key people who aren't on the scene at the moment.

Find an undistracted time and place. Reflect on, and list, your key qualities as a person. This might look something like:

- Intelligent
- Shy or Social
- Im/patient
- Sensitive
- Creative
- Athletic

- Un/organized
- Un/opinionated
- Hard working
- Loyal
- Stable
- Playful

. . . and so on.

If you're as normal as I suspect, you may not have included some of your less thrilling attributes. Review your list, be honest, and see if any other qualities appear:

- Messy
- Put things off
- Controlling
- . . . ?

- Often late
- Forgetful
- Critical
- . . . ?

As with the "Hello" exercise on p. 155, imagine that each of these traits is the main gift or ability of an individual member of your inner family. How does that feel? Study your roster, and pick out the ones who are often evident during "average" (non-emergency, non-conflict) times. Initial them "R" for "Manager" ("general staff."). Star ("*") or highlight the others.

Next, think of your self in several recent conflictual or crisis situations with, say, health, money, work, or key relationships. Do any other familiar personal traits come to mind?

- Unfocused
- Numb
- Obsessive

- Worry a lot
- Scared
- Easily frustrated

Asterisk these. They're (some of) your Inner Kid and Guardian parts. Several different traits may belong to one part.

Now review the list of common inner-family parts on p. 48. Reflect, and see if any of those fit you as either an "R" or an "*" part. If so, add them to your roster. Title them differently, if that feels better to someone.

Look over your whole team, now, and imagine them as a group. Ask your self: *"Most of the time, who's in charge of them? Which of these parts gets their way, most often?"* Trust any response that comes to your awareness. At this point, many people naturally answer "I am," or "Me." Recall: the word "I" now describes (probably) over a dozen of your subselves. They can't *all* be in charge—or can they? Ask the question again, and be open to any inner answer, hunch, "feeling," or vision. Don't edit, compute, or analyze—just *listen.* Notice your breathing, as you do. If it's shallow, someone has probably blended with your Self.

If the answer to "who's in charge" seems to be one or several of the parts you've listed, circle them. If your inner response is "I don't know who's in charge of them all," notice how that feels. Who would you *like* to be in charge of your crew of subselves? What (or who) is in the way?

If you feel you do have an inner leader, but you don't see her or him on your roster, add "My Self" to your list. Alternative titles are my *Common*

Sense part, my *Adult*, my *Coach*, or the like. Pick a label that fits best, for now. I recommend you try out "*my* (vs. 'the') Self," unless some inner one is really uncomfortable with that label. If so, who, and why?

Finally, scan your list again, and see if you intuitively know which part is directing and guiding your parts work. It may be your Self. Some people have a separate inner family guide who is a spiritual energy, a *Wise One*, or a part like an inner wholistic psychiatrist. These parts work co-operatively with Self for overall harmony. Some people have a small healing committee. If no clear answer emerges at this point, that's OK.

Your initial list is comprised of the most easily identified members of your inner team. Underline or highlight any of them you feel a special interest in, or discomfort with. How would you describe your feelings about each of them, and all of them together? Pride? Indifference? Discomfort? Wonder? Startlement? Curiosity? Anxiety? Nothing?

As you see them assembled, what's your instinct: are all these parts of you usually unified and harmonious? Do they all know about and trust each other? Do they have a common purpose yet? Do they have a trusted and respected leader? How would you feel if you could solidly answer "yes!" to all these questions?

The last piece of this preparation step is to try out terms for all your parts together, and pick a name that fits comfortably. My Inner family? My Team? My motley crew? Clan? Community? Squad? Gang? Family? Troop? Band? The term you settle on should have a thoroughly positive feel to (all of) you.

Once you have an initial sense of who belongs to your inner team, then . . .

Pick Inspiring Models

Shift mental gears, and maybe your body and breathing. Review your life to pick some respected mentors to inspire, encourage, and lead you along your recovery path.

Recovery Hero/ines

Meditate on women and men you've met personally, or famous people you haven't met, whom you specially admire (hero/ines). See who comes to mind when you ask "Who do I know who seems to have lived an exceptionally balanced, serene, satisfying, productive life?" The target here is to establish a clear mental picture of a person who is living with their real Self consistently in charge of a harmonious inner family. The persons you pick as models don't have to be rich, famous, or the inventor of the wheel. You're seeking someone whom you instinctively know is clear on:

- Who they really are, and aren't;

- What their personal talents, limits, and life-mission are; and . . .

- Someone who seems deeply, authentically pleased and satisfied with whom they're becoming, and what they're doing with their life.

You may or may not wish to pick someone of your gender. Be wary of "having to choose" someone your parents or partner would necessarily approve of. This is *your* choice, not theirs! Also, be cautious if some subselves want you to pick unmatchable super-heroes like Christ, Buddha, Athena, Mother Teresa, Lao Tzu, Lincoln, Mohammed, Abraham, or the Pope. Perhaps you'd like to blend the qualities of several hero/ines into a composite. Perspective: this is about picking someone who *lives well*, vs. *achieves great things*.

As you do this, note with affectionate interest how your subselves react. *Teen* Inner Kids may want you to pick a rock or video star. Younger Inner Kids may urge their favorite cartoon character. Your *Historian* may nominate some famous or powerful person from world history. Your *Inner Olympian* may feel a sports superstar is the best choice. Your *Skeptic* may yammer reasons that this whole idea "is ridiculous." None of your parts may yet understand what a "recovery hero/ine" *is*, so acknowledge their choices respectfully, and stick to your quest. By the way, can your Self think of any reason why each of your parts can't have a hero/ine, as long as they don't promote false-self dominance?

Once you envision one or more inspiring persons, see what happens inside after verbally saying *"I will enjoy learning to be as serene, wise, joyous, Self-satisfied, and wholistically healthy as (my hero/ine) seems to be, over time."* If all your inner crew cheers—terrific! More likely, you'll hear a Babel of Guardians and Inner Kids shouting all the reasons this is a brainless, stupid, idiotic, unrealistic fantasy. Can your Self listen tolerantly, and hold onto your hero/ine vision? Repeat this exercise periodically, and notice how the inner responses change . . .

The next parts-work recovery resource to choose is . . .

An Effective-Team Model

Meditate on your whole life. Recall if you've ever *experienced* being part of _ a truly harmonious adult or adult-child group, with _ a clear, common purpose, and _ a trusted, skilled, motivated leader. If so, recall vividly what it *felt* like to be part of that group. If you haven't experienced that, muse or journal in detail how you think it would feel.

Ask other people if they've ever belonged to a group that really worked *well* together. Learn why they thought it did, and what participating in the group felt like to them. The group might be a family; a class; a competitive or investigative team; an artistic troupe or cast; a business department or task force; a church or civic committee; a set of neighbors; a book, prayer, bridge, or investment club . . .

Journal and/or vocally describe your impressions in detail. Option: record it on tape or in a computer file. Build an accessible, detailed vision of the qualities and characteristics of a really harmonious, effective family or team. Try out the belief that you can evolve your own parts into a group like that—despite any inner naysayers. Imagine each of your parts feeling about your Self and each other what you may have felt about your real-life team, and it's excellent leader. Meditate on how it would feel to belong to a really unified and harmonious group of adults and kids. That's exactly what your inner family can become!

Get clear over time on _ how such a group comes to be, _ how it effectively handles conflict and differences of opinion between members, and _ how the leader facilitates resolving these. If helpful, write these ideas down and highlight them in your inner-family journal. Ask others their opinion on this, over time, and collect a rich sample of responses and experiences.

As your parts-work experience unfolds, revisit and refine your vision of a truly effective, integrated team. If someone inside says "*We* can never be like that!" (e.g. your *Doubter* or *Pessimist*) reassure them you hear their disbelief, and that you're setting out (anyway) to discover how to do this thing that they and/or your Self hasn't experienced yet.

Pick Inspiring Nurturers

Here "nurturing" means "Taking deep satisfaction from wanting to fill someone's key needs, and acting on that with steady awareness and mutual respect." How does that compare with your definition? Significant parts work *always* involves meeting, rescuing, and nurturing a group of scared, lonely, rageful, shamed Inner Kids (p. 48). The good news is that we all seem to have one or more parts whose natural skill and motivation is to nurture in a healthy way.

If you're not familiar with, or distrust, that part of yourself, it can help to identify one or several people you know who seem to be really effective, balanced, loving caregivers (vs. care*takers*). This includes caring well for *themselves*, too! Can you think of a really nurturing *man*? Male and female nurturers have some common qualities, and some gender-unique ones.

Hold these models in your consciousness as clearly as you can. Vividly imagine them comforting, guiding, protecting, confronting, soothing, and loving. Notice what they do and say, and how they look. Begin to realize clearly why you think they're effective nurturers. What makes them specially successful in this role? As you get clearer on this . . .

Begin to imagine (regularly) how it would feel to have one or more such Nurturers always available within you, to gladly and tirelessly minister to your needy Young subselves. As you begin to get in touch with your inner *"Good Mom / Dad / Parent"* part, learn appreciatively how s/he reacts when your inner kids "act out." As your parts work progresses, stay alert for inner and outer examples of what *effective* caregiving looks, feels, and sounds like. When you can verbally describe these in some detail—you've laid a solid foundation.

Now you have _ a rough draft of many of your parts; and clear, inspiring models of _ some person who seems harmonious, and well led by their Self and Higher Power; _ a consistently harmonious, dedicated, well-led team or family; and _ one or more effective nurturers. Now you're ready to . . .

Affirm Your Personal and Social Strengths

A useful early-recovery resource is to acknowledge and quiet any inner resistance, and build a realistic list of your unique talents, abilities, and social skills. You can use this summary to bolster your inner crew if you get stuck in recovery, or (someone) feels pessimistic, scared, or insecure. The same skills you use with physical people, you can use to advantage among your inner tribe. That's specially true if you've had caregiving experience with kids of various ages. For example—if you have an inner *Diplomat*, or *Chair(wo)man, Peace Maker, Advocate, Humorist, Limit Setter, or Inspirer*—enjoy the reality that you can call on the parts that bring those talents to you to help your *internal* process and relationships. How do your subselves react to this idea? Option: keep your *Strengths* list where you can see it in the course of an average day.

Clarify Your Initial Parts-work Goals

To provide purpose and direction to your explorations, invest some up-front time identifying specifically what you're trying to do for yourself. Start with your . . .

General Inner-family Targets

My experience is that initial parts workers' goals are vague, very general, or very narrow. That's fine! There's a wide range of start-up parts-work goals available. For example:

• "I'll try parts work out, and see what happens."

• "I want to change my whole attitude about life. Have I been (controlled by) a false Self for all these years?"

• "I want to find out what to do with my life."

• "I want to understand why I do certain things . . . "

• "I want to be less depressed." And/or . . .

• "I want to have more fun . . . "

Whatever your initial parts-work goals, _ write them down as clearly as you can; _ say them out loud, and see what thoughts or feelings bloom; and _ choose an attitude of "My goal/s and priorities can change along the way."

Work patiently over time to refine your first inner-family targets into simple, concrete, specific objectives. For example, an initial goal of "I want to have more good friends" can evolve into "I want to significantly increase my confidence about _ dancing, _ being authentic and assertive, _ dealing better with aggressive and _ unempathic people, and _ resolving interpersonal conflicts." That can become "I want to find, meet, rescue, and free my self-doubting and anxious parts, and redirect their Guardians, over time." See the layers of awareness?

Experts who study *effective* inner "self-talk" suggest that we're often better off using positive assertions or goals than negative ones. Positive statements focus on building, healing, and increasing things, rather than reducing, destroying, "fighting," harming, or limiting. Notice whether it feels better to say "I have to stop being so *pessimistic* and negative," or "I'm steadily learning to be more realistically *optimistic* and hopeful."

Your choice of words counts in defining your inner-family goals. Black and white imperatives ("I must be happier!") tend to be limiting, and can raise your parts' "performance anxiety"—specially if you have a fierce *Inner Critic*. See how simple, clear, positive-action, here-and-now goal statements work for you, like: "I am steadily learning to feel more balanced, serene, and joyous, at a pace that's just right for me." (Can you get into that one?)

The risk of omitting or minimizing this initial goal-setting step is that you may "ride off in all directions." That invites your false self to persuade you that parts work is useless to you or others. Like life in general, setting and adjusting your inner-family aim/s is an ongoing *process*, not an event.

Another helpful preparation step for your inner-family work is to . . .

Rank Key Life "Problems"

As your general parts-work objectives become clearer and more specific, prioritize them periodically to avoid trying to work on too many things at once. For example: if you find from initial parts-work experience that the process really does bring positive changes to your life, your *Achiever*, *Perfectionist*, and other parts might push hard to work on "lose that weight for good / stop being so shy / improve your (or have a) sex life / make more money / stop interrupting others / make more friends / sleep better / end these migraines / break my ice cream habit / stop obsessing about ____:!"

This can feel like being in Disneyland and wanting to take all the rides at once. As an effective leader, your unblended Self is likely to say something like "Look, we have to pick one or two projects at a time. There is enough time and energy to attend each of these. Probably the best choice for us right now is to focus on being less "busy," and to make time to meditate and do some parts work each day without too much guilt or anxiety. How does everyone feel about those two goals?"

Notice that the specific steps outlined in this book provide ready-made goals. Avoid adopting them wholesale, unless you find a way to rewrite them in *your* language and style, and make them yours. The whole point here is to strengthen your trust in your own judgment, over time.

Once you've picked a specific inner family target, try vividly imagining your daily life after fully achieving that goal. Expect some distrustful or scared Inner Kids and Guardians to interfere with this, at first. Notice with interest and respect how they try to block (protect) you from "risky" change. Begin to wonder why . . . ?

Rank Your Inner Family Work

Let your unblended Self poll everyone inside, and decide: "what life activities are generally more important to me (us) these days than parts work—and which are less?" A few activities will normally come before this work, like your job, caring for any dependent people, physical health, and nurturing other important relationships. Consider making a contract or commitment with yourself to invest Manager un-distracted time and effort in high-priority parts work until . . . (what?)

Affectionately expect your shamed, self-doubting, skeptical, and catastrophizing Guardians and Inner Kids to resist and sabotage such a contract. How would your model hero/ine and team leader handle such anxieties? Try trusting that your Self knows just the right way to respond, if unblended and free to decide.

Clarify Self-ish vs. selfish

Typical novice inner-family explorers say "I feel so selfish focusing on me like this!" Teach your *Inner Critic*, *Humble One*, and *Shamed Child's* the difference between being "*selfish*" and "*Self-ish*." The former means to intentionally act to fill your own needs without caring about the needs or feelings of others. *Self-ish* means to attend the needs, feelings, and welfare of all your personality parts and body equally with those of the key people around you, by letting your Self lead. See if any of your inner crew rejects this distinction, and work patiently with them to re-evaluate their opinion. Promote your self from one-down to equal human dignity and worth—without undue guilt or shame. *Self-ish* is healthy and helpful, despite what your black/white naysayers (and other wounded people) decree! Notice your self-talk now . . .

Check Your Initial Inner-family Attitudes

Another helpful thing to do before meeting your whole inner team is to _ get clear on and _ edit some of your key inner-family beliefs. Your parts-work goals, experience, and outcomes will be strongly shaped by them.

Like members of any group, each of your parts carries its own beliefs about the real world, including parts work. Their beliefs are likely to conflict, significantly. The goal here is to get clear on some initial inner-family beliefs that your Self can use as productive parts-work guides. As your recovery work progresses, other subselves usually revise their beliefs, based on the new experiences you'll have.

Here's a brief exploration of some key attitudes. Notice your reaction to each, as you read. Take your time, and add more that occur to you:

1) Your belief about changing your beliefs

Most people have initial doubts or disbeliefs about some parts-work basics. They also may feel (protectively) "I probably can't (won't) change what I believe." That's normal and OK. Revising our old beliefs and forming new ones requires new information and experience. It takes time. Here are several exercises to help form helpful, realistic initial inner-family attitudes:

___ Describe as clearly as you can out loud or in writing what "a belief" or "an attitude" is. How would you explain the concept to someone just learning the English language, or a visiting space alien?

___ Recall one or more key beliefs you've had earlier in your life that has changed substantially. Letting go of believing in Santa Clause, the Easter Bunny, ghosts, and the Tooth Fairy are pretty common Western examples. Learning what married life and child raising are *really* like are others.

___ Speak a comfortable form of these affirmations several times. Close your eyes and listen, or say them to your image in a mirror:

"I can get clear on my key beliefs now."

"I can safely change certain key beliefs, if I learn credible new information."

___ Go over the set of inner-family basics outlined in Chapter 3, and write down your current belief or attitude about each one. You may find "I have no reaction to this one, now," or "I have several reactions!" Just write down whatever thought or feeling appears, without judgment. These are your initial inner family beliefs and feelings—your jumping-off point.

___ For each belief you've identified which might interfere with reaching your inner family goals, draft a simple affirmation that leads towards dissolving the interference. For example: if you discover . . .

"I'm not sure I have an inner Self part who is instinctively an effective leader that my other parts can completely trust"

. . . then draft and try out something realistic, simple, and freeing like . . .

"Over time, I can thoroughly research whether I have an effective inner Self part or not. I can maintain an open mind on this until I do enough research."

See how the attitudes below feel. React to them honestly, to discover your own core attitudes. Edit those until they're comfortable enough—at least for your Self:

2) <u>Your attitude on self permission</u>

"I give myself full permission to do parts work now, in a way that suits me, with confidence and calmness. I need not please anyone else as I develop my own inner-family ideas, goals, style, pace, and results."

3) <u>Your attitude on change, risks, and loss</u>

"Using parts work to free my true Self, and to increase my inner-family harmony, will require my subselves to make important changes. Together, we can find a safe-enough way to make the changes I need."

"Making healthy inner changes requires taking some risks. My unblended Self can determine what a safe risk is for me at any time. S/He can co-ordinate my resources to safely take the risk, and gain new learning."

"Making personal changes always involves losses (broken emotional bonds) and gains. I am fully capable of safely and healthily grieving any major losses I experience from doing my parts work."

"I can find an effective way to reassure and calm any terrified parts that they're in no danger of being 'killed', 'fired', "forgotten," or 'thrown out' as we do this exploration safely."

"I can develop effective ways over time to safely rescue any of my parts trapped in the past, and redirect my misguided parts' energies in a healthier way."

4) <u>Your attitude on your personal safety</u>

"As I do my parts work, I (my Self) am the ultimate authority on what feels safe at any time. I will stop any aspect of work that feels unsafe; learn what my parts' anxiety is about; and then decide how to proceed—without major guilt, shame, or anxiety."

"I can trust my Self and other parts to direct the pace and course of this work so that anything that comes up can be safely handled. Nothing awful or evil will be loosed to significantly harm me or others."

"If I do discover that I have many personality parts and an inner family, I am not, and never was or will be, 'crazy'. I am, and always have been, normal and OK, given the traumatic experiences I've had."

"My Higher Power / Guardian Angel/s / Sprit Guide will help my Self keep me safe enough, as we do this work."

5) <u>Your attitude on realistic optimism</u>

"I (my Self) can maintain a cautiously-positive open mind about the possible benefits of parts work for me. I don't need all my parts to believe this right now, and won't criticize them if they don't."

"I can honor my Inner Kids' and Guardians' needs to believe our inner family efforts 'won't work'. I will move us ahead with this vital project anyway."

6) <u>Your attitude on affirmations</u>

"I will learn to draft and effectively use realistically-positive affirmations in achieving my key inner family goals, over time."

7) <u>Your attitude on tolerances</u>

"I can learn to tolerate not knowing what changes this parts work will bring about in my life, without undue anxiety. I can also tolerate not knowing how long this process will take us."

8) <u>Your attitude on handling parts' resistances</u>

This is a *key* inner-family belief. Some of your parts will normally be scared, skeptical, and even hostile to your inner family work—specially if it involves an unknown professional helper. In pursuing their prime objective to keep you and themselves safe, some subselves will probably give you some intense initial thoughts or senses like these:

- "This (parts work) is stupid. You're a real jerk to believe this junk!"

- "You don't have time (to do it)."

- "You know you've never been any good at meditating."

- "(Parts work) won't work for me."

- "Nothing comes—and nothing will" (when trying to contact a part);

- "You're going to release or discover something really bad, terrifying, or fatal. Don't do it!"

- "I just can't do it alone."

- "It's too abstract and vague—I just can't do that."

- "If I 'go inside,' I'll go crazy (or 'get stuck in there'). I'll certainly be put away in a nut house."

- "Other people will surely: laugh / say "You are weird!" / tell me to stop / reject and abandon me / get upset."

Anything sound familiar here? As you notice well-meant inner warnings like these, notice the pronouns: "I" refers to the part that's "speaking," not your (unblended) Self. "You" refers to your whole inner family or self.

Some of your parts may also manifest their anxiety ("resistance") through unpleasant physical symptoms. Your Self and they can learn to understand and resolve each, with time, empathy, teamwork, and patience.

See what these attitude statements bring up among your crew:

"Some of my parts will naturally resist and try to sabotage my inner family work. When they do, they're unaware or misinformed, and are trying to protect me and themselves."

"None of my parts are evil or bad now—nor have they ever been. My parts always mean well, from their (limited) point of view. They can and will safely learn to change their views, if needed."

"I can respect and empathize with each protective part of me, as it expresses its fear and distrust, without agreeing and impeding our inner-family teambuilding."

To honor any pessimistic (i.e. scared) Guardians, meditate or journal. Give them a chance to express their views on the specific personal risks they see to your doing inner family work. What's the worst thing that could happen (according to them)? Why should you *not* do parts work to recover from significant false-self wounding?

Now invite the "other side" of you to speak: what could happen if you *don't* free your Self and teambuild your inner clan? Write both views down in your journal, and review them regularly. Monitor your attitudes for change, as your experience grows.

Recap: an important parts-work preparation step is to consciously identify, edit, and *use* a set of attitudes, or beliefs, about yourself, your inner family, parts work, and your recovery. Keep these where you can see them, to steady yourself during times of confusion or regression!

A last consideration before you start to meet your inner clan: who should you invite to share and support your inner family experience?

Picking Initial Supporters

A fundamental theme that weaves through every aspect of successful recovery work is building related inner senses of *trust* and *safety* among all your parts. The real-world people around you are a vital element in nurturing these two core factors. Let's look at some options . . .

Who should I tell?

Let's face it: the idea that you, or all of us, are walking collections of "inner voices" and "energies" is pretty weird for typical people. Recall your own initial reactions: Amusement? Skepticism? Curiosity? Disbelief? Hostility? Righteous indignation, and sarcastic criticism?

Most of your subselves are acutely aware of the people around you, and how they seem to feel about "you" (i.e. them). If you describe inner family concepts or aspects of your work to people who jeer, shame, ignore, discount, or threaten you (all)—it will scare certain young parts, activate their Guardians, and risk inner chaos and disempowering your Self.

Be selective, then, about which people you confide in, and what you disclose. As you sense another person's genuine interest, understanding, empathy, and support, trust them with more. Other people who are doing their own parts work are probably safe—unless they're in pseudo recovery and their Self is not solidly in charge. Doing parts work with one or several others can be a rich and intimate experience. Trust your own "intuition" on whom to trust, with what, when—and "take it easy!"

As always, there are many alternatives—remember the 88 piano keys (p. 129)? One is to tell close others "a little" about your parts and inner team. That can sound like *Well, I'm just meditating and learning about myself in an interesting way these days. I'll let you know if anything intriguing comes up.*

By the way—you don't *have* to tell anyone about your work. However, getting trusted others' caring reactions, validations, and encouragements can often really deepen your insights, and speed your inner-family healing. I agree with John Bradshaw's opinion that "We all need *mirroring* (feedback)"—specially during new ventures. What's your opinion?

Whom to ask for help

For those of us from low-nurturance childhoods, our Guardians and Inner Kids' combined fear, distrust, and shame can hinder or block our natural growth towards wholistic health. We try diets, and the weight returns. We take assertion courses, and the shyness and anxiety remain. We go to counseling, and key relationships still don't "work" well. We make a budget, and then disregard it. These are examples of fruitless "first-order" changes—which change surface behaviors, but leave our inner-family structure and belief system untouched.

Picking a Parts-work Therapist

Because of this, it can help to have an experienced parts-work counselor to keep you focused and motivated in doing (some of) your inner-family work. Borrowing their Self's clarity, nurturing motivation, and clear leadership for a while can overcome your other parts' fear until they free your Self to "drive your own bus." Because parts work is not yet widely accepted or taught among clinicians or clergy, finding a qualified professional to help may be hard.

If you *do* find someone with inner-family experience, look for these things in deciding whether to ask their help:

_ Can the person clearly and credibly describe inner-family theory—i.e. some version of the ideas in this book—in some detail?

_ Has s/he done her or his own kind of parts work, and is s/he willing to describe some of it?

_ Do you and s/he both feel her or his true unblended Self is solidly in charge of them?—i.e. does s/he seem to manifest the characteristic traits of a Self being in the lead? (p. 67)

_ Can s/he coherently describe _ the main steps to follow, and _ the ultimate typical goals, in doing inner family work?

_ How does s/he propose to handle your subselves who may be in current or chronic conflict?

_ Does s/he include some form of rescuing parts stuck in the past) in his or her inner-family techniques? If not, is s/he willing to learn as you do? Depending on many factors, Rescuing is an important or essential recovery skill.

_ Does s/he believe we each have a naturally-effective executive Self, or does s/he feel inner families are leaderless, and run by group consensus?

_ Is s/he willing to flex (within "reason") and work with *your* inner family beliefs (above), or does s/he require you to adopt her or his attitudes and beliefs?

Notice the theme of these questions, and develop your own. If you have a shamed inner child and an anxious *"People-Pleaser"* Guardian who quails at assertively questioning an authority—reassure them that you (all) have the perfect right, as a human and a consumer, to evaluate whom you ask for help. You'd probably do that with a car mechanic, a dentist, tax consultant, baby sitter, realtor, or a plumber. Hiring a parts-work helper is no different. See the sample "Bill of Personal Rights," on p. 350.

If you can't find a qualified and experienced inner-family professional, the next best thing is to find a trustworthy and experienced therapist who accepts inner-family concepts, and is motivated to learn about them with you. Many people eventually find their true Self without having done this kind of inner-family work. If you can find such a grounded, centered, trustworthy therapist, see if they'd companion you as a supporter, guide, and inner-family co-learner. Recall that one of the six false-self wounds is excessive dis/trust . . .

Recap

We've just reviewed a set of preparation steps you can take before meeting and harmonizing your team of subselves. Each of these small projects is part of your early recovery work. If young or Guardian subselves really need you to skip some or all of these foundation steps, know that you can pause anywhere along the way and do them then. I propose that the earlier you do them, the more fulfilling and effective your recovery work will be.

As you do each of these "prep steps," note with interest any inner voices, images, and impulses (like defocusing) that tend to hamper or block the step. Try out the idea that each of these reactions is one or more protective Guardian subselves—part of your false self—who is distrustful, uncertain, and scared about what you're doing, rather than "bad." Be alert for patterns of inner "resistance"—they're fertile areas for significant inner-family work and growth.

Now—do you feel ready to meet your inner clan?

7) BASIC PARTS-WORK TECHNIQUES

"One must have chaos in one's self in order to give birth to a dancing star."

—Fredrick Nietsche

Your DNA (genes) and personal history guarantee that the way you do inner-family recovery work will be unlike anyone else's way. The following techniques are a buffet of options, rather than a rigid fixed course. Scan this whole book to get a feel for its scope. Then reread in whatever level of detail that initially feels "right." The basic techniques here are:

- Getting ready for a parts session
- Communicating with your parts
- First meetings: what to ask
- Build an inner-family roster
- Unblending
- Freeing your Self
- Owning (accepting) your subselves
- Re-doing old traumas
- Rescuing parts stuck in the past (Exiles)
- Resolving inner-family conflicts
- Reassigning certain parts (usually Guardians)
- Reclaiming disowned parts
- Using inner council meetings
- Building inner-family trust and teamwork
- Guidelines for healing the six false-self wounds
- Measuring your progress

Option: use this chapter to start evolving your own parts-work "manual." That could be a loose-leaf binder with tabbed dividers, or PC files, for each of these techniques. As you explore the recovery path, you surely will develop your own insights, variations, and observations on each one of these topics, or invent new ones. Encourage yourself to get and keep the curiosity of a student (learner) as you go . . .

Getting Ready For A Parts Session

You can optimize the outcome of your parts work with some simple preparations for each inner-family session. The more you do the work, the more routine these steps will become. First . . .

Reserve Enough Undistracted Time

Like meditating or praying, if you try to jam parts explorations in between other pressing life activities, you risk inner distractions spoiling your concentration and efforts. With experience, you'll evolve a sense of how much time to allocate comfortably to meet with your inner staff. For starters, try at least 15 minutes. Expect some parts to resist, and reassure them that there's time enough to attend "the other important things." Next, . . .

Gather Helpful Materials

Options: your journal and a pen/cil; and possibly: art markers or crayons; a newsprint pad; clay; magazines for pictures; photographs of key people or places; soothing background tapes or CDs (e.g. harp music, waves, "Nature sounds"); candles or incense; an alarm clock; sacred items (e.g. a Holy Book, crucifix, icon, crystal, or amulet); toys or stuffed animals; a footstool, Kleenex; a blanket and pillow; slippers; a special garment; water or fruit; a book of meditations or affirmations; and this book. Do *not* bring your cordless phone, checkbook, Walkman, or pet parrot!

Any resources that add to your parts' comfort, and enhance ways they can safely express themselves, are worthy. As your inner-family style develops, you'll evolve your own took kit. At some point, it may be helpful to add tools to allow safely expressing parts' repressed anger—like a tennis racket and target pillow, a rolled-up newspaper or magazine, or a padded "encounter bat."

Pick An Appropriate Site

"Appropriate" means a place that . . .

- Is free enough from distracting noise, smells, movement, and interruptions;

- Is comfortable in temperature, light, decor, space, and furnishings; and a place that . . .

- Feels "right." Parts work can be intensely personal, and increasingly spiritual. Doing it in a place that feels like your safe space—a den, study, alcove, or sanctuary—is a great help. A setting close to or in Nature is often optimal. The alternative is to try parts work in a site that has uncomfortable memories, associations, or feelings for some of your inner members.

- *Appropriate* also means a place where your parts can yell, storm, or cry freely, without unduly disturbing or arousing other people.

Ideally, furnishings will include a comfortable chair or sitting place, and a couch, bed, or futon where you can lie down comfortably if (someone) needs to.

Try to do your work in the same place. Accumulating positive inner-family experiences there will strengthen hesitant parts' expectations of safety, comfort, and good outcomes. A strategic exception is when your current work may benefit from visiting places associated with earlier life-trauma. These can include, early homes, schools, neighborhoods, churches, cemeteries, and other emotionally evocative sites.

Review Your Attitudes and Goals

When you've allocated enough time, arranged for no interruptions, and are settled in your "inner family space," then . . .

- Read or review your initial beliefs and affirmations about parts work from your journal—perhaps out loud.

- Close your eyes to shut out visual distractions, if that suits you, and mentally get clearer on what you want to do this session. Optionally, invite your inner *Health Director* or Higher Power to guide the session, trusting that parts who need attention will appear, and help form your work.

• Without judgment, notice any distracting thoughts, feelings, or sensations that some parts may be giving you. Calmly accept any doubts, fears, "blanknesses," or confusions, as their legitimate protections—and use them as opportunities to guide your work.

As you gain experience, you'll develop your ability to do effective parts work in an increasing range of situations and places. Building your own "inner-family space" is a helpful way of getting started.

Communicating With Your Parts

Our subselves each have unique feelings, wants, and opinions. When they feel safe—or excited—enough, they express these as thoughts, day and night dreams, hunches, intuition, visions, senses, moods, memories, urges, impulses, knowings, and (some) physical sensations. As you explore your inner community, you'll discover that at any given moment there's usually a *lot* going on!

The next discovery is that—when your parts feel safe enough, they'll respond to communications from your Self, each other, and "outside" people. Our subselves talk, listen, argue, interrupt, whine, whimper, moan, bellow, demand, and question, all the time!

Before going on, check these ideas out. Pause, be still, and notice your individual emotions and thoughts now. Imagine each feeling and thought is brought to your Self by another part of your personality. Ask (think), "Who are you?" or any other question that occurs. Notice any reaction—like another thought, a shift in feelings, or a body sensation. If it feels "right," let an inner dialog develop. If emotions occur as you do so, those are subselves reacting. What's going on in there—who needs what?

If "nothing is going on," recall that some parts have the protective ability to "drop a curtain," "numb out," or "blank" your inner perceptions. If that's your experience now, respectfully ask the part responsible to show you why s/he needs to do that. S/He may or may not feel safe enough to answer in some way.

If it still seems really far-fetched that you can talk to your own parts (without being crazy!), experiment further. If you believe enough that your Self and your parts really can communicate, then continue getting to know them.

How Do I Communicate?

There's a wide range of ways to learn about each of your parts. You can . . .

- Have inner-thought dialogs, and . . .

- Written monologs or dialogs; and . . .

- Use pictures or other media, and . . .

- Use your body. You can also . . .

- Ask one part to pass communications back and forth between you (your Self) and another subself that's known but isn't ready to interact. As in outer groups, some parts will tell you things about other parts—which may or may not be accurate (!)

With a trained inner-family guide or helper, you can . . .

- Choose "indirect access" to one or more subselves, with your Self as intermediary and translator, and/or elect . . .

- Direct access, where the helper talks directly with a part, while your Self observes.

- You and a helper can also work co-operatively together to interview, instruct, (retrain) or negotiate with parts.

Each subself may have a preferred way of communicating. Some will do so via thoughts and/or inner images or memories, some will use your vocal cords, and some would rather write prose or poetry, or sketch in your journal. Some very young Inner Kids are pre-verbal, or even pre-birth. They can communicate basically via body sensations (muscle spasms, aches, tingling, numbness, hot flashes, chills, goose bumps, heart racings, shallow breathing, dizziness, . . .), emotions, or mental images, not coherent thoughts.

As your parts-work experience grows, you'll develop a facility with each of these communication "channels." Let's take a look at the main modes:

Using Your Inner Voices

What is a "thought"? We all have them, yet it's hard to describe exactly what they are. For most of us, they're (usually) coherent streams of internal words and phrases—sometimes linked to images or emotions, other times not. The inner-family concept suggests that our thoughts are the voices of our subselves. Before adopting the inner family concept, most of us would say, "I'm thinking." That changes here to "part of me is talking, or expressing."

Say to your self (think) now: *"A part of me is forming these words."* Notice that you can will (or more accurately, allow) inner talk to happen. Actually, you can will inner sound: try laughing (or bellowing) inside, or silently "hum" part of a favorite melody. Interesting, huh? You may have an internal barbershop quartet or whole chorus waiting to perform!

Inner-family work uses this universal ability to communicate "inside" to interact with most parts. To meet a part, then, you (your Self) focuses on them, and form an inner question or comment—like "Are you the one who's waking me up at night?" Then be *quiet*, and notice any response: a thought, feeling, body sensation, or several of these. "No response" *is* a response. If a thought forms, that's some part "replying" to you. By alternating willed comments or questions from your Self with sensed responses, you can have dialogs with one or several parts.

Such conversations can be internal, or you can speak out loud. I've shared profound moments with clients who encouraged a part to use their lungs and vocal chords to make sounds for the first time in their life.

Instead of "I'm talking to my self," which may feel silly or weird, try saying "I'm giving one of my parts a voice." The experience of talking in parts work, either alone or with a helper, can feel much different!

Pause and notice your thoughts and feelings now. Is anyone commenting on the ideas we just covered? Who?

Changing Chairs or Locations

Psychologists Hal and Sidra Stone have developed an inner family process they call "voice dialog." In *"Embracing Our Selves"*, they write about many clients who would change their seats during a parts session to access different inner "voices." I've experienced the same thing. A woman

I'll call Joan would blend regularly during our sessions. An angry adolescent part would talk on the left end of the couch; a sad one spoke with a very young voice from a separate chair, and Joan's Self would speak confidently from the right side of the couch. This evolved spontaneously. It wasn't true when we began, nor did I coach it.

Imaging and Sensing

Some people are more visual, and others are more sound, touch, or movement oriented. They easily see or sense inner images of real things ("picture" your kitchen), and non-real things like dream-scenes and imagined sights. For instance, image a mouse and an elephant having tea. If you can't, you're still OK! Visual people can develop the ability to see or sense symbolic images of their parts, and often the parts' actions and surroundings. Such images are rich sources of information about your inner team and it's members.

If you are visual, two options for your Self are: _ intentionally pick an image that seems to fit a subself, or _ invite the subself to show you it's own preferred visual symbol. I recommend the latter, because asking a part how it wants to represent itself is more respectful than "forcing" an image on it.

My experience is that depending on how safe they feel, some parts will pick an initial image (or none), and then adopt a more authentic one later in the work. Others don't need to do that. Some parts can use several different images at different times, depending on inner and outer circumstances.

The majority of parts' images I've met are of full or partial human adults and children—including infants and even embryos. Other typical images have been "a pile of black dirt," "a ferret," "a huge gray boulder," a "soft white light," "a fairy like Tinker Bell," "a high wall," "a bronze door," and other non-human forms. There is no right way to image a part, other than what they and you feel is fitting.

Note also that the image of a subself is a symbol—it's not the part itself. As with many inner-family explorers, one client discovered that her Guilt-tripping part used the image of her younger real-life mother: frowning, angry, and critical. Stay clear that such a part is not "my mother." It is a unique personal energy who uses the image of "my mother" to represent herself, like a costume. This distinction is important to avoid projecting feelings you have about the real person onto an inner part of yourself.

If you're visual, use steps like these to develop your ability to "see" or "sense" the images your parts want to use:

• Get quiet, relaxed, and physically comfortable, in a non-distracting place. Breathe comfortably from your abdomen, vs. your chest. Learning to breathe well is a great help. Many survivors of low childhood nurturance have an unconscious habit of breathing shallowly or not at all, in crises. That inhibits *feeling*—a vital source of inner-family communication! People who use tobacco also muffle their emotions by reducing the amount of oxygen in their blood.

• "Clear your inner space" in your own way. Perhaps imagine erasing a blackboard, clearing a tabletop, being by a calm pond, raking sand into smooth patterns, or focusing on a pleasant pastel color. Quiet your thoughts. Think or say softly "*I am still now*," or the like, several times.

• Focus your thoughts on the part you want to "see." With peaceful interest and expectancy, invite (vs. demand) a related image to form. *Trust the first thing that happens*, including "no image."

• Be alert to other parts having a significant reaction to the image. If some judgmental or analytic part wants you to edit or reject the image that comes (inner voice: "That doesn't fit—that's crazy!"), acknowledge and bypass their opinion. If some parts are upset, scared, or even disgusted by the image, acknowledge and reassure them—and *stay focused*. Use such reactions to learn more about those parts, after you're done with the current project.

• Focus on the image and it's surroundings. Neutrally notice as much as you can, like an objective reporter. For instance: "My sad part looks like a barefoot seven-year-old girl in a brown dress. She has stringy blond hair, and is sitting hunched in a corner with her arms around her knees. I can't see her face yet. The corner is sort of dark gray, and bare. The floor seems to be wood. I can't see anything else now."

• Notice your feelings and attitude about the part. If other than a compassionate interest, know that another part has probably blended with you. Work with that part, if it feels right at the time. See "Unblending" (p. 193).

- When the experience ends, journal (soon) about what you experienced, thought, and any emotional or physical reactions you noticed along the way. As always, there is no right or wrong—just *awareness*.

Memories

In inner-family work, memories are another channel with which some of our subselves communicate fluently with us. A related parts symptom is amnesia, which may be seen as a *Vault Keeper* Guardian or Inner Child's habitual protective action to keep us from imagined harm or pain. Some people doing patient meditation and parts work can safely regain some repressed memories. That is, a subself can gain enough trust in current inner and outer safety to "release" the old images. Typically the repressed material is about events that were experienced at the time as exceptionally painful, threatening, or overwhelming. See also "Body Memories" and "Flashbacks" below.

Writing and Drawing

Some members of your inner family are most comfortable and fluent communicating non-verbally. Here are some options:

Monologing

Using your inner-family journal, focus on a given part and invite it to express itself by writing it's current thoughts, feelings, goals, fears, and frustrations. A key here is to accept and write (or draw) anything that comes up. As you do, other parts may want to critique, comment, or block the Writer. Reassure them (your Self) that there's enough time for each part to be attended to, and stay focused: honor the part that's currently communicating. As you do, your other parts will gain trust over time that you'll honor them, too (if you do!). That's part of effective teambuilding.

As your inner-family recovery experience grows, you may notice that different parts have unique handwriting, vocabularies, and styles. This helps in times where you're not clear on who's communicating.

Right or Left Hand

Experiment with writing or drawing with each hand. Many parts explorers discover some inner members have a clear preference or aptitude for one hand or the other. Using your non-dominant hand may empower some subselves to communicate for the first time. If you have protective parts that scoff at this, acknowledge them with good humor—and try switching hands anyway.

Using Different Media

Try writing or drawing with a variety of media. Some parts may feel freer to express themselves with a pen, a marker, crayons, a pencil, or paints. Some may like prose, others poetry, while still others want to draw, sculpt, make a mural, a collage, or just *scribble*.

Dialoging

Sometimes it's illuminating to let a conversation between two or more parts develop on paper. One way to do this is to divide a blank page into two equal columns separated by a vertical line. Invite your Self (or another part) to write on the left side, and record another part's responses on the right side. An alternative is to let a dialog unfold on the page the way the lines in a play or transcription are written:

S(elf): *"Are you the part who's giving me the angry feelings?"*
P(art): *"What if I am?"*
S: *"I'd like to know more about why you're angry. Will you tell me some?"*
P: *"Maybe. I don't know . . . "*

Using Physical Feelings and Sensations (Body Signals)

Some subselves use body sensations and "conditions" to express themselves. From this view, headaches, stomach aches, facial tics, muscle tightness and cramps, diarrhea or constipation, tingling, goose bumps, "skin prickling," rashes, jaw clenching, local skin warmth, flushing, or coldness, numbness, heart pounding, nausea, faintness, and the like take on a new meaning. Experiment with this idea, and form your own conclusions.

Noting physical reactions can be specially helpful when you're just establishing contact and developing trust with new parts. If they're not ready to use thoughts or images, they may give you a body signal. For instance, if you get quiet, and ask within: "Will the part of me who causes me to procrastinate show itself now?," stay alert for any noticeable reaction like a sudden tightness in your stomach or throat muscles, a tremor in one foot, a "fluttering" of your heart, eyes watering, a "catch" in your breath or throat, a "sinking feeling," or similar.

If you do notice a physical reaction, work with it: e.g. "Are you causing the tingling in my right hand?" If "Yes," ask "What do you need from me now?" or "What do you want me to know (or do)?" Then *listen*, and trust what you "hear." If you get "No, I'm not," try "Can you show or tell me who is making my hand tingle (or causing a flashback, headache, or any other sign) now?"

Once your parts begin to know your Self, they often like agreeing with you on a safe way to get your attention if they need something. One way of doing this is to have them give you an acceptable physical signal—like a yawn, a sigh, a muscle twinge, an itch, skin warmth or coolness, or whatever. The next time you notice the sign, get quiet, "go inside" for a moment, and focus on that subself to see what it needs. For parts that have never felt known or noticed before, this can feel as miraculous as an island castaway suddenly being given a working videophone. Frequently, dialogs like this lead to re-doings, and/or rescuing Exiles from eternally re-living past trauma

Body Memories

After working with a gifted, veteran massage therapist, I now accept without question that some (all?) people store records of past traumatic events in certain muscles and/or organs. These body memories can be triggered by external events (music, activities, sights, smells, etc.), internal events, or tactile experiences. Massage and movement therapists and chiropractors are familiar with clients feeling spontaneous waves of anger, sadness, or fear when certain body areas are touched or manipulated. Amputees report body memories of their lost limbs. Physical and sexual abuse survivors often experience uncomfortable spontaneous body memories (burning, hyperventilating, pressure, pain, gagging)—without any clear connection to related thoughts or non-physical memories.

I believe such "psychosomatic" experiences are triggered by excited parts that have blended with the Self, and are urgently signaling for attention. They use certain body parts or sensations as communication instruments or channels. As with flashbacks, these physical parts-messages can first be understood, and later reduced, with patient, caring inner-family dialogs, re-doings, and rescuing Exiles from the past.

Flashbacks

A flashback is a spontaneous multi-media reliving (vs. remembering) a traumatic real past event. It is a powerful combination of physical sensations, memories, thoughts, and emotions that can feel temporarily overwhelming. Sexual or ritual abuse survivors frequently have periods of flashbacks at unexpected times day or night. These incidents can be very disorienting, frightening, and embarrassing. They may increase for a while with parts work, before receding. I believe flashbacks are usually caused by Inner Kids and related Guardian subselves living in the past, which are very agitated about an actual or expected event that reminds them of the past trauma. When true, flashbacks invite well-planned internal re-doings and/ or Exile-subself rescues. Flashbacks and body memories are both examples of normal inner-family blending with your Self.

Dreams, Hunches, and Intuitions

These seem to be other non-thought ways parts communicate with our conscious mind (Self). Decoding the meaning of dreams has fascinated people for centuries. Try out the idea that one of your parts is your *Dream Maker*, who wants to help you in their own way.

What is s/he trying to tell you, with both day and night dreams? What if every being (vs. every person) in a dream is a part of you, perhaps using a new symbolic image? The fields of Gestalt therapy and Active Imagination explore this idea in depth. Full discussion of this aspect of parts work is beyond the scope of this book. A helpful guide to Dream work and Active Imagination is "*Inner Work*," by Robert Johnson.

Do you have hunches, intuitions, and instincts? Most of us experience mild or strong "knowings" from time to time. Are these messages from one or more of your parts? Who? One possibility is that these knowings are the still, small voice of a benign *Spiritual* part—e.g. a *Guardian Angel, Indwelling Christ, Higher Power, Wise One*, or *Higher Self*.

Another possibility is that hunches are another channel besides thoughts that our Self uses to guide us on the right path. A third possibility is that some or all of these non-thought communiqués come from pre-verbal parts.

Do you have a hunch as to whether, and how, to use your intuitions in harmonizing your inner family? Are you currently even aware of them? Becoming clearly aware of these quiet, distinct messages is one benefit of personal meditation. Typical options:

- Build your sensitivity to these inner messages;
- Experiment with following them, and noting the outcomes; and . . .
- Note your other parts' reactions to your doing these two steps, and use them as useful inner-family information.

Using Your Moods and Emotions

Becoming non-judgmentally aware of—and learning to differentiate and name—your emotional feelings and moods is a powerful inner-family tool. Some people (e.g. most females) do this easily, while others have to develop their abilities. On a scale of one to 10, how easy is it for you to name your current emotions now?

Try out the idea that each of your parts (including your Self) has it's own unique emotions at any given time. One implication is that—because you probably have well over a dozen parts—you really can have several different emotions at the same time, without being crazy in the least.

This explains the confusing experiences of "loving" and "hating" a key person, or wanting to do something and also wanting to avoid it, at the same time. Sound familiar?

Many inner-family clients have independently reported feeling better saying "*Part* of me is really angry (or depressed, sad, confused, etc.) vs. "*I* am so ANGRY!"

With practice, you can learn to name and sort out your current emotions, and connect them each with their subselves. This skill helps in both identifying parts and in unblending (freeing your Self).

Any time you're experiencing intense emotions and perhaps related body sensations, You can go inside and ask "Who's feeling so _____ now?" Once you know which subself is generating a particular feeling, your Self can explore what that s/he currently needs, and why. Often, just being noticed and respectfully heard by your Self, and perhaps a trusted outside person, enables an over-excited part to calm down. This frees your Self to lead effectively.

Are *moods* different than *emotions* for you? For some, a mood describes the experience of having the same dominant feeling/s and bodily sensations (e.g. "heaviness") for a significant period of hours or days. I see moods other than serenity as prolonged periods when one or more excited non-Self parts have blended, and are in charge.

If this is true, note the implication: by identifying and working to satisfy the key needs of the upset part/s involved, your Self can learn to intentionally shift out of unpleasant moods. If you developed this ability, how would it affect the quality of your daily life?

We've just reviewed the wide range of ways your Self can communicate with your other inner-family members. Were you aware of all these options before you read this? Let's look now at how you can begin to use these ways of communicating . . .

First Meetings: "What Should I Ask?"

Imagine you've just inherited a small business, and you want to meet the staff and management. How would you do that? What would you want to know? How long would it take? When would you be "done"? Meeting your inner family is just the same, with some "extras." Here are some things you can seek to learn about each subself

- Approximate age
- Image (if any)
- Type of part
- Gender (if any)
- Main strategies
- "Enemies"
- How they "talk"
- Preferred title, or name
- Time "zone"
- Key beliefs
- Inner allegiances
- Goals and role/s
- Key abilities
- Origin
- Who they guard (if anyone)
- Degree of awareness of your Self, and of all other subselves
- Degree of trust in your Self and other subselves
- Attitude toward your High Power

If you have 15 or more parts on your staff, "getting to know them" each is not a trivial research project. Specially because some distrustful parts will mislead your Self to see how you react, before giving you their truths;

and others won't show themselves at all for weeks or months, until they feel safe enough.

Build an Inner-family Roster

Inventorying your subselves involves identifying each of them, and learning their unique traits (above) over time. As with real people, you'll evolve answers to some of these questions intuitively and quickly, and other answers from a series of encounters over time.

A client I'll call Alice developed a physical notebook with a fact page on each of her ~15 active parts. She had an entry on each page for the variables above—including "I don't know," or "unsure so far." She found the notebook helpful in keeping clear on her crewmembers while she first met them. After several months of recovery work, she no longer needed to use her "personnel file."

Another client created a colorful collage built with symbols of many of her parts—magazine pictures, cartoons, snapshots of herself as a child, and small physical objects. Some of her younger parts loved making and having it, though they were shy about showing it to some people!

After beginning her own parts work, an artist client brought me a 1976 news clipping. It described a Buffalo, New York artist who had painted her 15 "inner selves"—long before meeting an "inner child" became OK.

As you see, there are many ways of building a description of your inner crew. Some people keep their parts' roster internal, and don't do anything physical like the examples above. Note that composing a parts roster can be fun—even playful—rather than having to be some heavy psychological task. Your own unique style will shape what form/s your inner-family album takes. The point here is: learn clearly who's on your personality "bus," who's (usually) driving it, and with what usual results? Which of your subselves would be best at compiling your roster?

Unblending, and Inner Chaos

Inner-family pioneer Dr. Richard Schwartz proposes that agitated parts can paralyze, push aside, or merge (blend) with our Self in situations they see as threatening. When any of these occur, a false self controls your true Self and your body.

My clinical and personal experience validates that blending happens regularly to most of us, including kids. When they do, we lose our Self's wisdom and balanced perspective, and feel, see, think, and believe what the dominant subselves do. This is like a skilled teacher being temporarily shoved aside or "taken over" by one or more scared, angry, bored, or insecure students, who then try to run their class successfully.

Some people rarely blend, some do "once in a while," some do several times a day or week, and *some people have been ruled by a false self their entire lives.* The latter adults can't recall or even imagine the experience of being unblended (guided by their true Self). The concept and possibility seem like science fiction, or an absurd fairy tale. So "unblending" can refer to single instances of freeing your Self from a parts "take-over," or it can mean discovering the clarity and serenity of an unhindered Self for the first time ever. Needless to say, parts work is probably more challenging—and rewarding—for the latter folk.

How often do *you lose your Self's wise guidance?* How does that affect the quality of your daily life?

Initial Awareness

The inner-family skill of unblending begins with growing your conscious awareness that your Self (capital "S") is not in steady control of things now. How can you tell when this happens? Your current feelings and actions are keys. Again: when your unblended Self is in charge, you feel *calm, centered, energized and alert, clear and focused, grounded, "up," light, decisive, patient, compassionate, aware, assertive, and confident*—"alive."

Any time you feel significantly different than that in the present moment, you're probably in the protective custody of your false self (blended). This is, of course, a subjective judgment.

Some common symptoms of false-self dominance:

- (Some) sleep, eating, social, digestive, and sexual disorders;
- Excessively self-harmful, self-critical, or self-neglectful thoughts and acts (e.g. addictions, avoiding medications or medical care, and inner verbal abuse);
- "Excessive" moods—e.g. depressions or elations;
- "No" thoughts ("Uh, I don't know what I think about that");
- "No" emotions (numbness); *or* unusually intense current emotions—e.g. "unreasonable" rage, anxiety, terror, confusion, apathy, lust. Also, impulsive actions;
- Ceaseless thoughts ("mind churning" or "mind racing")—specially if disorganized or unfocused;

- "Excessive" ambivalence, and/or inner-voice "wars" or fights;
- Feeling preoccupied, distracted, compulsive, upset, hyper, or obsessive;
- Situational or "unusual" day dreaming;
- Feeling "odd"; or other people saying things like "Hey, Helen—you're not yourself, today" or "That's not like you!"

You can see the theme here. For more symptoms, see pp. 267 and 288. Once you sense or know that you're false self is in control (i.e. one or several young or Guardian subselves have blended with your Self)—what can you do? First, *stop*, and get clearer on which is happening:

Inner Chaos vs. Blending

Two different inner situations can yield the same symptoms of blending. If you have two or more overexcited parts "talking" or fighting at once, there may or may not be blending. Seek to learn "Is this just inner uproar without blending, or has one or more parts blended with my Self ('Me')?" In other words, are multiple students in the classroom rioting with the teacher still free to lead, or has the teacher (your Self) been infused (blended) with the feelings, beliefs, and immediate needs of one or more parts?

In the first case, the appropriate inner family strategy is "crowd management," like your effective-leader "hero/ine" (p. 151) would do. If you sense from the intensity of your thoughts or feelings, or just "knowing," that you're blended, then the "step aside" strategy is best.

If you're not sure what's going on, ask your subselves to tell or show you (via inner images) what's happening. Recall that hunches and intuitions are normal inner-family communications. Asking for spiritual insight or guidance is another option here, if you're not clear enough on what feels "right" at the moment. Notice any response you get, including "no response."

Freeing Your Self (Unblending)

If you're Self is disabled or overwhelmed . . .

First, accept that Inner Kids and Guardian subselves have taken control of your inner family because they urgently need something "right now" or "very soon." Your excited part or parts are probably scared, hurt, shamed, confused, or protectively angry. *Neither they nor their intense neediness are "bad"!*

If you think, "I disagree," that's probably your vigilant *Inner Critic* doing her/his job. Parts that take over or overrule your Self usually either don't know about your Self yet, or don't trust your Self and other competent Manager parts like your *Nurturer, Achiever, Adult,* and *Warrior/Amazon* to fill their urgent current needs. True recovery changes these to clear awareness and trust, over time.

Next, check your attitude: if you believe "I *can* learn to harmonize my inner family," go for it. If not, work to meet the part that brings you that protective distrust and pessimism, and empathically (and persistently) negotiate for change. Small experiential steps add up, over time . . .

Third, imagine one or several upset subselves as being like octopuses who have wrapped their tentacles tightly around your Self for security. Imagine asking each subself firmly and respectfully to release you, keep their feelings and needs, and "move aside." Doing this is easier if you have previously identified each part its name and function. Reassure them that when they do, you'll listen carefully, and work to fill their needs. If they agree to do this, thank each part, and notice how your feelings and thoughts change.

If they don't step aside or calm down, compassionately accept this as a signal of their fear and protective distrust. Watch for your *Inner Critic* badmouthing the blending part/s (symptoms: blameful thoughts or angry feelings). If s/he does, clearly acknowledge that ["You really dislike (the blending part/s) for taking over control now . . . "], and ask *Critic* firmly to stop doing that now because it distracts you. ["I (Self) can't sort this out and act until you step aside."]

If there are several blending parts, focus on one at a time, and try to learn clearly what each needs now. Listen empathically and patiently to what they each say, or give them an undistracted chance to write, draw, yell (if you can) or otherwise express themselves. When you feel you know what they feel or need, describe that to them clearly and simply ("So you feel hopeless and really scared that we'll never have any real friends, and so we'll always be alone, forever.") Note their reaction. My steady experience is that once upset narrow-focused parts feel respectfully noticed, and empathically *heard* (vs. agreed with), they'll usually step aside (unblend) from your Self.

Once you've unblended and/or calmed your overexcited subselves, the general theme to follow is . . .

- *Listen* respectfully to each separate part's needs,

- Reassure, clarify, validate, and prioritize,

- Stay focused, and . . .

- Patiently problem-solve one thing at a time, within local constraints (time, energy, etc.)

- Your *unblended* Self is naturally skilled at doing these steps effectively! Notice your immediate reaction . . .

If someone inside you is doubtful or skeptical now, patiently acknowledge that, and encourage them. Keep developing and practicing unblending and "riot control," and keep the faith. You *can* develop a style that works reliably for you (all). Doing so will increasingly build your parts' trust in your Self, over time! The more they do, the faster your recovery will progress.

Another basic parts-work technique is to . . .

Own Your Subselves—Pronouns and Names

Early in their inner-family work, it seems natural for people to talk about *"the* Self," or *"the Flirt,"* as though these personality parts existed neutrally "somewhere else." When encouraged to consciously shift their thoughts and language to *"My* Self," *"My* Guardians," and *"My* Dirt Pile (part)," most clients have reported a positive shift in the feeling of their work. It becomes more intimate, personal, and real. This is no different than talking about *"my* heart, hand, ear, and gray hair."

Until you *experience* your personality parts, it's often tough to really believe that you have a set of interdependent subselves that you (your Self) can interact with. This is very different from what we've been taught all our lives. Using *"the"* instead of *"my"* to describe your parts, or *"it"* instead of *"he"* or *"she,"* keeps them abstract concepts rather than aspects of you as real and vital as your liver or lungs. That makes your recovery an impersonal, intellectual concept, vs. an unfolding personal experience. I assume you wouldn't say "The lungs have pneumonia," referring to your own—or would you?

Habitually saying *"the* Self" and *"the* inner family" is a way your Guardian parts try to protect other fearful and shamed parts from accepting what's *real*, and related intense emotions. That's a form of well-meant reality distortion. Your recovery terminology and *language* is important, in many ways!

What's in a Name?

Another way of owning your subselves and making them more real and personal is to experiment with naming some or each one. Your inner-family work may feel and proceed differently if you think and say (for instance) "Rhonda" rather than "my sad little 6 year-old." If they're asked (and feeling safe enough), some parts will quickly announce a name and/or title they'd prefer. Others will seem, or really be, indifferent. As with images, your Self forcing a name or title ("my Inner Dunce") on a part without consulting them can feel insulting and disrespectful. How would you feel if a key friend or relative declared "I'm going to call you *Porky* from now on, because I just get a kick out of it"?

In settling on parts' names and titles, recall that a key inner-family objective is to build group identity, pride, and respect, over time. As a part's self-image improves via inner-family work, it may be appropriate sometime to have a christening party or ceremony to bequeath a more respectful and dignified name and/or title. One client (spontaneously) did just that, calling an inner "board meeting" to announce and celebrate the transition of "my little *Saboteur*" to "Cindy, our Prayer Director." This work makes "self respect" (and Self respect) a *team* effort!

Inner-family names and titles are powerful, because of un/conscious emotional associations. For instance, if the name "Lucy" reminds you of the daffy and lovable TV character played by Lucille Ball, it may feel shaming if applied to a female part of you who currently feels insecure or stupid. From time to time, check out the + /—emotional "tone" of the names and titles you're using in your inner family work. An option at any time is to ask one or all your parts what they think, feel, or want about these important symbolic labels.

Incidentally, note that true recovery causes some people to change their real names, informally or even legally—e.g. "Patricia is my real name, and sounds more dignified to me than Bubbles." This is also true when parents and children have the same first name, and kids have historically been called "little" Art, Sharon, etc. to distinguish them. If the child is shame-based, "little," or "junior," may *unconsciously* lower their self worth. I believe my (very wounded) wife suffered because her mother named her for a dead baby. She may have felt she was a kind of "substitute" girl without her own identity, rather than a beloved unique child.

Recall: this book is about assessing for major false-self dominance, and learning to empower your true Self. Parts work is a particularly effective way of doing the latter. We've just surveyed some basic parts-work, or inner-family work, techniques: ways to communicate with your parts, first meetings, preparing for a parts work session, building a membership roster, unblending, and owning and naming your subselves. Now we're ready to look at some special ways of using parts work proactively to reduce any false-self wounds affecting your life.

Ask your inner crew if anyone needs to take a break now, or attend some responsibility, before continuing. Also consider journaling, and/or discussing what you just read with a supporter. Other options are to try a first meeting, or visit with one or several subselves you've already met. Who's driving your inner-family "bus" right now? How do you know?

Awarenesses . . .

8)   SPECIAL PARTS-WORK TECHNIQUES

This chapter builds on the basic recovery techniques you just studied. It outlines powerful ways you can reorganize and harmonize your inner family, over time, under the expert leadership of your true Self:

- Using inner council meetings for important decisions

- Parts work and your spirituality

- Re-doing past traumas

- Rescuing young subselves stuck in the past

- Resolving inner-family conflicts

- Identifying and accepting disowned subselves

- Reassigning Guardians to new inner-family roles—"job retraining," and . . .

- Building inner-family teamwork and harmony.

With focus, practice, and patience you can master each of these. Together, these techniques empower you to make lasting (second order) changes to the group of subselves that determine the quality of your life.

If a false self has controlled you much or all of your life, these concepts and techniques bring the potential of setting you free from protective custody, and "driving your own bus" for the first time. Use a marker to highlight key ideas, jot margin notes, and/or journal or tape-record your reactions to these ideas as you read. If you haven't recently, review the basic attitudes you forged on p. 169, and use them as you study and experiment. Do you (all) have "the open, curious mind of a student?" Is your Self in charge now? Look forward to interesting reactions from your subselves as you read and react.

Notice your self-talk, body state, and breathing, as we tour each of these recovery skills.

Using Inner Councils

In chapter 6 (p. 133), did you mentally identify an *effective*, well-functioning, well-led class, team, or group that you've belonged to? If not, do so now. If you can't think of an effective group, think of an ineffective one. Recall how major decisions were made in the group, and how that process affected group morale and teamwork. Keep that experience and image in mind, as you read about creating an effective team *within* you . . .

How would you describe how your subselves have generally made important decisions, to date? Very cautiously, with a lot of worry and indecision? Impulsively, for "instant gratification"? Fearfully? Belligerently? Intuitively? Hesitantly? Un/emotionally? Proactively, or reactively (letting life control *you*)? Asking others' opinions (including God's), and following their suggestions, or "trusting your own counsel"? We each develop a decision-making "style," which generates typical "outcomes"—satisfying and successful, to frustrating, regretful, and unsuccessful. Significantly-wounded people aren't famous for making healthy short or long-term decisions for themselves and those who depend on them.

To improve the outcomes of major decisions (e.g. "Should you and I conceive a child now?"), you can use inner council meetings. This is best done after you have a clear idea of all the subselves that comprise "you," and the key traits and limits of each one. Here are key ideas on how to conduct an effective inner-council, chaired by your Self. An option is to have a spiritual subself advise you all, as you meet.

Site—All parts agree on comfortable, safe outer and inner places to meet. Your real site should be quiet, physically comfortable, and as undistracting as possible. Clients who have tried inner-family councils often evolve a preferred physical location to hold their inner meetings, though such gatherings can take place anywhere.

Some people go inside, and image their parts convening in a richly appointed boardroom. Others imagine a custom-designed retreat center by the water or in a forest glade, or by a sacred council rock on a mountain or shore. What kind of a setting would help your parts meet most productively? (Option: poll them!) The best choice promotes feelings of *security*, *comfort*, *quiet*, and *peace*. You can use a real (remembered) site, or create one in your "mind's eye."

Empathic Leadership—Your Self calls each meeting, and is clearly in charge of it. S/He may delegate portions of the meeting to another part, or ask small groups to do some of the overall task at hand. Your stage of parts work will determine who comes. At first, expect distrust, and some "no shows." If that happens, meet with individual subselves to learn what they need. Also, note your (Self's) option to invite timid parts to attend and "just observe and listen." Meeting alone with each of your subselves, over time, and then perhaps in small groups, is a good way to prepare for convening most or all parts at once for key discussions and decisions.

A first council meeting might be to re-introduce your Self, and then each subself. Invite each one to describe their main inner-family goals and strategies, one at a time. You may be surprised at how much your subselves don't know about each other! After introductions, an agenda item might be to evolve ground rules for "How can we have *effective* meetings?"

Clarity and Focus: Your Self decides who attends, with counsel from others. S/He helps all attending parts understand what the specific current objectives are, and keeps them on track (focused) on one thing at a time throughout the meeting. For long or conflictual meetings, s/he can summarize at the end, what was agreed, and who is to do what. Some councils can be to brainstorm or to fact-find ("does anyone know about . . . ?"). Others can focus on evolving goals and plans, shifting or clarifying your parts' responsibilities, or clarifying and evaluating complex life-decisions.

Respectful Order, and Rules: Through experiment and experience, your parts will learn that they (usually) each have contributions to make, and have a right to be respectfully heard by all. Your Self will have each subself speak without interruption, and balance who gets "air time"—e.g. firmly confront any part who hogs the meeting. S/He will invite the opinions of quiet parts, and genuinely care about all your parts' ideas, anxieties, and needs.

As with any gathering, some rules of order need to be observed for the group to get anything done. A key guideline is that only one part talks at a time, and that all others really *listen*. Other guidelines are to *respect* all different viewpoints, and *stay focused* on the issues at hand, rather than on power struggles or parts' traits and character. Each part brings the potential for valuable insights and suggestions!

Clear Communication and Decisions: help your subselves to learn and use effective communication skills: process awareness and metatalk (talking about your communicating), respectful assertion, empathic listening, and win-win problem-solving—brainstorming and compromising skills. Do you know what each of these are? Together, they can strengthen all your inner and outer relationships To learn more about them, see this Web page: **http://sfhelp.org/cx/links2.htm**; or see the related guidebook *Satisfactions* (Xlibris.com).

Your Self's learning, modeling, and coaching these skills with patience and humor will increasingly lead your councils to clear, healthy short and long-term decisions.

Inner council or staff meetings help all your parts to know and appreciate each other, and to build trust in the leadership skills of your Self. Periodic meetings nourish inner-family morale and coherence, and ensure that all parts feel noticed, informed, important and appreciated. Can you imagine a successful sports team, acting troupe, or business enterprise that didn't have Manager well-planned and led staff meetings?

Before continuing, pause and reflect on what you just read. Get quiet, go inside, and imagine most or all of your inner family coming together as a group, now. What do you notice?

Parts Work and Spirituality

Shelves of books have been written on spirituality and religion, but I've seen little writing on the spiritual aspect of inner-family work, so far. A basic premise here is that all persons—including you—have a spiritual "dimension." It develops over time and has major effect on your experience of daily life. Your wholistic health is the interactive mix of your (*spiritual* + emotional + physical + cognitive) well-beings. What do *you* think?

I believe leaders of high-nurturance families prize each member's unique spiritual needs, growth "stage," and beliefs. They try to respect and attend those needs equally with physical, emotional, and mental needs. Typical wounded people usually didn't get that balanced childhood nurturance, so their wholistic recovery usually needs to include "spiritual growth" as a conscious element. This can shape your process of inner-family harmonizing in various ways, such as . . .

- Validating the reality of one or more spiritual inner-family members, and including them in your council meetings.

- Exploring the reality of a benign Higher Power, and the fourth (spiritual) group of subselves outlined in p. 49.

- Developing an effective way of communing with inner and Higher spiritual parts or presences, to nurture and guide your recovery, over time. Learning to get quiet, listen for, and *trust* your "still, small voice" seems to be an effective way to do this. Typically, it tends to speak in very short sentences, and may manifest as a "feeling," "hunch," "sense," "urge," *and/*or an inner image. Are you aware of such a "voice" in your life now? Do you *heed* it? How do your inner-family members react to it, so far?

Because spiritual belief and experience are personal and subjective, only generalities are possible here . . .

In my experience, true recovery seems unlikely or impossible without most or all inner-family members accepting *on faith* that there is a real, benign, caring Higher Power and/or Higher Self *always* there to rely on when life gets overwhelming. The evolution of that faith, and the degree that each subself feels it, develop with experience and reflection, over time.

Some people in pseudo recovery are spiritually indifferent. Others will insist vehemently that they needn't believe or need any spiritual help or nurturance to heal. The false self of other wounded people needs to disparage others who manifest spiritual faith ("Belief in so-called '*God,*' and needing *church* is a crutch for wimps who can't make it on their own.") I suspect such disparagement signals a false self who is terrified of the true *surrender* necessary to "Turn it (your life and will) over" to your Higher Power. It demonstrates the toxic dis/trust and fear traits that we wounded people work to reduce, over time.

Early in life, some people were taught toxic religious and spiritual beliefs and practices. These promoted their forming and later maintaining a false self, until thoughtfully reviewed and revised. Some people may begin recovery while participating in a toxic religious community. *Toxic* means, "consistently promoting a mix of significant fear, shame, guilt, and reality distortion, (false-self dominance)."

Common Western examples of toxic faith are beliefs that all people are inescapably born unworthy "sinners" (shame and guilt), and need "salvation" to avoid "burning in a lake of fire for eternity" (fear). Most major religions preach that they are "the one true way," (competition) and that non-believers should be pitied, converted, shunned, persecuted, reviled, or killed.

These hardly sound like inner-family harmony in action, which is characterized by genuine compassion, empathy, mutual respect, limited tolerance, and love. Justification for these toxic spiritual and religious beliefs and related behaviors sounds like "But it's for the safety of your immortal soul, and it's God's will, not *mine!*" Avoidance, denial, and reality distortion at work.

People who choose to believe in righteous "spiritual warfare" against "Satan," and "Evil," may be unaware of carrying on a ancestral legacy of projecting their *inner* war against feared or reviled personality parts they've been taught to disown.

For such people, true recovery involves their key subselves becoming aware of (1) the toxic nature of their present beliefs and worship practices and (2) the existence of alternatives; and then (3) convincing narrow-minded Guardian parts that it's safe and healthy to experiment with new spiritual beliefs, experiences, practices, and environments, as part of the over-all recovery process, and (4) gradually evolving a new high-nurturance spiritual and perhaps religious environment which promotes true recovery.

A specially powerful option here is to evolve a comfortable inner (or outer) image of "my spiritual part(s)," or "my Higher Self." I've witnessed a number of clients spontaneously calming and reassuring terrified, lonely, or shamed inner kids by introducing them to a comforting, protective "Angel," or "My Inner Jesus." Intentionally including such spiritual parts in inner imagery and outer journaling can richly nourish the recovery experience and speed harmonizing. Dr. Ed Smith promotes a form of this he calls "Theophostic" therapy. He and his colleagues report impressive healing results with Christian believers and others. See www.theophostic.com on the Internet.

Related spiritual aspects of inner-family work are optionally including your spiritual part/s in recovery projects like re-doings, rescues, and inner councils. This will make more sense as you learn about each of these.

A basic theme in building nurturing personal spirituality is to empathically identify and confront Inner Kids and Guardian parts who have toxic spiritual beliefs. If you've ever tried to argue "religion" with someone with a different faith, you know that *logic, reasoning,* and *explanation* rarely convert others' beliefs, unless they're desperate. Your Self and Higher Power will know the best strategy for gently and respectfully inviting such parts to try out new beliefs, over time. True recovery inevitably seems to promote and *use* spiritual awareness, gratitude, and guidance.

Often "blind (toxic) faith" and righteous zealotry is founded on deeply buried (denied) personal and family shame, guilt, and fear, garnished with ignorance. These can be maintained by living in a toxic (low-nurturance) social environment that would shame and reject evidence of "blasphemy" and "leaving the faith." Patient inner-family toward identifying the parts who carry those emotional burdens, and helping relieve them, usually promotes more wholistically-healthy spiritual beliefs in even the most zealous inner "believers," over time.

Recoverers raised in the Christian tradition can find a recovery-friendly version of "liberal" faith in the Unity church movement. Among the books many Unity members recommend is *"Conversations With God,"* by Neale Walsch. Another is *"When God Becomes A Drug,"* by recovering Episcopalian priest Fr. Leo Booth. There are certainly other denominations and individual congregations that genuinely support the theme of faith-based wholistic recovery from childhood neglect and trauma.

Another powerful parts-work technique is . . .

Re-doing Old Traumas

A 40-ish client I'll call Jack had been abandoned early by his (traumatized) mother, and raised by a highly critical grandmother and uncle. He had spent most childhood years in two stern Midwestern Catholic schools in the 1960s. He and I were working toward healing his anxiety, distrusts, and pervasive shame and guilts.

Jack had grown aware of over a dozen personality parts, including a frightened, lonely pre-teen part he called "Little Jack." He also discovered a powerful adult male Guardian he named "Billy," who reminded him of an iron-strong and resourceful character in the movie "The Dream Team." These subselves had become quite real to Jack.

One session, he tearfully described a powerfully shaming fifth-grade experience. He'd been called up in front of two combined classes to recite a poem that he hadn't been able to memorize. As this became obvious, the nun in charge sarcastically ridiculed him, took him by the ear, and led him past his smirking classmates into a coatroom at the back of the room. There (as he remembered), she continued to loudly belittle him, and at one point angrily slammed his head against the wall. It was a shattering experience, in part because when he told his custodial grandmother later, she angrily said "Don't you whine to me, young man—you deserved that!" Jack couldn't recall having ever felt protected or valued as a child. This was having a major negative effect on his work, health, finances, and social relationships.

He courageously agreed to try re-living the old poetry-class trauma in a new way. I asked "Who would you like to protect Little Jack from the shaming he got?" The bearded, slender man thought "I'd like Billy, . . . my Self, and . . . you." I warmly agreed. Jack got quiet and physically comfortable, went inside, and focused on the memory of the old classroom full of students. I suggested he take all the time he needed to note the details: the sounds and smells, the colors, the temperature and time of day, the feel of the chair he was sitting in, and what he was wearing.

Eyes closed, he described these clearly and quietly. I asked Jack's Self to stand in the cloakroom with Billy and me, first looking at us, then out at the class. He did, describing us two men, and then seeing the back of Little Jack's head, and the teacher's features, voice, and actions. He named several of the students in the class, and recalled hearing a distant bell.

The scene unfolded, as it had countless times in Jack's memory—shaming him anew each time. This time, however, when the woman dragged the shaking boy into the coatroom, she met three grown men there. Jack's Self had said earlier he wanted Billy to lead, using his talent at forceful assertion. He did—sternly confronting the surprised teacher. Billy told her to let go of Little Jack, and put his arm around the boy.

Eyes closed, Jack filled my office with Billy's powerful voice. It was notably deeper and stronger than the voice he usually used. He spoke to the nun real time, telling her that she was abusing young Jack, and that he would not tolerate that—now or *ever* again. Jack described her righteous, arrogant, indignant reactions. I asked him "What would Billy say?" Billy (in Jack's words) firmly told her to go back in front of the class and apologize to them and to Little Jack for what she'd done. She fumed and resisted, and he firmly re-asserted. "How's Little Jack?" I asked. "He's stunned! He's just standing next to Billy with his mouth open."

Eyes still closed, the man on my couch described the woman going to the front of the class and apologizing haltingly. At Billy's demand, she introduced him, me, and Jack's Self to the children, and said that we'd come to "take care" of Jack. Billy told her and the class "I'm going to be around from now on. If you don't believe that, just try me out."

As this unfolded, physical Jack was crying on my couch, and shaking his head as he described this new outcome to the hateful old abusive experience. After a few minutes of quiet and collecting, he opened his eyes. I asked what he was aware of. "Little Jack feels different. I feel different! I've never felt anything like that before in my life . . . " He seemed awed. I said, "We just re-did a powerful shaming experience that you remember."

In later sessions, we re-did several other shaming and terrifying experiences that Jack recalled—including him at five years old finding his gruff, scary uncle dead in his bedroom. Some months later, he spontaneously described these re-doings as "life-changing" events for him. Prior to the re-doing, Little Jack (the subself) had lived in the past, believing he was all alone. Later, this Young subself shifted to living in the present with Jack's other parts—his first nurturing family.

This vignette shows the main steps in Re-doing. The purpose of this inner-family technique is to give a wholistically healthier outcome *experience* to key remembered traumatic events. This is not magic, and it obviously doesn't change the real past. It *can* change your present feelings about the past. Re-doing can be a powerful healing tool, in proportion to your abilities to *own* your parts (accept their realness), and to immerse yourself safely in key past events.

Key steps to successful inner family re-doings are . . .

_ **Over** "enough" time, clearly establish the identity and traits of most or all of your key inner-family members (chapter 7). Work patiently to reduce any (parts') ambivalence or doubt about all your parts' reality and impact on your daily life.

_ **Identify** the specific Young subselves that carry your terror, shame, distrust, rage, and loneliness. Over time, help them meet and accept your Self, key Guardian parts (like Billy, above), and any involved outer-family nurturers (like me, above). When it feels right, pick one or a few related Inner Kids to work with in a re-doing experience, and prepare:

_ **Pick** a remembered childhood or adult trauma that involves the Young subself/s. Focus on a single experience at a time—not your whole life!

_ **Build** a (small) re-doing team. Identify one or more trusted strong, nurturing parts. These are usually, but not always, adults. Consider including spiritual parts, and any special real or mythical hero/ines as possible members of your re-doing team. Also consider safe professional helpers, and key trusted, well-grounded, outside partners, friends or kin. See if each candidate part (1) knows the Young subself/s, and (2) is willing to participate in a re-doing experience for him, her, or them. Honor any responses.

_ **Everyone** get clear on *why* you're going to re-do the selected traumatic incident, and generally *how*. Who will do the talking or lead the action? What's the main job of each participant? In the example above, Jack's Self was the delegating leader. He and "I" were there for continuity and moral support, while Billy took the lead. Jack's Self chose that part because of Billy's gift of forceful, focused assertiveness and courage.

_ **Avoid** planning to kill, harm, or abuse any "bad" characters in the remembered event. This technique is *not* about fostering violence or revenge as a way of healing and problem solving. (You may have subselves that relish fantasizing those!) Re-doing is about you *experiencing* clear, respectful assertion of your needs and healthy limits, and effective, loving nurturance and protections.

_ **The first time** you re-do, check first to see if there are any Guardians who are catastrophizing, pessimistic, belittling, or are likely to sabotage the event. If so, work with each to gain their trust and support. Appeal to them to trust you, and just try re-doing to see what happens. As with any team, if some subself is too scared, don't force it. Work respectfully and patiently with them to find a safe-enough way for them to try re-doing as a learning experience. Shoot for an open-minded "let's see what happens" attitude among all players.

_ **Pick** a safe comfortable, distraction-free place to do the exercise. Ideally, your site should be one where—if you need to yell or cry—you can do so without worrying about scaring or disturbing other people. Allocate enough time, including time afterward to debrief and integrate your reactions. If you need some resources (journal, stuffed animal, water, background sounds, Kleenex, tape recorder), assemble them.

_ **If it feels "right,"** let your Young subself know in advance generally what you're doing, and why. Note their reactions, answer questions, and agree how to involve them. Offer any appropriate reassurances. An option is to call a council meeting to discuss this healing plan.

_ **If you're using** an outside helper, get clear together on their role/s. Do you want them to actively coach? Silently support? Be careful about physical closeness and contact—even reassuring touching can distract from your inner re-experience.

_ **Breathe** comfortably. Get centered, close your eyes (if you wish), focus on the remembered image of the traumatic event, and invite your chosen helper/s to "be there." Play out the event, and generate a "better" outcome together. Take your time. Allow anything to happen that "wants to." If your Analyzer part wants to evaluate the process, ask them to wait until you're finished. Trust your Self's ability to do "the right thing"!

_ **When** everyone involved feels "done enough," return your focus and energy to your real site. Debrief your inner family and any outer helper/s. Note in particular how your Young subself seems to be. Recap what you did, why, and what you experienced. Ask within non-judgmentally: "what am I aware of now?" and (later) "what did I (we) learn here?" Check with any inner skeptics to learn their reactions.

_ **Thank** and appreciate any part/s and helpers involved in each re-doing project, as seems fitting at the time. Let yourself be open to the possibility that some healing reactions may evolve later. Stretch, breathe well, be fully "back in" your body again, and "move on . . . "! Consider journaling soon after each re-doing experience. Invite all your parts to comment . . .

Other than these guidelines, there is no "right way" to re-do. There are only new experiences, awarenesses, and learnings. If "nothing" seemed to happen, or if you were distracted by "mind-racing," "blankness," or "felt nothing," see these as useful reactions in themselves that you can do productive parts work with. Seek respectfully what part/s caused such reactions, and work patiently to meet them, and gain their trust and cooperation.

If this re-doing concept is new to you, notice non-judgmentally where your thoughts and feelings are. Where's your Self? Who's "driving your bus" right now?

Rescuing Parts Stuck in the Past

One of the most powerful aspects of inner-family work is finding an Exile subself that is trapped in a past traumatic time, and—when all parts are ready—bringing them to live the *safe* present.

As a practical ex-engineer who had little inner-family experience, I was pretty skeptical when I first heard about internal "rescues." After practicing parts work since 1990, I now firmly believe that most previously traumatized people *do* have one or more parts who live each day and night "back then." Such trapped parts are typically young Inner Kids and sometimes their devoted Guardian parts. Because these subselves lack clear perspective on what *was* vs. what *is now*, their inner reactions to current life cause minor to major inner-family conflict and disharmony.

The good news: with patience, compassion, and sensitivity, such trapped parts of yourself can migrate to permanently join their inner kin in the safe present.

Before reading how, notice your reactions to the idea of rescuing some "stuck" parts. Do you "hear" skeptical, cynical, or anxious inner voices (thought steams)? If so, acknowledge them affectionately. The speaker/s are probably steadfast Guardians doing their self-appointed job of shielding you from unsafe risk. Muse a little: if you do have one or several parts who live in the past, who would they be? If it seems risky to discover them—what's the threat? How might your life feel different if they joined you all in the present? Intuition counts, here.

Timing

My experience is that it's unwise to try rescuing too soon, in the flow of your inner family work. Give yourself plenty of time to . . .

*   Get familiar with your parts' roster,

*   Learn how to communicate well with your inner members (p. 180)—specially with key Guardians and Inner Kids, and your spiritual part/s; and . . .

*   Evolve your own comfortable style of doing this recovery work. Effective subself rescues hinge on patiently establishing inner trusts, safeties, and realistic expectations via experience.

Generally, any time a person has clearly self-disturbing, self-harmful, or self-limiting behavior patterns, they probably have one or more parts trapped in the past. Inner-family pioneer Dr. Richard Schwartz calls these parts *Exiles*.

If you suffered profound childhood trauma and emotional-nurturance deficits, it may take months of inner family work before you (all) feel ready enough to begin rescuing your Exile/s. If you're uncertain, listen for the clear guidance of your "still, small voice." Trust and follow it, even if it "makes no sense."

Recognizing Stuck Parts

The biggest clues that one or more of your inner-family member are caught in a time trap are repeatedly distorted reactions to inner and outer current events. These behavior patterns are often dubbed *obsessions*, *compulsions*, *impulses*, *addictions*, and *denials*. Some recurring physical conditions may also be symptoms. Examples:

• Despite her partner's verbal and behavioral assurances, a woman can't ease her fears that he really doesn't love her, and will eventually choose someone else. Her insecurity, distrust, and jealousy increasingly strain their relationship;

• A clearly successful salesman can't acknowledge or enjoy his achievements, and feels relentlessly driven to "do better!";

• A mother is constantly overanxious about her competent grown daughter's welfare, and remains over-enmeshed with her despite her daughter's exasperated protests and growing resentment;

• A young father swears he'll never abuse his children the way his own father did—yet despairingly acknowledges "I'm acting just like Dad!"

• An attractive single woman cycles through repeated approach-avoid relationships. "Something goes wrong," before or after engagement, and she always breaks up—despite longing for marriage and her own home and family.

• An experienced and well-trained marketing executive develops an embarrassing stutter when she makes follow-up calls to some (not all) new male clients. Her efforts to control the stutter fail;

• A single woman in her 30's reports a recurring strong feeling of dread around mid-afternoon, and a powerful compulsion to "get home"—though there's no practical reason to do so;

• A grandfather describes a recurring life-long nightmare dream of being attacked in a forest by unseen wild "things," and being unable to run or hide.

See anything familiar here? If so—what can you do? Here's an overview:

Steps to Rescuing

- Choose an attitude of patient, positive expectancy about rescuing any stuck parts—even if you don't see how yet.

- Identify a stressful behavior trait, and seek to identify one or more related Exile subselves.

- Identify and befriend any parts guarding the Exiles.

- Choose or build (vividly imagine) a *safe* inner haven in the present.

- Consider one or more Re-doings with the Exile/s (optional).

- Brief all your parts, and patiently help the Exile/s relocate to your safe inner haven. Over time, integrate them with your other inner-family members and evolve their role/s.

Here's more detail on each step . . .

Pick a Behavior Pattern, and Seek an Exile

Look for a self-limiting or self-harmful behavior pattern like the examples above. Write or say as specifically and objectively as you can what the pattern is—ideally in a phrase or one sentence: e.g. "I've always been afraid to show my anger to my Father," or "I have recurring sleep problems."

Get quiet and undistracted, go inside, and (your Self) ask the part or parts that "cause" or "know about" the behavior to identify themselves. Your inner invitation might sound like "Will the part who interrupts my sleep please show itself now, in some way?" If more than one part appears, separate them, and work with one at a time.

Until you've experienced the results several times, this vital question may sound absurd: ask a part you feel may be stuck "What year is it?" Trust the very first thought or "sense" you get to this, before various parts try to judge, discount, or deflect. I've seen dozens of clients react with amazement when their part says "1965," or some date many years in the past. Other options of confirming a part's being exiled are to ask "What house do you live in now?"; "Who is living with you now?"; "What do you see outside your windows?"; "Where do you sleep?"; "How much do you weigh now?"; and so on.

Note that some very young Inner Kids may not know how to answer questions like these, or may be too bewildered and confused, at first. If this happens, Your Self and your Nurturer will know how to react. *Listen*, and trust your "intuition"!

Identify and Befriend Guardians

Often, before you can meet an Exile (usually a young subself), one or more of their distrustful Guardian subselves will intervene. Until s/he knows and trusts your Self and any outside helpers involved, and clearly understands what you're trying to do—and why—s/he's likely to repeatedly interfere with your rescue attempts.

Typical Guardians often fear that if the Young subself/s they protect "leave," or are effectively cared for by another part, they'll lose their inner-family jobs. If you've ever been in a work situation where you felt your position was about to become obsolete, you can empathize!

Recall that providing effective protection is a Guardian's sole purpose in life. If a subself stubbornly hinders your rescue plan, be compassionate, vs. angry, impatient, or critical—for they may see the sure outcome as their own "death" or demotion. Genuine *respect* and *compassion* for each of your subselves is the key, just as you'd wish physical people to treat you (all). The Golden Rule applies *internally* too!

As you first seek to identify and meet a suspected Exile, be alert for a Guardian who "blanks" you (experience: "My Exile won't respond"), or who brings you feelings other than compassionate interest about the Exile, like anxiety, or an inner voice saying "that part causing my overeating is really stupid! I wish s/he were dead!"

If you encounter a "blanking" or "numbing" Guardian, respectfully invite it to identify itself. Through inner dialog, imaging, or other means, empathically learn what this part fears. These fears are likely to be catastrophic, vague, and emotional, vs. logical, like "all hell will break loose!"; or "you'll get sick and go crazy!"

Honor, vs. discount, such fears. Avoid "reasoning" with the fearful part, and work over time to replace their fear with tentative trusts and new hope. If appropriate, reassure each obsessive (i.e. frightened) Guardian that their energy and gifts are unique and valuable, and that there will always be a valuable role for them to play in your inner community. If appropriate, invite them to help plan and perform (not lead) the rescue. Assess whether they may be stuck in the past, too. If so, switch to rescuing them first.

If a Guardian projects negative judgments about a suspected or known Exile, affirm the Guardian's feelings ("You really feel Baby Annie is worthless and dumb")—*then respectfully and firmly ask them to step aside.* If they balk, listen to and affirm them again, then reassert. Often their fierce judgments mask powerful unidentified fears. Invite your scared subself to talk about their fears, and *listen* (vs. argue, reason, discount, threaten, explain, etc.). Stay clear: *listening is not* agreeing. If their judgmental feelings persist, refocus on this Guardian, and defer the rescue exploration until they're more stable and trusting. Trying to rescue too soon can build toxic distrust among your parts that this technique is ineffective or dangerous.

Build a Safe Haven in the Present

Before rescuing any Exiles, evolve an inner "place" that feels safe to all known parts. Imagine this place as clearly as you can. Describe it out loud, or on paper. It may be an actual place you know of, or you may enjoy creating it. Let your imagination soar! One client experienced a strong feeling of peace and safety on an imaginary tropical beach by a soothing lagoon. Another vividly pictured a snug mountain cabin in a forest clearing. Another found that her parts felt best gathered together around a beautiful crystal rock, in a cave. Later this became a "pure," warming fire. Some people find that their parts naturally want to live in their current physical home—or in a comfortable imaginary addition to it.

Furnish your Special Place with anything you want: a fountain, music, a fireplace, comfortable places to rest, games, food, sacred items, a garden, beautiful views, a moat, walls, . . . Option: look through magazines or Websites for ideas and inspiration. If you have an inner *Artist*, sketch, model, or paint your haven. When it feels right, invite (vs. demand) your known parts to congregate there. Patiently let your Haven evolve, with their input.

As with other aspects of parts work, there is no absolute right or wrong in designing or picking a safe haven. As you vision yours, notice with affection if some inner voices insist "This is really stupid!" and "What if other people knew you were daydreaming about this junk?" If you feel ambivalent about trying this recovery step, affirm that this is *your* life, not someone else's. Imagine how some scared, lonely, sad young subselves might feel, experiencing a safe place and a resident family that is truly welcoming and caring—perhaps for the first time in their lives.

Does anyone feel you have something to risk or lose by trying this?

Consider a Re-doing

Each Exile rescue is unique. Your success depends on all subselves involved feeling *respected* and *safe* enough throughout the process. Keep in mind that against all logic, parts trapped in the past don't know about your current world. They probably won't believe you, if you just describe it. If they're endlessly recycling one or a series of traumas, you may have to re-do (p. 204) one or more old scenarios first, to gradually free them to migrate to the present.

A client I'll call Sylvia became aware of a part about five years old who was trapped on a vacation lake beach. She (the Exile) endlessly relived the terror of watching helplessly as her drunken father tried to drown her mother. This incident had actually occurred to Sylvia as a girl, 26 years before. To begin to rescue her little Inner Child, Sylvia planned a re-doing, and "went inside."

She (her Self) took her strong *Adult Woman* part, her present (large!) male partner, an Angel part, and me, back to the beach. We re-did the incident, stopping the father's assault, bringing the mother and father safely to the beach, and calming the five year old. Later, Sylvia brought her Exile ("Nina") to her present-day home to meet and join her unknown companion parts. The little one was dumbfounded and shy, at first, and then (temporarily) overwhelmed with relief and wonder.

Pause, and notice what your self talk is now—including memories and images . . .

Brief All subselves, and rescue the exile

At each rescue step along the way, keep all your known parts informed as to what you're doing. Respect any suggestions or anxieties they have. If your circumstances warrant, call one or more inner councils to plan or discuss a rescue. Recall: your Self or a trusted delegate is in charge of such meetings, and every rescue. Your Higher Power will guide and support you all as you plan.

Imagine what it would feel like if you were small, alone, scared, and hopeless (remember?). A kindly adult appears "out of nowhere" and says "Come with me now. I'll take you to a wonderful place where you'll always feel safe and comfortable." Would you do it? Often it can reassure distrusting Exiles if you gently invite them to visit the present with you first—taking anything the want with them they need to link them with "home." After they've explored your safe haven, and perhaps met some or all of your other parts, Exile's anxieties will usually subside. By the way—do "fairy tales" take on a new meaning here?

Young subselves may not understand the concepts of "time," or "years." Before a rescue, it may help them realize what's happening if you show them a calendar, and explain that each Earth trip around the sun is a "year." Be patient as they grapple with the concept of coming to live in a different time. One client found it helpful before a rescue to show his Exile the cemetery where his mother was presently buried. He then visited her physical grave. His trapped young part had been convinced that his mother was still alive, and couldn't be abandoned. Frequently, trapped parts feel a strong sense of duty to younger siblings or infirm relatives who "live with them." They need to build trust that those dependent beings will be OK if the Exile "leaves."

Before migrating, ask your Exile whether they want to say goodbye to anyone or anything in their present place. Help them do that safely, without rushing. See if they want to bring anything special with them. Reassure them that they can come back to visit any time they want. Demonstrate that, if it helps to build faith. With each of these steps, *take your time*. Be alert for your *Impatient One* and your *Achiever* protectively trying to push the process too fast.

Some rescues are planned (or spontaneous) single events. Others unfold in stages. One sexually abused client's young Exile revealed herself living under a bed in the woman's past. It had no "center" (no body trunk), just arms, legs, and a head. The first rescue step was to find her body, and rejoin it with her limbs and head. The next was to cautiously peek into the kitchen (of the house in the past), to see that her abusive (i.e. majorly wounded) Grandmother wasn't there.

Next, my client's Self took her young Exile into the (past) backyard garden, which she had only seen through the bedroom window before, and never visited. Then her young subself hesitantly agreed to try a "nice vacation trip" into the present. Eventually she agreed to live there. The whole multi-step rescue took many weekly sessions, and solo journaling, imaging, planning, and praying in between. Patience, faith, creativity, awareness, courage, and optimism are keys here, as with other inner-family techniques.

Rescues get easier with practice. My experience is that adults who were greatly neglected and traumatized as kids often have several Exiles. One such client did nine rescues, over time. Other people have one trapped part—or none. I've never experienced an Exile that wasn't a young (i.e. infant through teen) Young subself. Guardians seem to know the past and the present, and move easily back and forth. Those that do so aren't trapped, and need no rescuing.

While these ideas are fresh, pause and reflect—do you feel you have one or more parts stuck in the ever-unsafe past? What do you sense might happen to your life if you used this recovery technique to bring them to real safety and fellowship?

Resolving Inner-family Conflicts

Perhaps the most common evidence of inner-family reality is the daily discussions, debates, or screaming matches, going on inside our heads and bodies.

"You should go visit your brother in the hospital now!"

Another voice quickly says . . .

"But I need to cut the lawn, balance my checkbook, and I really want to watch the playoffs on TV. I don't have time today. Go see him later. He won't really mind."

Perhaps a third voice joins in:

"You pathetic, selfish wimp. Never can make your mind up, can you? Always thinking of yourself first. It's a wonder your brother even speaks to you. He's in pain, and you want to watch TV. You're a real scumbag, pal."

Sound familiar? When is the last time you had an inner struggle "with your self" like this? How often does that happen? When it does, how do you feel? Is there a pattern to the voices? Who (which inner voice) usually "wins"? Can you imagine finding a way to successfully mediate these battles? If unblended, your Self can do so *every time*. Note your first reaction (i.e. thoughts and memories) to that idea. Do your *Skeptic* and/or *Cynic* pipe up? What would your life be like if you could really resolve many or most of these inner battles effectively?

For reference, recall a time you were conflicted with another person and you reached an acceptable compromise together. How did you two do that? Here's an overview of the way it can work between your battling parts:

_ Authorize yourself to take enough time to mediate, and find an undistracted place to do so.

_ Adopt the "=/=" (mutual respect) attitude that each of your parts has legitimate needs, no matter how "unfair" or "wrong," and deserves *respectful* attention. Recall: you have no "bad" subselves. They each want to protect you—and themselves—in some way.

_ Trust your Self to find a workable compromise to any inner hassle, given time and freedom from blending. This increases with experience, as your inner team harmonizes.

_ Identify the parts that are opposed, and sort them out. If you have an image of one or all, focus on it, and tell the part you (your Self) are there to help each one get their needs met safely. Expect initial disbelief and resistance, without judgment—and go ahead anyway.

_ If things are too heated, ask your opposed parts to separate for now. Focus on and work with them one at a time. Ask each in turn what it wants, specifically—and *listen*! Repeat back concisely, without judgment or comment, what you hear. Like physical people, excited parts will start to calm down when they feel someone accepts and respects them, and *hears* (empathically validates) them *without judgment*. This doesn't imply *agreement*!

_ Be alert for your parts' *real* needs "beneath" their stated needs. As with people, one way of probing for *real* current needs is to ask "What do you feel will happen if you don't get (the surface need) filled right now?"

The (*Dutiful*) part above might say . . .

"Well, that's obvious. If you don't go see your brother, people will think you're selfish and insensitive—specially Jackie. If you're ever in the hospital, they won't come to see you, and you'd be all alone. I don't want that to happen."

A *Caregiver* (Nurturing) subself might say . . .

"You'd really feel good going to see him. You know how much it would mean to him, and you really do care about your brother . . . "

The third (*Achiever*) voice might disclose . . .

"But I'm afraid if you don't cut the grass this afternoon, it'll get out of hand and take three times as long, later. And you know what happens when you put off balancing the checkbook—checks start to bounce, and you get in trouble. So get going!"

Finally, a fourth voice might surface, belonging to an early-teen inner *Competitor* or *Athlete*:

"But you're always busy! C'mon—relax and have a little fun for a change. Watch the game! Ned will understand . . . "

Let (vs. force) your Self mediate and seek a win-win compromise among all parts involved. In this example, that might sound like . . .

"OK, how 'bout this: The checkbook should only take about 10 or 15 minutes. We'll do that now. Then I'll go to the hospital for an hour or

two. Maybe Ned and I can watch the game together there. I'll get back here by four-ish, and at least get the front lawn mowed. I'll do the back yard tomorrow after work, if I have to. Can you all live with that?"

As each of your parts experience the calm, ability of your Self to (1) hear and accept their current real needs, and (2) balance them fairly with other parts' needs, their trust in your Self's judgment, reliability, and leadership will rise. A nifty spinoff: as you develop your inner conflict-resolution process, you'll probably find yourself mediating conflicts with people around you in the same mutually respectful, win-win way.

Notice your reactions now. Do you think these steps will work for you? Are you willing to try them out? What might get in your way? Listen to your inner voices, and feel your emotions and physical reactions, without judging them . . .

Inner-family Conflict Resolution Tips

Obviously, many inner struggles aren't as neat as the example above. Here are a few guidelines for your Self to raise your resolution success rate. These apply to *outer* conflicts too!

Stay focused on the current conflict. Avoid getting snarled in related (or non-related)—or past—issues. One problem at a time!

Stay clear on what aspects of the current situation you can impact or control, and which you can't. See the *Serenity Prayer* on p. 361. If a subself fears that global warming will kill you soon, compassionately acknowledge their fear, and underlying wish to protect you; and that there's really nothing you can do about that, so you (Self) choose to worry about other current things.

Watch out for a *Catastrophizer* part making exaggerated or future (vs. current) threats. Acknowledge their well-meant warnings, and stay focused on the present.

Avoid assuming past experiences are always valid guides for the present. You've never done this inner recovery work before, so at least inner (and therefore outer) results may well be new and different . . .

Avoid the limiting bipolar (black/white) thinking that *Super-Controller* parts promote ("Do it!" // "Don't!"). Usually, there are *many* possible solutions to a conflict, not just two.

If one or more of your conflicted parts are young Inner Kids who can't understand realistic practicalities, consider having a nurturing or companion part stay with them for reassurance while your Self works the current conflict out. Your inner kids need your Self or inner *Nurturer* to be a compassionate leader, not a buddy. They'll usually feel better knowing someone's in charge of setting and following (enforcing) safe limits, even if they don't like the limits.

If useful, agree on a signal that anxious or distrusting parts can use to get your Self's (or a delegate part's) attention along the way. That can be an image, a physical symptom, (like finger tingling or stomach "rumbling"), or a special thought or memory.

When some inner kids are scared of an impending event, consider inviting them to "go play," or "stay home in your safe place" while your older, wiser parts handle the real-world situation. Help your Inner Kids trust *without guilt* that they don't have to handle outer (or inner) conflicts. Their important job is to be curious, contribute their priceless energies and gifts, and to experience and learn, over time. Most of us low-nurturance survivors grew up over-responsible, never questioning that we were asked to do what our wounded caregivers were responsible for, but unable to do.

Learn the special strengths and abilities that each part brings you, and *use* them! Delegate aspects of a current conflict solution to subselves with suitable skills and abilities, rather than feeling your Self has to "do it all." For example, if a part is very adept at respectfully keeping parts focused, include her or him in complex resolutions. See "teamwork" below . . .

As you experiment with this inner-resolution concept, focus on and grow what works. Acknowledge your inner *Perfectionist's* need to have conflict resolution work exactly, every time—and focus on learning from those times that aren't "perfect" or "totally successful." Aim for compromise, and meeting each part's needs *enough*, vs. completely, for now. Go for "*Progress, not Perfection*"!

Here's another vital inner-family technique, to add value and impact to your inner councils, re-doings, rescues, and conflict-resolutions . . .

Reassigning Certain Parts

A middle-aged client I'll call Debbie discovered to her discomfort that one of her Guardian parts brought her intense feelings of insecurity and overt jealousy in her primary relationships. Even when her partner was consistently trustworthy, this part doubted and accused him. This in turn corroded the relationship, promoting the very thing the *Suspicious One* feared. This pattern had happened with several men, over prior years. Debbie felt helpless to change the pattern.

One core element of the pattern turned out to be a very young Exile, who carried Debbie's deep shame and abandonment fear. Over time, Debbie rescued "Gretchen" (who carried her shame), and put her in the loving care of her Inner *Nurturer* ("*Good Mom*") and a tender "Golden Angel" part. As some healing months went by, Gretchen began to feel better about herself. As this happened, the Guardian who had brought the feelings of jealousy interfered.

Patient parts work disclosed that "Miss Jealousy" was really frightened that as Gretchen improved, she (the part) was out of a job—and would be somehow discarded or forgotten.

Learning this, Debbie's Self called an inner council. She appreciated the years of service that Miss Jealous had put in protecting Gretchen, and affirmed Gretchen's healing progress. Debbie asked her team for suggestions on how Miss Jealous' energy and skills could be better used. Some spirited discussion evolved the idea that the team needed someone to take charge of remembering important commitments.

Miss Jealous felt that was an important role, and enthusiastically agreed to shift her focus from protecting Gretchen to acting as a staff consultant in charge of "responsible follow-throughs." Gretchen and Debbie's other parts all felt comfortable-enough with, and even *excited* about, this change. This is inner-family "harmonizing" and team-building in action.

Some weeks later, Debbie reported that her feelings of relationship anxiety seemed less, (vs. gone), and that her partner had noticed, and was "relieved."

This story shows how misdirected, unaware subselves can shift their inner family "job," (role) and redirect their talents and energies to help all parts prosper in the present. At times this happens in one parts session. Other times it takes longer. Reassigning is usually useful with Guardians who's related Inner Kids are rescued and become safe and secure in the present. It also helps with Inner Kids (or even Manager parts) who no longer need to have act in a primarily protective way because of successful parts' integration, rescuing, and team building.

My inner-family mentor Dick Schwartz said that in his decade of experience, most Guardians were weary of their endless protective missions—and despaired of ever putting them down, because they saw safe no alternatives. When your Guardian parts come to trust that the Inner Kids they're protecting really *are* safe enough under the care of your Self and trusted delegates, they're often delighted, relieved, and enthused about using their talents in another way. My own parts-work experience with clients verifies this.

The larger recovery target here is to patiently rebalance the roles each of your parts play in your inner family (personality), and empower your Self to lead, to promote growing group co-operation, wholistic health, and your personal clarity, serenity, courage, and effectiveness. Remember the inspiring model of an effective team that you chose? Muse on how that team evolved the responsibilities of each member.

More parts-work recovery techniques . . .

Reclaiming Your Disowned Parts

Most of us have a few "traits" (subselves) we've grown to fear, dislike, and feel ashamed of. A natural reaction is to deny, repress, overcontrol, or "banish" such unpleasant parts—or at least judge them mercilessly as "bad," "awful," or "disgusting" (as in "I hate my snotty *Procrastinator!*")

In their intriguing inner-voice book *"Embracing Each Other,"* psychologists Hal and Sidra Stone suggest such disowned parts inevitably cause powerful reactions in some of our relationships. The Stones feel that the people we're most intensely repelled by or attracted to display active parts similar to those we're trying to disown ("opposites attract"). Such intense reactions often cause stressful or hurtful relationship decisions.

I agree with the Stones' proposal that learning to accept and even welcome our "awful" parts into our inner team promotes wholistic health and daily harmony. Doing this reunites subselves who have previously been paralyzed, rejected, or exiled. Could this need for "personality integration" cause the deep, universal human yearning for "wholeness"?

It takes constant life-energy to repress and deny a subself. Recoverer John Bradshaw likens this effort to trying to swim while holding one or two buoyant beach balls under water. Therapist Virginia Satir said it's like trying to constantly hold the kitchen door closed against a pack of ravenous dogs. Inviting disowned parts "in" can free up vital energy to fill other needs.

Note that acknowledging and *accepting* such parts does *not* mean allowing them to control or strongly influence your decisions!

Here are ideas on how to reclaim your valuable disowned inner-family members:

Identify Rejected Parts

Accept that you may or do have such rejected personality parts, and that you can learn to genuinely welcome them into your inner team. If you experience strong disbelief or resistance to these ideas, identify and learn about the Guardian parts that bring you those protective feelings and attitudes. Negotiate with them to at least allow you to explore, and see what happens.

Review the people in your life you've had extreme feelings about—particularly revulsion, disgust, dislike, fear, and rage. See if there's a common pattern to the qualities in those people that you react very strongly to. For example, most of us dislike others who often lie or hedge; are insincere and phony; are egotistical, selfish, and/or insensitive; constantly blame and criticize; or never admit their mistakes. Any bells ringing? If you have a particularly strong judgmental reaction to such traits in one or more people, you may have a part carrying that trait in yourself that you don't want to acknowledge.

For each such trait you identify: go inside, and invite the part that carries that characteristic in you to identify itself in some way. If "nothing happens," convene your known parts and ask them if they know of any hidden part who carries the target quality.

If "No," then focus on your parts who hold the strong feelings of disgust, disdain, or revulsion. Ask them where they learned to have such intense reactions, and why they have them. See if this leads to recalling a traumatic time when you, or someone or some thing you prized (like a pet), were greatly hurt or scared somehow by a person with the target quality.

If so, explore to see if you have a current or exiled young subself who is related to that incident. If you do, stay alert that the Guardian with the strong "negative" feeling may be protecting that Inner Child against a feared subself who hasn't "come out" (come into your awareness) yet. Explore this patiently and gently over time.

For instance: as a child, my client Jack was abandoned by his mother, and severely shamed and neglected by his (wounded) grandmother. He (i.e. some false-self parts) developed an intense dislike for, and rage at "women who avoid commitment and responsibility." As a young man, he fell in love with a woman who died several years later while they were discussing marriage.

By middle age, Jack had never married or conceived a child—and often felt sad, angry, and lonely. With persistent, inner work, he discovered a hidden (adolescent) part of himself who fiercely didn't want him to commit to *anyone*, for fear of expected agonizing abandonment. Jack's inner *Judge* was furious at this part (i.e. frightened and deeply ashamed of it), and worked ceaselessly to "keep it down and out." Parts work helped to moderate this, over time. Recently, Jack became engaged.

Including Your Disowned Parts

If you locate a rejected part of yourself, what are your choices? Options:

Refresh your attitude: try out the belief that any part can, with respectful encouragement over time, shift its energy to new goals and strategies. Every part of your personality is a potential asset!

As with any unknown subself, meet and learn about your disowned One (Chapter 7). With time, develop a trusting relationship between it, your Self, and other key parts. Trust, safety, listening, patience, and acceptance are the keys.

Identify each part that wants to reject this shunned aspect of your self. *Non-judgmentally* learn why, acknowledge their specific fears, and work patiently to reduce them over time. Reassure any anxious or distrusting inner members that you'll see to it that this new part won't "take us over" or "get out of hand." Ask them to trust you (your Self), and then follow up. Take small, respectful steps, and safe-enough risks. Use *listening* and inner-conflict resolution skills (p. 216).

Evaluate compassionately whether the part is an Exile trapped in the past. If so, rescue it safely when the time seems right.

Pay attention to the name and/or title you and other parts use to identify the newcomer. If their current name or title is derogatory, pick a more respectful or neutral label that fits. For example, if at first your disowned part is dubbed "*The* (vs. *my*) *Whore*" or "my *Stupid Sex Addict*"—see if a nick/name without negative associations would feel OK—like "Tex," or "Willow." Subselves often will tell you a name or title they prefer. The idea that they can ask for one they like may be an amazing new concept.

Work with the disowned part and your inner crew to see if job retraining (reassigning, above) is appropriate and currently possible. If so, go for it! Recall: all parts mean well—but may be misinformed, frightened, and/or living distorted lives in an earlier traumatic time. All parts bring energy and unique, valuable abilities. With steady love, acceptance, and patience, any of your inner teammates can be re-motivated and redirected in more healthy and productive ways.

If for some reason retraining isn't appropriate or possible for now, steadily remind everyone that this reunited subself is only one part—not *all* of you. If you identify and reclaim a "selfish," "dishonest," "weak," or "voyeuristic" part—stay aware that they alone don't determine who you, the whole person, are. As with all parts, help the newcomer feel safe and accepted, stay calm, and not "act out." As with insecure kids, this often means lovingly providing and *enforcing* firmly-flexible limits and consequences.

Include your newly accepted part in all inner-community councils and relevant decision discussions. Invite, acknowledge, and consider their input—and keep your Self in charge!

For perspective, think about your best friends. Do they each have some unpleasant qualities? On balance, you still accept and value them for the greater good they bring you, and vice versa. You can do the same with any of your disowned parts, prizing your self as much as your do your best friend. True recovery inexorably leads us to the Golden Rule. Reality-check that with your recovery hero/ines.

All these basic and special techniques will empower you to work toward the real payoff of your inner-family recovery work . . .

Harmonizing: Building Inner-family Trust and Teamwork

The overall aim of this work is to increase your inner harmony, wholistic health, and productivity, over time. These things "happen" naturally, as you . . .

- Build respect, safety, appreciation, and esteem among your inner family members;

- Patiently resolve their conflicts, fears, and distrusts; and . . .

- Enlist and include them together in pursuing your short and long-term life goals, including raising the nurturance level of your outer environment in safe-enough steps.

Does this seem reasonable? Possible? If not, who's "speaking" for you?

Building your inner family into a truly effective team is an art and an achievable skill. What are the keys? Use this suggestive checklist to define your current inner family strengths, and areas to improve:

_ Each team member knows all the other members, and is clearly living in the present time.

_ All members maintain a clear vision of—and genuine high desire for—common goals.

－ Each subself stays clear on their own and others' skills, team roles, and responsibilities. Boundaries between subselves, and between the team and the "outside world" are firmly flexible, and consistently clear enough to all.

－ Each of your inner team member feels steadily recognized, respected, trusted, and valued "enough" by all other members—and themselves.

－ Each subself is clear enough on—and willingly abides by, or proposes constructive changes to—your inner family's key rules and values.

－ All personality parts usually communicate clearly, and problem-solve effectively, with each other.

－ Each member steadily respects the team leader—your Self—and trusts that subself to consistently . . .

• Provide clear focus, vision, goals and explanations; guidance; believable optimism; and steady inspiration and encouragements;

• Resolve major conflicts, and adapt creatively to unexpected life conditions;

• Recognize achievements, and forgive mistakes;

• Get effective help and protection, when needed;

• Delegate responsibilities wisely and fairly;

• Set and adjust paces, balances, boundaries and limits, when needed; and . . .

• Stay fully committed to the team, the job, and the objectives, no matter what.

－ Each of your inner-family members stays clear on your group's purpose and identity, and feels appropriate satisfaction and pride in belonging.

During undistracted reflection, edit this list to fit your own experience and beliefs. Does your teamwork-traits list fairly characterize the "ideal" team you thought of before (p. 164)? Does it describe your present *outer* family? The family you grew up in? The schools and church/es you went to? Your current work environment? One way of seeing this recovery goal is: create nurturance, safety, and harmony conditions internally, that you didn't get enough of as a child, despite your wounded caregivers' best efforts. See checklist A) on p. 257 and the checklist at **http://sfhelp.org/ gwc/hi_n_org.htm** for perspective.

Notice with interest where your thoughts go now, and how you feel. Does this checklist honestly describe your inner crew now? If not (yet), can you envision all your parts closely fitting this list "sometime"? What would have to happen? Who's responsible to see that it does? (I propose your unhindered Self is). What if your inner family never becomes a truly effective team? What if it does? How might either of these outcomes affect any dependent (grand)kids in your life?

If shooting for these inner-family traits seems inviting and useful, how high a priority do you assign to achieving them? Typically, what do you do each day instead of working towards these personal objectives—i.e. what are your current priorities?

Which of your subselves is setting your daily priorities and goals, these days? How well are their decisions "working" for you all?

As a naturally talented leader, your unblended Self is skilled at directing the communications among your parts into effective discussions and problem solvings. S/He can also learn to improve this skill, and teach it to your other parts. Doing so is one key to successful inner teambuilding, for many of our parts don't know how to communicate effectively. Hence our recurring times of inner confusion and chaos.

See Scott Peck's interesting book *"The Different Drum"* for thought-provoking stories and ideas on the process of building a truly harmonious community. Though his book focuses on groups of people, I propose that his ideas apply to *inner* communities like yours, too. See what you think.

Let's sum up. We've just reviewed key techniques that comprise "inner-family recovery work." These include . . .

- Using Self-led inner councils or staff meetings.

- Identifying, validating, and using your spiritual part/s and Higher Power in all your recovery work.

- Experimenting with meeting, validating, and communicating with your parts.

- Unblending: persuading distrustful, needy parts to "step aside" and allow your Self to attend them, and make life decisions.

- Re-doing old real-life traumas.

- Rescuing young Exiles from an endlessly unsafe, agonizing past.

- Identifying, accepting, and including rejected ("disowned") subselves.

- Recognizing and resolving *inner*-personal conflicts.

- Reassigning, or job "retraining"—changing selected parts' inner-family role/s, goal/s, and/or priorities.

- Harmonizing: building inner-family teamwork and cooperation, over time, under your Self's leadership—with guidance from your spiritual resources.

There are other important recovery techniques you can study and experiment with—like intentionally releasing subselves' rage and sadness, using healing rituals, and unlocking body memories. Other options include using hypnosis, art, sculpture, movement, aromas, and an emerging new therapy called EMDR (eye movement desensitization and retraining) to validate, access, express, and integrate your subselves.

Recall: this book is about understanding, assessing for, and replacing unseen false-self dominance with natural Self-leadership. An early premise here was that controlling false-self parts usually cause people (like you?) some mix of six mutually-reinforcing psychological wounds. Can you name them?

Now you have the basic tools and ideas to draft a meaningful personal recovery framework. How can you apply the parts-work recovery techniques we just reviewed to liberating your talented true Self?

9) TYPICAL RECOVERY PHASES, STEPS, AND RESULTS—WHAT TO EXPECT

EXAMPLE: REDUCING EXCESSIVE FEARS

"Free your true Self to lead, and harmonize your inner family" is pretty vague and abstract. A more concrete way of defining your recovery goals is "Over time, transform your mix of the six false-self wounds into their opposites. That is, transform . . .

- Stressful false-self domination into consistent true-Self inner-family leadership, and grow inner-family harmony.

- Excessive shame and guilts (a shame-based personality) into (1) genuine self-love and self care, and (2) genuine forgivenesses of self and others.

- Excessive fears (a fear-based personality) to acceptance of what *is*, and *serenity*, based on confidence in Self, Higher Power, and selected other people.

- Chronic overtrusting and/or undertrusting into solid reality-based trust in your own perceptions and judgments, selected other people, and your Higher Power.

    These recovery conversions over time will help you . . .

- Transform chronic reality distortions into clear awareness and acceptance of inner and outer realities; and . . .

- Grow the abilities to (1) choose and emotionally attach to (bond with) wholistically-healthy other people and groups, and to (2) give and receive genuine Self and mutual love.

Use the self-assessment checklists in Part 3 to identify which os the six false-self wounds you want to reduce. Fully exploring the conversion of each of these into it's opposite condition (e.g. converting toxic shame into genuine self respect, self-care, and self love) merits individual books.

Here are some general recovery options for each trait, using inner-family techniques and other strategies. This chapter offers a representative example of transforming toxic fears, to illustrate all six of these recovery goals.

A basic premise here is that each of these wounds is brought about by combination of Inner Kids and Guardian subselves that blend with your Self, because they don't trust her/him. For example, "excessive shame" occurs when one or several intensely shamed personality parts—usually young Inner Kids—blend. Then "you"—i.e. your body and conscious mind—*feel* the emotions, perceptions, memories, and values of these shamed parts, and you lose the perspective and wise judgment of your Self.

You're also influenced by the thoughts and feelings of the Guardian parts who specialize in soothing your shamed inner child(ren)—e.g. your *Denier, Procrastinator, Blamer (Inner Critic), Magician,* and *Perfectionist* subselves. They may blend with your Self also—with, or instead of, the *Shamed Child(ren).*

A recovery opportunity grows from this blending > innerwound concept wound. Using an appropriate combination of the inner-family techniques you've just read about, do steps like these:

_ **Identify** the young and Guardian subselves that "cause" each trait, one at a time.

_ **Work** patiently and respectfully with each Guardian to . . .

- Introduce your Self to these other parts gently and respectfully (safely). Usually this involves a lot of *listening* to each part at first; and then . . .

- Earn their trust that your Self and any outside helpers genuinely share their desire to protect and nurture the Inner Kids, and are not trying to demote, fire, exile, or "kill," the Guardians.

_ **Introduce** the target Inner Kids to other subselves who can companion, protect, and nurture them—e.g. your *Good Mom, Good Dad, Healing Spirit, Older Sib*, and/or *Nurturer* parts—and patiently build a trusting relationship between them;

_ **Rescue** each Inner Child who seems stuck in the past, _ re-do any major traumas that promote their and their Guardians blending with your Self, and _ re-integrate any disowned parts that contribute to the target trait you're transforming.

_ **Identify** and promote respectful change in other parts—usually Guardians—which maintain the target trait. For example, for her or his own reasons, your *Inner Critic* needs to constantly heap blame, shame, and guilt on "you." That promotes your *Shamed Child* and *Guilty Kid* "activating" (feeling badly) and blending—which activates one or more Guardians like *Blamer, Denier, Abuser*, or *Addict*. That promotes more blending, and the temporary or chronic loss of your Self's abilities and wisdom.

_ **Identify** and courageously change major outer events, relationships, and surroundings that promote the target Inner Child's burden—e.g. shaming relationships, and home, work, and/or worship environments. This usually involves one or more very conflictual and scary confrontations with key (wounded) people—like a parent, mate, "acting-out" child, or sibling—whose false selves fear your changing. This step often includes retraining existing Guardian parts to behave in new ways toward such people, like an *Inner Blamer (Critic)* shifting to the new role of (protective) *"Peaceful Warrior,"* or *"Truth Teller."*

Learning about communication skills (*Satisfactions,* Xlibris.com) and high-nurturance relationships and environments (p. 257), and then using them while trying new safe new social behaviors, helps make this challenging step more impactful and effective, over time.

_ **Raise** your awarenesses of _ this whole evolving process, and _ it's inner and outer *results*, via meditation, journaling, and accepting caring feedback from trusted, empathic companions—e.g. fellow recoverers and guides.

Tailor these baseline trait-recovery steps to fit your unique inner and outer circumstances, history, and personality. Notice several themes: these steps . . .

- Involve both inner and outer *second-order* changes—i.e. major shifts in your core attitudes, values, behaviors, and relationships. That involves taking and tolerating safe-enough *risks*.

- Take courage, patience, creativity; and often, appropriate human and spiritual help.

- Take months or years to traverse and stabilize, though initial positive results usually appear quickly.

- Use most of the inner-family techniques described in chapters 7 and 8.

- Are orchestrated by your emerging true Self, with help from inner and outer supporters.

From this outline, can you see how working on each of the six wounds will help reduce the other five? They all interact and promote each other, so decreasing each trait helps to heal them all! Because of this, the pace of your recovery progress tends to accelerate naturally, over time, because inner healing promotes itself. The reverse is also true: unseen and unhealed, the six wounds tend to interact with the environment and amplify each other over time. That promotes low-nurturance inner and outer environments. Those promote accumulating pain, despair, self-neglect, apathy, sickness, and premature death.

If this is happening to you and you're a co-parent, an inevitable spinoff is a decline in your family's nurturance level for any dependent kids. That fosters automatic adaptive false-self development in them. If you're wounded, that's probably what happened to you, your sibs, and many of your ancestors, as kids.

Example—Reducing Excessive Fears

What might these steps look like if you decided to transform a primal fear of *rejection* and *abandonment* that had long skewed your life? Based on searing early childhood experience, this core fear cripples many of us without our awareness, until we're well into true recovery. It is one of a group of primal anxieties that burden our Young subselves and some Guardians, including fears of . . .

- Physical pain, injury, and death.

- Change, risk, and the unknown.

- "Failure," in our own and/or others' eyes.

- Loss of (emotional) control, and fear of . . .

- Strong emotions in ourselves and others (and therefore of conflict and intimacy);

- Fear of excessive fears, combined with a sense of powerlessness;

- Loss of freedom and autonomy (self-choice); and for some, . . .

- Fear of success.

The *causes* of these fears are different. The *experience* of fear is the same for each and all of them—pain, anxiety, and degrees of hesitance, defense, or paralysis. Are any of these fears significantly shaping your life, so far? Any of your kids' lives? Your partner's life? Before true recovery, typical people ruled by a false self minimize, numb, intellectualize, or repress these fears, and awareness of their impacts on daily life and loved ones.

How might you or another apply the inner-family recovery steps above to reduce an old fear of rejection and abandonment—i.e. the terror of experiencing *aloneness* and *disconnection*? For brevity, this example is in outline form. It presumes you've done some version of the "getting ready" steps in chapter 7. This example would be the same for any of the fears above, or any of the other five inner wounds.

Overall, the recovery theme to follow with any toxic fear is to gradually and intentionally transfer the dependence of the frightened subselves from *outside* people, events, and conditions to internal resources: Self, other dependable parts, and spiritual nurturer/s and/or your Higher Power.

This doesn't mean to become indifferent to or detached from other people. It does mean to break the adult illusion that we must depend totally on others for survival, safety, and comfort, as we had to when we were infants and toddlers. The target for reducing fear of abandonment is to build the credible belief in the youngest Young subselves and *Catastrophizer* Guardians—"If we ever have to live alone for a while, we'll be OK enough." In other words, the target is to safely connect the frightened parts with the strong, caring, reliable personality parts who *want to* nurture and protect, vs. feeling they *have* to.

1) Identify the Subselves Involved (chapter 7)

Typical findings might be . . .

Inner Kids: *Fearful Child* (say, about five years old), *Lonely, Shy Child* (say about 11), and *Shamed Child* (about 3). Use any suitable titles or names—specially those that individual parts prefer; and . . .

Active Guardians: *People Pleaser* ("Always Be Nice; *Never* be mean or selfish!"), *Inner Critic* ("Don't you mess up!"), *Catastrophizer* ("No one will love you, You're gonna die lonely, sick, and unloved!"), *Numb-er* ("There, there—don't *feel* anything"), and *Distracter* ("Let's watch some TV now, instead of worrying and feeling bad, OK?").

Your set of protector parts would probably be different. These are typical and illustrative.

2) Earn the Trust of Your Guardians

Meaningful parts work can't happen unless all affected inner-family members know what's going on, why, how it will affect them, who's in charge, and that the process is *safe enough*. If you've done some parts work already, you may not have to do much "set up" to begin building trust with your Guardians. If it's your first major parts work, your Guardians and Inner Kids will need a lot of patient, genuinely *respectful* disclosure, listening, validating, explaining, clarifying, and reassuring. They'll need time to mull, reflect, and deliberate. Doing these is part of building experience and skill in communicating with your subselves.

You can "get permission" from the several Guardians who protect these three Young subselves one at a time, in a small group, or with your whole inner family at once. Take small steps, and declare clear goals along the way. "First, I (your Self) want to say hello to our three Inner Kids, one at a time. Then I want to learn from them what they're so afraid of. I want to do this so they can feel more secure more often. How do you (Guardians) feel about this idea, so far?"

Commonly, Guardians who don't yet trust your Self will hold open or covert fears that s/he is going to "fire," "forget," or "do away with" them. So part of this second wound-reduction step is reassuring all Guardians that them that (1) these won't happen, and that (2) one result may be that they'll get an important *better* (inner family) "job," if they wish it. Expect initial resistance and skepticism. Self will know what to do with it, and when it's safe to proceed.

To strengthen your (Self's) sincerity and authority on this vital reassurance, recall that physiologically, your personality parts are semi-independent regions of your brain. They *can't* be "killed, fired, or banished," any more than your kidneys can! Note another possible reassurance: invite ambivalent Guardians to be present when you meet with the young subself they guard.

3) Engage the Young Subselves

When your Guardians OK it, gently approach each of the Inner Kids one at a time, to do several things:

Introduce your Self, so they know who you are and why you're focusing on them.

Gently and non-judgmentally, explore how each part feels and thinks about the possibility of being abandoned by key physical people (friends, relatives, perhaps pets) in the present. Use language appropriate to their age. If you find a "five year old" part talking like a Ph.D., you're really dealing with a distrustful Guardian part.

Learn from each young part who they rely on now for safety and comfort—i.e. other parts, imaginary or spiritual "Ones," pets, and physical people. Ask specifically if they know your Inner *Nurturer*. I've never met a recoverer without one, though some Nurturers are more confident than others. This step lays the groundwork for the young part to shift from looking outside (to other people) for reliable comfort and safety, to looking *inside*.

If they haven't yet, evolve a way to have your *Nurturer* safely meet them. Make sure other parts know what you're doing, and why. If an over-responsible older Child has been watching out for the young part (e.g.

a "*Little Parent*" Guardian subself), invite her or him to be present at each inner meeting, and make sure s/he knows what's going on.

When s/he trusts your Self enough, ask each Inner Child what year they think it is. If s/he's too young to understand the question, your Self can ask other parts for advice on how to get clues. You're learning to "sense" whether any rescuing from the past is needed.

Ask your part which other inner-family members s/he knows. If this subself is stuck in the past, or is isolated from others in your inner family, find safe ways of introducing them to each other, one or a few at a time. Watch out for overloading, and respect your Inner Child saying, "No, I don't want to meet new 'people' (parts) now." Just as with a physical child, don't over-force your needs here—and stay in charge.

If it's relevant, trust your Self's wisdom, and rescue any involved child-part from being trapped in the past when it seems "time" to do so. When the time seems right, gently ask each Young subself about any rejection and abandonment traumas s/he _ remembers or _ expects. Use *their* perception, memories, and judgment, not your adult ones! *Fluency in the communication skill of empathic ("reflective") listening is very helpful here* See the Web article at **http://sfhelp.org/cx/skills/listen.htm.**

Consider having your *Nurturer* and any spiritual parts present as you do this. Do a lot of affirming, validating, and empathizing, to the extent that you genuinely feel them. If you don't feel them, be alert that some Guardian has silently blended with your Self because they don't yet trust what's going on, or why.

If you detect such a well-meaning *Blocker* part, stop working with the Child (explain why), and work to build awareness and confidence in that Guardian subself so s/he'll unblend. Ask what assurances they need from you (your Self) that would ease their anxieties, and negotiate how to provide those. When you have, return to your fearful, shy, lonely, or shamed young subself, and continue.

Follow your Self's wisdom and instincts on whether, when, and how to do any re-doings with each Inner Kid's abandonment traumas. Go slowly, and keep everyone informed and *heard*. If you have an *Impatient* part, affectionately acknowledge it—and don't rush!

A key goal here is to "connect" each Inner Child with one or more nurturing parts that they can talk with any time their rejection/abandonment (or other) fear erupts—just like a child on a stormy night seeking the comforting arms of a loving, secure parent. The other half of this is credibly reassuring any scared Guardian subselves that they can depend on you (your Self) to reassure and problem-solve with them. The need to do this dwindles as all your parts *experience* your Self's wisdom, good judgment, and reliability, over time.

Vignette: Well into learning parts work, a 30-something nurse/single-mom client of mine I'll call Sue described an old trauma. She told me vividly and emotionally of being left alone in a hospital for several days and nights when she was six years old. She recalled the absolute terror she felt believing that her mother, a cold, intellectual (badly wounded) woman, was going to leave her there for good. Young Sue had been relentlessly taught that her fears (in general) "were silly," and that her Mother would pay them little attention—just like her own mother had.

After much discussion and planning, my client agreed to do a re-doing for "Susie"—a young subself who replayed the remembered hospital terror over and over again because she was stuck in the 30-years' distant past. Sue decided to have her grown *Nurse* self, her warm, strong *Nurturer*, a kindly androgynous *Angel*, and her own 12 year-old daughter accompany her into the remembered hospital room. I was to provide moral support in the therapy room, but wasn't included.

My client relaxed on the couch, centered, and "went inside." Her Self brought all her supporters to Susie's remembered bedside. They introduced themselves, and told the little one they'd stay and play until Susie went home. As the re-doing evolved, Sue experienced her Mother entering the hospital room. Her Nurturer confronted "Mom," firmly and with compassion. She said from now on, this team was going to help her care for little Susie whether "Mom" liked it or not. Initially resentful and defensive, Mom broke into tears, (in the redoing), and admitted her guilt and sense of maternal inadequacy.

The whole experience lasted over half an hour, in real time. After debriefing, Sue decided to rescue Susie (the Young subself), and to have a conversation with her real Mother about the actual past experience. Her intent was not to blame or fault-find, but to give her parts the real experience of overcoming guilt and anxiety about talking to her Mother about a past traumatic event—whether her mother was "comfortable" or not.

This kind of respectful, calm, confrontation notably built her skeptical parts' trust of her Self, and of the real benefits of inner-family risks and events. Their conversation went well, and Mother and grown daughter felt "closer" afterward. Sue also described the re-doing experience to her own daughter, and the girl got interested in trying parts work and meeting her own inner family.

Patiently done, these first three recovery steps can bring initial relief to your scared subselves, and strengthen your inner family's bonds, trust, and teamwork. Further experience and experimenting strengthen both of those, when your Self is free to lead. The next step is often *fun*!

4) <u>Reassign Selected Guardians</u>

Typical Guardians develop in childhood because there was no real-life (Self-directed) adult to guide and protect adequately. As you rebalance your inner family, Guardians find that they don't have to do what they've been doing, for so many years. That creates the wonderful problem of having a "free resource" to apply to other personality tasks.

In this example, five Guardian parts are involved in comforting three inner kids who react to expected abandonment by "outside" people: *Pleaser*, *Critic*, *Catastrophizer*, *Numb-er*, and *Distracter*. As your Inner Kids learn to refocus their need for security *inside*, each of these Guardians can relax part of their responsibility—and focus on doing "something else" (that promotes your productivity and well being). The more they relax, the less often they'll blend—the more your Self will be free to lead—and the more they'll trust her or him!

Typically, *Pleaser* parts exist to comfort and protect young parts who carry the burdens of excessive shame, guilt, and fear. As each of those burdens diminishes via effective recovery work, the *Pleaser* part finds s/he doesn't have to work so hard to keep "the kids" safe enough. That frees the subself up to relax, help other parts, and/or do something entirely new.

Reflect: if you could change your behavior in some moderate way, what would you like? Better recall of names and dates? Have an inner coach that affirms you in tough situations, or reminds you to "Stay focused" or "Keep balanced" in confusing times? To slow down and see the humor and beauty that surrounds you every day? To exercise more? To be more assertive? More creative? The options are only limited by your creativity and awareness.

Does your *Skeptic* or *Cynic* pipe up protectively now with ideas like "This 'subself retraining' is *ridiculous*. It won't work!"? If so, respectfully ask her or him to acknowledge the reality that you (all) have been able to learn new behaviors, build new abilities, and "change your habits" through the years. This demonstrates the unarguable reality that your personality parts can and do change *all the time*. That's all "job retraining" is—using your parts' natural ability to learn new things, change their minds, and willingly shift their daily energy and focus. This shift is powered by their quenchless wish to be useful and "do good" for you and each other.

Do you (all) believe this?

5) Change Your Outer Environment

As your Inner Kids learn that reliable safety and comfort are available *inside*, and their loyal Guardians relax and shift control to your Self and Higher Power, your attitudes, and then your behavior, will change. That will delight some well-wishers, and will annoy, worry, or scare others whose insecure false selves need you to remain "the old (toxic) way."

In this case, as your *People Pleaser* relaxes and s/he and your Inner Kids stop blending, your Self will be freer to respectfully confront other people, ask new things of them, and set new limits with them. Your *Pleaser's* pre-recovery job was to minimize other people's displeasure—i.e. minimize the risk of their painful criticism and rejection (result: guilt and shame), and terrifying abandonment.

Pleaser's other goal was to protect your *Shamed* and *Guilty* Inner Kids from scathing blasts from your Inner *Critic*. As you all feel safer, you're Self is freer to say to other people . . .

- "No (I choose not to do what you want me to do),"

- "Not now," or . . .

- "Not that way,"

. . . with less alarmed yammer from and blending by your *Critic*, *Catastrophizer*, and *Perfectionist* parts.

Pleaser's relaxing also frees your Self to be more proactive, as you lighten your fear and shame burdens. S/He can now selectively intervene if s/he feels someone else's actions are harmful or dangerous. Either way, you'll become more "independent and assertive," less "easy going," and express your unique individual values and preferences with less worry about "what others will think or do." Some other people won't *like* this assertive new you!

Kids in low-nurturance families and settings learn to endure and avoid high anxieties and fears. Living anxiously becomes *normal* and unconscious. That promotes choosing and tolerating fear-promoting adult relationships and environments. These can manifest as relationships where one partner implies or threatens to cut off emotional or physical contact, or approval and acceptance, or "commit suicide," if the other person doesn't behave "right." It also looks like keeping an uncertain or demeaning job, or inappropriate responsibility.

Changing your environment to reduce being held hostage by toxic fear (a terrified young subself and related Guardian/s) means your Self and supporters leading your inner family to risk change and temporary confusion to find new higher-nurturance relationships and jobs.

On a practical level, that can mean sadly ending a co-dependent (toxic) love relationship, or nervously seeking a higher-nurturance job. It can also mean accepting the harsh, sad reality that a needy, wounded relative (e.g. Mom, brother) may say, "If you insist on being so selfish and inconsiderate (i.e. respectfully assertive), I'll have nothing more to do with you." Difficult choices like these are inevitable in true recovery. In pseudo recovery, your false self will urge alluring ways of avoiding the pain, anxiety, and guilt of "standing up for yourself" with critics who don't know or care about (or fear) your recovery.

Guardians' persuasions can be tough: "You know God says in the Bible you have to 'Honor Thy Father and Thy Mother.' You can't let Mom cut us off, or we'll burn in Hell forever! Are you too stupid to see that?" (A chorus of *Critic*, *Perfectionist*, *Catastrophizer*, and *Magician* subselves all together, because they don't yet trust your Self and Higher Power). Heavy duty, huh? Your Self hears a very different message from your Higher Power. See *"Conversations With God,"* by Neale Walsch for possibilities.

Bottom line: as you free your Self, reorganize and harmonize your inner family, and heal your mix of wounds (recover), you'll encounter a series of confusing, scary choices about significantly changing your *outer* life. The theme that guides your choices at these times will be taking courageous responsibility for the quality and outcome of your own life, and respectfully encouraging other people to do the same. This is not about being *selfish* (not caring about other people's needs and feelings). It *is* about being *Self-ish*: promoting your own needs and well being to be *equal* to other people and living things you care about—*without undue anxiety, guilt, doubt, and shame.* How does that sound to (all of) you?

6) Learn From Your Experience

A periodic (vs. last) step in working to reduce each of the six false-self wounds is to pause and reflect on what your recovery experience is teaching you. In this example, reducing fear of rejection and abandonment, what could you learn from patiently working at the other five steps? Perhaps things like . . .

- I'm clearer on how to identify my parts, and communicate with them.

- I've learned more compassion for my burdened young subselves, and more appreciation for the tireless, dedicated—and narrow-visioned, ill-informed—efforts of their Guardian parts.

- I'm changing from disliking my *Inner Critic* to respecting him (her). S/ He's trying to protect my inner kids, though I don't agree with how s/ he's been doing it! I'm learning I can negotiate with Critic, as s/he trusts me (Self) more, and our teamwork builds.

- I've gained more trust in, and skill at, inner-family re-doing, rescues, and team meetings. I'm feeling more confident and resourceful. I'm seeing change-possibilities that didn't exist before.

- Instead of resentment or disdain, I'm learning to feel compassion for other people who are unaware of their own blending and false selves, even if they mistreat me. I'm learning genuine forgiveness—for *my* sake!

- I'm strengthening my spiritual faith, and my ability to receive guidance and comfort from my spiritual part(s) and Higher Power.

- I'm learning how and when to use journaling to help me in this healing work.

- I'm learning who I can get real recovery support from, and who I can't.

- I'm learning to mourn all the years I've lived a prisoner of misplaced shame, guilt, and fear—and I'm letting go of the need to blame (or idealize) my parents.

- I'm learning to trust my Self's judgment, skill, wisdom, and dedication—and I'm learning to really *believe* I can recover from false-self dominance, over time!

So far, we've focused on reorganizing your inner family, and shifting leadership to your true Self and Higher Power. If you courageously commit to using recovery steps and techniques like these, what may happen?

The Other Half of Recovery

These parts-work concepts and techniques are basic skills you can develop to help intentionally reduce your mix of psychological injuries. Learning and applying these skills is *half* of your recovery work. The other half is learning or expanding three or four basic life skills, over time . . .

- **Effective communication skills**: awareness, clear thinking, "digging down," metatalk (talking about communicating), empathic listening, respectful assertion, and win-win problem solving. If you can't describe each of these clearly, you're probably nots using them—or teaching them to your kids. See *Satisfactions—7 relationship skills you need to know* (Xlibris.com), or http://sfhelp.org/cx/links2.htm.

- **Healthy three-level grieving** attitudes and practices. See *Stepfamily Courtship* (Xlibris.com) or http://sfhelp.org/grief/links3.htm for a series of articles.

- **Effective relationship skills**, including effective (high-nurturance) parenting skills. See http://sfhelp.org/relate/links4.htm for concepts and tools.

Co-parents and kids in typical divorced families and stepfamilies—over half our U.S. population—have one or two groups of complex adjustment tasks to master, in addition to these life skills. See **http://sfhelp.org/sf/co/kid_needs.htm** and **http://sfhelp.org/sf/basics/tasks.htm** for what they are.

True (vs. pseudo) recoverers simultaneously (1) learn these skills, and (2) reorganize their inner family; while (3) making a living; and—for many, (4) co-managing a home and family; and (5) having periodic fun, relaxation, and rest stops along the way. Your overall recovery goal is to gradually raise your inner, physical, and social environments from low-nurturance to high (pp. 257 and 281)—and enjoy the results!

Seeing this whole grand scheme, can you appreciate why having your Self leading your unique, talented inner crew can optimize your long-term satisfaction, health, and fulfillment ("success")? Until it's transformed, major false-self dominance covertly hinders each of these second-half recovery learnings and skills. For instance:

False-self dominance makes effective communication and conflict resolution with key people difficult or impossible—even if you learn the seven skills above. This is largely due to unconsciously sending "I'm 1-up" or "I'm 1-down" "*R(espect) messages* to communication partners, instead of the mutual-respect messages we all need. *Two* shame-based people have exceptionally hard times trying to negotiate and problem-solve—specially over emotional parenting, financial, and intimacy (relationship) conflicts. Protective reality-distortion (denial) blocks seeing this, until each mate is well into true recovery.

Learning and applying the seven communication skills can be a great help in resolving *inner* conflicts among your subselves!

Frozen grief promotes "depressions," addictions, and various physical illnesses, until it's freed up. Because fear-based recoverers unconsciously repress or numb their emotions, and often live in low-nurturance (anti-grief) environments, they're prone to frozen grief.

Alternatively, wounded people may never risk real emotional-spiritual attachments (bonds) with others, to avoid expected agonies from rejection and abandonment. Such fear-ruled people have few losses to grieve. Learning about healthy three-level grieving without also reducing the dominance of a protective false self probably won't free up blocked grief. Conversely, empowering your true Self without learning the healthy grieving basics can slow the thawing of frozen mourning.

Most survivors of low childhood nurturance grew up among toxic family relationships that *unintentionally* promoted major fears, shame, guilts, and anxieties. As recovering adults, we often have to learn "from the bottom up" how to choose and nurture wholistically healthy relationships—i.e. ones which promote mutual respect, satisfaction, safety, trust, and growth. A special category of this is unlearning the toxic parenting values and reflexes we were raised with, keeping the good traits of our caregivers, and evolving and practicing new concepts of high-nurturance caregiving. These are often as alien as learning to speak fluent Norwegian or Swahili.

What to Expect from Recovery

Replacing false-self dominance with Self-led inner harmony is an evolving, organic process. This transformation develops unevenly, at it's own pace. Like growing trust, love, and a healthy fetus, recovery can't be rushed. Like most natural processes, making these second-order (core attitude) changes can be loosely divided into early, middle, and late phases. There is no real "end" to the process.

To give you a sense of this, here's a general profile of the inner-family recovery stages that I've seen typical clients experience . . .

Early Phase

- Accumulate enough pain, weariness, hopelessness, and despair to "hit the wall," and accept that core life changes *now* are essential and unavoidable. This often occurs in early middle age, sometimes triggered by a divorce, death, addiction, or a child's pain.

- Discover the inner-family concept, and have some alarmed Guardians reject it as "stupid," "ridiculous," "too weird," "dangerous New Age silliness," or "for other people"; *or* . . .

- Start exploring and experimenting slowly, skeptically, and intellectually; *or* . . .

- Start quickly, with intuitive complete acceptance of your conflicted inner crew, *or* . . .

- Start somewhere in between.

A few women or men with overly "male brains" (see *Brain Sex*, p. 371) may not get into parts work because they're neurologically too logical and intellectual to feel or sense their parts' communications and reactions. Other forms of personal-growth work can be effective for them.

Many recovers have early-phase "false starts," like trial attempts to quit smoking. Each one contributes to getting ready to heal, for "failure" (to change) builds weariness, hopelessness, frustration, anxiety, and self-disgust. These combine to build motivation to break through the fears, and commit to Self-motivated second-order changes.

Most true recoverers take 20 to 40+ years to move through this phase.

Middle-phase Recovery

Highlights . . .

"Catch on," and put moderate to intense energy into exploring and meeting your inner family. Begin to experience individual subselves and/or voices (i.e. parts) as *real*. Start to "see" and intuit the personal implications and possibilities of this work. Tell other people of the concept, and get various reactions;

At this point, some people dominated by *People-Pleaser* and *Catastrophizer* parts will stop their inner-family work because of painful social disbelief or disapproval. Others continue privately—perhaps with some parts' added anxiety, guilt, and shame. Self-focused ("centered") people feel far less of these;

One or more "AHA!" or "WOW!" experiences occur along the early way. In them, people experience clear physical, emotional, and/or behavioral changes unmistakably related to their parts work. Ambivalence shrinks or vanishes. Inner-family enthusiasm may spurt, and then settle back. People at this stage may try enthusiastically "selling" others on inner family work, and learn to be selective about this;

Experience and skill grows with inner-family communications, re-doing, rescuing, conflict resolution, and real-time awareness of blended vs. non-blended Self-states ("Man, I'm really split (blended) now. Let me find out who's taken me over . . . "). Initial enthusiasm and wonder mellow, and the work becomes more methodical and "long-distance." Expectations become increasingly realistic. Patience, self-awareness, and compassion for early caregivers, self, and other wounded people grow.

Depending on their goals and experience, recoverers may elect (i.e. their Self suggests) other forms of therapy instead of, or along with, parts work. These might include massage or group therapy, art or movement therapy, chiropractic treatments, temporary medications, changing or joining a high-nurturance (p. 257) church, and attending a 12-step or other type of recovery-support group.

The typical middle-phase of recovery continues with . . .

False-self dominance recedes, as measured by shrinking symptoms of the six inner wounds. That yields increasing periods of inner calm, balance, clarity, and productive serenity. People burdened by co-dependence (relationship addiction) become more equally self-and-other focused, *without crippling guilt and anxiety*. "Narcissistic" ("self-centered") recoverers become genuinely more empathic and aware of other people. Habitual self-abuse and neglect, and automatic blending, become conscious—and diminish noticeably. Physical and emotional symptoms related to these may decrease. Calm, natural assertiveness, living in the present, lightness, and humor grows unevenly, with some temporary relapses to "the old ways."

As your Self becomes more internally trusted and influential, you may evolve calm vocal or written confrontations with people whose actions were traumatic recently or earlier in life. The outcome of such events is (usually) a marked release of old resentments, guilts, and frustrations, and an increasing focus on the present, vs. obsessing about (or denying) the past. Genuine *forgiveness* of self and others grows. Some of these relationships improve, and others decline. Ripples from these confrontations may extend to other similar relationships.

Other people may comment on "The new you," "Something's different about you," or question "What's gotten into you?" Their responses strengthen your trust that you really *are* recovering! Patterns of impulsive conflicts or emotional outbursts with—or avoidance of—others, shift. Sleep, eating, worship, meditation, breathing, and/or dream patterns may change subtly or obviously. Styles of grooming, clothing, and housekeeping may relax or shift (recovery slogan: "A perfectly clean house indicates a disabled Self.")

Eventually, inner-family change slows, and parts-work integrates comfortably into a larger personal-growth process. Parts-work habits, rituals, and reflexes develop, lessening the need for conscious evaluations and decisions. Language may shift—e.g. "we" (subselves) may increase, and "I" decrease, or becomes more selective, because "Self" takes on new meaning. Inner-family terminology weaves naturally into normal thinking and conversation ("I took several excited parts with me on vacation, and left my anxious ones at home.")

For most (all?) true recoverers, spirituality deepens—promoting escalating inner harmony and serenity. Conception of, and faith in, a *real*, benign, accessible Higher Power grows. Some recoverers seek church for the first time, return to prayer and/or church, or change to a high-nurturance congregation that is more supportive of real wholistic recovery.

Recoverers' human relationships alter gradually or suddenly, as they meet others who share their interest in, or are powerfully threatened by, recovery work. Informal or formal parts-work support groups may form for a while.

Key relationships often become more or less stressful, as awareness of the complex interplay between "my parts and yours" grows. (See Stone and Winkleman's *"Embracing Each Other."*) Key relationships often improve if (significantly-wounded) partners are Self-motivated (vs. "required") to develop their own recovery. Family relationships can be enhanced, if kids are encouraged to meet their inner families, and relatives become comfortable talking about everyone's parts.

All these shifts combine to promote well-deliberated changes in dwelling, geography, employer or occupation, church, social circle, and daily priorities and time management. All such changes result in gradually raising the nurturance levels of your inner and outer environments. As this happens, the pace of your recovery generally accelerates, with intervals of uncertainty and change-related anxiety. Paradoxically, your life-pace is likely to slow down across this multi-year middle recovery phase.

Late-phase Recovery

People pause or end parts-work at any point along their recovery path. If they work to "completion" (a relative term), some typical occurrences are:

If you've been using a professional inner-family or recovery guide or coach, you'll eventually "feel right" about phasing them out, and continuing your healing work alone or with someone else. You may return for a brush-up or consultation on special situations, or just to exchange pleasure in reporting recovery progress. You may or may not refer special others to your coach or guide.

Your recovery work becomes reflexive and often unconscious, like tying shoelaces. It becomes integrated into normal living patterns, and dwindles as a discrete activity. Recovery veterans become selective teachers and facilitators for others who are ready to explore harmonizing their inner families—including kids.

Conscious mental focus on recovery-related events and goals fades, and is replaced by a gradually increasing "attitude of gratitude." Clear real-time awareness of your internal and external processes becomes second nature, and empathy usually grows for other people's processes. You come to prefer and guard a high-nurturance lifestyle, and promote it for interested others, without becoming a zealot or bigot about it.

Some recoverers become seriously interested in identifying and *living* their true life purpose. That usually presents minor and major risks, changes, uncertainties, "failures," and adventures. The end result can be inexpressible satisfaction and joy, as Earthly death approaches. You may feel serenely "I lived most of my unique human potential, and I gave what I was created to give to the world, in a way that deeply pleases me." What would you most like to think and feel as you approach your death?

If your present lifestyle continues, how likely is it that you'll feel some version of this?

How Long Does Recovery Take?

Early in her parts work, one middle-aged client's young subself kept asking us anxiously "How long will this (therapy) take?" She was frustrated by my saying "Sounds like you'd feel much better knowing you'd be done with this work by a certain time. All I can say is 'it takes as long as it takes.'" Two years later, we both smiled affectionately as we recalled that *Anxious Girl*. Feeling far safer, she had stopped asking, months before.

Generally, the lower your childhood family nurturance, the greater your false-self dominance and chaos, and the longer it will take to replace your mix of the six wounds with Self-led inner harmony.

A key variable is how motivated and successful you are in at least stabilizing (vs. solving) current external stressors like kids, work, money, relationships, and health. Until your outer life is consistently calm "enough," it's hard to find time and opportunity to get quiet, and do meaningful inner focusing, calming, learning, and healing. Growth towards inner and outer harmony seems to be interrelated, and happen in small, irManager steps that include temporary relapses and setbacks.

A related recovery-time factor is the nurturance level of your present home and workplace. Most wounded adults and kids seek—and even *create*—low-nurturance environments at home or work unconsciously, because they're *familiar*. Obviously this isn't about "logic." It is testimony to the narrow vision and ignorance of our governing young and Guardian subselves. So if you live, work, or study among people who will shun, ridicule (shame), or ignore you, your overall recovery process will take significantly longer than if your human environment accepts and appreciates you, and encourages your striving to make second-order (core attitude) changes. I believe our American social norm now is low-nurturance groups. What do you think?

Use the 11 worksheets in Part 3 to help you assess the nurturance level of your home, family, and work environments. High-nurturance equals "pro-recovery." Stay clear that this assessment is not about *blaming* other people. It's about freeing yourself from anxiety, blame, guilt, and shame, toward achieving your life's purpose and helping others do the same.

Another major influence on how long recovery "takes" is how soon you can take full, unambivalent responsibility and authority for the quality of your own life. As long as you ignore your life ("I only live for my kids"), blame or dwell on others, or look to others to "fix" (your life)—your recovery will stall or move glacially. These behaviors usually signal that protective Guardians and reactive inner kids are disabling your Self, and running your life.

A final timing factor is how soon, and how genuinely, your inner-family members acknowledge that you (all) cannot recover alone. One of the biggest milestones in true recovery is the moment your most skeptical, independent subselves say, "I surrender" the fierce need to *control* inner and outer events and beings. You can do forms of inner-family work without totally accepting a benign Higher power, but their results and scope will be limited and may be temporary.

This (distrust + fear) factor alone blocks millions of suffers from even preliminary recovery from an addiction—because they resist or spurn (i.e. are frightened of and misinformed about) "that 12-step religion junk," or "that namby-pamby b.s. about a loving God." Other millions of holier-than-thou and falsely pious (wounded), "fundamentalist" worshippers are trapped in a self-amplifying form of toxic religious delusion based on denied fear, shame, and secular power.

"God" takes many forms and has many prophets. Accepting the possibility or certainty of a Power greater than ourselves who can help us *if invited to*, seems essential to true long-term recovery from false-self dominance. If you're skeptical or blocked on this acceptance—try interviewing the "voices" inside like a reporter. Learn what such faith in an unconditionally nurturing Higher Power would mean. What are those protective parts afraid of—*really*? I write this as an ex-atheist, raised in a home with no Higher Power or spiritual focus, conversation, inquiry, or reverence. My parents unwittingly passed on the spiritual neglect that they were raised with.

Notice that "take full responsibility for your own life and healing" implies that using "Holy Books" like the Bible, Torah, Talmud, Bhagavad-Gita, or Koran as the ultimate authority on how you and others conduct your lives is giving responsibility to the ancient authors of those (useful) books, and those who promote them. Many recoverers discover that clear, meaningful, loving guidance from their Higher Power comes from within—*right now*, not from ink on a page or someone else's interpretation of the ink.

Notice with interest what your inner crew wants you to know now . . .

So there are a number of identifiable factors that will combine with your unique history and personality to determine "How long will recovery take?" In general, expect small benefits to start happening within several weeks or months of this leg of your journey. These benefits can manifest as, for example, a repeated conflictual communication with an adult or child "turning out a little differently, this time." Rewards come at every step, if you're calm and aware enough to perceive them . . .

Measuring Your Progress

Decide if recovery is working for you by assessing for desired changes in the quality of your inner and outer lives and relationships.

The greatest measure of recovery effectiveness, I believe, is in how often you experience the symptoms that your unblended true Self is leading your inner family well—specially in conflicts and crises. Other recovery-researchers validate my experience: true recovery symptoms are unmistakable periods of clarity, groundedness, "lightness," relaxed energy, calmness, optimism, purpose, focus, gratitude, and peacefulness—with unexpected blooms of *joy*. Other symptoms include . . .

- A growing, nurturing (vs. fear and shame-based) spiritual faith and personal serenity.

- Growing self-awareness, clearer identity and personal boundaries, and increasing self confidence.

- A growing clarity on your special talents, traits, limits, life purpose, and related priorities.

- An increasingly automatic ability to make healthy, win-win short-range and long-range decisions, and to calmly *trust* these decisions, despite uncertainties.

- An increasing number of high-nurturance relationships, work and social settings, and activities, and fewer toxic ones.

- An increasing comfort in choosing responsibility for your own life, and compassionately and firmly giving others responsibility for theirs i.e. less "enabling" of other wounded people.

- A clear decrease in ambivalence, uncertainty, confusion, and self doubt—and a related decrease in sending other people "double (mixed) messages."

- A growing ability to laugh appreciatively (vs. derisively) at personal, human, and Nature's foibles, sillinesses, and ironies.

- A growing acceptance of personal Rights (p. 350), and of other people's equal rights—and responsibilities. A symptom of this is increasingly effective respectful assertiveness (asking for what you need, without guilt or anxiety), and win-win problem solving. This leads to an increased willingness to admit and accept conflict, and to negotiate respectfully, vs. fighting or avoiding.

- More signs of true recovery . . .

- A growing tolerance for ambivalent situations, a decrease in black/white rigidities, and a decreasing need to *control* feelings, relationships, and events—without major anxiety.

- A growing ability to feel and exchange true Self-love and mutual love every day. This includes a growing empathy and compassion for others (like ex mates and parents) who are unaware of being controlled by a false self.

- Spontaneous, genuine forgiveness of Self and others, for past "mistakes" and betrayals.

- Notable improvements in eating (diet), sleeping, and exercising habits, and seeking appropriate health care.

- Increasing periods of genuine centeredness, balance, happiness, hope, productivity, contentment, energized peace, clarity, and firmness of beliefs and decisions; and . . .

- An increasing deep attitude of gratitude for recovery, human and spiritual support, and the beauty, wonder, richness, and opportunities of daily life on Earth.

Sometimes as a wounded person breaks old protective denials and starts to recover, other family members "catch it," and start to heal also. When committed primary partners *both* need and choose personal recovery, their relationship can grow exceptionally rich and strong.

Other times, kin and/or partners (i.e. their false selves) are unconsciously threatened by the recoverer's changes, and their protective denials and defenses increase. This eventually requires the recovering person to choose between continuing to heal, or valuing key others' insecurities as being more important. This enables (unconsciously encourages and promotes) others' denials, and is usually a symptom of pseudo recovery.

Recap

You've just read an overview of recovery from significant false-self dominance, and an outline of one way to recover: Self-directed *inner*-family ("parts") work. This conceptual framework proposes that wholistic recovery has three parts:

- Years of accumulated pain from false-self wounds, leading to . . .

- Some form of "hitting bottom," or "hitting the wall," which often happens in middle age. That leads to . . .

- More years of gradual awakening to who's *really* been running your life, and the impacts of that, and then intentionally discovering how to free your Self from protective custody.

Pause and reflect. Breathe easily, from your belly. Can you name the characteristic emotions and sensations that signal that your Self is leading your inner family? Is that how you feel right now? Relax, and notice with non-critical interest what your inner voices are saying now. Do you know who's "speaking"?

What have you learned here? Can you now clearly describe to another person . . .

- _ "low family nurturance?"
- _ "subselves," or "personality parts"?
- _ "inner family" and _ "the three or four functional groups of subselves"?
- _ your _ "true Self" and _ "false self"?
- _ typical symptoms a true Self is in charge?
- _ the _ six false-self wounds, and how those affect _ courtship, _ marriage, and _child-raising?

- If you've already used the 11 worksheets in Part 3, what have you concluded?

  - _ I feel confident that my true Self is making my key life decisions often enough, and I don't really need some form of personal recovery now; or . . .
  - _ I am often dominated by a false-self team of subselves. I need some sort of recovery program now; or . . .
  - _ My partner is (not) significantly wounded, and I (don't) need to alert her/him to the ideas in this book.
  - _ The nurturance level in our _ home and _ family is (not) high enough for me, and I (don't) need to raise it now.
  - _ I (don't) need to help a dependent child in my life to empower her/ his true Self.
  - _ If you're a human-service professional: I (don't) need to change something in my _ work or _ work setting to help my students / clients / patients / employer / colleagues become more aware of their false selves, and to empower their true Selves.
  - _ I'm unclear on one or more of these things, and I need further reflection and study, and/or _ help from a qualified professional guide.

- If you haven't yet worked with the 11 worksheets in Part 3, is there anything (or anyone) that's hindering you from doing so now?

If you feel done enough with these, and you haven't read chapter 11 recently, I'll meet you there to finish our part of the journey together.

PART 3

Wound-assessment Worksheets

This section provides 11 ways to help you judge who's *really* running your life—your Self, or some false-self personality parts. These worksheets are synthesized from the observations of well over a dozen recovery authorities. Some of their published works are listed in Selected Readings (p. 369).

- **Worksheet A)** summarizes 28 high-nurturance family (or group) traits. Early false-self formation seems to occur if too many of these are absent from a child's environment too often. Such factors also strongly influence whether an adult's true Self leads their inner family, or other subselves do.

- **Worksheet B)** gives 42 common behavioral traits of (unrecovering) survivors of low-childhood nurturance. The media calls such survivors "Adult Children" of toxic parenting or family "dysfunction."

- **Worksheet C)** provides a way to check your family tree for symptoms of inherited low psychological-spiritual nurturance.

- **Worksheet D)** proposes a rough way to estimate the nurturance level (low to high) of a human group by typical behaviors and attitudes of its members. The group can be a classroom, committee, company, team, troupe, congregation, a home, or a whole family. Low nurturance suggests the group's leader/s are significantly ruled by a false self.

- **Worksheets E-J)** give common behavioral symptoms of each of the six false-self wounds; and . . .

- **Worksheet K)** is a reprint of the two-part Codependents Anonymous (CoDA) checklist of traits of co-dependence—a form of relationship addiction common to *many* psychologically wounded people.

Chapter 10) Evaluating Your Results

Chapter 11) Summing Up, and Next Steps

Perspective on Assessing for Inner Wounds

These assessment tools have evolved over 17 years of clinical study and practice. Worksheets A, B, and K are shaped by the work of other respected professionals, and the others are largely original—influenced by scores of teachers. These worksheets are not formally research-validated, so view them as suggestive, vs. "proof," of low family nurturance and significant false-self dominance.

All 11 worksheets are shaped by my clinical work with over 1,000 typical Midwestern-U.S. divorced and stepfamily co-parents since 1981. These good people were either considering re/marriage and seeking stepfamily education, and/or sought clinical help with divorced-family and stepfamily relationship problems. A number of them wanted help in wholistic recovery from addictions, major trauma, and loss.

I've been in self-motivated recovery from major inner wounds since 1985. My experience and study in this life-changing process has profoundly influenced the design of this book and these worksheets. In the scores of lay and clinical authors I've (compulsively) read to understand why I—and so many of us—have major intimacy, health, and relationship problems, I've rarely seen other authors acknowledge their own personal recovery experience in their writings. I believe that's partly from normal denial, partly from fear of public discounting and rejection, and partly from the understandable *surface* wish for privacy and dignity.

Often, underneath those lurks the most insidious trait of significant false-self dominance—primal *shame*. This manifests as a mix of semi-conscious thoughts and feelings that yields a *certainty* that "I am a worthless, unlovable, damaged, inept, despicable person."

I encourage you to wait until after doing all 11 assessments before making any solid judgments. The protective subselves that result from low childhood nurturance are experts at well-meant distortion and denial. So these worksheets look for the *effects* of personality anarchy because it's difficult to measure a false self's dominance directly. All the worksheets together provide many composite clues. Suggestions about evaluating your results follow the last worksheet in chapter 10.

How to Best Use These Worksheets

Mark this page with a paperclip. Rereading these suggestions before doing each worksheet will help you get the most from them.

Adopt and keep a long-range mental outlook. Assessing yourself for false-self wounds and acting on the results aims to raise the quality of the rest of your life.

Coach your parts to choose attitudes of curiosity and cautious optimism—a "glass half full" mindset. Any outcome of your assessment here is positive: either you're not significantly wounded, or if you are, discovering that enables you to heal it, over time. The alternative is unawareness, a truncated life of significant pain or numbness, illness/ es, and unintentionally passing the six psycho-spiritual wounds on to dependent kids. As you prepare to die, you will surely encounter your own judgment about how well you chose to live your life . . .

Pick distraction-free times and places in which to fill these worksheets out. Distractions include weariness, worry, hunger, physical discomfort, noise, temperature, movement, lights, etc. Overlooking or ignoring this suggests false-self dominance.

Rest and meditate between each worksheet. Consider journaling your thoughts and feelings as you go—your awarenesses may be just as important as what the worksheets indicate. Slower is better, despite our (low nurturance) media's relentlessly glorifying *speed.*

Re-word or modify any items, if that makes them more useful to you. Use colored markers, underline, and jot notes or symbols like *, !, and ? as you go. Make these sheets *work* for you!

Allocate plenty of time to do each worksheet—e.g. 30" or more. If other things distract you, do the worksheet another time. You have the rest of your life to "finish" them.

Copy each worksheet before you use it. That allows you to do another version in the future to track your changes, and/or to give copies to people you care about. See the Internet versions at **http://sfhelp.org/gwc/links1.htm**

First, scan all the worksheets and the "scoring" suggestions at the end of this section, to get an overall sense of how these tools fit together. If an impatient, curious, or anxious subself is urging you to do these worksheets before reading Part 1 of this book, I encourage you to affectionately say "no." Your attitude, awareness, and motivation toward honest assessments here will probably improve, if you read Part 1 first. You'll get better results, long term. If you disagree, your false self is probably "driving your bus."

Stay aware as you go: *these worksheets are not about blaming you and/or your caregivers*. They're also not about you or someone else being "sick" or "crazy." They are about seeing what's *real*, improving your life satisfaction and wholistic health, and raising the nurturance level of your family and other groups you contribute to.

Pause and reflect—what are your subselves "saying" now? What does that mean to you? "I don't know" is OK!

A) 28 TRAITS OF HIGH-NURTURANCE FAMILIES

A FRAMEWORK TO SHOOT FOR

W as the family you grew up in psychologically and spiritually *healthy*? Did it work (function) well enough? How can you assess the nurturance level of your birthfamily or your current one? *Nurturance* is the process of respectfully and lovingly filling key personal and mutual needs. Let's define a high-nurturance (*functional*) family as one whose leaders consistently and effectively . . .

• Fill the physical, intellectual, spiritual, and emotional needs of all it's members—including their own—*equally*; and . . .

• Nurture and strengthen their family's social and ecological environments, over time, vs. deplete or stress them.

How does this compare to your definition of a wholistically healthy family?

People who grew up in childhoods with too little psycho-spiritual nurturance often don't *know* what a high-nurturance family or group looks, feels, and sounds like. To us, low family nurturance is normal and unremarkable. If we're asked, "Was your birthfamily (or your childhood) pretty healthy?" we'll say sincerely "Sure!"—when it *wasn't* wholistically healthy at all.

Social-science researchers and clinicians suggest that high-nurturance families and other groups (schools, churches, teams, and committees) have many of the traits below. Did—or does—*yours?* Premise: leaders of high-nurturance groups are seldom wounded, and usually guided by their true Selves.

Prepare

- *Review* the suggestions starting on p. 255. Then . . .

- Read a brief summary that validates the premise behind this worksheet (and book) at **http://sfhelp.org/parent/news/ucla.htm**

- *Decide who to assess*: your birthfamily; past marriage family; single-parent family; present home or extended family; or a class or school, a work group, a neighborhood, an agency, or a church community. If you're rating a group, substitute *group* for *family* or *household*, and *leaders* for *co-parents* below.

- *Decide* specifically *who comprises this family or group*: just those people who live/d or work/ed together, or emotionally-important *absent* members, too—including living and dead grandparents and/or other relatives or special friends.

- *Pick a time frame*: now, or a specific past time—e.g. your childhood at a certain age.

- *Check to see if your Self is in charge, right now.* If you're unsure, see p. 67.

- One at a time, thoughtfully *note your target family's or group's traits*. Check each item below that you feel fits well enough. If you're unsure about an item, use "?", or come back to it. Decide whether it's OK to check a trait if the group doesn't meet all the sub-criteria in that trait.

- If some of these items don't lend themselves to a clear *yes* or *no* answer, consider using a number to indicate the degree of trueness (1) or falseness (5).

Again: this exploration is not about *blaming* anyone. It is about breaking protective old denials, and uncovering whether you and/or another have significant false-self wounds. Note the Web version of this worksheet at http://sfhelp.org/gwc/2_famtraits.htm. **As I start**, I'm aware of . . .

I believe that . . .

- As far as psychological and spiritual nurturance, my childhood family was (check one):

  _ *very un*healthy _ fairly *un*healthy _ neither _ fairly healthy _ *very* healthy.

- This had _ growthful _ hurtful _ no significant effects on me as a wholistically-healthy person. Option: very hurtful = 1, very growthful = 10.

- As individuals, the odds (0% to 100%) that my main childhood caregiver/s were significantly wounded, psychologically, are:

- (person 1) _____, (person 2) _____, (person 3) _____, and (person 4) _____

Reduce distractions, give yourself at least 30 minutes, *take your time* with each item, and breathe comfortably as you go. Option: journal your thoughts and feelings as you reflect, noticing which of these items evoke the strongest emotional responses. There are no right or wrong answers! For each item, imagine describing the key reasons for your assessment to an interested stranger. Try to avoid impulsive "snap" answers, and trust your first solid responses—even if you don't like them! Decide how you feel about checking an item if you can't confidently check all sub-parts of it as "true."

How you *feel* as you do this assessment can be as important a source of awareness as what you write.

28 Traits of a High-nurturance Family or Group

_ 1) *All* members feel basically good about _ each other _ *and themselves*—i.e. they have high self esteem, most of the time.

_ 2) *All* members usually feel free to express their _ thoughts and _ emotions spontaneously, without fear of being ridiculed, ignored, attacked, or shunned. This includes _ feeling safe to disagree openly with the leader/s and other members of the family or group.

_ **3)** The balance between individuals', kids', adult couple's, and family activities is generally satisfying enough to all members.

_ **4)** Family problems are discussed _ *honestly* and _ *promptly*, and _ are usually *resolved*, rather than being denied, ignored, minimized, deferred, or endlessly rehashed.

_ **5)** The resident co-parent/s are _ clearly and _ consistently in charge of the home, without dependent kids feeling _ smothered, _ over-controlled, _ ignored, or _ afraid to be themselves—i.e. without having to be "hyper alert." _ *Everyone is clear on who is running the family, and _ everyone usually trusts the leaders' decisions,* even if they don't like them.

_ **6)** *Each* family member has _ good friends, and _ Manager activities outside the family, vs. being socially isolated. _ Kids' and _ adults' friends move freely in and out of the family's home, feeling welcomed, valued, and respected by all members—without violating either family or individual privacies and boundaries.

_ **7)** *All* family members usually feel _ valued, _ *listened* to (vs. agreed with), and _ *respected* by each other, _ *even during conflicts and disagreements.*

_ **8)** Children basically *trust* their primary adult caregiver/s to care consistently and adequately for their major fears and hurts. Kids trust their adults to _ guide and _ protect them, vs. minimizing, ignoring, or even causing shame, guilts, fears, and hurts.

_ **9)** Each member child and adult feels _ safe, _ appreciated, _ positively valued, _ supported, and _ respected (i.e. loved) *unconditionally*, most of the time; (take your time with this one!)

_ **10)** Children feel that _ their caregivers and _ each other are basically _ happy and _ secure *enough*, regardless of current situational health, work, financial, security, or relationship problems.

_ **11)** Household rules and consequences are usually pretty _ clear, _ appropriate, and _ consistent for everybody. Child discipline is _ "firmly flexible," and is usually enforced _ consistently, _ promptly, and _ lovingly. Co-parents are generally united in _ setting limits and _ providing consequences.

_ **12)** Adult caregiver/s are _ often open to hearing and considering constructive feedback and new ideas about family functioning, from all family members and knowledgeable others. Even when feeling criticized, leader/s _ are usually able to *listen* to the upset person/s, vs. attack, defend, explain, pull rank, or leave.

_ **13)** Spontaneous (vs. dutiful or manipulative), genuine praise, appreciation, and encouragement are exchanged often _ among *all* family members, and _ with others.

_ **14)** Family members feel comfortable _ interchanging roles, within their abilities. For example, the kids may plan and make some meals, or various people may do the laundry (without excessive griping!), depending on schedules and other responsibilities. _ A basic feeling of spontaneous teamwork and co-operation exists, most of the time.

_ **15)** Individual and family humor, play, and kidding are _ spontaneous, _ have no big hidden agendas or double messages, and _ usually feel balanced enough with serious times.

_ **16)** *All* _ adults and _ children tend to take _ responsibility and _ credit for their own choices and actions, vs. blaming, mind-reading, denying, feeling victimized by, or constantly "rescuing" each other.

_ **17)** The welfare and activities of each person in the family are usually of real interest and concern to other members. *All* members are regularly open to both _ discussion and _ confrontation, without smothering ("enmeshment"). Family _ integrity and _ loyalty are highly valued by everyone, and _ all members spontaneously feel family *commitment* and *pride* (vs. shame or indifference), _ without being obsessed by them.

_ **18)** Interpersonal conflict and confrontations happen _ spontaneously and real-time. They're generally _ supportive, _ mutually *respectful*, and _ constructive, rather than blameful, shaming, belittling, or manipulative. _ Minor kids can *safely* confront the adults, as well as the reverse.

Such confrontations often result in _ empathic listening, _ respectful assertion, and _ effective problem solving, vs. justifying, arguing, blaming, counterattacking, condescending, withdrawing, or ignoring.

_ **19)** There are no major taboos or family secrets (e.g. addictions, miscarriages, abortions, desertions, job losses, illnesses, affairs), either _ about the current family, or _ other relatives or ancestors. *There is no rule that says "we don't talk openly about that in our family."*

_ **20)** All members—specially kids—are encouraged to _ acknowledge and _ grieve their physical and invisible losses, without impatience, shame, guilt, or anxiety. Members are consistently comfortable with _ talking honestly about their losses; _ openly crying when sad or joyous; _ sharing despair, when felt; and _ showing anger (within appropriate limits) at each other, other people, or "life."

_ **21)** The adult caregiver/s _ *value* and _ *actively promote* spiritual awareness and growth in _ themselves, _ each other, and _ younger members. Shared and private _ spiritual and _ religious activities consistently yield *warmth, peace, hope, strength, serenity, and closeness*, vs. shame, guilt, anxiety, dread, cynicism, and/or confusion. _ Members are respectfully encouraged to make their own decisions about spirituality and worship, vs. having to "do it *our* way."

_ **22)** Family members _ spontaneously express their love and affection physically, _ within appropriate sexual limits. Adult sexuality is _ private, and _ mutually enjoyed. The caregivers consistently and sensitively guide kids to _ understand, _ accept, and _ appreciate their own _ gender, _ sensuality, and _ sexuality—within age, family, and societal norms—*without excess _ excitement, _ shame, or _ guilt.* All family members usually feel comfortable *enough* in _ discussing sexual issues with each other, and _ can comfortably assert personal limits and needs about doing this, without major anxiety, shame, or guilt.

_ **23)** The adults prize and maintain their _ identities and _ emotional boundaries as _ individuals, and as a _ committed, loving couple. They consciously try to balance time with the kids, with each other, with friends, their job/s, and by themselves. Adults consistently take their _ relationship and _ co-parenting as separate, high-priority concerns—each warranting significant time, thought, integrity, and commitment.

_ **24)** *All* members typically _ disclose most mistakes, disappointments, and "failures" to each other _ without undue anxiety, shame, guilt, or embarrassment. Most mistakes _ are viewed as chances to *learn*, rather than as personal flaws. _ Adults and _ kids can often laugh at themselves appreciatively, vs. with excess guilt, shame, or embarrassment

_ **25)** *All* family members are generally positive and optimistic: each person usually feels that . . .

_ Most people are good and trustworthy, and mean well;

_ Life problems may usually be resolved with time and patient, honest effort; and . . .

_ It's usually OK to ask for help from others and a Higher Power, without guilt, shame, or fear;

_ **26)** No one in the family is probably or surely addicted to, or regularly over-uses:

_ TV, sports, computers, or other hobby

_ Real or fantasy (e.g. media) sex

_ Special relationship/s

_ Fitness, exercise, and health

_ Work, studying, or "busy-ness"

_ Rage, excitement, or another emotion

_ Food (e.g. sugar and fat) and/or eating

_ Alcohol, and/or illegal drugs

_ Caffeine and/or nicotine

_ Conflict or excitement

_ God, worship, or spirituality

_ Cleaning and neatness

_ Power and control

_ "Fairness," "justice," or a social cause

_ Acquiring, spending, counting, gambling, investing, or saving money, or other assets

_ **27)** The family leaders agree *enough* on a _ clear and _ consistent set of _ realistic goals for the group, and _ willingly share responsibility for achieving them, over time.

_ **28)** Each co-parenting adult's own birthfamily had most (e.g. over 20) of the items above.

*   *   *

Note without judgment how you *feel* right now. "Nothing" is a feeling: "numbness." What do your feelings mean to you?

Options

Only a rare family or group would have all 28 of these traits all the time. Can you think of one who does? Recall: the premise here is that more of these traits a family or other group has consistently, the higher its nurturance level. Conversely, the fewer of these characteristics you feel exist in a family, classroom, church, or work group, the lower the wholistic nurturance the group provides its members—i.e. the harder it is for some or most members to get their core emotional, physical, spiritual, and mental needs met.

Many low-nurturance families may be described as *shame-based*, because most members unconsciously or secretly feel they're basically flawed, damaged, incompetent, worthless, unlovable, or "bad" people. Therefore, until committed to genuine (vs. pseudo) personal recovery, typical members will usually minimize or deny that their family had few of these high-nurturance traits. Knowledgeable friends or professionals would compassionately disagree.

Wait until you finish all these worksheets before deciding whether a false self significantly controls you or another person. Meanwhile, consider some key options:

If You Rated Your Childhood **Birthfamily**

- Note the specific strengths you checked, and decide whether you carried them forward into your marriage family (if any).

- Consider discussing your conclusions with any siblings, for validation and more perspective.

- Consider acknowledging the strengths you checked to your original caregiving adult/s, with *thanks*!

- Reflect on, and/or discuss with key other people, how the items you *didn't* check have affected _ you, _ your choice of

- mate/s, and your _ primary relationship and _ parenting successes.

If You Rated Your **Prior-marriage Family**

- Note all the strengths checked, and congratulate yourself and your former mate!

- Consider discussing the worksheet with your "ex" and/or (older) children for their input and mutual awarenesses.

- Consider the likely effects of those items you *didn't* check on your child/ren, and discuss this with relevant other people.

- Use the latter as guidelines in setting current parenting and therapy goals, to strengthen and heal your minor child/ren.

If You Rated Your **Present Family**

- Congratulate yourself, your partner, and any grandparenting adult/s on the high-nurturance traits you checked!

- Use unchecked traits as guidelines for revising family or parenting behaviors or priorities, or therapy goals, over time.

- Rate your and your partner's respective childhood families, compare and contrast, and discuss patterns and implications.

If You Rated Your Prior or Present **Romantic-partner's Family**

- If checks (strengths) outnumber blanks, appreciate those responsible. If blanks predominate . . .

- Reflect on why you chose this partner, and . . .

- Discuss this with knowledgeable and caring others, perhaps including a counselor, for added awareness. Be gentle with yourself, and discourage any critical or shaming inner voices!

* * *

Regardless of whom you assessed, you can increase your awareness and learnings by reviewing this worksheet and journaling *nonjudgmentally*. Write about, or tape record, your specific thoughts, images, memories, and feelings on each item. Remind yourself that *there is no right or wrong here*—just what's real now, and what (you perceived) happened. Note particularly any item that brings up strong feelings in you—i.e. activates certain subselves. Who are they, and why do they react like that?

If you have minor or grown children—how do you suppose they each would fill out this worksheet, if they understood the theme of each item well enough? What would they feel? How would you feel about showing this to them, or inviting them to fill out a copy and discussing the results with you?

Consider using some version of these 28 high-nurturance factors as input to creating a meaningful family or group *mission* statement, and co-parents' job descriptions.

As I finish this worksheet, I now believe that . . .

- As far as emotional and spiritual health, my birthfamily was (check one):
  _ *very un*healthy _ fairly *un*healthy _ neither _ fairly healthy _ *very* healthy.

- This had _ growthful / _ hurtful / _ no significant effects on me as a wholistically healthy person. Option: "1" = very hurtful, "10" = very growthful.

- As individuals, the odds (0% to 100%) that my main childhood caregiver/s were significantly wounded, psychologically, are . . .
  (person 1) _____, (person 2) _____, (person 3) _____, and (person 4) _____.

Thoughts / Awarenesses . . .

B) COMMON TRAITS OF SIGNIFICANTLY-WOUNDED PEOPLE

P remise: survivors of low childhood nurturance display predictable, observable behaviors that better-nurtured people do not.

Suggestions

- Refresh yourself on the worksheet guidelines on p. 255.

- Pick a present or absent adult or child you wish to assess for significant inner wounds. If it's useful, pick a time frame—now or other. Then take your time, and thoughtfully answer each item.

- Consider journaling as you do this worksheet. Your thoughts and feelings as you do this are as valuable as what you write.

- This is about discovery and recovery, not *blame*. These traits are not good or bad, they're *symptoms* of false-self dominance.

- Hold your final conclusions until finishing all the worksheets.

- Check each sub-trait before deciding to whether check the whole trait. Option: use 1 to 5, instead of check or blank.

See the Web version of this checklist at **http://sfhelp.org/gwc/1_gwctraits.htm**.

* * *

_ 1) S/He _ usually thinks in black/white ("bi-polar") terms: s/he sees things as either right or wrong, good or bad, relevant or not, logical or "stupid"—not somewhere between, or a mix. S/He's _ mildly to very uneasy with ambivalence, vagueness, or uncertainty.

_ 2) S/He is _ often a (compulsive) perfectionist: achieving perfection is just "normal" (vs. special); S/He _ has trouble enjoying her/his own achievements, and _ is often uncomfortable accepting merited appreciation and praise.

_ 3) S/He is _ often rigid and inflexible. S/He _ thinks obsessively, and/or _ acts compulsively, even if personally unpleasant, unnecessary, or unhealthy; or _ s/he is often overly passive, cautious, and compliant, fearing to take personal, social, and occupational initiatives.

_ 4) S/He is usually _ serious, intellectual, and analytic, wanting to understand life and situations, and _ know in great detail why things are as they are. S/He _ may be interested in psychology, counseling, and/or study and discuss human behavior "endlessly."

_ 5) S/He is often _ confused, disorganized, overwhelmed, and "helpless," or s/he _ is fiercely independent, domineering, over-organized, and overcompetent. S/He _ depends excessively on, or _ stubbornly avoids, medical, psychological, social, and/or spiritual help.

_ 6) S/He is _ uncomfortable being silly, spontaneous, or child-like ("doesn't know how to play"), or s/he _ is usually silly, simplistic, superficial, and joking.

_ 7) S/He is either _ extremely responsible (over-willing to take charge, organize, and fix things, even if personally taxing); or s/he _ is frequently irresponsible and undependable; and probably _ denies, minimizes, or rationalizes (explains) doing either one.

_ 8) S/He often _ has trouble feeling and/or expressing strong emotions, and/or _ tolerating them in others—specially anger, hurt, fear, and sadness. S/He _ often feels "nothing," or s/he _ has frequent unpredictable or inappropriate outbursts of rage, sadness, weeping, "depression," or anxiety. S/He may _ never apologize, or _ apologizes "all the time."

_ **9)** S/He compulsively _ needs to control personal emotions, key relationships, and interpersonal situations. S/He is either _ overly aggressive, rigid, and domineering, *or* _ subtly, persistently manipulative—e.g. using guilt trips or a "helpless victim" stance, striving to "always" get her/his way. Where true, s/he probably _ denies, _minimizes (e.g. jokes about), or _ rationalizes this ("I have to, because . . . ").

_ **10)** S/He has _ significant memory gaps about early childhood years and events, and one or both parents. S/He _ knows little about one or both parents' childhood experiences and feelings, and finds that unimportant or unremarkable.

_ **11)** S/He's socially _ very shy *or* very adept, and _ has few or no real (intimate) friends. S/He has a history of relationship _ avoidances and/ or _ "failures," including divorce/s. S/He feels _ high discomfort with interpersonal commitment and/or intimacy, and _ consistently denies, minimizes, or rationalizes (intellectually explains) this.

_ **12)** S/He _ may be sexually dysfunctional—e.g. impotent, frigid, or compulsively avoids sexual contact; *or* _ s/he is harmfully seductive, voyeuristic, and/or promiscuous. S/He may be secretly uncomfortable with, or ashamed of, her or his _ gender, body (parts), and her or his _ sexual feelings, _ fantasies, and/or _ behavior.

_ **13)** S/He _ "never gets sick," *or* _ suffers chronic illnesses like migraines or other headaches, back, neck, or other muscle pain; insomnia or apnea; obesity; asthma; gastric, intestinal, or colon problems; anxiety attacks; phobias; allergies; or other emotional or physical maladies which may not respond to appropriate medications or therapies.

_ **14)** S/He is _ highly uncomfortable about revealing personal thoughts, feelings, and experiences (excessively distrustful), *or* s/he _ often discloses personal things inappropriately (insensitive, over-trustful).

_ **15)** S/He is _ uncomfortable giving, getting, and/or observing affectionate and appropriate touching and hugging ("stiff" or "cold"), and/or _ touches others dutifully, awkwardly, or inappropriately.

_ **16)** S/He _ often avoids personal conflicts with or between others, by changing or controlling the conversation, getting intensely angry, "collapsing," or withdrawing physically and/or emotionally ("numbing"); *or* s/he _ seems to often enjoy triggering or experiencing conflicts with or between others.

_ **17)** S/He is _ very reactive about—and/or _ is (or was) addicted to—one or more of these:

_ Alcohol in some form
_ Illegal ("hard") drugs
_ A special hobby
_ Sugar / fat
_ Another person
_ Food / dieting / nutrition
_ Work or "busy-ness"
_ Sex / masturbation / porn
_ Material possessions
_ Prescription drugs
_ Excitement / drama
_ Pain / death
_ Caffeine / nicotine
_ Cleaning / neatness
_ Health / exercising
_ "Justice" / "fairness
_ A social "cause"
_ Emotional "recovery"
_ God / worship / church / salvation / hell / Satan
_ Lying / secrecy / truth / honesty
_ Personal image / others' opinions
_ Money / wealth / saving / spending / gambling

_ **18)** S/He has _ children,_ relatives, and/or_ past or present partners, who _ excessively obsess about, or _ are or were addicted to, one or more of the above.

_ **19)** S/He has _ recurring depressions, apathy, and/or tiredness "for no reason." S/He may have _ periodic sleep disorders (e.g. insomnia) and/or _ nightmares.

_ **20)** S/He often feels vaguely "empty," "something's *missing* (in me)," or "I'm *different* (than other people) somehow . . . ," without knowing why.

_ **21)** S/He is _ fairly to very uncomfortable being alone; *or* s/he _ prefers solitude to an unusual degree, and _ seems socially isolated.

_ **22)** S/He _ has consistently low self esteem; Often harshly self-critical; _Discounts her/his own successes and/or merited praise; _Constantly apologetic or defensive; _Consistently avoids making or keeping solid eye contact with some or most men / women / authorities / people; S/He _ commonly uses "you" or "we" rather than "I."

_ 23) S/He _ often experiences "mind-racing" or "mind-churning": ceaseless "inner voices" (thought streams), which _ are frequently anxious, fearful, critical, argumentative, and/or chaotic.

_ 24) S/He is _ often hypervigilant: i.e. anxiously alert to the present and expected future actions of other people. S/He tends to _ assume others' (usually negative) beliefs or intentions, and _ often reacts to things that haven't happened yet as though they had.

_ 25) S/He often _ smiles and/or chuckles automatically and inappropriately when nervous, hurt, confused, scared, angry, or worried (i.e. often). If so, _ s/he is usually unaware of this habit, _can't explain it, and _ may minimize, intellectualize, defend, or joke about it to hide related anxiety.

_ 26) S/He _ often feels vaguely or clearly victimized by others or "fate"; _ regularly avoids taking responsibility for her or his own choices, and _ denies or _ endlessly rationalizes doing so—*or* s/he _ assumes *too much* responsibility, and _ blames herself / himself harshly (feels guilty) for things beyond her/his control.

_ 27) S/He is _ highly sensitive to real or imagined criticism from others, and _ unnecessarily rationalizes, explains, and defends her / his own actions and values. S/He is _ quick to blame others, *or* _ often empathizes with "the other guy's" situation and defers to them.

_ 28) S/He commonly _ fears, distrusts, is tense around, and/or argues with some authority figures. S/He either _ feels very anxious without clear instructions, *or* _ compulsively resists them, and acts independently.

_29) S/He often _ fears saying "no," and setting appropriate limits (boundaries) with others. S/He _ feels guilty about asserting her or his own _ needs, _ tolerances, and _ ideas; and may do so _ expecting others to discount them.

_ 30) S/He _ confuses pity with love, and/or _ associates love with pain. S/He _ usually focuses on others' needs first, and tends to _ rescue or "fix" them; or _ s/he is overconcerned with her or his own needs ("self centered"). S/He_ avoids intimacy, or _ cyclically seeks, then runs from it—i.e. has a history of "approach-avoid" relationships.

_ **31)** S/He tends to be "over-loyal"—i.e. _hangs on desperately to toxic relationships which regularly cause significant shame, fear, guilt, stress, and pain; S/He _ may repeatedly cycle between intense jealousy and guilt. _Major personal relationship-choices are often largely based on fears of criticism, "being wrong," rejection, and abandonment.

_ **32)** S/He _ feels bored, restless, or uneasy without current personal or environmental crisis, chaos, or excitement. At times _ s/he seems to seek or *make* crises, and _ denies, minimizes, jokes about, or rationalizes (justifies) this.

_ **33)** Typically s/he _ is passive and reacts to situations, *or* s/he _ is often self-harmfully impulsive, spontaneous, and proactive.

_ **34)** S/He often _ feels alone, disconnected, or lonely, even in a group or crowd. S/He _ rarely feels s/he really *belongs* anywhere, and may or may not disclose that to others.

_ **35)** S/He _ often seeks pleasure and gratification *now*, vs. later; S/He _ may defend or minimize this, _rationalize by saying "I can't help it," or _ minimize or deflect from it by joking.

_ **36)** S/He prefers to work independently (e.g. as a consultant, craftsperson, or entrepreneur) and/or in a solitary setting. S/He either _ changes jobs often, *or* _ stays at the same job for years. S/He _ works in a human-service occupation or avocation (nurse or doctor, teacher, counselor, lawyer, beautician, case worker, special ed teacher, clergyperson, nanny, day care worker, professional consultant, . . .)

_ **37)** S/He either _ rarely *or* _ frantically initiates social activities. S/He habitually _ avoids *or* _ compulsively seeks being the center of social or occupational attention.

_ **38)** S/He is frequently either _ self-centered, grandiose, and hyper health-conscious; *or* s/he is _ subtly or clearly self-abusive, self-deprecating, self-sabotaging, and/or self-neglectful (e.g. never seeing a doctor, dentist, gynecologist, or oculist).

_ **39)** S/He _ habitually withholds or shades the truth, or lies, to avoid expected criticism, rejection, or "hurting others." S/He _ denies doing so, and _ secretly feels righteous, or guilty and ashamed.

_ **40)** S/He is _ secretly or openly critical or ashamed of her or his "looks," appearance, or body. S/He may be _ either extremely modest *or* _ very immodest; S/He consistently grooms and dresses either _ shabbily and drably, *or* _ "loudly," over-formally, or "perfectly."

_ **41)** S/He _ ignores, minimizes, or intellectualizes personal spiritual, _ confuses spirituality with *religion or church*, and/or _ chooses relationships and settings compulsively from rigidly religious/spiritual beliefs that foster denial, guilt, shame, fear, and c/overt bigotry. S/He discourages children from exploring other beliefs because they are "not the (one) True Way." If confronted on this, s/he will _ rigidly deny and/or _ earnestly justify it as "godly," "righteousness," and trying to reddem (save) sinners from Hell and eternal damnation." S/He may do significant social good based on these beliefs.

_ **42)** S/He repeatedly chooses people with many of these traits (i.e. other psychologically-wounded survivors of low childhood nurturance) as mates, friends, and associates.

_ **43)** S/He _ denies having many or most of these traits *to excess*, _explains them defensively, and/or _ minimizes their personal significance; and _ s/he probably denies this denial, _jokes about it, or _ is defensive about it.

Because none of us grew up in perfect childhoods, *everyone* has mixes of these traits! To help you in your final conclusions, note how many __ of these 43 traits you checked about yourself.

Awarenesses . . .

C) SCAN YOUR FAMILY TREE FOR CLUES

WOUNDS PASS DOWN THE GENERATIONS

Basic premises, from 17 years' study and decades of clinical and personal experience:

- Low-nurturance family trees have telltale patterns of personal and social traits that higher-nurturance families don't have.

- People ruled by false-selves tend to unconsciously pick each other as partners. That raises the odds that they'll unwittingly pass on major false-self wounds to their dependents and descendents.

- Chronic emotional/spiritual stress (anxiety) can trigger genetic predispositions for illness and addiction, and weaken the immune system. Significantly wounded people tend to neglect their wholistic health, and to minimize or deny that. Implication: "chronic illness" in your family tree *may* be a symptom of low childhood nurturance, and false-self dominance.

- Many personal, interpersonal, and social problems—like addiction—are symptoms of significant false-self dominance among some or all the people involved.

- Individual siblings will react differently to low household and family nurturance. Social, environmental, and circumstantial factors will shape how individual kids react to emotional/spiritual nurturance deprivations

- Low emotional and spiritual nurturance and related psychological wounding unintentionally migrates down the generations (spreads), until a descendant spots it and *stops* it—i.e. chooses true personal recovery.

Overall premise: assessing your family tree honestly can reveal clues about whether you and/or key relatives (including your children) are often controlled by false selves.

Directions

You'll need a large piece of paper, like two 8.5" x 11" sheets taped together on the long edge. On this, draw in pencil your three-generational family *genogram*, like the example on page 276. Draw the genogram *large*, with lots of white space, for you'll be making notes all over it. Option: see the Web example of a stepfamily genogram at **http://sfhelp.org/sf/basics/geno.htm.**

- Use circles for females of any age, and squares for males—or another convention you prefer.

- Solid horizontal lines mean legal marriage, and dashed lines mean emotional commitment. An "—x—" means a divorce, and "—//—" means emotional detachment and/or legal separation. Solid vertical or slanted lines denote biological parent-child (genetic) bonds. Use double lines ===== to denote specially strong bonds. Dotted lines can mean emotional but not biological bonds, like an adoption. A zigzag (..WW..) between two people (symbols) can symbolize significant tension.

- Put ages, names, dates (birth, death, marriage, divorce), and other pertinent information by each person, including a "?" if little is known about them. Put an "X" or slash through the symbol of a dead person. Option: note the cause and date of death. Option: if a child was a surprise or unwanted conception, note that.

- Include foster and adopted children, key caregivers (e.g. a baby sitter), etc—in general, anyone who had a notable effect on the wholistic (emotional + spiritual + physical + mental) health of one or more of your family members.

- Draw at least three generations. Include aborted fetuses or stillbirths, children, and adults—i.e. anyone of unusually intense emotional and/or biological significance to one or more family members.

- If you were or are married, draw the multi-generational genogram of your partner(s), as best you know it.

- Now—honestly and thoughtfully, note by any person on your map each probable or sure instance of any of the following traits. Use colored pencils to help you see emerging patterns. Expect to erase or amend some early marks. If you're unsure about a trait, add it with a "?" Look over the several sets of family-tree traits below, before using them to finish and assess your ancestral map.

Consider journaling or tape recording your thoughts, feelings, images, and memories, as you do this exercise. They can be a rich source of learning, self-awareness, and discussion, now and later.

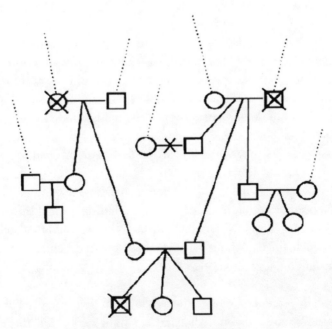

Basic Three-generation Genogram

Family-tree Symptoms of False-self Wounds

- Attempted or actual suicide
- Physical abuse*
- Unwanted / unplanned pregnancies; abortion/s; harassment
- Stalking; sexual or other
- Marital affair/s
- Kidnapping or abduction
- Incest, rape, or other *sexual* abuse*

- Chronic lying or stealing
- Chronic *exhaustion* without clear medical cause/s
- Obsession with *cleanness*
- Major trouble with the law unemployment
- "Excessive" reclusion
- Chronic *depression*; using mood-controlling medication/s

- Chronic *sleep* disorders—e.g. insomnia, nightmares, night terrors or sweats
- Self-mutilation, including unusual tattooing
- Chronic digestive disorders problems / ulcers
- Religious, social, or political fanaticism or bigotry
- Excessive secret-keeping, suspicions, or distrust

- Stillbirth/s
- Emotional abuse*
- Excessive hoarding
- Committing chronic or major crimes
- Separations or divorce/s
- Spiritual abuse*
- Attempted or actual murder
- Chronic illness/es
- Addiction/s to substances, activities, relationships, and/or "emotional states"
- Serious cult or gang involvement and/or hygiene
- Chronic job losses and/or and/ormilitary
- Marital or family desertion/s or social isolation
- Hospitalization for "nervous breakdown/s" or mental "conditions"
- Inability to focus; excessive "mind-wandering" or "mind-churning"
- Self-neglect—e.g. refusal to get medical checkups
- Hypochondria—obsession or with personal health
- Obesity; obsessive weight-loss regain cycles;
- Excessive emotional numbness or volatility

*see p. 279

(more) **Family-tree Traits of False self Wounds**

- Multiple Personality Disorder or "Schizophrenia"

- Repeated failure to graduate from Manager or trade school/s
- Rabid atheism *or* excessive piety and "penances"
- Emotional *cutoffs* family (kin "not talking")
- Reported animal sacrifices, torture, or entrapment
- Chronic or "unreasonable" legal suits
- Chronic anxiety attacks; major phobias, delusions, or reality distortions
- Bankruptcy or excessive indebtedness—or excessive fear of same

- Chronic eating disorders
- (e.g. anorexia, bulimia, food phobias)
- Church excommunication or obsession
- Minor kid/s regularly parenting younger siblings
- "Enshrining" dead or lost member/s
- Ancestral mystery figures (little or no knowledge of them)
- Homelessness—living "on the street"
- Chronic rage attacks; teeth-grinding; chronic major muscle
- tics or spasms
- Excessive sexual promiscuity, addiction, or dysfunction

When you're done assessing individuals on your map, go back and assess each family or person for natural or man-made disasters: earthquakes, floods, plagues, wind storms, tidal waves, droughts, rape, war, riots, burglaries, muggings, lightning strikes, fires, vehicle crashes, job losses, and the like. These traumas often promote or amplify inner wounds in adults and kids. Use colored markers to note any of these on your family map.

Perspective

None of these individual traits *prove* low family nurturance and false-self wounds. Some—like sexual abuse or torture, murder, suicide, abortion, and addiction—are more suggestive than others. Note that "no knowledge" of an ancestor or a branch of your family tree may be an indicator of significant wounding by itself.

Everyone has *some* of these conditions in their ancestry. Key: watch for clusters of these traits among several members of a particular generation, and/or down the generations of one person. My rule of thumb is—if there are probably or surely five or more of these traits in any person's current and past two generations, the person was probably moderately to greatly deprived of the high-nurturance family traits on p. 257. That raises their odds of significant wounding, *regardless* of their current surface behavior, health, or family situation.

Assigning any of these traits to an ancestor or family relationship is a judgment call, often based on hearsay and tradition. Deciding what "*excessive*" is in any family member must be subjective. To improve the objectivity of your research here, ask knowledgeable kin, close family friends, or involved professionals to reality-check your opinions about the existence of any family-tree trait you're unsure of. If you do, note their reactions to what you're doing.

Caution: if you're an unrecovering survivor of a low-nurturance childhood, you're apt to unconsciously minimize, ignore, "forget," or deny some or many of these ancestral traits. Another possibility is that some of these family-tree traits were family secrets (implying fear, guilt, and/or shame), and you were never told about them. A third is that they were exaggerated, invented, or misunderstood, for various reasons. Moral: go easy on drawing any firm conclusions from this worksheet alone—use the results from all 11 of them.

* **"Abuse"** **is** a provocative and biased term, and is often misused. What I mean by "abuse" here is "when a person in authority or power, like a parent or teacher, willfully uses their position of power and authority to harmfully inflict their own needs or opinions on a dependent person who can't _ defend themselves or _ leave." The abuser may do this one traumatic time, or repeatedly. If the receiving person can withdraw and/or defend safely, the other's actions are *aggressive*, not *abusive*. "You were *aggressive* with me" is less likely to provoke a defense/counterattack spiral than "You *abused me*."

- *Emotional* abuse includes repeated verbal or physical humiliation, excessive criticism, threatening, belittling, teasing, name-calling, discounting, ignoring, abandoning, and shaming.

- *Physical* abuse can include *any* physical activity (e.g. relentless tickling, over-feeding, forced enemas) that produces *excessive* pain, fear, confusion, shame, guilt, and/or bodily harm.

- *Sexual* abuse covers a range of passive and active activities which result in *excess*ive shame or humiliation, gender or role confusion, personal-boundary distortion or loss, psychological blending, excess sexual fear or dysfunction, self-mutilation, personal degradation, and severe distrust of Self or some others. Immature children—specially in low-nurturance homes—exposed to media or real adult sexual behavior can suffer serious emotional/spiritual trauma.

- *Spiritual* abuse happens when an authority (caregiver, teacher, clergy, mentor) . . .

  _ intentionally imposes ideas ("truths") about God, Hell, Demons, the Devil, etc. on . . .
  _ an immature, defenseless person which . . .
  _ promote *excessive* terror, shame, and guilt in, or . . .
  _ the self-harm of, the receiver.

Aware nesses . . .

D) TRAITS OF HIGH-NURTURANCE GROUP MEMBERS

TRUE SELVES PROMOTE HIGH MORALE

Premises:

- People form groups, including families, to achieve vague or specific conscious goals. Underneath these goals, every group member has a set of fundamental emotional, physical, mental, and perhaps spiritual needs. These include needs for respect, inclusion, role clarity, appreciation, free expression, learning, rest, privacy, stimulation, and emotional and physical comfort and security.

- The degree to which *all* members feel these core needs are met in their group over time can be called the group's *nurturance* level. Implication: family adults need emotional, spiritual, and physical nurturance just as much as minor kids do.

- The nurturance level (low to high) of any group is directly proportional to how psychologically wounded its most influential members are. "Low nurturance" means the same as "dysfunctional."

- The average nurturance level among the several homes comprising a multi-generational family, or the departments in an organization, reflects the degree of false-self dominance in the large group's most influential members.

- Typical members of a low-nurturance group will feel and behave differently toward the group than members of a high-nurturance group will.

If these premises are true, then . . .

- A quick test for any group's nurturance level ("functionality") is to judge the average primary emotions most members usually feel in the group, after they get used to being a member. There are many variables that shape the validity of this premise for any group member, *so this checklist is at best a rough indicator of a family (or other group's) wholistic health. It is not "proof."*

Note that "low nurturance" behaviors in the members may indicate the leader/s' ineptness at group-leadership (lack of knowledge or skill), rather than the leader/s' being controlled by a false self.

Directions

- Review the worksheet guidelines on p. 255.

- Pick an adult or child you want to assess for false-self wounds. I suggest you start with yourself.

- Focus on a group this person regularly participates in, or did, as a child—e.g. their birthfamily or marital family, a school, classroom, team, committee, or church congregation. Then . . .

- Estimate the main emotions or attitudes you feel the person often experience/d as they participate/d. Recall: this is about getting clearer, *not* about blaming anyone!

Typical Group-member Traits

Higher-nurturance	_Group_ _Lower-nurturance Group_
(Leaders probably not significantly wounded)	(Leaders probably have significant wounds)
_ Serene / peaceful in the group	_ Nervous / anxious / worried
_ Calm / relaxed doubting / ambivalent /	_ Stressed / tense / uneasy at ease in the group _ Self-

_ Self-confident /   uncertain
Self-assured / sure   _ (Very) ashamed / guilty

_ Appropriately proud of membership
_ Energetic / interested   _ Apathetic / bored / listless
in group activities   _ Defensive / irresponsible
_ Responsible in group roles and tasks
_ Sociable / sharing   _ Isolated / extra shy / withdrawn
in the group   _ Rigid / over-controlling

_ Spontaneous / free   _ Secretive / suspicious / on guard
_ Trusting / open   _ Resistant / defiant /
_ Cooperative / team player   rebellious / loner

_ Recognized / appreciated   _ Ignored / discounted /
by others   unappreciated
_ Loyal / accepted /   _ Detached / rejected /
involved with others   indifferent
_ Important / valued /   _ Invisible / unwanted /
needed by others   unimportant

_ Competent / adequate / able   _ Incompetent / inadequate /
_ Happy / satisfied / fulfilled   unable
_ Upset / frustrated / unfulfilled _ Despairing / gloomy /
(usually)   cynical / pessimistic

_ Hopeful / optimistic /   _ Feels unsafe / uneasy /
motivated (usually)   in scared / anxious
_ Feels safe and secure _   Overwhelmed / disinterested
the group   **_ Dreads going to /** "hates"
_ Challenged / stimulated   / being in / the group
alive / "dead"

_ Looks forward to / enjoys
being in / the group

Recap: the more members of a group that display these "high" or "low"
behaviors, the more likely the group's leaders are _ inept in their role, and/
or _ significantly controlled by a false self. Leaders who are controlled by

false selves unintentionally promote inner chaos (stress) in their group's members. Results: I checked _ of the 19 traits, (for whom, in what group?). Also see the related worksheet at **http://sfhelp.org/gwc/hi_n_org.htm**

* * *

Awarenesses . . .

WOUND-ASSESSMENT WORKSHEETS
E) - J)

PREMISES AND DIRECTIONS

These symptom checklists allow assessing for each of six false-self wounds. Honestly recorded, the results can help you (1) decide if personal recovery will benefit you, and (2) identify specific healing targets and yardsticks within an overall personal-recovery plan.

Premises

* Growing up in a low-nurturance childhood promotes two to six psychological wounds:

1) Significant **dominance of** a group of reactive, shortsighted personality parts—**a false self**. This dominance disables the true Self, and causes combinations of . . .

2) **Excessive shame** ("I'm bad and unlovable") **and guilts** ("I've done bad things");

3) **Excessive fears**—e.g. of abandonment (aloneness), emotional overwhelm, the unknown, and "failure."

4) Unconscious **reality distortions**, including denial, repression, minimization, numbing, projection, and exaggeration.

These four wounds combine to cause . . .

5) **Overtrusting** unsafe people and events, **and/or undertrusting** safe people and environments, and . . .

6) **An inability to *feel* and/or bond** (emotionally/spiritually attach), and/or to give and/or receive genuine love.

- Each of these traits is caused by two or more personality parts who don't know or trust your true Self. Patterns of behavior suggest which personality subselves are disabling (blending with) your Self.

- These six inner wounds tend to amplify each other—e.g. shame and fear promote reality distortions, and vice versa. Conversely, healing one wound tends to reduce them all.

- Some behavioral symptoms are common to several of the six wounds, and others are unique.

- Individual behavioral traits don't "prove" the wound or who the key controlling subself is (like a *Shamed* or *Fearful Child*), but they are suggestive. The more symptoms you check, the higher the odds of false-self dominance and the particular wound.

- What qualifies as *excessive*, *irrational*, *obsessive*, and *compulsive* behavior below is a personal opinion. Many low-nurturance survivors use this reality to "prove" (deny) that they do not have major false-self wounds ("I am *not* obsessive about . . . ").

Directions

Fill out each of these six checklists thoughtfully for yourself. Check each symptom that you feel usually or surely applies to you. Then re-do the checklists for each other adult or child you want to assess for major false-self dominance. Use a different symbol or initials for each person. Options: assess each of your parents or grandparents, siblings, marital partners, children, and/or your employer, colleague, or a key friend. If you're unsure about a trait (a possible wound symptom), come back to the item later, or use "?"

Reassure yourself along the way that having some or many of these traits does *not* mean you or another is "crazy," bad, or sick. It may mean that you or they grew up in a low-nurturance childhood and unconsciously adapted by developing a protective, over-dominant false self.

Stay aware that assessing for these wound symptoms honestly is the first step toward *healing* them. The biggest blocks to personal and family healing are *ignorance* and *unawareness*—i.e. false-self denial and repression.

Suggestions about evaluating your results from all of these checklists begin on p. 322.

If you haven't recently, review the suggestions for doing these worksheets on p. 255. Be gentle with yourself—don't feel you have to do all six at one sitting! You may amplify your learnings if you journal your thoughts and reactions to each of these checklists as you fill them out. Your process is just as important as the results. Again—there is no "right" way to do these . . .

It's OK to give copies of these checklists to others. For checklist copies, see the Web versions at **http://sfhelp.org/gwc/links1.htm**

E) COMMON SYMPTOMS OF
FALSE-SELF DOMINANCE

Premises

- Human personalities are naturally many-sided, rather than a single monolithic entity. Each of our semi-independent personality "parts," "sides," or "subselves," has unique talents, limitations, values, goals, perceptions, and strategies.

- A "false self" is one or more personality parts, or subselves, which often *blend* with, or paralyze, the personality's natural skilled leader, the true Self. Typically, these subselves are reactive Inner Kids and/ or their protective Guardians. False selves typically make ineffective to unhealthy decisions, situationally and over time. They're far more concerned with immediate comfort and gratification than long-term outcomes.

- There are *many* behavioral symptoms of false-self dominance. They're so numerous and socially widespread (*"normal"*), they tend to disappear. Symptoms of true-Self personality leadership (# 10 below) are far rarer in our culture. This worksheet is a composite of the traits in worksheets F-J.

Pick an adult or child you want to assess for living from a false self, and see how many of these traits you feel usually or "significantly' describe them. I recommend you assess yourself before anyone else.

These false-self symptoms are typical, but not exhaustive:

_ 1) S/He has _ frequent marked "mood swings," and/or _ did or does regularly take "mood control" (e.g. anti-depression) medication.

_ 2) S/He feels _ "little" (child-like), and/or _ acts "childish" or "immature," either chronically or situationally—e.g. when with a bioparent or authority figure.

_ 3) S/He has one or more active addictions to _ substances, including sugar, carbohydrates, and fat; _ relationships (see p. 316); _ activities, like work, gambling, sex, spending, or "working out;" and/or _ mood states, like excitement, rage, or sexual arousal and release.

_ 4) S/He has periodic "attacks" of _ rage, _ mania, _ depression, _ panic, and/or _ crying. An "attack" is an episode where the primary emotions seem unwarranted and uncontrollable.

_ 5) S/He often acts impulsively and "thoughtlessly," even if results are painful or hurtful personally and/or for others.

_ 6) S/He is chronically "hard on myself"—i.e. relentlessly expects perfection; and is _ over-demanding and/or _ over-critical of his or her own _ behaviors, _ values, or _ traits.

_ 7) S/He has _ unusual and/or _ frequent episodes of amnesia and/or "forgetfulness" ("absent-mindedness.")

_ 8) S/He has an unusual reliance on "lists" to "stay organized" and "be productive."

_ 9) S/He often has tense or "achey" shoulder, neck, jaw, back, and/or stomach muscles.

_ 10) S/He seldom feels mixes of *clear, grounded, focused, serene, decisive, strong, centered, resilient, purposeful, aware, light,* and *energized*—the symptoms of true-Self inner-family leadership.

_ **11)** S/He often has "mind-racing"—i.e. has _ "many voices (thought streams) in my head all the time"; _ "arguments with myself"; and feels _ frequent "confusion." Related symptom: S/He _ often experiences unfocused, vague, illogical, "fuzzy" thinking.

_ **12)** S/He is self neglectful—i.e. frequently does personally-unsafe or unhealthy things "anyway."

_ **13)** S/He has "a short attention span"—i.e. s/he has trouble _ getting and _ staying focused, alone and/or with others.

_ **14)** S/He often feels aimless or purposeless about life—"I'm going through the motions."

_ **15)** S/He often feels anxious, distracted, or "spacey," without knowing why.

_ **16)** S/He has significant _ compulsions (e.g. unnecessary cleaning, organizing, or list-making), and/or _ obsessive thinking.

_ **17)** S/He often _ feels uncomfortably ambivalent and indecisive; _ changes his or her mind often, and/or _ frequently "second-guesses" (doubts) personal decisions or perceptions.

_ **18)** S/He has frequent _ nightmares, and/or _ unusual or _ unpleasant fantasies.

_ **19)** S/He habitually _ sends "double messages" to others (words and actions don't match); and _ denies, _ defends, _ jokes about, and/or _ minimizes this.

_ **20)** S/He habitually _ breaks appointments, commitments, and/or promises; and then _ feels remorseful or defensive, and _ says "I don't know why!" or "I can't help it."

_ **21)** S/He has _ repeated or _ significant "time lapse" episodes—i.e. has no memory of recent events or periods of time. See (7) above.

_ **22)** S/He often feels vaguely or clearly odd, confused, uneasy, irritable, intimidated, envious, and/or distracted in the prolonged presence of

Self-guided people, families, and/or other groups (#10 above and p. 257 and 281). S/He _ tends to avoid such people consciously or unconsciously.

_ **23)** S/He has non-organic "sexual dysfunctions"—e.g. impotence, frigidity, low desire, sexual or pornographic addiction, promiscuity, excessive fantasizing, sexualizing all relationships, and/or compulsive masturbation.

_ **24)** S/He is secretly or openly unable to identify or empathize with most of the traits of wholistically-healthy (high-nurturance) families.

_ **25)** S/He feels "irrational" or unexplainable emotional pain, sadness, or anger with _ real and/or _ media-portrayed scenes of parent-child love, comforting, tenderness, bonding, and shared enjoyment and closeness.

_ **26)** S/He often feels numb—i.e. unable to _*feel* or _ name any significant emotions. A subset of this is _ feeling some emotions but not certain others—like anger, lust, regret, sadness, or empathy. A form of this is _ a marked inability to feel pleasure (anhedonia). This *numbness* symptom inhibits healthy grieving and intimacy. A coping response to this numbness is to semi-consciously _ guess what others would feel, and _ pretend to feel that.

_ **27)** S/He has significant _ paranoias, _ hallucinations, _ neuroses, _ delusions, and/or _ "mood" or "dissociative" disorders, like "bi-polar" manic depression. "Schizophrenia" seems to have biological roots, and may be promoted or triggered by being raised by seriously wounded caregivers.

_ **28)** S/He has significant symptoms of the other five inner wounds: _ toxic shame and guilt, _ excessive fears, _ dis/trust problems, _ reality distortions, and _ inabilities to bond or to exchange genuine *love*.

_ **29)** S/He is judged by other people who know him / her as "phony," insincere, "plastic," "shallow," "narrow," or "distant."

_ **30)** (add your own trait)

*   *   *

Which of these traits invoke the strongest reactions in you (your inner family)? Do you know why? Consider journaling or tape recording your reactions to this worksheet now, or soon. To help your overall assessment, record how many of the 29 symptoms of false-self dominance you checked: ___.

Recap: The more of these traits a person has, the more likely s/he is often controlled by a group of protective false-self personality parts. Such dominance becomes "normal" in early childhood, so seldom raises any inner alarms.

Awarenesses . . .

F) COMMON SYMPTOMS OF EXCESSIVE *SHAME* AND *GUILT*

Shame is the painful feeling of (1) being inept at an important role (lover, parent, child); or of (2) being a totally bad, damaged, worthless, disgusting, unlovable person. *Guilt* is the normal emotion we feel if our *Inner Critic* decrees that we've "done something wrong"—s/he believes we've broken someone's "rule"—a should (not), must (not), or ought (not). "Embarrassment" happens when our shame and/or guilt is made public. Reality check: recall the last time you felt embarrassed.

Shame and guilt often *feel* the same, though they have different roots. Unforgiven guilt fosters shame—"I break rules, so I'm a bad person." In moderation, each of these normal emotional reactions is healthy and helpful. Significantly-wounded people feel excessive (toxic) shame and guilts. The unseen dominance of a shame-based false self appears to be the most pervasive block to feeling and expressing self-love and love for others. This trait appears to be rampant and unremarked in our current society.

These related wounds are healed differently. Toxic shame is usually carried by one or several young personality parts. This shamed "bad me" part is "born" well before puberty—often by age three or so. Often, shame-based caregivers with low self-awareness *unknowingly* promote shame and guilts in their young kids. That's why toxic shame has been called "the gift that goes on giving." For more perspective, see *"Healing the Shame that Binds You,"* by recovery mentor John Bradshaw.

Review the guidelines for using these worksheets on p. 255. Then focus on an adult or child, and check the traits below that seem often or generally true of them. This checklist of common symptoms of excessive shame and guilt is illustrative, not exhaustive.

*   *   *

_ **1)** S/He has a deep semi-conscious core belief that "I am a bad, weak, unlovable, undeserving, inept, unattractive, stupid, powerless, worthless (person / man / woman / partner / parent / child.")

_ **2)** S/He is excessively zealous, defensive, rigid, dogmatic, and/or "preachy" about "sin;" moral righteousness; "spiritual warfare;" God; the Devil, or Satan; the Bible, Torah, or Koran; Hell; "the one true religion," and/or about being "damned" or "saved."

_ **3)** S/He is _ habitually self-centered, "egotistical," or "narcissistic." If confronted, s/he _ denies, _ defends, or _ rationalizes this; or _ disparages herself / himself, and says, "I can't help it."

_ **4)** S/He has one or more active addictions to _ substances, including sugar, fat, and carbohydrates; _ activities, like work, spending, gambling, se, or working out; _ unhealthy relationships (co-dependence); and/or to _ an emotional state, like excitement, anger, or sexual arousal.

_ **5)** S/He constantly belittles, discounts, and criticizes herself / himself, and/or others—and _ apologizes or _ blames herself / himself for this.

_ **6)** S/He repeatedly _ chooses unchallenging, menial jobs below her/his personal capabilities; S/He _ avoids responsibilities excessively, and may be judged "lazy" and/or "unmotivated."

_ **7)** S/He compulsively _ rescues needy or hurting others; and/or _ defends and _ identifies with disadvantaged, sick, wounded, and/or oppressed people or animals ("underdogs").

_ **8)** S/He _ has few or no *real* friends, and _ is consistently drawn to other shame-based (wounded) people as companions and colleagues.

_ **9)** S/He is _ excessively isolated, socially; or _ socializes compulsively, striving to be the center of attention.

_ **10)** S/He is _ excessively sensitive to, and _ defensive about, imagined or actual criticism or rejection.

_ 11) S/He tends to compulsively over-explain her actions, opinions, or decisions, when other people haven't asked for such information or don't care.

_ 12) S/He habitually _ avoids eye contact, and is _ apologetic, _ self-critical, _ indifferent, _ jokes about, or _ is defensive about this.

_ 13) S/He _ chronically mistakes respectful feedback for criticism, and/ or _ often wrongly *assumes* unspoken criticisms.

_ 14) S/He is _ excessively concerned with "Who's to blame?," and _ is apt to assume others blame her or him, when they really don't.

_ 15) S/He feels "irrationally" guilty or "uneasy" about earned successes and recognition.

_ 16) S/He obsesses about "my rights" or "I (don't) deserve . . . ," or "equality" or "fairness."

_ 17) S/He "endlessly" reviews and anguishes over past "mistakes."

_ 18) S/He _ routinely puts her/his own opinions, needs, and welfare last (vs. equal), without complaint; and _ feels "selfish" or "uneasy" if invited to rank herself/himself as a person of equal human dignity.

_ 19) S/He has an unreasonable and/or chronic fear of "failure" or "making mistakes."

_ 20) S/He rarely _ apologizes or _ admits "mistakes;" or s/he _ reflexively apologizes all the time, and may _ apologize for apologizing.

_ 21) S/He _ habitually wears unflattering, inappropriate, and/or "sloppy" clothing; and/or _ s/he has notably poor grooming and/or hygiene. S/He may _ joke about this, _ apologize for it, _ defend it defiantly, or _ be self-critical about it.

_ 22) S/He focuses excessively on _ personal, professional, social, and/or dwelling *appearances*, and/or _ the financial value of personal assets. S/He seems _ excessively focused on getting and possessing valuable "things," and _ specially admires rich, famous, and/or powerful people.

_ 23) S/He is compulsively _ perfectionistic ("I can't help it"), and/or _ driven to "win," "succeed," and/or "be number 1" or "the best."

_ 24) S/He compulsively "shades the truth" or lies, directly or by omission; and _ denies, _ blames others for, _ ignores, _ pokes fun at, or _ justifies that.

_ 25) S/He is self neglectful—i.e. s/he resists or avoids seeing a doctor, dentist, or eye specialist for checkups or illnesses; and _ ignores getting or taking prescribed medications. This can also be a symptom of reality distortion and excessive fear (p. 299).

_ 26) S/He chooses unhealthy _ diets, _ habits (e.g. smoking), _ lack of exercise, and/or _ emotionally or physically toxic environments; and s/he _ ignores, _ defends, _ minimizes, _ intellectualizes, or _ jokes about this.

_ 27) S/He rarely _ buys anything "nice" or "special" for herself / himself, or _ takes fun trips or vacations.

_ 28) S/He usually _ deflects and/or discounts others' sincere compliments, and _ says "I'm very hard on myself," or "I'm my own worst critic."

_ 29) S/He _ chronically gives time and energy to others, and _ asks little or nothing in return; people see her / him as a "saint," or "selfless martyr." Alternatively, s/he gives to others, and _ expects them to *want* to give back to her / him ("conditional friendship or love).

_ 30) S/He openly or covertly _ avoids and/or _ disparages this inner-wound assessment, and the related need for personal recovery.

_ 31) S/He repeatedly _ chooses, _ justifies, and _ tolerates "toxic" relationships, situations, and/or environments—i.e. those which promote major shame, guilt, anxiety, frustration, and/or confusion.

_ 32) S/He repeatedly takes impulsive risks that result in self-harm, humiliation, toxic guilt, and/or loss of self respect.

_ 33) S/He _ rarely asks for what s/he wants or needs, or _ asks anxiously and expects rejection, rather than declaring or asserting calmly. S/He is _ notably "unassertive," "passive," and "quiet," *or* _ s/he is an "insensitive," aggressive, demanding "bully."

_ 34) S/He doesn't _ set and/or _ enforce wholistically-healthy limits (boundaries) with herself / himself, _ and/or others. S/He is often "undisciplined."

_ 35) S/He _ accepts or _ reinforces a core belief like "I don't deserve or expect success, love, security, comfort, friends, and/or nice things."

_ 36) S/He repeatedly self-sabotages—i.e. sets herself / himself up for failure, disappointment, frustration, and/or losses; and _ feels or says things like "I can't help it," or "It doesn't matter."

_ 37) S/He frequently _ chooses long-suffering victim, saint, or martyr roles in key relationships and social settings; and _ rationalizes that, or _ doesn't complain or question why.

_ 38) S/He chooses a direct-contact human-service profession—e.g. clergy, counseling, medicine, education, law (enforcement), consulting, . . . (yes, there are *many* exceptions!)

_ 39) S/He feels uneasy or anxious about _ describing this assessment project, and/or _ showing these worksheets to key others; and/or _ discussing the results and what they may mean.

_ 40) (Add your own symptom/s.)

Which of these symptoms invoke the strongest reactions in you (your inner family)? Do you know why? Consider journaling or tape recording your reactions to this worksheet now or soon. For later evaluation, note how many of the 39 symptoms you checked for yourself: ___.

The more of these behavioral symptoms a person displays, the more likely that their inner family is often dominated by a *shame-based* false self. That is, that one or more personality subselves deeply believe they and other subselves are fundamentally flawed, unlovable, and unworthy. Because feeling unlovable is shameful, Guardian subselves diligently provide many mental, emotional, and social camouflages for this, like reality distortions (p. 308).

Toxic excessive shame (I am a damaged, unlovable person) can be converted into realistic self-appreciation, self-respect, and self-love, over time—with clear awareness, courage, patience, intentional effort, and appropriate supports. Similarly, toxic guilts (I break key rules) can be greatly reduced. See p. 114.

Awarenesses . . .

G) COMMON SYMPTOMS OF EXCESSIVE FEARS

Fear is a normal emotional/physical response that protects us against injury, pain, and death. Moderate fears ("worries and anxieties") are usually helpful guides to local decisions. When extra-anxious, distrustful subselves control the *inner* family (personality) of an adult or child, the person's reaction to daily life may be "fear-based." Their controlling subselves don't trust their Self, other people, and/or a benign Higher Power, to protect them adequately from a mix of . . .

_ Criticism, rejection, betrayal, and emotional or physical abandonment—i.e. protect them from being alone, unloved, and unsafe; and . . .

_ Being hurt badly or killed by the unknown. This can manifest as excessive dread of environmental and inner-personal change and risk-taking; and . . .

_ Strong emotions in themselves and/or in others overwhelming them (causing inner-family chaos.) This can manifest as _ fear of "losing control" (symptom: being "manipulative" or "very controlling"); _ fear of "intimacy" (loss of identity), and/or _ fear of conflict (loss of boundaries). And/or the fear-based person's inner family is over-alert to . . .

_ "Failure" (amplified by toxic shame), and/or _ "success."

Fear ranges fluidly along this continuum:

vague unease > discomfort > worry (anxiety)
> fear > dread > panic/terror > hysteria

From prior experience, kids and adults can be unconsciously fearful of "too much fear." Often the other false-self wounds of reality distortion, shame, and excessive distrust unconsciously amplify toxic (excessive) fears—and vice versa. Combined with toxic shame and guilt, toxic fears seem to promote the stressful condition of co-dependence—relationship addiction (p. 316).

Review the guidelines for using these worksheets on p. 255. Then focus on an adult or child you want to assess for toxic fears. Stay aware that freeing your Self to harmonize your inner family (personality) is your recovery target, not just reducing excessive fears.

These are typical behavioral symptoms of a fear-based false self:

_ 1) S/He over-avoids _ *inner*personal and _ interpersonal conflicts; "My partner (child, parent, friend) and I *never* fight!"

_ 2) S/He is obsessed with _ pleasing, _ helping, and/or _ rescuing her / his mate, kids, and key friends.

_ 3) S/He _ freezes, _ panics, _ flees, and/or _ manipulates when others emote strongly, or appear likely to do so.

_ 4) S/He equates a raised or intense voice or angry face with "You're *yelling* at me" (also a symptom of reality distortion.)

_ 5) S/He repeatedly rationalizes and tolerates toxic, demeaning, and depleting relationships.

_ 6) S/He _ habitually uses "bi-polar" (black/white) thinking, and _ feels high discomfort with ambivalence or uncertainty.

_ 7) S/He feels "unreasonable" _ guilt and/or _ anxiety over crying or raging privately, or in public.

_ 8) S/He feels chronic, major "free-floating" anxiety, worries, or dread.

_ 9) S/He apologizes compulsively, whether warranted or not (also a symptom of toxic shame).

_ **10)** S/He often _ "walks on eggshells" with key others, and _ denies it, _ rationalizes it, and/or _ laughs about it; and _ does nothing about it.

_ **11)** S/He rarely _ asserts needs and opinions, or _ says "no"—i.e. s/he _ has trouble setting clear, appropriate personal limits and boundaries and/ or _ enforcing them.

_ **12)** S/He _ identifies with, *or* _ vehemently denies or disparages, *co-dependence* (also a toxic shame symptom.)

_ **13)** S/He compulsively _ chooses and _ tolerates approach-avoid relationships, and may _ joke about, _ deny, _ overanalyze and explain, and/or _ righteously defend this.

_ **14)** S/He automatically _ represses ("numbs") and/or _ withholds (doesn't express) some or most emotions, specially anger, shame, and sadness. This may contribute to blocked grief and situational or chronic "depression."

_ **15)** S/He _ feels compelled to *control* people, events, perceptions, and/ or feelings; S/He is _ preoccupied with "what if . . . " (also a symptom of excessive distrust).

_ **16)** S/He is _ highly uncomfortable with, and/or _ avoids, changes in environment or routine. S/He _ lives an overly structured, ritualized life; and may _ rarely or never "go out."

_ **17)** S/He repeatedly _ picks emotionally unavailable (wounded) partners, and either _ complains about this, _ jokes about it, or _ "doesn't notice" it.

_ **18)** S/He compulsively _ "shades the truth" or _ lies, directly or by omission; and _ denies, _ minimizes, or _ justifies doing so ("I have no choice, because . . . "). This is amplified if s/he chooses over-critical (wounded) companions who make truth-telling unsafe.

_ **19)** S/He has a history of relationship "failures," and/or _ avoiding committed relationships (a symptom of several inner wounds).

_ **20)** S/He has an obsessive need for clear rules, plans, order, and organization—"structure."

_ **21)** S/He avoids, or can't tolerate, true (vs. pretended) _ emotional and/or _ physical intimacy.

_ **22)** S/He _ avoids, or _ is high ambivalent about, personal commitments; S/He has _ an excessive need for _ personal freedom and _ self-responsibility, and is _ uncomfortable asking for, and/or _ accepting help (also a symptom of toxic shame).

_ **23)** S/He is often unconscious of _ smiling and _ chuckling inappropriately—e.g. when scared, confused, hurting, or angry (also a symptom of toxic shame).

_ **24)** S/He is often unable to authentically describe her/his _ current emotions and/or _ body sensations. S/He _ may anxiously *guess* at them, if asked, or _ may *compute* "What I (should) feel now," vs. spontaneously *feeling*.

_ **25)** S/He is _ habitually late and/or _ "forgetful;" and _ claims "I can't help it." (may also indicate repressed rage).

_ **26)** S/He has _ facial or other muscle tics, _ jaw grinding, and/or _ chronic muscle, head, or stomach aches or pains (possible source: subselves' fear of feeling and expressing *anger*.)

_ **27)** S/He is "always" _ analytic, _ intellectual, and _ "in my head" (fear of *feeling*.)

_ **28)** S/He is unable to describe clearly "what I like (or don't like)." A co-symptom of toxic shame.

_ **29)** S/He _ feels or _ shows no appropriate shock, anger, and sadness over major physical or abstract losses. This is also a symptom of an inability to bond (p. 312).

_ **30)** S/He frequently _ breathes shallowly, or holds it; and _ isn't aware of that, until someone points it out. Related symptom: _ nicotine overuse or addiction (fear of *feeling*.)

_ **31)** S/He _ "never" argues, or _ gets angry or _ "upset" in conflict. This is often from a Guardian protecting one or more Inner Children from feeling intense fear of emotional overwhelm, loss of boundaries (identity and emotional control), and feeling unable to defend adequately against expected major pain.

_ **32)** S/He usually has _ an expressionless face, _ a "frozen" body," and/ or a _ "flat" voice. Alternatively, s/he appears _ "plastic", "phony," and "hollow,"—insincere, and not "authentic," or "real."

_ **33)** S/He has periodic uncontrollable _ rage, _ weeping, and/or _ depression "attacks;" despite painful personal and social consequences like post-attack shame, guilt, and anxious self-distrust.

_ **34)** S/He often "catastrophizes"—obsesses about, and assumes the worst possible outcomes of, human or natural situations. This is an example of a Catastrophizer (Guardian) subself trying to protect ("be prepared!"), despite scaring one or more inner kids (Inner Kids).

_ **35)** S/He sets unrealistically high standards (perfectionism)—i.e. s/he _ sees high achievement or perfection as "normal," and _ meriting no special praise or recognition from Self or others. This is also a symptom of reality distortion and toxic shame.

_ **36)** (Add your own symptom.)

*   *   *

Which of these traits invoke the strongest reactions in you (your inner family)? Do you know why? Consider journaling or tape recording your reactions to this worksheet now or soon. For later summing up, record how many of these 35 symptoms you checked for yourself: ___. For options on reducing excessive fears, see p. 116.

Awarenesses . . .

H) COMMON SYMPTOMS OF
EXCESSIVE DIS/TRUST

Trust is a conscious or unconscious attitude (belief) about the degree to which a person, situation, or thing is *safe*—i.e. whether they or it will probably cause pain or pleasure. Trust grows from direct experience and from association—e.g. "A spider bit (hurt / scared) me once, so now I don't trust any crawly insects."

Amplified by the other five inner wounds, most survivors of inadequate early nurturance either trust too easily—and get repeatedly hurt and betrayed; or they aren't able to really trust truly-safe people, places, things, and events, and live anxious, restricted lives. Subjectively, this feels "normal."

Mixed with toxic shame and fear, excessive distrust blocks real intimacy and spontaneity. This mixes with other factors to promote remaining single, marrying without true commitment and intimacy, "approach/avoid" relationships, and/or a series of psychological and legal divorces.

Mixed with toxic shame, another symptom of this common false-self wound is *Self* distrust—chronically doubting one's own perceptions and decisions. Another symptom is distrust of, or confusion or ambivalence about, a benign spiritual Higher Power.

Excessive dis/trust problems usually stem from one or several Guardian personality parts protecting one or more scared young subselves. Overtrusting can come from false-self dominance of a *Naïve* or *Needy Child*, and a protective *People Pleaser* Guardian subself. It can also stem from Guardian parts wanting to shield young Inner Kids subselves from (shameful, scary) conflict, scary realities, and agonizing rejection and abandonment. These excessive trust imbalances fade as your subselves increasingly trust your true Self, other safe people, and a caring, non-punitive Higher Power.

If you haven't recently, re-scan the guidelines for using these worksheets on p. 255. Then focus on yourself or another person, and check which of these typical symptoms of overtrusting and undertrusting seem to apply. Look for the themes here, and identify other symptoms like these:

* * *

_ 1) S/He constantly "second-guesses" (doubts) her / his own past and/or current _ perceptions, _ reasoning, _ conclusions, and _ decisions.

_ 2) S/He constantly _ over-researches decisions, and/or _ consults others "too much."

_ 3) S/He has frequent trouble _ making clear decisions, and _ sticking to them, or _ acting on them.

_ 4) S/He feels excessive, unwarranted _ jealousy, _ suspicion, and/or _ possessiveness about one or more key people or possessions.

_ 5) S/He habitually over-analyzes other people for what they *really* mean, think, feel, or want, and _ denies, _ explains (justifies), and/or _ jokes about that.

_ 6) S/He risks personal harm or exploitation by disclosing personal information to strangers.

_ 7) S/He often avoids conflicts for fear of "blowing up," "lashing out," or "going out of control" (self distrust.)

_ 8) S/He has a history of small and large hurtful betrayals by trusted others ("broken promises.") Excessive fear of abandonment (p. 299) can promote tolerating these woundings.

_ 9) S/He is unable to _ exchange and _ sustain true emotional/physical intimacy—i.e. s/he is unable to trust that key people are reliably, authentically safe. This is a co-symptom of toxic shame and reality distortion.

_ **10)** S/He is _ excessively anxious about revealing personal dreams, hopes, fears, emotions, and thoughts. S/He _ keeps personal secrets, and _ promotes family secrets ("You don't tell strangers our family's business." This is also a symptom of toxic shame and guilt.

_ **11)** S/He compulsively "mind-reads" others—i.e. distrusts them to tell the truth, and assumes "I know what you're *really* thinking / feeling / wanting!" This is also a symptom of fear of the unknown.

_ **12)** S/He has great trouble accepting merited compliments—"You're just saying that to be nice." ("I don't trust that you really *mean* that.") This is also a symptom of toxic shame.

_ **13)** S/He has a history of procrastinating (putting things off), despite repeated painful personal and social results (distrusts that certain things will be enjoyable or safe.)

_ **14)** S/He has a pattern of _ thinking and/or _ accusing various others of _ "lying," _ "pretending," or _ "withholding."

_ **15)** S/He is excessively self-responsible—i.e. s/he over-avoids trusting some or all other people to help fill key personal needs. This is also symptomatic of toxic shame ("I don't deserve help.")

_ **16)** S/He is excessively _ watchful and _ strict with minor kids or other people—s/he doesn't trust their judgment. This is also a symptom of toxic fear (of the unknown).

_ **17)** S/He often avoids _ new situations, _ people, _ experiences, and _ major life changes—i.e. s/he distrusts that they'll be safe (pain-free) enough—and/or that s/he's competent to handle unexpected challenges (self distrust).

_ **18)** S/He is often skeptical, cynical, apathetic, indifferent, and/or disparaging of _ God, _ religion, _ church, _ prayer, and/or related ideas, programs and materials. S/He may vow or pretend personal spirituality or piety, but his / her actions don't bear that out.

_ **19)** S/He compulsively needs to manipulate and control certain other people excessively—i.e. s/he distrusts that they or others are competent, safe, and reliable. This becomes a symptom of toxic fears.

_ **20)** (Add your own symptom.)

*   *   *

Which of these traits invoke the strongest reactions in you (your inner family)? Do you know why, and in whom? Consider journaling or tape recording your reactions to this worksheet now or soon. Note how many of these 19 symptoms you checked for yourself: __. For options on improving your dis/trusting, see p. 118.

Awarenesses . . .

I) COMMON SYMPTOMS OF *REALITY DISTORTION*

Here, "reality distortion" means unconsciously seeing inner and outer events, circumstances, and relationships in ways that other knowledgeable, grounded people don't. Usually, chronic distortions indicate one or more Guardian subselves ceaselessly protecting young subselves from expected or current shame, guilt, and/or fear. Guardian subselves like the *Magician* use well-meant distortion strategies like . . .

- Denial ("I'm *not* ruled by a false self!")

- Repression ("No, I'm *not* hurt / angry / scared!")

- Numbing ("Well—I don't feel anything special, right now.")

- Minimizing ["Nah—(some trauma) is no big deal"]

- Exaggerating ("You have never been on time in your life!")

- Projecting ("You're screwed up, not me!")

- Catastrophizing ("Global warming will bring civilization down—you'll see.")

- Mind-reading ("I know what you *really* want / feel / think / mean!")

- Idealizing—seeing people, relationships, or other things in unrealistically approving ways.

- Mis-remembering, ("Yes I did tell you about the gas leak!"), and . . .

- Amnesia, "forgetting," and blackouts ("I have no memory of that.")

- Reread the guidelines for using these worksheets on p. 255. Then focus on one or more persons you wish to (compassionately) assess for false-self wounds—one at a time. Check which of these common symptoms of reality distortion seem to fit. Be open to similar symptoms that occur to you, as you review these . . .

*   *   *

_ 1) S/He vehemently and rigidly insists that events, feelings, conversations, and decisions that others witness _ didn't happen—*or* _ happened at a different time, place, or circumstance ["I / you / they) never (said / did / thought / felt) that!"; I am *not* a workaholic!"]

_ 2) S/He fervently declares that major disappointments, losses, or traumas _ "aren't that important," and/or _ "don't effect (or bother) me."

_ 3) S/He (false self) genuinely believes that a key relationship is "fine," when others see major problems.

_ 4) S/He believes a partner is (not) having an affair when they aren't (are). This also is symptomatic of excessive *dis/trust* and toxic fear.

_ 5) S/He is _ steadfastly resistant to taking full responsibility for her / his own life, health, and happiness. S/He _ adopts a "martyr" or "victim" role, and insists, "I can't help it," or "(someone else) won't let me (be responsible.)" Often, this comes from a combination of shame + Self-distrust + reality distortion.

_ 6) S/He often reads incorrect meanings into others' statements and/or actions—e.g. "You *are* angry at me—don't you deny it!"

_ 7) S/He projects her / his own shameful traits onto others ("You're the shopaholic here—not *me!*") This is a co-symptom of toxic shame and guilt.

_ **8)** S/He often refuses to see "flaws," "weaknesses," and/or these behavioral wound-symptoms in _ herself / himself, and/or _ a revered or desperately needed partner, parent, hero/ine, mentor, or child.

_ **9)** S/He frequently rationalizes that clearly abusive, criminal, self-harmful, neglectful, and/or unethical acts are "really OK, because . . . "

_ **10)** S/He automatically minimizes her / his own _ needs, _ risks, _ feelings, _ consequences, _ responsibility, and/or those of others—e.g. "Hey, no big deal (to me)!" and "You're making a big thing out of nothing!"

_ **11)** S/He finds most or all of these false-self symptoms trivial and unremarkable: "So what?"

_ **12)** S/He has _ distorted or _ no clear ideas about what _ emotional, _ spiritual, and/or _ physical abuse, and _ child neglect or _ self neglect are; and s/he _ tolerates any of these without much complaint. Possibly a co-symptom of toxic fear.

_ **13)** S/He believes and justifies clearly unhealthy _ parenting and _ relationship goals, priorities, and techniques.

_ **14)** S/He fervently believes "My childhood and early family were fine / wonderful / healthy / loving / "functional" (high nurturance, per worksheet A) when they clearly *weren't*.

_ **15)** S/He mistakes _ pity, _ neediness (co-dependence), _ control, _ companionship, _ duty, _ rescuing, and/or _ sexual intercourse for *love*; and _ defends, _ rationalizes, or _ denies doing so.

_ **16)** S/He _ believes "My parent/s really loved me," and _ cannot clearly describe how they demonstrated that; and/or s/he _ amplifies, _ misinterprets, or _ invents parental behaviors to "prove" their love.

_ **17)** S/He vehemently blames God, Satan, devils, "evil powers or forces," or the like for unhealthy or immoral personal decisions, or family or world events.

_ **18)** S/He has excessive _ admiration of, _ reliance on, or _ affiliation with, groups, ideologies, or movements that espouse hate, terror, violence, anarchy, crime, superiority, or other wholistically-unhealthy behaviors.

Other knowledgeable people describe her / him as "a bigot," "racist," "redneck," or "hate monger."

_ **19)** S/He constantly thinks and says " . . . never . . . ," or " . . . always . . . ," and may deny this, or get defensive about it.

_ **20)** S/He is unrealistically concerned with "the end days," "final judgment," "the second coming," 'the Rapture," "the false prophet (anti-Christ)," prophecies of global war, famine, pestilence, destruction, alien invasion, and similar catastrophes.

_ **21)** S/He regularly reduces complex life events to two alternatives—i.e. habitually does black/white thinking.

_ **22)** S/He has had—or now has—what others deem a "major paranoia," "delusion," or "neurosis" about some feared person, group, event, object, or situation. S/He _ resists and rejects all contrary evidence, despite painful personal and social consequences.

_ **23)** (Add your own symptom.)

* * *

Which of these symptoms invoked the strongest reactions in you (your inner family)? Do you know why—and in which of your subselves? Consider journaling or tape recording your reactions to this worksheet now or soon. If you want to, record how many of these 22 symptoms you checked: ___. For options on converting major reality distortions to clear perceptions over time, see p. 120.

Awarenesses . . .

J) COMMON SYMPTOMS OF AN INABILITY TO *BOND* OR *LOVE*

Toxic shame is the absence of self-love. It usually comes from not experiencing genuine, consistent, unconditional love as a young child, or (subselves) fearing to trust it when it's offered. In "*Scripts People Live*," Psychologist Claude Steiner wrote that some unhappy people seem to unconsciously choose a "loveless" life script, or plan, despite the resulting emptiness and pain. Camouflaged false-self dominance helps explain why this is so, and what may be done to reduce it.

The experience or feeling of this common wound is hard to describe, yet many people have it. It has been described as feeling empty, alone in the crowd, disconnected, alien, and having a "hole in the soul." Many recovering people report becoming aware that because of denied childhood trauma, they (their inner family members) unconsciously associated love with pain—so they (their false self) reflexively avoided it, while other subselves yearned and strove for it. That can result in a discouraging series of roller-coaster "approach/avoid" relationships and pseudo (pretend) intimacy and mutuality.

If you haven't recently, re-scan the guidelines for using these worksheets on p. 255. Then focus on yourself or another person one at a time, and check which of these typical symptoms of bonding and love barriers seem to apply. Look for the themes here, and identify your own symptoms. These are common signs of being unable to emotionally/spiritually attach or bond with one's Self, other people, and/or a benign (vs. shaming, frightening) Higher Power . . .

*   *   *

_ 1) S/He often feels alone with ("disconnected from") other people.

_ 2) S/He periodically feels "there's something missing in my life, but I don't know what."

_ 3) S/He is unable to relate to the personal reality of "a still small (spiritual) voice within."

_ 4) S/He harshly criticizes religions ("a crutch for the weak,") clergy, church, worship, "do-gooders," missionaries, etc.

_ 5) S/He periodically feels sad, down, or depressed "for no reason."

_ 6) S/He often feels like "being on the outside looking in (at others' lives)."

_ 7) S/He often feels "There's something basically different about me—I'm not like other people."

_ 8) S/He is "religious" but not spiritual; and _ denies, _ defends, _ minimizes, or _ justifies (explains) that.

_ 9) S/He has an _ intellectual, or _ no real (impactful, emotional) relation with a personal Higher Power ("God").

_ 10) S/He is _ puzzled by, and _ unable to empathize with, others who talk about "feeling God's presence" or "having a personal relationship with God."

_ 11) S/He _ is often unable to identify clearly "what I want (or need) now, and may _ "compute" what s/he "should" need, to appear or feel "normal."

_ 12) S/He doesn't really _ understand or _ empathize with any of these symptoms.

_ 13) S/He isn't aware of confusing "love" with pity (for a needy partner)—so "I love you" means "I feel sorry and compassionate for you." This promotes marrying to rescue an alluring (needy) wounded person.

_ 14) S/He _ emotionally and/or _ physically withdraws when real unconditional love is offered, and _ denies, _ rationalizes, _ deplores, and/or _ minimizes this.

_ 15) S/He is unable to articulate clearly and authentically what adult-partner love _ feels like or _ means.

_ 16) S/He becomes anxious, evasive, defensive, mute, "touchy," or "frozen (cold)" if intimate _ conversation or _ behavior turns to love.

_ 17) S/He says "I love you!" but the receiver doesn't feel loved—which may also be a symptom of their own wounds.

_ 18) S/He isn't aware of confusing "love" with lust and sex: so "I love you" really means "I desire you sexually."

_ 19) S/He complains that a partner never says or demonstrates their love enough, or "right." This can either be true, or an inability to receive love because of false-self defenses like reality distortion, distrust, and emotional numbing.

_ 20) S/He _ righteously expects something in return for providing "love," and _ can't understand why this promotes relationship conflict. S/He probably has never *felt* unconditionally loved, or has repressed that agonizing awareness.

_ 21) S/He isn't aware of confusing "love" with dependence: so "I love you" really means "I (mainly) need and expect you to fill my needs."

_ 22) S/He shows "love" by providing physical things and/or "good times."

_ 23) S/He isn't aware of confusing "love" with duty: "I love you" really means "I'm supposed to feel 'love' for you (but I can only guess what that is, so I'll pretend.)"

_ 24) S/He is chronically self-abandoning: i.e. s/he is unable to genuinely feel and demonstrate consistent, unconditional love for herself / himself, by putting healthy food, rest, exercise, and medical care at high authentic priority. Amplified by toxic shame.

_ **25)** S/He is unaware of confusing "love" with obligation: "If you really loved me, you would/n't . . . "

_ **26)** S/He is _ habitually uncomfortable with, or _ avoids, spontaneous physical expressions of love: i.e. s/he avoids appropriate caressing, hugging, stroking, and kissing. Alternative: s/he _ pretends to want to do these ("fakes it"), and _ denies that pretense internally and/or interpersonally (reality distortions).

_ **27)** S/He _ has acquaintances, but few or no real friends. S/He may _ pay professional counselors to listen, because "there's no one else (that I trust to care about and hear me)."

_ **28)** S/He often experiences social events as "chores" to be endured or avoided, vs. enjoyed. S/He may _ acknowledge, _ discount, or _ deny this.

_ **29)** S/He has (had) affair(s), and/or _ is emotionally or _ legally separated or divorced one or more times; or s/he has _ never married.

_ **30)** S/He . . . (add your own symptom.)

*   *   *

Reflect: which of these symptoms invoked the strongest reactions in you (your inner family)? Do you know why—and in which of your subselves? Consider journaling or tape recording your reactions to this worksheet now or soon. For overall assessment conclusions, record how many of these 29 symptoms you checked: ___. For recovery options on improving the ability to *feel* and bond (care), see p. 122.

Awarenesses . . .

K) SYMPTOMS OF *CO-DEPENDENCE*

This last wounded-assessment worksheet offers a two-part checklist of common traits of adults with the psychological condition (vs. disease) of *co-dependence*. This term evolved in the 1980's from *co-alcoholic*, which mental health workers used to describe someone who is emotionally enmeshed with someone addicted to ethyl alcohol. Many now view this unhealthy enmeshment as a relationship addiction. A "co-dependent" is someone with many or most of the behavioral symptoms below.

People burdened with this condition obsessively over-focus on the current welfare and activities of another (wounded) person—often another addict. In doing this, they consistently lose sight of their own personal needs, abilities, feelings, goals, and lives. Until in effective recovery, they lose healthy me/you *boundaries*, and their own personal *identity*.

Typical co-dependents are unconsciously attracted to alluring, needy wounded people. As with addiction to substances, activities, and emotional states, co-dependence significantly reduces both the quality and length of life, and puts dependent kids at risk of major false-self wounding.

Typical kids trapped in significantly low-nurturance childhoods are in a chronic state of fluctuating inner pain. Therefore, they're at significant risk of becoming dependent on the temporary relief ("comfort") of one or more of the four types of addiction—including *relationships*.

After 23 years' study, I believe any addiction is initially powered by a false-self's instinctive drive to self medicate—i.e. to numb or mentally distract young subselves from emotional and spiritual *agony* and *emptiness*. Those come from psychological wounds and unawareness of healing alternatives. That's *woundedness*, not *sickness*!

Like other true addictions, as co-dependence progresses, it generates *more* emotional pain, and is self-amplifying. Managing (stabilizing) any addiction ("sobriety") is the gateway that enables significant progress on freeing your true Self and reducing these wounds (*full* recovery). "Dry drunks" are people who have stabilized their addiction, or exchanged one unhealthy compulsion for another, but have not recognized or healed their false-self's dominance. They are in pseudo recovery.

Real, vs. pseudo, recovery provides true emotional/spiritual comfort, and helps breaks addiction distortions and toxic dependencies. Healing the twin roots of inner-family shame, and terror of abandonment (aloneness), usually permanently reduces the roots and symptoms of co-dependence or "love" addiction.

The two sets of traits below are gratefully adapted from public Codependents Anonymous ("CoDA") 12-step materials. The more traits you check, the more likely that you or others are (1) significantly controlled by a well-meaning false self, and (2) that you have (or had) a *dependent*, vs. a balanced *inter*dependent, relationship. If not acknowledged and healed, both of these inexorably put you and any dependent kids at significant risk of escalating stresses, and potential (re)divorce.

Co-dependence is a *normal*, widespread psychological condition *that can be reduced.* It is *not* a sign of *craziness, badness, failure, weirdness*, or a *"character defect"*! It *is* a significantly harmful psychological-spiritual condition that deserves serious attention, awareness, and patient, corrective effort. Since the 1980's, a great deal of effective help has become available. See, for example, the Hazelden Institute's catalog (**http://www.hazelden. org**) on the Web.

Directions

Review the guidelines for using these wound-assessment worksheets on p. 255. Then mentally focus on your relationship with _ your present partner, _ a former partner, or _ another key adult like a parent, sibling, relative, child, co-worker, or friend. With that relationship in mind, fill out the two checklists below, slowly and thoughtfully.

Mull whether each trait usually or generally applies to you, and separately, to your chosen other. Try not to focus on what others may think of your answers. You don't *have to* show them to anyone—and—it may be helpful to do so. If you're unsure about an item, use "?." Optionally, use 1 to 10 to indicate the importance or frequency of an item.

As you do the worksheet, notice your images, thoughts, and feelings—or their absence—*without judgment.* Also notice your breathing, posture, and sensations. These reactions are clues to "the truth." They're just as important learnings as your written responses.

If it feels right, change the wording of any item, and/or add items.

About Our Relationship

Me / You

_ 1) My good feelings about who I am depend on feeling liked by you.

_ 2) My good feelings about who I am depend on getting approval from you.

_ 3) Your struggle affects my serenity. My mental attention focuses on solving your problems, or relieving your pain.

_ 4) My mental attention is usually focused on _ pleasing you, and _ protecting you.

_ 5) My Self esteem is bolstered by _ solving your problems, and _ relieving your pain.

_ 6) My _ hobbies and _ interests are put aside. My _ time is spent sharing your hobbies and interests.

_ 7) Your _ clothing, _ personal appearance, and _ behavior follow my desires, as I feel you are a reflection of me.

_ 8) I'm seldom aware of how I feel; I'm mainly aware of how you feel.

_ 9) I'm seldom aware of what I want; I ask or assume what you want.

_ 10) My dreams of the future are mainly linked to you.

_ 11) My fears of your _ rejection and _ anger strongly shape what I say and do.

_ 12) I use giving as a key way of feeling safe in our relationship.

_ **13)** My own social circle diminishes as I involve myself with you.

_ **14)** I put many of my values aside in order to stay in relationship with you.

_ **15)** I value your opinions and ways of doing most things more than mine.

_ **16)** The quality of my life hinges largely on the quality of yours.

_ **17)**

_ **18)**

Awarenesses . . .

Shift mental gears, sort out your reactions to what you just did, and relax. When you feel ready, again focus on yourself and, optionally, on a past or present partner. For each of you, check which traits you feel probably apply. As you do, recall: this assessment is not about judging you or another to be "bad," "sick," or "crazy"—it's about discerning inner disharmony that needs to be healed!

General Traits of Codependents

Me/You

_ **1)** We automatically assume responsibility for others' feelings and/or behaviors.

_ **2)** We have trouble identifying our feelings; invalidate them; and/or often feel _ confused or _ guilty about, or _ ashamed of them.

_ **3)** We have trouble freely expressing feelings: i.e. "I'm happy / sad / joyful / hurt / confused / enraged / scared / anxious / numb / . . . "

_ **4)** We often fear or worry about how others may respond to our feelings and behaviors.

_ 5) We can't say "no" to others _ at all, or _ without major guilt and anxiety.

_ 6) We automatically equate love with pain, anxiety or fear, and/or pity.

_ 7) We generally have trouble making and keeping close relationships.

_ 8) We greatly fear being hurt and/or rejected by others—and often expect these, despite all reassurances.

_ 9) We often have trouble making firm decisions.

_ 10) We often minimize, alter, and even deny the truth about how we really feel.

_ 11) We typically react to others' actions and attitudes, rather than act on our own.

_ 12) We usually put other people's needs and wants well before our own—automatically.

_ 13) Our fear of others' feelings (e.g. anger, indifference, and disapproval) largely determines what we say and do.

_ 14) We question or ignore our own values in order to be accepted and liked by significant others. We often value others' opinions more than ours.

_ 15) We often feel empty, different, and depressed, "for no reason."

_ 16) Our self-esteem is bolstered by events outside of us. We have great trouble acknowledging good things about ourselves.

_ 17) Our serenity and mental attention is determined by how others are feeling or acting.

_ 18) We tend to judge everything we do, think, or say, harshly, by someone else's standards. Few things we do, say, or think are "good enough." Perfectionism feels normal to us.

_ **19)** We don't know or believe that being vulnerable and asking for help is OK and normal.

_ **20)** We don't know that it's OK to talk about personal problems outside the family; or that feelings just are—and that it's better to share them than to deny, minimize, or justify them.

_ **21)** We're steadfastly loyal, even when we're repeatedly discounted, shamed, neglected, or used.

_ **22)** We have to feel clearly and steadily *needed* to have an OK relationship with others.

_ **23)**

Notice the similarity of many of these items to others in these other wound-assessment worksheets. Also reflect on which of these symptoms invoked the strongest reactions in you (your inner family)? Do you know why—and in which of your subselves? Consider journaling or tape recording your reactions to this worksheet now or soon. If you want to, record how many of these 38 (combined) symptoms of co-dependence you checked: __.

Awarenesses . . .

10)   USING YOUR ASSESSMENT RESULTS

If you've had the courage and stamina to use most or all of these 11 wound-assessment worksheets, I congratulate you! Doing so suggests that you're in significant discomfort, and/or you have a clear vision of a more fulfilling, enjoyable life for you and any dependent kids. How can you use these assessment results to get that life? Start by answering these core questions:

- "Who has *really* been running my life? Has an unseen false self been making many or all of my key life decisions?"

- "Am I, or was I, committing to a partner who is significantly wounded?"

    If you have dependent children:

- "Are my kids at risk of false-self wounding because of too little emotional/spiritual nurturance? See p. 257.

    If you're a clinician, clergyperson, doctor or nurse, educator, family-law professional, caseworker, or mediator, another vital question is . . .

- "Does my professional work promote my clients', students', or patients' awareness and acceptance of their inner-family, and who's leading it?"

Here are some options and suggestions about answering each of these vital questions.

1) Are You Ruled by a False self?

If you feel without doubt "Yes, I am," then skip to question two. If you're unsure, *or feel "No, I'm OK,"* read on.

Answering this question honestly can be as hard as answering "Do I have a life-threatening disease?" If you are wounded, your false-self Guardian parts are fiercely dedicated to protecting you *now* from fear and other discomfort. Unable or unwilling to see the long-range implications, these subselves will persistently distort your reality by using one or more strategies like these:

- Denial ("No, I'm not significantly wounded")

- Minimization ("Well, I'm wounded a little, but everyone is. No big deal.")

- Intellectualizing or rationalizing ("Let's really analyze *why* I might be wounded, and what it might mean—but let's not *feel* anything, or decide to *do* anything to reduce the wounds.")

- Procrastination ("These are definitely important questions. I'll use my worksheet results to answer them *later*, after I . . . ")

- Persuasion ("This is too complicated and boring. Put the book down.")

- Catastrophizing —"Oh my God—if I *really* face what these worksheets mean, my life will be a disaster!"

- Deflection—("I'm pretty sure my mate (and/or child) is badly wounded. I've got to save her/him! I'll take care of *me* later.")

Against well-meant defenses like these, how can your Self answer the vital questions above? Reality: if your false self is running your life now, your Self may not be able to break free and use what you found from the worksheets. If you're hurting enough, weary enough, and/or scared enough for your kids' sake—you can break free now.

From experience with many recoverers (including myself), I trust that *your unblended Self knows how to meaningfully interpret your results here.*

Quiet your other inner and outer "voices," breathe well, trust what your "still, small voice" says, and *listen*. If your false self will let you, you'll become aware of a "sense," "hunch," or "certainty" about each of the relevant questions above.

Collect Your Results

Only you can decide what "significantly wounded" is. If you aren't sure whether a false self dominates you "too much," look at the results from all 11 worksheets together:

1) I checked __ of 28 traits of a high-nurturance birthfamily (more is better).
2) I checked __ of 43 common behavioral traits of significantly-wounded people.
3) Family-tree clues: do my ancestors clearly show five or more of the traits? Yes / No
4) I checked __ of 19 high-nurturance behaviors, relative to my birth family.
5) I checked __ of 29 symptoms of being dominated by a false self.
6) I checked __ of 39 symptoms of excessive shame and guilt.
7) I checked __ of 35 symptoms of excessive fears.
8) I checked __ of 19 symptoms of overtrusting or undertrusting.
9) I checked __ of 23 symptoms of major reality distortions.
10) I checked __ of 29 symptoms of an inability to bond or to love.
11) I checked __ of 38 symptoms of co-dependence (relationship addiction).

Looking at all these results together raises the odds that your Self will get a clear reading on whether you're significantly wounded despite any Guardian subselves' well-meant, misguided attempts to protect you from knowing. Generally . . .

The more symptoms of all the worksheets you check for yourself or another person, the more likely it is that you or they are held in protective custody by a defensive, reactive, short-sighted false self.

"Significantly" means if you work to empower your true Self, you'll feel your life will be noticeably "better"—calmer, healthier, and more productive, satisfying, and enjoyable. A rough rule of thumb: I suspect if you checked over half of these traits, you *probably* (vs. surely) are ruled by a false self much or most of the time. Other key indicators:

- From these worksheets, the partners I've been most attracted to are probably or surely wounded: _ yes _ no _ unsure

- From these worksheets, I believe that one or more of the adults who raised me as a young child was (then) probably or surely dominated by a false self: _ yes _ no _ unsure.

- I _ have had, or _ now have, a major addiction to a substance (including food), an activity (like work, gambling, exercise, or sex), a relationship, and/or a mood state (like excitement).

- I _ probably or _ surely was sexually molested, as a child.

- _ I am now, or probably will be, divorced at least once.

If some of your subselves feel uneasy or scared here, comfort them by noting that everyone, probably including your most revered mentors and hero/ines, has some of these wound symptoms! The *degree* of wounding, and its *effects* in your and your kids' lives, are the main issues.

Recall that a typical false-self trait is rigid black/white thinking. That might manifest here as "I'm either wounded or I'm not." Recall that wounding ranges from "a little" to "significant" to "extreme." Extreme wounding was called Multiple Personality Disorder, now known as Dissociative Identity Disorder, or "D.I.D." Because false-self dominance seems to be our cultural norm, the *real* questions are . . .

- "How wounded am I—low, moderate, or high?"

- "What might I experience if I work at empowering my true Self, and harmonizing my inner family?"

I again encourage you to avoid false-self dominance as meaning you're sick, weird, crazy, or bad. This is also not about blaming your parents and caregivers, their ancestors, or "society." Ignorance is a burden and limitation, not a fault!

True-Self Symptoms

A final way of estimating who's *really* running your life is to assess how often you feel the symptoms of a true Self in control: *light, centered, grounded, alive, aware, focused, purposeful, compassionate, serene, firm, resilient, realistically optimistic, patient, grateful, humble, confident, and energized.*

Over the last several years, I have felt combinations of feelings like these . . .

_ never
_ one to several days a month, on average
_ several days a week, on average
_ most of the time
_ all the time

Option: to reduce inevitable subjectivity and bias, explain these Self-in-charge traits to several people whom you trust, and know you "reasonably well." Then ask their honest opinions about how often they see you manifest these traits. If you or they are uneasy with "the truth" here, that's probably a sign of inner wounds in someone.

False-self dominance is no different than having a major physical injury. Once it's identified, you and others can reduce it, over time, using our amazing human ability to regain impaired health. In true recovery, your Self will choose inner and outer environments that activate that ability.

Self-directed parts work (Part 2) can help you identify and get to know your inner-family members better. Doing this is the second step in true recovery, after deciding that you want to reduce false-self dominance. Vital awarenesses that will evolve from your inner-family work are learning "Which of my subselves are *really* running my life, and how does that dominance affect my (and my children's) serenity, joy, health, and relationships recently?"

Whether you now think or "know" you're significantly wounded or not, you have several options: learn more, get qualified help, and/or decide on your best options with your partner, and with any dependent kids. Here's some perspective on each of these.

Learn More

Read some or all of the selected titles following p. 369. Option: journal your thoughts, feelings, and awarenesses (and inner voices) as you read. Be patient here—this research is about improving the rest of your life!

If you haven't yet, read Part 2 before deciding what to do next. Doing so will widen your perspective on your recovery options and resources.

Be alert for other people who are in some form of high-priority personal recovery, and learn from them. Their specifics will differ, but their goals are the same as yours—a healthier life, and protection of minor kids. Most people who attend 12-step ("Anonymous") meetings are seriously dedicated to the first phase of true recovery—addiction management (vs. "cure.") All are probably significantly wounded, and I suspect very few know it.

Some local mental-health agencies, hospitals, and community colleges may sponsor periodic seminars on some form of recovery. If they do, they probably won't use terms like "false-self dominance" or "inner family harmony." Your unblended Self will know whether you should attend.

Try journaling, without pre-judging what you think you'll experience or learn. If you do this regularly for several weeks—without distractions—I suspect you'll learn some useful, interesting things about what's going on in your inner family! I recommend Julia Cameron's upbeat book *"The Artist's Way"* as an interesting, inspiring, practical guide.

A related option is to thoughtfully write your own autobiography, using what you learned here and from other sources. (Notice what your subselves say now about this possibility!)

Get Help from a Qualified Professional

There are at least two reasons to get professional help in evaluating your need for recovery, and guiding you on your way.

First, your view of yourself is self-protective—i.e. skewed. Friends' and caring relatives' judgments are probably biased toward your comfort, too ("Naw, you're not majorly wounded!") An objective, knowledgeable professional can help your Self guard against accepting biased inner and outer conclusions as to whether you're significantly wounded. Option: review this book and the worksheet results with any consultant you hire.

Secondly, if a false self often rules you, the odds are high those vigilant subselves are trying to protect you via one or more self-comforting addictions. These may include chemicals (including nicotine, sugar, and fat); toxic relationships (co-dependence); activities (e.g. workaholism); and/ or mood states (like *love, arousal,* or *excitement.*) If you have an addiction and aren't working an active "recovery program," you're probably denying or minimizing it (false-self reality distortion). That raises the odds you'll skew your assessment conclusions here, and defer or cripple your healing.

That in turn puts any dependent kids at high risk of false-self formation and wounding.

Veteran recoverers and trauma-recovery professionals consistently suggest you should be addiction-free for at least a year before working on full recovery. A licensed addiction counselor can help you assess whether you have a true addiction, and guide you toward managing it, over time. Your local mental-health agency or hospital can tell you what initials identify local addiction professionals—e.g. in Illinois, C.A.C. means "Certified Addiction Counselor."

The next major question these worksheets can help you start to answer is . . .

2) Is (or Was) My Partner Significantly Wounded?

If you're committed to someone you feel is probably or surely dominated by a false self, what does that mean, and what are your choices? Note: if you have "many" of the traits of co-dependence (p. 316), it's *very* likely _ your excellent partner (and/or any ex mate) is significantly injured, and _ you'll have a distorted view of this.

Bottom line: if your present partner, and/or a former one, is or was dominated by a false self . . .

• That's added evidence that *you* have significant inner-family chaos to quell, because false selves seem to choose other dominant false selves, over and over again.

• Despite vows to the contrary, their self-protective false selves are apt to sabotage or discourage your true recovery. And . . .

• If you co-parent minor kids (or grandkids) with them, each of those youngsters are at major risk of false-self wounding.

So: if you haven't already, re-do the 11 assessment worksheets. Focus first on your present partner, if any, and then on any ex mate/s. Preliminary clue: if you and/or they are psychologically or legally divorced and unrecovering, that's a strong clue that one or both of you are controlled by a false self. If you two have had major legal battles over money or kids, the odds of you both being dominated by false selves approach 100%.

If your present partner and/or a co-parenting ex mate is probably wounded, what are your options? The choices you lean toward will reflect who's making them—your Self, or someone else. False-self choices might include one or more of these:

- Avoid creating a firestorm (conflict), and keep your opinion to yourself.

- Triumphantly show them this book, and/or the worksheets, to confirm that the accusations you've made about them have been right all along. ("See—this *proves* you're nuts!")

- Hint or vaguely suggest that they "might benefit" if they "skim or scan" this book or another recovery resource. Leave the book "lying around," hoping they'll pick it up. Another indirect option is to begin using inner-family (subself) and recovery terms in your conversations, and/or telling anecdotes about "people in recovery," without explaining why you're doing that. Note that covert communications *always* breed anxiety, doubt, and distrust.

- Demand that your partner "get into recovery right *now*," or (some calamity will happen.)

- Try to manipulate your partner into assessing and/or recovering, by threatening dire consequences to any kids involved ("If you were any kind of responsible parent, you'd want to . . . ")

- Continue to focus and obsess on them, and ignore your own recovery.

If your Self is "driving your (personality) bus," s/he may ask your partner to read this book and any other writings you've found useful. Talk with your mate directly about the ideas here, and recommend that s/he use the worksheets to evaluate for false-self symptoms. If s/he procrastinates, defers, refuses, or says, "I've already done that (healed)," or gets "upset"—*red* light! In responding, to you, does s/he display the true-Self traits?

Be aware (beware) of feeling anxious about, or responsible for, your partner's reactions and decisions. Avoid *enabling* them: i.e. taking responsibility for what they must do for themselves. Helping them "for their own good" (rescuing) is a sure sign of co-dependence (false-self dominance) in *you*. The paradoxic alternative is to help them by encouraging them, but not doing *for* them: help by *not* helping. Note that these wounds often produce the paradox ("double message") of someone in pain pleading, "*Please* help me"—and then criticizing or ignoring the help that you or others offer.

If you're courting a wounded person, postpone any long-term relationship commitments until you and your partner make clear, solid choices about any relevant personal recoveries. Needy, unaware, wounded people (their false selves) are at high risk of mistakenly believing that getting married, and/or having a child, will *help*—i.e. provide the comforts they've been self medicating for. This is *vital* if either of you already have minor custodial or non-custodial kids.

From 22 years' experience with hundreds of troubled couples, I believe (re)marriage and child conception or adoption will *never* really solve any major psycho-spiritual problems either of you have, long term. Validate this with people in true, vs. pseudo, recovery for five or more years. I believe (denied inner wounds + a group of unawarenesses) are core causes of our tragic U.S. (re)divorce epidemic. See **http://sfhelp.org/hazards.htm**

Perspective: two wounded people who are each committed to their individual recoveries can build an exceptionally strong, nourishing relationship! Two resources that can promote that are "*Embracing Each Other*," by Hal Stone and Sidra Winkleman; and "*Getting the Love you Want*," by Harville Hendrix.

If you're a divorced parent of young or grown kids, what are your options here?

Use these 11 worksheets to evaluate your ex(es) for false-self symptoms. Do this for your kids' sakes, not your former partner's. If both of you co-parents are significantly wounded, which is very common among divorced American families, it's likely your kids are developing protective false selves.

Option: use awarenesses from this book to convert disdain or hostility into genuine (vs. dutiful) compassion for your ex. If you've blamed, resented, and disrespected her or him for past behaviors, don't blame yourself—*and* try seeing him or her as a majorly wounded person from a low-nurturance childhood, vs. a "bad" person or prior mate. Genuine compassion breeds forgiveness—which helps *all of you* heal. Your distrustful false self will probably resist such an attitude shift, specially if those subselves are shame-based.

If s/he's receptive, alert your ex to this book and related sources and materials. Avoid hidden agendas or expectations. Again—be alert for co-dependent urges to rescue, blame, analyze, preach, or condescend. Those are typical disrespectful false-self behaviors that *invite* reciprocal wounding in other people.

Be patient, and avoid black/white pronouncements ("Gerry will never change.") Stay aware that accumulated pain, weariness, and hopelessness are powerful recovery motivators. As wounded people in protective denials turn middle-aged, they can "hit bottom," and start true recovery literally any day. If, when, and how that may happen is beyond your abilities to control or predict.

3) Is a Beloved Child Ruled by a False self?

If you can really bond and love—i.e. *care*—(p. 312), perhaps the most painful conclusion you'll draw here is that one or more kids you care about is probably or surely burdened by psychological wounds. The flip side of that is, you can apply the ideas here to protect such kids from further wounding, and do what you can to help them empower their true Selves (heal), over time. The positive results of your efforts to do this will spread down the future generations in ways you'll never know.

Though each child and family situation is unique, there are some general guidelines you can tailor to strengthen your chances to be of real help . . .

- *Work steadily on your own recovery*, and use it to intentionally increase the nurturance level of your kids' environment (p. 257).

- *Sharpen your understanding of what your kids need*, so you can "nurture (fill their needs) strategically." Typical minor kids of divorce or parental death have at least three concurrent sets of adjustment needs:

a) Their age-dependent set of over 20 *normal development tasks*, like learning to socialize, study, set goals, problem-solve, balance pleasure, work, and rest; and so on;

b) Heal their mix of the six inner wounds. Kids can't heal themselves. When present, the traits will hinder mastery of these other several sets of concurrent tasks. A third set is . . .

c) *Divorce-adjustment tasks.* Average kids and adults each may have over a dozen mental and emotional adjustment needs to fill, so their reorganized (vs. "broken") family can grieve, stabilize, and resume growth.

Typical minor and grown stepkids have a fourth set of needs, which are often concurrent with the prior three sets:

d) *Stepfamily adjustment.* When one or both bioparents seriously courts a "new adult," all co-parents, kids, and kin face a stunningly complex emotional + financial + physical + social merger of three or more extended biofamilies, over four or more years after re/wedding.

Providing such needy kids with a consistently high-nurturance environment—while managing marriage, personal recovery, and lesser life responsibilities—is no small challenge! For more on these four sets of needs, see *Build a High-nurturance Stepfamily* (Xlibris.com), or **http:// sfhelp.org/sf/co/kid_needs.htm** on the Web.

- If one or more of the kids' other caregiver/s seem to be dominated by false selves, tailor the options above to fit your situation, and patiently apply them within your limits. Avoid trying to plead, con, or force other co-parents into recovery. These are fruitless and usually self-defeating. By definition, true recovery must be Self-motivated and self-serving.

- If you're a divorced or widowed parent dating an alluring new partner who seems significantly wounded, one of the best things you can do for your child(ren) is to *not* commit to this person and related stepfamily stress until you get a clear reading on whether s/he'll start self-motivated recovery.

- Depending on how serious you feel the child's mix of the six inner wounds is, take responsibility for finding appropriate professional help. It's unlikely you'll find anyone familiar with the ideas in this book—and veteran child therapists can be a major help anyway. Option: if you feel this book merits it, show it to any clinician you hire, and use it—and the four sets of tasks highlighted above—as a framework for defining how you're trying to help your child/ren.

In my experience, many people ruled by false selves gravitate to "the helping professions." If you work directly with people to improve some aspect of their wholistic health (clergy, counselor, teacher, doctor, lawyer, caseworker, etc.) a fourth question for you to evaluate here is . . .

4) Am I Promoting My Students' / Patients' / Clients' Recoveries, or Not?

Fully exploring this vital question merits a separate book. Two key points to mull:

- Your choice of profession may indicate that *you* are significantly wounded and unaware of it, so far.

- Despite professional training, our inherited one-brain, one personality myth promotes professionals being unaware of wounds in themselves and those they serve. Therefore, they often ignore, minimize, and/ or misdiagnose false-self dominance as something else—e.g. "addiction," or (some) "depressions." In so doing, they miss the root problem—protective false self-dominance—so often the symptoms recur in the same or different forms. This includes some (most?) psychosomatic conditions.

Whether you're significantly wounded or not—if you're not consciously focusing on assessing those you serve for false-self symptoms, and not teaching and promoting self awareness and internal Self leadership, you risk spending your and their resources on solving surface problems (symptoms). My experience suggests that their presenting problems will eventually return in the same or different form.

If you need to recover and defer that, you're false self will probably skew your professional service to hide your set of the six false-self wounds. In other words, by practicing your profession in denial of your own major false-self wounds, you risk providing inadequate or even harmful (wound-enhancing) service to your clients, patients, and/or students. This is specially impactful if you teach, advise, or evaluate other human-service professionals. As far as I know, ethical codes of professional conduct don't yet evaluate for this.

You also risk working in, and contributing to, a low-nurturance organization (ref. worksheets A and D). Doing so will probably hinder or block your personal recovery, and unintentionally promote wounding in your co-workers and those you all serve. Option: use copies of the worksheets here to estimate whether your immediate supervisor and the top executives in your organization are significantly injured. If they are, a medium-range personal recovery goal becomes leaving this organization, and finding another with a higher nurturance level.

Clergywomen and men are in a particularly vulnerable and powerful position. They are uniquely positioned to explain false-self dominance and wounds to couples seeking sanctified marital union, and to encourage or require courting couples to assess themselves for significant false-self dominance *before* conceiving children in a low-nurturance environment. They have perhaps the best chance at breaking our insidious ancestral cycle, and sparing couples and their kids years of future heartbreak and agony.

Those who train and ordain clergy have an even greater implied responsibility to include this complex "taboo" topic (inherited false-self wounds) in their curricula and ordination requirements.

An incendiary extension of this concept is far beyond the scope of this book. If the 13 premises on pp. 29-33 are true, our society must eventually confront itself: we currently require no licenses or parenting-competence certification for couples that procreate and add a child to our global society. I believe psychological or legal divorce is a clear symptom that a false self significantly dominates one or both mates. The stark fact that almost half of U.S. marriages fail legally, and untold millions more exist in misery, testifies that most U.S. families are relatively low-nurturance. We are taxed to fund billions of dollars to treat the *symptoms* of false-self wounds, without looking squarely at the root cause: *many couples are too wounded and unaware to competently raise kids with dominant true Selves*. I don't know of any school systems that consciously try to promote their students' true Selves. Do you?

This chapter has offered ideas on using your worksheet results to answer four core questions:

- "Who has *really* been running my life? Has an unseen false self been making many or all of my key life decisions?" This is the central question posed by this book.

- "Am I, or was I, committed to a partner who is significantly wounded?"

- "If you have dependent children: "Are my kids at risk of psychological wounding because of too little emotional/spiritual nurturance?

If you're a clinician, clergyperson, doctor or nurse, educator, family-law professional, caseworker, or mediator, another vital question is . . .

- "Does my professional work promote my clients', students', or patients' awareness and acceptance of their inner-family, and who's leading it?"

Whatever your answers to these, note your feelings, and collect yourself. Recall why you first picked up this book. What's happened among your inner family members since you did so? When you feel ready, let's recap, and finish this part of your journey together . . .

11) SUMMING UP, AND NEXT STEPS

Evidence across the centuries suggests that though we have one body and one physical brain, our human personality has the natural capacity to be multi-faceted. We are the first generation of people to be able to see images of living brains at work. PET radiology scans show many separate parts of our brains activating simultaneously to produce all our "unitary" daily experiences. For instance, the "simple" automatic act of discerning and decoding these words is probably activating well over a dozen interdependent regions in your brain at this moment—yet you have no awareness of that. The further marvel is that you're digesting, breathing, listening, tasting, hearing, feeling, imaging, blinking, fighting off germs, cellularly dividing, pumping and filtering blood, producing and monitoring hormones—all at the same time you're "reading"—without conscious awareness. Awesome!

Your multi-faceted *personality* can be viewed as a dynamic *inner* family of "parts," or subselves. They are semi-autonomous centers in your brain, and interact like the individual members of an orchestra or sports team. Every personality appears to include a natural leader part called (here) your Self (capital "S"). If allowed to, s/he acts like a seasoned musical conductor or athletic coach to promote group harmony, growth, and effectiveness.

Personality formation is powerfully affected by early childhood family experience. Families exist to fill primal needs of their members, because other human groups can't do so as well. Because of their leaders, some families and other human groups are more wholistically healthy than others—i.e. their members get their emotional, spiritual, and physical needs met more often. Restated—any family's nurturance level can be ranked low to high. Nurturance level means the degree to which caregivers spontaneously fill a young child's primal needs for safe touching, validation, encouragement, securities, respect, companionship, stimulation, play, listening, and protections from unsafe choices. Adult members have the same needs, but have more social options to fill them. From various sources, Worksheet A (p. 257) gives 28 high-nurturance family traits.

Though unverified by formal research, my personal and clinical experience since 1985 with over 1,000 average American adults and some of their kids strongly suggests why some personalities fragment more than others. The *emotional-spiritual* nurturance level of a young child's home greatly affects whether a false self forms, how it behaves, and how their caregivers and environment respond. Caregivers in low-nurturance families are usually significantly wounded—meaning their various subselves often *blend* with, or take over, their true Self. Such people choose each other unconsciously as mates again and again—and unconsciously replicate low-nurturance homes, just as their wounded, uneducated ancestors did. True (vs. pseudo) personal recovery can break that toxic bequest.

Most (all?) young children automatically develop a neural group of semi-independent subselves. The subselves can be grouped by function and traits as . . .

- Managers, including the Self, who control the inner family when no threat is apparent;

- Young subselves, who activate when they perceive danger, shame, guilt, fear, or loneliness; and . . .

- Narrow-focused Guardian subselves who distrust and take over the true Self in order to comfort, soothe, and protect the Inner Kids around the clock. Each Guardian has one or more unique current strategies to do this—which paradoxically may be harmful to the person long range.

- Many people believe in a fourth group of one or more *spiritual* subselves or "energies."

When they perceive inner and outer *danger,* young and Guardian subselves can "blend with" (take over) or paralyze your Self, usually without you knowing it. When that happens, you and others do harmful things to yourself and each other, including kids, "against my better judgment." Typical survivors of low childhood nurturance believe that their (false self's) behaviors are *normal,* even if displeasing or harmful. They *are* normal—for significantly wounded people. We routinely and protectively blame "other factors" for our life problems, rather than our reactive, impulsive, short-sighted, misinformed false self crew of personality parts.

When false selves frequently dominate inner-families (personalities) like yours, typical adults and kids have mixes of these six psychological wounds:

- Often being controlled by a well-intentioned, short-sighted, reactive false self, which causes . . .

- Excessive shame and guilts,

- Excessive fears,

- Compulsively overtrusting or undertrusting yourself, other people, and a Higher Power.

- In proportion to their degrees, these four wounds combine to cause . . .

- Protective reality distortions—e.g. denials, repressions, exaggerations, intellectualizing, black-white thinking, emotional numbing, mind reading, and "forgetting;" and . . .

- Difficulty bonding (attaching emotionally and spiritually to others), and feeling and exchanging genuine love.

Unacknowledged, these injuries combine to cause major health and life problems: chronic illness and self-neglect, addictions, "depression," isolation or failed relationships (e.g. divorce), unintentionally passing on false-self wounds to dependent kids, unrealized or unborn dreams, and often premature death—well short of living up to personal potentials.

When an adult or child is currently or often controlled by a group of Inner Kids and Guardian subselves—a "false self"—they typically exhibit characteristic personal and social behaviors. The 11 worksheets in Part 3 provide different ways of assessing whether you or another person have those traits and behaviors to excess. Ultimately, your unblended Self is the best judge of this.

Children who form a false self are naturally adapting to their emotional and spiritual environment—they are *not* sick, crazy, or weird. A small percentage of highly traumatized (neglected) kids are extremely fragmented, and develop what used to be called "Multiple Personality Disorder." Moderate to major false-self dominance seems to be our cultural and human norm—yet we don't acknowledge that yet, out of fear, superstition, and inherited ignorance. Because normal personality anarchy is socially labeled as "going crazy" and "acting out (badly)," most wounded kids quickly learn to camouflage the symptoms of their emerging false self to appear "normal" to themselves and others. Their wounded, shame-based caregivers often instinctively mute or hide the symptoms of their and their kids' inner family anarchy from themselves and others, because they (i.e. their Young subselves) fear role failure, rejection, scorn, and/or pity.

In very low-nurturance homes, typical kids are overwhelmed, and the emotional, physical, and social symptoms of false-self control are painfully obvious. Our national runaway, school dropout, delinquent, and teen-parent subcultures are composed of such highly wounded kids. Our 12-step subculture and related multi-billion dollar addiction-recovery industry are populated by kids and adults usually dominated by false selves.

This book is for lay and professional people who want to learn if they—and others they care about—are significantly wounded, psychologically. Part 1 overviews the concept of your *inner* family of personality subselves. The first half of Part 2 overviews the life process of psychological wounding and coping attempts, hitting the wall, and then proactively recovering from false-self wounds over many years.

The second half outlines a tested, effective way of recovery: meeting and reorganizing (harmonizing) your inner family and empowering your Self, via "parts work," or "inner-family work." Parts work applies proven family-therapy techniques to our *inner* families of dynamic subselves. The details of this work are unique for each recoverer, but the theme is the same for all. Inner-family work leads toward recognizing and safely freeing your Self from "protective custody" by a distrustful group of "false self" parts. That allows reorganizing and harmonizing them all, over time—producing permanent, beneficial second-order (core attitude) life changes.

Part 3 of this book offers 11 self-assessment worksheets to allow overcoming normal false-self resistances and deceptions, and learning if a false self dominates you. Part 4 provides a set of resources to help recoverers along the way. The good news: there are *many* useful recovery resources available now. The bad news: there are *millions* of adults and kids who desperately need them, and the great majority doesn't know it. The recent trend of increasing public and professional awareness of "Adult Children" (wounded people) and the need for recovery is hopeful for us all . . .

Pause and reflect: do you remember why you initially picked up this book? What was it that caught your attention, and what were you curious about, or interested in? Did you note that inside the front cover, as the Introduction suggested? The title asks, "Who's *really* running your life?" Do you have a clearer answer to that now? Which of your subselves is replying?

What Now?

As always, you have many choices . . .

- If you haven't yet, try meeting and talking with one of your subselves. Use the "Hello" and "First Meeting" guidelines on pp. 155 and 190. Your subselves are more likely to remain skeptical or indifferent to these ideas until you *experience* a real conversation with one or more of your personality parts. If you (i.e. some subselves) hesitate trying this—what's the risk? Notice your thoughts right now. Who's speaking—and making your decision? Or . . .

- Do nothing now. Mull, reflect, and discuss these ideas, but don't act on them yet. Re-read or scan this book at a later time. Like a seed, recovery "blooms" when the seed, soil, and weather are right. If you're held in protective custody, your present job may be building the "wall" you need to "hit" later. Or . . .

- Defer judgment on your (or others') need for recovery, and learn more. For example, see which book titles (p. 369+) "call you," and invest some time absorbing their authors' ideas. Give copies of this book to any co-parenting partners, siblings, parents, close friends, and/or professionals (therapists, doctors, teachers) who are significant in your life. Discuss the nurturance-level, inner-family, and true/false-self concepts as teammates and fellow-journeyers, not adversaries! Or . . .

- Re-scan this book and highlight ideas or sections that give you the strongest emotional reactions. These high-energy "trigger" ideas or words are strong clues to what's going on in your inner family, and which passengers are fighting to control your "personality bus." Or . . .

- Scan the summary of typical Inner Kids and Guardian subselves on p. 48. See which ones give you the strongest reactions, and wonder "Why?" Reflect on "Which of these normal personality parts is dominating my recent life? How does that feel to me?" Or—you may . . .

- Confront the question "Should I begin recovery from false-self dominance *today*?" Listen without judgment to the voices in your head, and to your intuition. Make an effort to get quiet, and hear or sense your "still small voice." Whose voice is most persuasive?

- Relax, breathe well, and close your eyes. Vividly imagine yourself as a clear-minded old person, shortly before your death. Envision sitting by your Future Self's bedside, and listening to what s/he says about your life choices and efforts, across the years. If you have grandchildren, reflect together on how you feel about what you and your peers bequeathed to them—and how their lives seem to be "turning out." Notice whether the conversational focus is on deep satisfactions, or regrets.

What does your Future Self advise you about whether to forge an effective personal recovery plan now?

- If you (may) have one or more kids, imagine yourself as an old person on a platform in the center of a vast stadium. The seats are full of thousands of people that you and your conception partner/s gave life to and influenced—all the future generations carrying your genes and DNA. Your partner/s may be sitting with you on the platform. Imagine your describing to them over loudspeakers your decision about whether to work at personal recovery or not. Imagine their reaction, and how you feel.

Breathe comfortably and well. Mute all inner and outer distractions, and reflect . . .

Who is *really* running your life?

How do you like the results, so far?
Bon Voyage, worthy pilgrim . . .

PART 4

Resources

- The Internet as a Recovery Resource

- A Bill of Personal Rights

- The 12 Steps for recoverers

- Selected inspirations

- Selected readings

- Index

THE INTERNET AS A RECOVERY RESOURCE

Since ~1980, a swelling array of recovery-related ma-terials and resources has become available to the literate public. The popularizing of the Internet is opening up unprecedented ways to learn, and to exchange support with other recoverers and experts. As computers get cheaper and simpler, software evolves and stabilizes, telephones access widens and gets faster, and websites explode, the (World Wide) "Web" is becoming a dynamic *major* resource for people in recovery. The Web is the fastest growing part of the full Internet. There are at least four aspects of this amazing resource you can tap for help:

- Search engines

- Websites and Portals

- "Chat" groups, and Forums ("Message boards")

- Online booksellers

Here's brief perspective on each of these, which may be quickly outdated!

Search Engines

An Internet "search engine" is a computer program that takes a word or phrase you type and with lightening speed sends out little "robot" or "spider" programlets to scan most of the strands of the global information Web for matching documents or sites. Within seconds, you get a PC-screen ("page") of the findings, often sorted and organized by "best fit" first. Usually the findings provide you with many "links" which, if selected and "clicked" by your computer "mouse," will take you to the new Website in seconds. In reality, any search engine only examines a fraction of the information available.

The number of search engines is growing fast. All are competing to provide the best service and ease of use. They use different search strategies and "spiders," so identical inquiries often yield different results on different engines. Increasingly, one search engine will provide links to others—and even try a search on the others for you at the touch of a key, if you wish.

There are hundreds of general and specialized search engines. Several of the biggest now (8/02) are www.yahoo.com, www.altavista.com, www. directhit.com, and an interesting one called **www.ask.com**. It features "Jeeves, the butler," who attempts to answer your questions in conversational text. Most search engines have a "help" section that explains how to use their features.

You'll quickly find that learning to pick the right recovery-related search term or phrase is an art. Be alert for both spelling and capitalization choices, as you type your inquiry. Some relevant search words you might start with include . . .

- Recovery
- Recovery group
- Adult child
- 12 step
- Personality splitting
- Dissociation
- Toxic relationship
- Toxic parenting
- Incest survivor(s)
- Family dysfunction
- Anger management
- ACoA, or ACA (Adult Children of Alcoholics)
- Moodiness, or mood swings

- Codependence
- True self
- Personal growth
- Recovery group
- Emotions Anonymous
- Addiction recovery
- Abuse recovery
- Child neglect
- Personal healing
- Trauma recovery
- Search engines

As you experiment, you'll evolve your own search strategy and terms, and favorite search engines.

Websites and Portals

A "Website" is one or more collections ("files") of "pages" of information on one of the many computers ("servers") linked together on the World Wide Web. Each site has a unique Web address, or "URL" (Uniform Resource Locator), which is what search engines display when you seek a certain kind of site. The URL is like your unique postal address. The author or "Webmaster" of each site usually provides "key words" in their Web pages to tell inquiring search engine spiders what their site is about.

The unique URL of a website must end with a set of three letters which tell what category of site it is. Common ones now are . . .

- ".com"—commercial, for profit
- ".org"—(usually) non-profit
- ".edu"—a school or university
- ".gov"—a national or local government site, and . . .
- ".net"—a communication company.

Servers in different countries are identified by unique letters in their URL address, like international telephone area codes—e.g. Australia is ".au". Web users (you) have a program on your computer called a "browser," which translates the pages on any server computer into readable images and words on your PC screen.

Websites have added multi-media sound, motion, and color to the original text-only Internet process of "uploading," locating, and "downloading" individual documents via "FTP," or File Transfer Protocol. There is wealth of textual information available on the ftp-server network within the Internet. "Downloading" means transferring information to your personal computer from a remote server.

A class of emerging Websites is called "Portals." They are kinds of super search engines that compete like information shopping malls. Their creators try to provide Web users with easy access to all possible information and service that they seek, like news headlines, weather, horoscopes, games, shopping, entertainment, free e-mail accounts and home web-pages, etc. Their "links" to information (other Websites) are organized into hierarchical "trees" of subjects, which are searched via a user's typed command. Website providers often submit their site's address (URL) to be included in the major Portals' index of sites. As the Web expands and evolves, the indices change all the time. Like (smaller) search engines, different Portals will point you to different collections of Websites, so try several.

As you explore this amazing new "virtual" (real but invisible) new territory, you'll meet some alien terms. One is "Intranet." This describes a mini-internet that links computers and terminals in different parts of an organization, like a state government, or university, all coordinated by a central "hub" server. This server may or may not be connected to the larger global Internet.

Chat Groups and Message Boards

Websites devoted to personal, relationship, and family health (and other topics) often have an interactive section called a "chat room," "forum," or "message board." These are focused on one topic of common interest (like "recovery"), and offer a place to "talk" directly to other people from around the country or world by typing comments into your local computer. Chat rooms are interactive, with real-time (typed) discussions among a group of "online" people, or "users."

"Message boards" or "Forums" are slower. You type in a comment or question ("post a message"), and other "logged in" (registered) members may or may not type in responses over the next several days. A series of messages and responses on a given theme or topic is called a message "thread." Threads can be searched by topic, so you can read "old" conversations. Some chatrooms and forums have a moderator, and others don't. E-mail, telephone, and in-person friendships, and (re)marriages can develop from such "virtual" online groups.

Internet chat rooms and forums provide recoverers with an unprecedented chance to meet each other and exchange information, resources, and encouragements. Compared to live support groups, chat rooms and forums can't give you a hug, friendly guffaw, or a smile, or react to your facial expressions and body language. Nonetheless, socially isolated recoverers can find these Web meeting places invaluable sources of comfort, information, validation, and inspiration.

Like effective in-person support groups, the best chatrooms and forums stay focused on realistic optimism, healing and problem solving. Others can degrade into ain't-it-awful whine, moan, and complain sessions that demoralize everyone, and hinder recovery. The moral: pay attention to how you feel in any such group, and shop around for one that feels consistently supportive and uplifting—i.e. one that offers you a high nurturance level.

Booksellers on the Web

Another rich source of recovery information is the growing number of online booksellers like ***www.amazon.com, www.bn.com*** (Barnes and Noble), and ***www.books.com***. Fiercely competitive, such commercial Website owners provide increasingly easy ways to find, evaluate, and mail order books, audiotapes, games, and other products via credit card. Larger online booksellers offer rankings on individual books or tapes, based on readers' posted opinions and ratings. Some of these sites offer book chatrooms or message boards, and are steadily expanding toward becoming media-oriented Web portals. An excellent Web source of recovery materials is ***http://hazelden.org***, which allows ordering, or browsing and reading, hundreds of books online, free. If this URL doesn't work for you, search the Web for "Hazelden."

Most major online booksellers offer site-wide search engines, allowing you to quickly locate books or tapes by title, subject, or author. "Brick-and mortar" libraries are computerizing to offer the same service, and are networking so readers can computer-search other libraries' databases.

An exploding new source of Internet information is the young industry of "e-books." A growing number of websites offer these "paperless" books for free or fee downloading to your computer, or on CD-ROMS available by mail. E-books have several advantages: they're portable, easily updated, compact, never go out of print, and may contain hyperlinks and multi-media effects (pictures, sounds, animations) that make them easier and more interesting to use. A possible disadvantage is that anyone can produce an e-book, now, so buyers need to be choosy about non-fiction authors and their credentials. This is specially true for topics relating to human health—like recovery. Ask any Web search engine to survey the Web for "e-book" or "electronic book" sites. Then search those for "recovery" or similar term.

Bottom line: the World-Wide Web portion of the exploding Internet offers you a rich, powerful, expanding resource for recovery information, products, services; and (virtual) fellowship and support.

A BILL OF PERSONAL RIGHTS

AN AFFIRMATION OF YOUR PERSONAL DIGNITY, FREEDOMS, AND RESPONSIBILITIES

Survivors of inadequate emotional and spiritual childhood nurturance (p. 257) are usually burdened with low self esteem—i.e. toxic *shame*. We learned early to automatically devalue our opinions, needs, and perceptions, and to not question or protest that.

A core aspect of true (vs. pseudo) recovery from false-self dominance is to validate and assert our personal dignity and equality with all other people—without undue guilt, shame, or anxiety. For typical recoverers, this is a difficult major second-order (core attitude) change.

An unambiguous, clear, authentic mental Bill of Personal Rights is the foundation for firm assertions. Assertions are needed for effective inner-personal and interpersonal problem solving. Kids of any age can have Bills of Personal Rights too! Is there anyone in your home or family that doesn't deserve to have such a declaration of personal dignity respected by you?

Use this sample Bill as an inspiration for creating your own. For real authenticity, it's best that your Bill of Rights comes from within *you* . . .

+ + +

These statements will clarify for me, and remind me of, my rights as a normal human being. I was not taught some of these as a child, and can strengthen my belief in them today. Affirming my personal rights repeatedly will help free me of old inhibitions and distorted beliefs, and empower me to be firmly assertive (vs. aggressive) with others in a clear, positive, respectful way.

It's healthy for me to honor and respect my own rights and needs as much as I do those of every other person. I can legitimately proclaim and pursue these rights without shame, guilt, or fear, in any way that doesn't interfere with other adults' and kids' equal rights. I need no one's permission to adopt and live from these beliefs.

Like every other person—no matter what my age, experience, or situation, I am a rare, unique, worthwhile human Being. I bring a blend of talents, perceptions, and motives to the world like no other person, past or present. I honor and respect my own uniqueness, and that of every other person. I claim the right to be *me*—without explanation, apology, or defense. I am responsible for being *me*, at all times. I also freely affirm others' equal rights and responsibility to be their own unique Selves.

I Now Declare My Human Right To . . .

1) Experience all my own emotions. They are a natural part of being human. They include fear, sadness, anger, shame, uncertainty, confusion, joy, lust, hope, pride, happiness, etc.—even "numbness." I am not "bad" or "wrong" for *feeling* any of these.

2) Describe and/or express my feelings to others if and when I choose to, without feeling obligated, guilty, or ashamed. I am responsible for this choice, but not for others' reactions.

3) Say "Yes," "No," and "I don't know," without undue guilt, shame, or anxiety—and to be responsible for the consequences.

4) Choose if, when, and how to meet others' expectations of me. If I choose not to meet them, I need not feel guilty—unless I've already committed to do so. I am responsible for such choices, and their consequences.

5) Choose my own friends and acquaintances, and how and when to spend time with them. I may, but don't have to, justify these choices to others.

6) Make my own mistakes—and learn and profit by them, if I can.

7) Choose if, when, and how to respectfully tell others clearly how their actions are affecting me—and to take responsibility for doing so.

8) Earn and maintain my own self-respect and pride, rather than depending on other people's opinions of me.

9) Seek, evaluate, and accept or decline help, without undue shame, anxiety, or guilt.

10) Give others the responsibility for their own beliefs, decisions, feelings, and thoughts, without feeling guilty, anxious, or selfish. Doing otherwise often burdens me, and blocks their chances to grow self-competence and Self-respect.

    And I further declare my unarguable personal rights to . . .

11) Seek situations, environments, and relationships that I feel are healthy, growthful, and nurturing for me. I do not owe—but may choose to give—others explanations of my decisions on these.

12) Be spontaneous, play, and have fun in ways that please me, as long as they cause me or others no harm or discomfort.

13) Develop and grow at my own pace, and in the directions I feel are best for me. This does not mean I ignore other's similar rights, or reject others' well-meant advice or counsel.

14) Appreciate my own efforts, and to honestly enjoy my own achievements without guilt, anxiety, or shame.

15) Act to fill my own wants and needs, rather than expect others to do so for me.

16) Periods of guilt-free rest, refreshment, reflection, and relaxation. These are as productive for me as times of work and action.

17) Choose whom I will trust, when, and with what.

18) Take on only as much as I can handle at any given time, and tell others if I feel overloaded, without shame, anxiety, or guilt.

19) Nurture, love, and value my Self as much as I do others who are special to me. Pride (Self appreciation), in moderation, is not a "sin," and never was. Being "Self-ish" (attending my own needs and nurturance) is OK—as long as I don't interfere with, minimize, or dishonor other's rights to equal Self-care.

20) Choose the goals and paths I wish for my life, and pursue them without guilt, shame, or the need to explain or justify them to others.

And I claim my unarguable rights to . . .

21) Take all the time I need to evaluate and make important life-decisions—even if this stresses others, somewhat.

22) Care for my body and Spirit lovingly and respectfully, in my own ways.

23) Decide on my own priorities and limits at any given time, and act on them as I see fit.

24) Distinguish between who my family, workmates, and friends say I am (or was), vs. who I *really* am.

25) Be heard and clearly understood. My thoughts, feelings, wants, and needs are as legitimate, worthy, and important as anyone else's.

26) Define my own standard of excellence in any situation, and choose whether to strive for this standard or not.

27) Enjoy and express my natural sensuality and sexuality in any way I choose that does not harm me or another person.

28) Choose how to balance and spend my time—and take the short and long-term consequences.

29) Tell others respectfully what I expect of them, realizing they may or may not choose to fulfill these expectations.

30) Choose how and when to peacefully fill my spiritual needs, even if my choices conflict with others' values or wishes. I do not have the right to force my spiritual or religious views, values, or practices on other people—nor do I grant others the right to force theirs on me.

And I further declare and affirm my unarguable rights to . . .

31) Heal past personal shamings and wounds, over time, and replace unhealthy inner messages I've lived by with more nurturing and productive ones.

32) Listen to and heed my "inner voices" with interest and respect, and to sort out my true voices from others' I hear.

33) Have my physical, emotional, and spiritual privacy and boundaries (limits) respected by others. I accept my obligation to respect theirs as well.

34) Ask (not demand) of others how they feel about me, what they think about me, and what they want from me. They may choose to answer or not.

35) Decide if, when, and how to forgive my mistakes, and any hurts received from others. I affirm that such forgiveness promotes *my own* healing, health, and growth.

36) Work respectfully and peacefully to change laws or rules I feel are unjust or harmful to me and/or others.

37) Evolve, declare, revise, and use my own Bill of Personal Rights, and learn how using it affects me and others. I validate and affirm others' equal right and opportunity to do the same.

Options

- Edit and rewrite this sample to make it *yours*. Read each statement out loud, and reflect: "Do I really believe this, or something like it, now?" If the answer is "No," or "I'm not sure," clarify what you *do* believe.

- Take your time. These are the basic un/conscious beliefs ("rules") by which you conduct your daily life!

- Acknowledge your parents' and other teachers' responsibility to have taught you their versions of your Rights, to get you started in life. Then accept *your* responsibility to rethink their opinions and beliefs, and decide clearly if they fit you, or if you need to adopt new standards. When is the right or best time to do this? What if you don't?

- Post this Bill somewhere in plain view, where you (and perhaps others) can see it daily and be refreshed on what it stands for.

- Give a copy of this to other people you live and work with, affirming their equal rights—and/or encourage them to evolve their own Bill. For a copy, see **http://sfhelp.org/relate/keys/rights.htm**.

- Consider if and how you wish to incorporate the concept and contents of your family members' Bills of Rights in any family mission statement and co-parent job descriptions you evolve and use.

- Any time you feel major inner and interpersonal conflicts, refer to your Bill to help get clear on your specific, respective personal rights, as you seek a win-win resolution.

Enjoy creatively choosing small reminders of all these rights ("anchors," or "triggers") to carry with you or have visible where you work or live. Any object, music, emotion, physical sensation, movement, inner image or memory, or word(s) can automatically remind you of any or all these personal rights, and what they stand for.

Awarenesses . . .

THE 12 STEPS FOR RECOVERERS

In 1935, "Dr. Bob," "Bill W," and a small group of inspired pioneers founded Alcoholics Anonymous to help people (vs. *families*) struggling with lethal addiction to ethyl alcohol. They did this because the best medical, religious, and mental-health treatment of the day rarely helped. The "12 steps" evolved as a succinct summary of their philosophy for "recovery" from (i.e. *management* of, vs. "cure" for) this lethal addiction.

In the three generations since then, the public and clinical concept of "addiction" has grown to include at least four groups of things:

- *Compulsive activities*, like workaholism, gambling, spending, worship, over-eating, Internet surfing, and sex;

- *Relationships*—"co-dependence;"

- *Other substances*—like fat and sugar ("comfort foods"), illegal and prescription drugs, nicotine, and caffeine; and . . .

- *Mood states*—like rage, "love," excitement, and sexual arousal and release.

All of these provide temporary comfort from inner pain and emptiness. They all ultimately *increase* the pain—until sufferers "hit bottom," and make some true second-order (core attitude) changes in their core perceptions, life values, and priorities.

In the last quarter century, "Anonymous" groups and some related national organizations have sprung up for families and persons struggling to recover from most of these—like Co-dependents Anonymous (CoDA),

Overeaters Anonymous (OA), Sexaholics Anonymous (SA), and Gamblers Anonymous (GA). Most adapted the language of original 12 steps to fit the unique traits of their target addiction. They haven't changed the philosophy, which seems to apply to all addictions.

Consider the American Constitution—the fundamental framework for our laws and social order, safety, freedom, and prosperity. Over centuries, the original intent of those authors has been thoughtfully modified to match social changes via publicly-ratified amendments. In exactly the same way, the semi-sacred precepts of the early recovery movement can benefit from thoughtful revisions to match new awarenesses and human truths—like false-self formation and wounds.

Part of the healing evolution that hasn't arrived yet is the public and media rejecting the old legacy of *shame* that our superstitious, ignorant ancestors attached to "addiction." The toxic adjective "Anonymous" in the titles of all these recovery groups witnesses the ignorant (false self) legacy of condemning addiction as being morally *bad*. This is as misplaced as saying shyness, warts, tooth decay, or depression is shameful.

As the Christian millennium dawns, a more fundamental change is accelerating: public awareness that *every* addiction, compulsion, and obsession is a symptom of underlying psychological wounding. Acceptance of that will promote awareness that addiction (false-self) *prevention* starts with educated, qualified parents providing high-nurturance environments for their families.

I envision our primal human need for wellness and child nurturance causing all recovery groups to eventually converge and merge into something like "Recoverers United." The recovery will be from unintended low childhood nurturance and resulting false-self dominance.

Hopefully, this will lead future citizens to demand that public policies prize and promote marital and parental education *far* more highly than they do now.

A Proposed Update of the 12 Steps

With veneration for the men and women who created and implemented the original 12 recovery steps, I propose an upgrade. It is based on the unvalidated premise that addicts, co-addicts, and all others struggling to free themselves and their kids from shame, confusion, emptiness, and fear, are *really* trying to restore their true Self to lead their inner families (personalities)—with the essential acceptance and support of their Higher Power.

Getting "sober" from any of the four types of addiction is a necessary *gateway* to potential *full* (spiritual + emotional + physical + mental) recovery—i.e. to empower our Self to harmonize and lead our inner families. Restated: addiction "sobriety" results from *preliminary* recovery.

Recognizing the need for broader recovery guidelines, the Adult Children of Alcoholics (ACoA) World Service organization has amended the language (vs. the philosophy) of the original 12 AA steps. The amendment is reprinted below. Most of the amended steps are followed by a proposed update, to acknowledge *false-self dominance*, not addiction, as the core condition we're trying to recover from. Proposed changes are in italics.

I offer this to fellow recoverers and their families and supporters as "wet clay," for much is new, uncertain, and unresearched. What *is* certain is that we each long for better lives for our descendants and ourselves.

1) We admitted we were powerless over the effects of alcoholism or other family dysfunction, and that our lives had become unmanageable.

I admitted *I* was powerless over the effects of *psychological wounds*, and that *my life* had become unmanageable.

2) Came to believe that a power greater than ourselves could restore us to sanity.

I came to believe that a power greater than *me* could guide *me* to *awareness* and *inner-family harmony.*

3) Made a decision to turn our will and our lives over to the care of God as we understand God.

I made a decision to turn *my* will and *my* life over to the care of God as *I* understand God.

4) Made a searching and fearless moral inventory of ourselves.

I made a searching and fearless inventory of *my inner family.*

5) Admitted to God, to our selves, and to another human being the exact nature of our wrongs.

I admitted to God, to *myself,* and to another person the exact nature of *my false-self's misguided choices.*

6) Were entirely ready to have God remove all these defects of character.

I was entirely ready to have God *help me accept my limits, and harmonize my inner family.*

7) Humbly asked God to remove our shortcomings.

I humbly asked God to help *me serenely accept my personal talents and limitations, and empower my Self and inner family to manifest my unique life purpose.*

8) Made a list of all persons we had harmed and became willing to make amends to them all.

I made a list of all persons *my false self* had harmed, and *I* became willing to make amends to them all.

9) Made direct amends to such people wherever possible, except when to do so would injure them or others.

I made direct amends to such people wherever possible, except when *doing* so would injure them or others.

10) Continued to take personal inventory and, when we were wrong, promptly admitted it.

I continued to take personal inventory and, when *I was* wrong, promptly admitted it *without undue guilt, shame, or anxiety.*

11) Sought through prayer and meditation to improve our conscious contact with God, as we understand God, praying only for knowledge of God's will for us, and the power to carry it out.

I sought through prayer and meditation to improve *my* conscious *and spiritual* contact with God, as *I* understand God, praying only for *awareness* of God's will for *me*, and the *will* to carry it out.

12) Having had a spiritual awakening as a result of these steps, we tried to carry this message to others who still suffer, and to practice these principles in all our affairs.

Having had a spiritual awakening as a result of these steps, *I am trying* to carry this message to others who still suffer, and to practice these principles in all *my* affairs.

*   *   *

Whatever expression of these ideas best fits you at this point in your journey, I believe the *spirit* of these 12 steps offers seekers a truly effective framework and guide for our challenging journey toward health, compassion, peace, and fulfillment—and for passing these on to living and unborn descendents.

Options

- Read each of the existing (ACoA) steps out loud slowly, and become nonjudgmentally aware of your thoughts, feelings, memories, and associations. These are your inner family's reactions to the amended set of 12 guiding principles. Is your Self present right now? How do you know?

- Now read the revised steps out loud. See how each and all steps "feel" to your inner crew. Notice the different tone from using "I" and "me." Why do you suppose the original authors omitted those? Consider journaling your reactions and awarenesses.

- Try composing your own version of these steps, based on your experience, vocabulary, insight, and wisdom to date. Your composition will change, as your recovery experience and awareness evolve.

- Post copies of the old or new steps where you can see them in your daily life. Use them to stabilize and guide your recovery, across the adventures and challenges of your emerging new life.

Awarenesses . . .

SELECTED INSPIRATIONS

This is a sampling from the rich trove of wisdom, humor, and insight that we inherit from wise fellow travelers and older mentors. Meditating on the *meanings* in comments like these can act like recovery "vitamins," any time you need wholistic nutrition. Option: build your own collection of inspirations over time, and read them regularly—e.g. at breakfast, and/or times of conflict.

Also explore the growing number of helpful published collections of "daily affirmations" for people in recovery. Use "(recovery) affirmations" in a Web search engine, or in an online bookseller's site, and see what you get. Ask other recoverers if they have any such resources to recommend.

My warm thanks to Jeannie McLennan for many of these . . .

The Serenity Prayer

"God grant me
the Serenity to accept the things I cannot change,
Courage to change the things I can, and . . .
The wisdom to know the difference."

—Reinhold Neibuhr, 1934

The Key to Mental Health

"Settle for disorder in lesser things, for the sake of order in greater things.
Therefore, be content to be discontent in many things."
—Anonymous

"The road to success is always under construction."

"Progress, not perfection!"

"Either way, it's going to hurt."

"Seek first to understand—then to be understood"

—Stephen Covey

"Go within, or go without"—Neale Walsch

"If you always do what you've always done,
you'll always get what you've always got."

—Steve and Carol Lankton

The Gestalt Prayer

"I do my thing, and you do your thing.
I am not in this world to live up to your expectations,
and you are not in this world to live up to mine.
You are you, and I am me.
If by chance we meet, it's beautiful.
If not, it can't be helped."

—Fritz Perls

"Three grand essentials to happiness in this life are . . .
something to do, something to love, and something to hope for.

—Joseph Addison

"Fatigue makes cowards of us all."

—Vince Lombardi

"H. A. L. T."—*H*ungry, *A*ngry, *L*onely, and *T*ired (the last three are often false-self symptoms—specially if excessive and/or chronic.

—12-step recovery slogan

"This is the true joy in life, the being used for a purpose recognized by yourself as a mighty one. I am of the opinion that my life belongs to the whole community, and as long as I live it is my privilege to do for it whatever I can. I want to be thoroughly used up when I die, for the harder I work the more I live. I rejoice in life for its own sake. Life is no brief candle to me. It is a sort of splendid torch which I've got ahold of for the moment and I want to make it burn as brightly as possible before handing it on to further generations."

—George Bernard Shaw

Mere longevity is a good thing for those who watch Life from the sidelines. For those who play the game, an hour may be a year; a single day's work an achievement for eternity.

—Gabriel Heatter

"Success at the expense of faith and family really is failure."

—Byrd Baggett, The Book of Excellence

"Making a living is necessary and often satisfying: eventually, making a difference becomes more important."

—David Campbell

"The problem isn't the problem the problem is the attitude about the problem."

—Kelly Young, age 19

He that gives good advice, builds with one hand; he that gives good counsel and example, builds with both; but he that gives good admonition and bad example, builds with one hand and pulls down with the other.

—Francis Bacon

"One must have chaos in one's self in order to give birth to a dancing star."

—Fredrick Nietzsche

"Whether you believe you can or you can't, you're right."

—Henry Ford

"Men occasionally stumble into knowledge: but
most of them pick themselves up and hurry off
as if nothing had happened."

—Winston Churchill

"I don't know the key to success, but
the key to failure is trying to please everybody."

—Bill Cosby

"Do what you know in your heart is right, for you will be criticized anyway."
—Eleanor Roosevelt

A pessimist is one who makes difficulties of his opportunities,
and an optimist is one who makes opportunities of his difficulties.

—Harry Truman

"Human beings have always employed an enormous amount of clever devices
for running away from themselves . . .
we can keep ourselves busy, fill our lives with so many diversions,
stuff our heads with so much knowledge, involve ourselves with
so many people, and cover so much ground that we never
have time to probe the fearful and wonderful world within . . .
By middle life, most of us are accomplished fugitives from ourselves."

—John Gardner

ON RISK

"To laugh is to risk appearing the fool
To weep is to risk appearing weak or sentimental
To reach out to another is to risk involvement or rejection
To show your feelings is to risk exposing your true self
To place your ideas and dreams before the crowd
is to risk their loss
To love is to risk not being loved in return
To live is to risk dying
To hope is to risk despair
To try is to risk failure
But risks must be taken—because

The greatest hazard in life is to risk nothing:
The person who risks nothing
Does nothing, has nothing, and is nothing;
S/He may avoid suffering and sorrow, but
S/He simply cannot learn, feel, change, love, or live
Chained by personal certitudes, s/he is a slave;
S/He has forfeited freedom.
Only a person who risks is free."

—Author unknown

"Did you ever notice how difficult it is to argue
with someone who is not obsessed with being right?"

—Wayne W. Dyer

"Learn to value spiritual things over material things.
They last longer, cost less, bring more."

—Linus Mundy in "Keep Life Simple Therapy"

"Everyone has his own specific vocation in life . . .
Therein he cannot be replaced, nor can his life be repeated . . .
Thus everyone's task is as unique as
his specific opportunity to implement it.
We detect rather than invent our mission in life."

—Viktor Frankl, "Man's Search for Meaning"

"Resolve to be thyself; and know that he who finds himself, loses his misery."
—Mathew Arnold, 1822-88; English poet and critic

"Learn to get in touch with the silence within yourself,
and know that everything in life has purpose.
There are no mistakes, no coincidences,
all events are blessings given to us to learn from."

—Elizabeth Kubler-Ross

"When you doubt yourself you doubt everyone else as well.
What is thought to be fear of others is really distrust of self . . . "

—Anonymous

Symptoms of Inner Peace

"Be on the lookout for symptoms of Inner peace. The hearts of a great many have already been exposed to Inner peace, and it is possible that people everywhere could come down with it in epidemic proportions. This could pose a serious threat to what has, up to now, been a fairly stable condition of conflict in the world

Some signs and symptoms of Inner peace:

A tendency to think and act spontaneously rather than on fears based on past experiences.

An unmistakable ability to enjoy each moment.

A loss of interest in judging other people.

A loss of interest in interpreting the actions of others.

A loss of interest in conflict.

A loss of the ability to worry. (This is a very serious symptom.)

Frequent, overwhelming episodes of appreciation.

Contented feelings of connectedness with others and nature.

An increasing tendency to let things happen rather than make them happen.

An increased susceptibility to the love extended by others,

as well as the uncontrollable urge to extend it.

<< WARNING! >>

If you have some or all of the above symptoms—please be advised that your condition of Inner peace may be so far advanced as to not be curable. If you are exposed to anyone exhibiting any of these symptoms, remain exposed only at your own risk.

—Saskia Davis

"Forgiveness is not the misguided act of condoning irresponsible, hurtful behavior. Nor is it a superficial turning of the other cheek that leaves us feeling victimized and martyred. Rather it is the finishing of old business that allows us to experience the present, free' of contamination from the past."

—Joan Borysenko, Ph.D.

The Invitation

"It doesn't interest me what you do for a living. I want to know what you ache for, and if you dare to dream of meeting your heart's longing.

It doesn't interest me how old you are. I want to now if you will risk looking like a fool for love, for your dreams, for the adventure of being alive.

It doesn't interest me what planets are squaring your moon. I want to know if you have touched the center of your own sorrow, If you have been opened by life's betrayals or have become shriveled and closed from fear of further pain!

I want to know if you can sit with pain, mine or your own, without moving to hide it or fade it or fix it.

I want to know if you can be with joy, mine or your own, if you can dance with wildness and let the ecstasy fill you to the tips of your fingers and toes without cautioning us to be careful, be realistic, or to remember the limitations of being human.

It doesn't interest me if the story you're telling me is true, I want to know if you can disappoint another to be true to yourself; if you can bear the accusation of betrayal and not betray your own soul.
I want to know if you can be faithful—and therefore be trustworthy.

I want to know if you can see beauty even when it is not pretty every day, and if you can source your life from God's presence.

I want to know if you can live with failure, yours and mine, and still stand on the edge of a lake and shout to the silver of the full moon—Yes!

It doesn't interest me to now where you live or how much money you have. I want to now if you can get up after the night of grief and despair, weary and bruised to the bone, and do what needs to be done for the children.

It doesn't interest me who you are, or how you came to be here. I want to know if you will stand in the center of the fire with me and not shrink back.

It doesn't interest me where or what or with whom you have studied. I want to know what sustains you from the inside when all else falls away. I want to know if you can be alone with yourself,
and if you truly like the company you keep in the empty moments.

—Oriah Mountain Dream, Native American Elder

SELECTED READINGS

Though many of these books refer specifically to people from chemically addicted families, most of what they say applies equally to adults raised in low-nurturance homes and schools where drugs weren't misused. Note that "addiction" includes compulsions with . . .

- *Other chemicals*, like sugar, caffeine, and nicotine; and prescription and "hard" drugs;
- *Activities*—like workaholism, gambling, jogging, sex, and Internet surfing,
- *Relationships* (co-dependence);
- *Causes*—e.g. animal rights, gun control, ecology, or abortion; or . . .
- *Emotional states*—e.g. religious or political zealotry, "love," sexual or other excitement, and rage (feeling powerful and impactful).

After 30 years' clinical experience, I believe all addictions, including addiction to an addict (co-dependence), are clear symptoms of significant false-self wounds and low-nurturance childhoods. Books discussing recovery from any of these symptoms deal with healing inner wounds by implication. Most authors or readers don't know that yet.

In these books, the term *"Adult Child"* (of family "dysfunction") means the same as "survivor of low childhood nurturance" in this book. I believe all unrecovering "Adult Children" are significantly wounded (dominated by a false self).

There are many other good books—these are representative. The "*" means "specially helpful, in my opinion." Some are out of print, and most online booksellers offer used copies. Note that almost all these titles have been published since 1985, many since 1990. Our ancestors, and most mentors, had no awareness of, or training in, this mosaic of concepts.

* * *

- **The Adult Children of Divorce Workbook**—*a Compassionate Program for Healing from Your Parents' Divorce*, by Mary Hirschfeld, J.D., Ph.D.; Jeremy P. Tarcher, Inc., Los Angeles, CA; 1992. The title speaks for itself.

- **Adult Children Of Abusive Parents**—*A Healing Program for Those Who Have Been Physically, Sexually, or Emotionally Abused*, by Steven Farmer, M.A.; Ballentine Books, New York, NY; 1990. One of many recent books for survivors of low childhood nurturance and psychologically-wounded caregivers.

- **The Adult Children of Alcoholics Syndrome**—*From Discovery to Recovery*, by Wayne Kritsberg; Health Communications, Inc., Deerfield Beach, FL; 1988

- **Adult Children**—*Secrets of Dysfunctional Families*, by John and Linda Friel; Health Communications, Inc., Deerfield Beach, FL; 1988. "Dysfunctional" equals "low-nurturance"—lacking many of the traits in worksheet A (p. 257).

- * **The Artist's Way**—*A Spiritual Path to Higher Creativity*, by Julia Cameron, with Mark Bryan; G.P. Putnam's Son's, New York, NY; 1992. Though this empowering work/book focuses on increasing personal creativity, it's really about personal recovery and wholeness.

- **Battling the Inner Dummy**—*The Craziness of Apparently Normal People*, by David L. Weiner, with Gilbert M. Hefter, M.D.; Prometheus Books, Amherst, NY; 1999. A zealous inquiry into what I believe are our false-selves' "illogical" behaviors. Despite a tremendous, sincere research effort, the authors somehow missed or discounted most of the books and concepts you see here. Worth reading, if for no other reason that it will widen your perspective.

- *** Brain Sex**—*the Real Difference Between Men and Women*; by Anne Moir and David Jessel; Doubleday Books, New York, NY; 1993. The biogeneticist and journalist authors offer an eye-opening research-based view of why "male brains" and "female brains" react very differently to the inner and outer worlds.

- **Children of Trauma**—*Rediscovering Your Discarded Self*; by Jane Middleton-Moz; Health Communications, Inc.; Deerfield Beach, FL; 1989. Specially touching and evocative.

- **Choicemaking**—*for Co-dependents, Adult Children, and Spirituality Seekers*, by Sharon Wegscheider-Cruse; Health Communications, Inc., Deerfield Beach, FL.; 1985

- **Coming Home**—*the Return to True Self*, by Martia Nelson; New World Library, Novato, CA, 1993. A spiritually-oriented view of recognizing and bridging the "wounded" between our "personality" (our inner family) and our true Self—a serene, caring, reliable source of "higher wisdom." The authoress changed her life work as she discovered her true Self.

- **Conversations With God**—*an uncommon dialog*, by Neale Walsch; G.P. Putnam & Sons, New York, 1996. A thought-provoking invitation to listen to God "directly." Whether you agree with the contents or not, this book will help you get clear on your spiritual and religious beliefs, and probably on some alternatives to ones you were taught.

- *** Daily Affirmations for Adult Children of Alcoholics**, by Rokelle Lerner; Health Communications. Inc., Pompano Beach, FL; 1985. This is a rich guide and source of focus and clarity for any recoverer, by a pioneering recoverer, teacher, and therapist. It offers a recovery theme and positive affirmation for each day of the year.

- **Different Drum**—*Community Making and Peace*, by M. Scott Peck; Touchstone Books, New York, NY; 1998. Best known for "*The Road Less Traveled*," Dr. Peck's book gives very helpful perspective from his extensive experience helping groups to become true communities. Applies directly to harmonizing your *inner* community.

- * **Discover Your Subpersonalities**—*Our Inner World*, and the People In It, by John Rowan; Routledge, London and New York; 1993. The most readable and realistic lay book I've found on our personality subselves. Rowan has written two other books on the subject for those wanting a wider perspective (below). He chooses to minimize the vital topic of what this book calls the Self. Read this one first.

- * **The Drama of the Gifted Child**—*the Search for the True Self*, by Dr. Alice Miller; Basic Books, Inc., New York, NY; 1984. This is a brief, sobering look at the results of low-childhood nurturance ("formation of a false self") by an eloquent veteran Swiss psychoanalyst. This classic, laser-clear book referenced by many other clinical authors.

- * **Embracing Our Selves**—*The Voice Dialog Manual*, by Hal Stone, Ph.D., and Sidra Winkleman, Ph.D.; New World Library, San Rafael, CA; 1989. A very helpful, interesting exploration of learning to listen to the voices within you—and discern who is talking.

- * **Embracing Your Inner Critic**—*Turning Self Criticism Into A Creative Asset*, by Hal Stone, Ph.D., and Sidra Winkleman-Stone, Ph.D.; Harper, San Francisco, 1993. A truly practical book on how to respectfully redirect the ceaseless voice in your head that keeps putting you down.

- **Facing Shame**—*Families in Recovery*, by Merle A. Fossum, and Marilyn J. Mason; W.W. Norton & Co., New York; 1986. Though written for clinicians working with low-nurturance (shame-based) families, this is still helpful for lay people interested in understanding how shame cripples many people, where it comes from, and what to do about it. See also John Bradshaw's *Healing the Shame That Binds You*.

- * **The Family**—*a New Way of Creating Solid Self Esteem*, by John Bradshaw; Health Communications, Inc., Deerfield Beach, FL; 1996. Update of a classic, impassioned description of childhood nurturance deprivations and consequences, by a recovering minister, father, and seasoned therapist and educator.

- * **Grandchildren of Alcoholics (ACoAs)**—*Another Generation of Co-dependency*; by Ann W. Smith; Health Communications Inc.,

Deerfield Beach, FL; 1988. I highly recommend this paperback, if you can find it. It will raise your awareness of how childhood traumas' psychological woundings can appear to "skip" generations.

- **Guide to Recovery**—*A Book for Adult Children of Alcoholics*, by Julie D. Bowden and Herbert L. Gravitz; Learning Publications, Inc.; Holmes Beach, FL; 1985. Particularly brief, clear, and straightforward—for all health-seekers.

- **Healing the Child Within**—*Discovery and Recovery for Adult Children of Dysfunctional Families*, by Charles Whitfield, M.D.; Health Communications, Inc., Deerfield Beach, FL; 1987. Helpful and thorough, though the author stops short of recognizing our chaotic inner family.

- * **Healing The Shame That Binds You**, by John Bradshaw; Health Communications, Inc., Deerfield Beach, FL; 1988. A helpful summary of his earlier book "The Family," (above) plus very useful ideas and exercises for working toward converting personal shame to healthy Self acceptance and love. I believe excessive shame is the most toxic of six common false-self wounds. See also Fossum and Mason's *"Facing Shame."*

- **How To Love Yourself When You Don't Know How**—*Healing All Your Inner Children*, by Jacqui Bishop, M.S., and Mary Grunte, R.N.; A P.U.L.S.E. Book, published by Station Hill Press, Inc., Barrytown, NY; 1992. One of the few books I've found (so far) that acknowledges the reality of (part of) our inner family.

- **Inner Time**—*the Science of Body Clocks, and What Makes Us Tick;* by Carol Orlock; Birch Lane Press, New York, NY, 1993. This is a readable, fascinating introduction to the new science of "chronobiology." It outlines convincing findings that help explain and validate the physiological "biorhythms," that amplify and clash with our inner-family dynamics.

- * **Inner Work**—*Using Dreams and Active Imagination for Personal Growth*, by Jungian analyst Robert A. Johnson; HarperCollins, New York; 1986. A clear, practical guide to meeting, understanding, and negotiating with the members of your inner family.

- **In Search of Your True Self**—*21 Insights That Will Revitalize Your Body, Mind, and Spirit!*, by Walter Staples; Pelican Publishing Co., Gretna, LA; 1996. I haven't read this yet, but the title and credits by others imply its helpfulness for people motivated to heal.

- **Is It Love, or Is It Addiction?** by psychologist Brenda Schaeffer; Hazelden Educational Materials, Center City, MN, 1987. A clear introduction to the trap of love addiction—which needy, psychologically-wounded people are vulnerable to at any age. Love addiction is similar to the emotional-spiritual condition of co-dependence.

- **It Will Never Happen To Me**, by Claudia Black, MSW; M.A.C. Printing and Publications Division, Denver, CO; 1991 (reprint). A brief, clear, classic introduction to the Adult-Child (ACoA) syndrome, by an insightful mental-health professional in personal recovery. Related recovery workbook available.

- * **Keeping the Love You Find**—*A Guide For Singles*, by Harville Hendrix, Ph.D.; Pocket Books division of Simon & Schuster, Inc., New York; 1992. This book for courting adults proposes we unconsciously marry Imagos—images of who we (our false-self parts) wish to see, vs. our real partner. Veteran counselor Hendrix implies how subselves interact, in most relationships. If you're already married, see *"Getting the Love You Want—A Guide for Couples"* (1988). Audio tapes and classes available.

- * **Legacy of the Heart**—*the Spiritual Advantages of a Painful Childhood*, by Wayne Muller; A Simon & Schuster Fireside Book, New York, NY; 1993. A marvelously positive, different, non-preachy way of looking at, and healing from, the traumas of a deprivational childhood. The author is a veteran therapist, and a Christian and Buddhist priest.

- **Lifebalance**—*How to Simplify and Bring Harmony to Your Everyday Life*, by Linda and Richard Eyre; A Simon & Schuster Fireside Book, New York, NY; 1997. A clear, realistic look at putting time and energy where it most matters. Specially helpful for chaotic inner families, and complex divorced families and stepfamilies!

- **Narcisssism**—*Denial of the True Self*; by Alexander Lowen, M.D.; Touchstone Books, Simon & Schuster, New York, 1997.

- **The Other Side Of The Family**—*a Book for Recovery From Abuse, Incest, and Neglect*, by Ellen Ratner, Ed. M.; Health Communications, Inc., Deerfield Beach, FL; 1990. The authoress is a professional with 16 years in the trauma-recovery field when this was published.

- * **The Plural Self**—*Multiplicity in Everyday Life*, edited by John Rowan and Mick Cooper; Sage Publications, London, and Thousand Oaks, CA; 1999. This is a *deep* book for those seriously interested in the origin and mechanics of personality fragmenting and dynamics. It documents that over two dozen respected clinicians, including Sigmund Freud and Carl Jung, have written over the past century about what the book you're reading now calls your *inner* family.

- **Recreating Your Self**—*Help for Adult Children of Dysfunctional Families*, by Nancy Napier; W. W. Norton, & Co., New York, NY; 1990. Nancy provides the interesting concept of inviting guidance from our Future Selves. Worth searching for.

- **Same House, Different Homes**—*Why Adult Children of Alcoholics Are Not All the Same;* by Robert J. Ackerman, Ph.D.; Health Communications, Inc.; Pompano Beach, FL; 1987. A clear, readable, 51-page overview of eight factors that shape why some kids are more traumatized than others in the same low-nurturance family. Unfortunately, this is out of print. The concepts may be summarized in Ackerman's more recent books.

- * **The Search For the True Self**—*Unmasking the Personality Disorders of Our Age*; by James F. Masterson, M.D.; Free Press, New York, 1988. Though written for clinicians, this book is the clearest I've found on how the false self may be born before age four. Masterson's portrait of the true Self encourages readers like you to empower theirs. *Inner*-family therapy provides an effective alternative to the expensive, intensive Freudian treatment Masterson has used effectively for healing and empowerment.

- **Secret Survivors**—*Uncovering Incest and Its Aftereffects in Women*, by E. Sue Blume; Ballentine Books, New York; 1991. A clear, factual introduction to assessing and starting recovery from the massive trauma of childhood sexual abuse. Includes a well-known, reliable checklist of symptoms. I believe true child abuse *always* causes adaptive false-self formation and dominance.

- **The Seven Spiritual Laws of Success**—*the Practical Guide to the Fulfillment of Your Dreams*, by Deepak Chopra: Amber-Allen Publishing / New World Library, San Rafael, CA.; 1995. A 115-page hardcover by a widely-respected leader in personal recovery and Self-actualization. See also his newer "*Seven Laws for* (high nurturance?) *Parents.*"

- *** Subpersonalities**—*The People Inside Us*, by John Rowan; Rutledge, London and New York, 1990. This is Rowan's own well-researched view of personality fragmenting and its implications and healing. He quotes learned others, including brain researchers, to provide helpful historical philosophical, and biological perspectives to the concept of psychological multiplicity. The 11-page bibliography implies personality splitting (subselves) is neither new nor trivial. Also see his other two books here.

- **Taming Your Inner Gremlin**—*A Guide to Enjoying Yourself*, by Richard D. Carson; HarperCollins Publishers, New York, reprinted in 1990. Carson's "Inner Gremlin" (singular) is what this book calls "subselves" or "personality parts." This brief, simple, whimsical book urges readers to become aware of their inner dynamics to enjoy life more. I disagree with Carson's idea that our "Gremlins" are intentionally malicious. This was first written in 1983, before the concept of "multiplicity" started emerging.

- **Touchstones**—*A Book of Daily Inspirations for Men*, by "M. A. F;" Hazelden Foundation, Center City, MN; 1986. One of many inspiring small books providing unique recovery inspiration and guidance for each day of the year—by a sensitive veteran recoverer who prefers social anonymity.

- **Toxic Parents**—*Overcoming Their Hurtful Legacy and Reclaiming Your Life*; by Dr. Susan Forward, with Craig Buck; Bantam Books, New York, NY; 1990. A New York Times best seller.

- * **When Rabbit Howls,** by "The Troops, for Trudi Chase;" Jove Books, New York, 1987. This sobering book will show you inner-family members in action, and where they came from. "The Troops" are the writer's inner-family members, who provide a compelling description of triumphing over childhood trauma. Note—this is a vivid example of extreme false-self dominance. The dynamics are common, but this degree of inner-family chaos is rare. See also *"The Mosaic Mind"* below.

- **You'll See It When You Believe It**—*The Way to Your Personal Transformation*, by Dr. Wayne Dyer; 1990 reprint; Avon, Eon, NY. An eloquent description of personal awareness and recovery from childhood abandonment and hatred. Related audio tapes available.

- **Your Many Faces**—*The First Step to Being Loved*, by Virginia Satir; Celestial Arts, Berkeley, CA; 1978. The availability of this short, clear book almost 25 years after first publication suggests its appeal and usefulness. Satir was a master therapist and empathic, positive student and facilitator of human behavior and potential. A fanciful, interesting, and *real* look at your inner family.

Both hardcover books below are written for human-service professionals. They are still helpful for most lay readers in real recovery. They propose and illustrate the full inner-family concept underlying Part 2 of this book. Both volumes have extensive bibliographies:

- * **Internal Family Systems Therapy,** by Richard C. Schwartz, Ph.D.; 1995; Guilford Press, New York, NY. This clear, readable book describes the basic theory.

- * **The Mosaic Mind**—*Empowering the Tormented Selves of Child Abuse Survivors*, by Regina A. Goulding, J.D.; and Richard C. Schwartz, Ph.D.; 1995; W.W. Norton & Co., Inc.; New York, NY. This book describes parts work in action. It's remarkable in that it excerpts the diary of an inner-family client, which vividly describes the interplay of her parts' thoughts, feelings, and motives as her recovery from severe childhood trauma progresses. See also **"When Rabbit Howls"** above.

Most books on Gestalt therapy or "Multiple Personality" (e.g. "*Sibyl*") will grow your perspective on the inner-family concept. True multiple personality disorder is the extreme case of the multiple-subself concept sketched in this book and related readings. Most of us do have a full inner family—and are *not* (pathological) "multiple personalities" or "crazy" at all!

INDEX

Symbols

N

O

P

R

S

V

W

X

Y